Fodor's

OAHU

Welcome to Oahu

The island known as The Gathering Place has many charms, from Honolulu's bright lights and Waikiki Beach buzz to the North Shore's big-wave meccas. Learn to surf or paddle an outrigger canoe, sample shave ice, and feast at a luau—all in one day. Slow down with a thought-provoking visit to Pearl Harbor or a leisurely drive along the coast and into the countryside, where island villages, ranches, farm stands, and vistas all await. This book was updated during the pandemic. When planning your travels, please confirm that places are still open and let us know when we need to make updates at editors@fodors.com.

TOP REASONS TO GO

★ **Pearl Harbor:** This historic memorial in Honolulu is a sobering, don't-miss sight.

★ **Waikiki:** Busy but beautiful, with a perfect beach for first-time surfers.

★ **Great Food:** Simple plate lunches, fresh sushi, creative Hawaii regional cuisine.

★ **Polynesian Cultural Center:** The famous luau provides insight into island culture.

★ **Nightlife:** From upscale jazz bars to local hangouts, Honolulu comes alive after dark.

★ **North Shore:** Shave ice, big waves, pro surfers, and a slower pace add appeal here.

Contents

Fodor's Features

MAPS

Chapter 1

EXPERIENCE OAHU

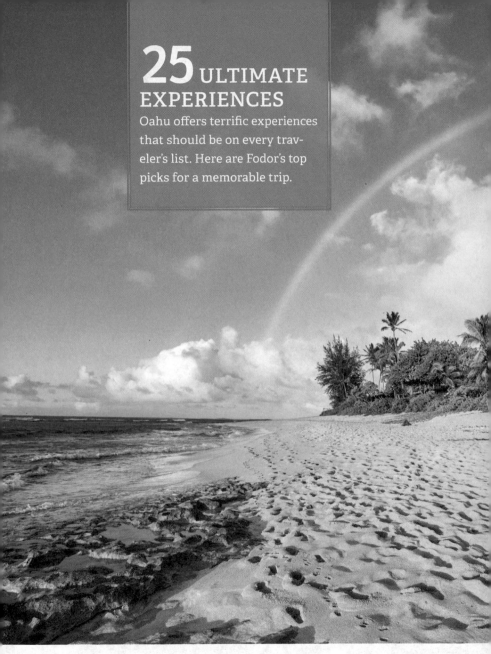

25 ULTIMATE EXPERIENCES

Oahu offers terrific experiences that should be on every traveler's list. Here are Fodor's top picks for a memorable trip.

1 Explore the North Shore

Spend a day on the North Shore. Start off in Kaneohe and drive up Kamehameha Highway all the way to Haleiwa, stopping along the way at fruit stands, shrimp trucks, beaches, world-famous surfing spots (don't miss Waimea Bay), and scenic overlooks. *(Ch. 5)*

2 Watch a Hula Show

For a more traditional, less touristy introduction to hula and Hawaiian music, go to the free hula show that's held several nights a week on Kuhio Beach. *(Ch. 3)*

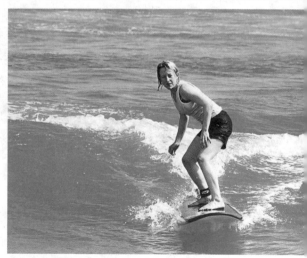

3 Learn to Surf

Waikiki's many surf schools make it popular with beginners. Less-crowded White Plains has better novice conditions as well as lots of surf amenities. *(Ch. 3, 4)*

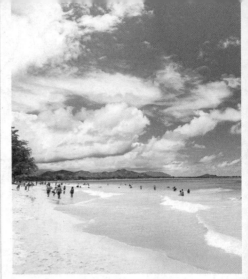

4 Have a Plate lunch

Everyone should try this bargain-priced Hawaii lunch tradition: an entrée with white rice and a scoop of macaroni salad. It's an island favorite. *(Ch. 3, 4, 5, 6)*

5 Relax at Kailua Beach

Looking for that idyllic, unpopulated stretch of white sandy beach and Technicolor blue water? Visit Kailua Beach for easy swimming waves and maximum sand. *(Ch. 6)*

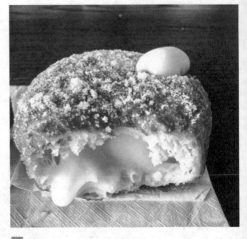

6 Paradise Cove Luau

Let's face it. There is no non-touristy luau, but Paradise Cove is where locals like to take visitors for traditional Hawaiian foods (give poi a chance) and a genuinely fun experience. *(Ch. 4)*

7 Munch on Malasadas

A must-eat, these deep-fried, sugar-coated doughnuts without holes (first brought to the islands by Portuguese immigrants) are an island fixture. *(Ch. 3, 4, 5, 6)*

8 Byodo-In Temple

Part of the Valley of the Temples cemetery complex, Byodo-In is a smaller version of the 11th-century original in Uji, Japan, but it's every bit as beautiful and peaceful. *(Ch. 6)*

9 Makapuu Lighthouse Trail

Less crowded than Diamond Head, Makapuu—popular with families because of its paved trail—offers an equally beautiful coastal panorama. *(Ch. 6, 7)*

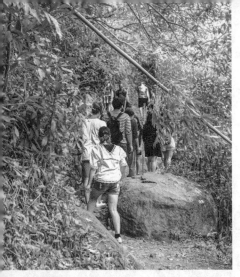

10 Seek a Waterfall on the Manoa Falls Trail

Manoa Falls is an easy (though occasionally muddy), 1½-mile rain-forest hike in Manoa Valley with the reward of a 150-foot waterfall at its end. *(Ch. 3, 7)*

11 Explore Chinatown

Oahu's Chinatown is a jumble of the historic and hip, with a revitalized dining scene, plus a mix of galleries, shops, and cultural sites. *(Ch. 3)*

12 Snorkel at Hanauma Bay

This nature preserve nestled in a volcanic crater with a vibrant reef is a phenomenal, family-friendly place to see colorful fish and other sea life. Advance reservations are now required. *(Ch. 6, 7)*

13 Explore the Kakaako Neighborhood

Filled with shops, restaurants, bars, and intriguing wall murals, this Honolulu district is vibrant, fun, and very cool. *(Ch. 3)*

14 Walk Through Waikiki

The best way to enjoy Waikiki's famed tourist strip is by foot: skip the traffic, burn off some mai tai calories, and catch the sights you might otherwise miss. *(Ch. 3)*

15 Take a Cruise or Kayak Trip

You've got to get out on the water, whether it's on a sunset catamaran cruise, a whale-watching trip, or a kayak excursion in the Mokulua Islands. *(Ch. 6, 7)*

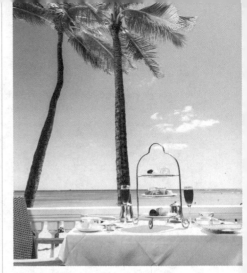

16 Take Tea at the Moana

Relaxed and refined at the same time, the Moana Surfrider offers high tea on its oceanfront Banyan Veranda, complete with dainty sandwiches, desserts, and a dose of glamour. *(Ch. 3)*

17 Visit Iolani Palace

The only royal residence in the United States gives you an introduction to Hawaii's monarchy era, which ended with the overthrow of Queen Liliuokalani in 1893. *(Ch. 3)*

18 Eat Out in Kaimuki

This unassuming neighborhood east of Waikiki and north of Diamond Head offers a diverse array of restaurants (both upscale and local) in a hip (but not-too-hip) part of town. *(Ch. 3)*

19 Explore the Nature Preserve at Kaena Point

Striking, stark, solitary: Kaena Point requires an easy (though not shaded) hike out to the island's westernmost point, which is considered a sacred spot. *(Ch. 5, 7)*

20 Relive History at Pearl Harbor

You can't go to Oahu and skip a visit to Pearl Harbor National Memorial, which preserves the USS *Arizona* and other World War II sites. *(Ch. 3)*

21 Treat Yourself to Shave Ice at Island Snow

Matsumoto's on the North Shore may be the most well-known, but we (and former president Barack Obama) prefer Island Snow in Kailua. *(Ch. 6)*

22 Try a Spam Musubi

If you want to eat like a local, you've got to try what is basically Spam sushi—sticky rice with seasoned, fried Spam wrapped up in seaweed. It's surprisingly tasty. *(Ch. 3, 4, 5, 6)*

23 Visit Doris Duke's Shangri La

Tobacco heiress Doris Duke's waterfront mansion here was inspired by the Middle East, South Asia, and North Africa. Don't miss it. *(Ch. 3, 6)*

24 Feel the Wind at Nuuanu Pali Lookout

On especially windy days, you can actually lean up against the wind, and on most days, you get spectacular views. *(Ch. 6)*

25 Watch the Pros Surf at Waimea Bay

During winter, when waves can crest past 20 feet, Waimea Bay is one of the best places in the world to watch the pros catch the big ones. *(Ch. 5, 7)*

WHAT'S WHERE

1 Honolulu. The vibrant capital city, home to the nation's only royal palace, has free concerts under the tamarind trees in the financial district and art galleries, hipster bars, and open markets in Nuuanu and Chinatown. It also encompasses Waikiki—dressed in lights at the base of Diamond Head, famous for its world-class shopping, restaurants, and surf—and Pearl Harbor, Hawaii's largest natural harbor and the resting place of the USS *Arizona*, sunk on December 7, 1941.

2 West (Leeward) and Central Oahu. This rugged western side of the island has become a "second city" of suburban homes, golf courses, and resorts surrounding lagoons in the Ko Olina area. Although the interstate cuts through the region, fertile Central Oahu is an integral part of Hawaii's rich cultural history. This valley, between the Waianae and Koolau mountain ranges, is an eclectic mix of farms, planned communities, and strip malls.

3 **North Shore.** Best known for its miles of first-rate surf breaks and green sea turtle sightings, the North Shore is home to the legendary laid-back surf town of Haleiwa. This plantation area also has farms, restaurants, and hiking trails.

4 **East (Windward) Oahu.** The sleepy neighborhoods at the base of the majestic Koolau Mountains offer a respite from the bustling city, with charming eateries, long stretches of sandy beaches, ancient Hawaiian fishponds, and offshore islands to explore. In the southeastern corner of Oahu, Honolulu's main bedroom communities crawl up the steep valleys that flow into Maunalua Bay. Also here are snorkelers' favorite Hanauma Bay and a string of wild and often hidden beaches.

Oahu Today

The third-largest Hawaiian island is also the most populated, with about 75% of the state's residents. Often called "The Gathering Place," Oahu is usually the first stop in Hawaii for visitors.

TOURISM AND THE ECONOMY

Tourism is Hawaii's primary industry, relying heavily on international travelers and generating $17 billion in revenue from some 10 million visitors in 2019. Although those numbers dropped considerably (more than 70%) in 2020 due to the COVID-19 pandemic, they're on the rise again. About a half-million tourists arrive on Oahu every month, the majority staying in Waikiki.

The pandemic led to concerns among residents, not only about developing a short-term strategy for reopening Hawaii's tourism safely, but also about the need to offer more culturally focused and voluntourism activities. As a result, the Islands have initiated a tourism sustainability plan that has instituted new fees and advance reservations at popular destinations across Oahu (and all the Hawaiian Islands). It's a good idea to check on such policies before visiting sites such as Hanauma Bay State Park and other natural attractions.

Up until early 2022, everyone in Hawaii had to wear masks indoors, and all bars and restaurants (indoor and outdoor) required a valid ID and vaccination card prior to entering. Before your trip, visit the Safe Travels Hawaii website (⊕ *hawaiicovid19.com/travel*) for updated COVID-19 information and requirements.

As the most developed island, Oahu's ongoing dependence on tourism has resulted in hardship for locals, including traffic problems, elevated housing prices, and general overcrowding that has strained the island's natural resources for years. Hawaii's average salaries don't offer enough economic stability for middle-to-low–income residents due to the state's high cost of living. Most people who live here have a long commute to their work in Honolulu (or they may hold multiple jobs), and it's not uncommon for many to live with extended family.

Adding to the problems, most Oahu neighborhoods, like much of Hawaii, saw home and condo prices skyrocket during the pandemic. In late 2019, Bill 89 (City Ordinance 19-18) passed, prohibiting short-term residential/apartment rentals, and some residents argue that the new law has unfairly limited an income stream they have relied on to make ends meet. At this writing, short-term rentals are allowed only in Waikiki, Ko Olina, and Turtle Bay.

SUSTAINABILITY

Oahu has begun educating its communities on the importance of keeping beaches and oceans clean and ensuring that marine life and reefs remain healthy. You won't find plastic straws in your cocktails on Oahu, where plastic shopping bags are also prohibited (so pack reusable bags, if needed). Further, all sunblock sold here must be reef-safe, the result of a January 2021 mandate, and the city of Honolulu has committed to create a carbon-neutral economy, using renewable energy, a green infrastructure, and sustainable waste management.

Hawaii Tourism's newly introduced Malama Hawaii program (⊕ *www.gohawaii.com/malama*) encourages travelers to be mindful while experiencing the Islands—by visiting with *kokua* (care) and *kuleana* (responsibility); by finding ways to *malama* (give back) to the land through volunteer programs; and by buying local to support the many great family-run shops and restaurants. A number of hotels are even offering special "Malama" packages.

EMBRACING LOCAL TRADITION

The arrival of Western Europeans in the late 1700s nearly led to the eradication of the Hawaiian culture. After Hawaii became a U.S. state in 1959, a process of Americanization further silenced some traditions: the Hawaiian language was banned from schools, cultural celebrations were forbidden, and children were distanced from local customs.

Hawaiian pride is now resurgent as islanders rediscover their heritage—from hula, lei making, and music to the methods for pounding poi and the nutritional and healing properties of native herbs, flowers, and other plants. There's also a renewed interest in building authentic Polynesian wooden canoes and learning traditional navigation. Several major educational facilities, such as Windward Community College, offer free Hawaiian language courses.

Visitors to Waikiki will experience Oahu's history as well. Landmark hotels such as the Royal Hawaiian and Moana Surfrider offer free (and fascinating) in-depth historical tours, as well as weekly lei making and other on-site Hawaiian ceremonies. You can also experience Hawaiian history by catching waves on a surfboard or a wooden outrigger canoe.

Most notably, the Native Hawaiian population is also on the rise in Oahu for the first time since the 18th century. Considered the first of its kind, the local settlement Puuhonua o Waimanalo—developed in partnership with the state in 1994 on the windward side of Oahu—is home to more than 200 mostly indigenous residents, who live on nearly 50 acres of land and support the culture and traditions of Hawaii.

TRANSPORTATION

The Honolulu Rail Transit system has been in development for over 40 years and is expected to cost more than $9 billion dollars (far more than originally budgeted) before it's eventually finished. This elevated rail line will span 20 miles—from East Kapolei to the Ala Moana Center, with several extensions, including a station in Waikiki. Although deadlines for completion are frequently changed, a small portion is set to open in 2022, with a goal of having the entire system operational by 2031.

AGRICULTURE AND OAHU'S CULINARY SCENE

Years ago, the major crops on Hawaii were sugarcane and pineapple, but those have nearly disappeared, at least commercially. Although most of Hawaii's food is still imported, a statewide movement to create a more sustainable food-supply chain has rekindled interest in local agriculture and inspired restaurants to emphasize farm-to-table cuisine. Weekly farmers' markets offer everything from fresh papaya or mango to small-batch honey, jam, and chocolate. Chefs and restaurateurs have partnered with the Hawaii Restaurant Association to ensure they are serving the freshest produce, meat, and seafood.

Having reopened after COVID-19, Oahu's restaurants are again thriving, especially in Honolulu's Waikiki and Kakaako districts, though a number of new, independently owned restaurants have opened around the island as well. You'll find every cuisine imaginable (and at every price point), from casual beach fare to multicourse tasting menus. These days, it's not unusual to see local, indigenous ingredients on menus, and chefs (some homegrown) who blend culinary styles, giving, say, Italian or French dishes distinctive Hawaiian twists.

Oahu's Best Beaches

HALEIWA BEACH/ALII BEACH PARK, NORTH SHORE

This legendary surfing spot hosts the Vans Triple Crown of Surfing each winter. Its beach park is popular (and often busy), with lots of shade, picnic tables, showers, and other amenities. The beach is one of the North Shore's few that are considered safe for swimmers. It's also great for snorkelers and novice surfers. Be sure to soak in some authentic island vibes by checking out the town of Haleiwa's shops and surf culture.

KO OLINA BEACH, WEST (LEEWARD) OAHU

Four picture-perfect, totally protected, man-made lagoons in front of three major resorts—including Disney's incredible Aulani—offer soft sand and calm, turquoise water. The Ko Olina area was truly made for family-friendly fun, with kayaks, SUPs (stand-up paddleboards), and snorkel gear readily available for rent and plenty of room for everyone, with grassy areas for relaxing and enjoying a pleasant beach day.

SUNSET BEACH PARK, NORTH SHORE

As its name implies, this beautiful beach, just down the road from the world-famous Bonzai Pipeline, is a favorite place to catch the sun's last brilliant rays before it dips below the horizon. It also offers calm waters and fun snorkeling in summer and big waves in winter.

ALA MOANA REGIONAL PARK, HONOLULU

Just a few steps away from the Ala Moana Center's shops and restaurants, this beach offers extraordinarily fine sand and smaller crowds than Waikiki, which is about 20 minutes away. With lifeguards and amenities (though little shade), this is a family-friendly spot with plenty of activity in and out of the water, including stand-up paddleboarding and snorkeling, as well as bicycling and picnicking. It's also a favorite local surfing spot, with several popular breaks just offshore.

BELLOWS FIELD BEACH PARK, EAST (WINDWARD) OAHU

Lovely, picturesque Bellows Beach is known for its striking stretch of wide, white sand and shimmering sapphire blue waters. Near Waimanalo Bay Beach Park and Bellows Air Force Station, it's usually open to the public on weekends and a favorite spot for body boarders and surfers. A fun place for camping, this eastward-facing crescent is famous for spectacular sunrises, shady ironwood trees, and strong afternoon breezes.

KUALOA REGIONAL PARK, EAST (WINDWARD) OAHU

With lots of shade and green space, this expansive park makes it possible for campers and other beachgoers to spread out. The sand itself isn't very wide, but the waves are gentle, and it's a great spot for swimming, kayaking, and paddleboarding. If the wind

Ko Olina Beach, West (Leeward) Oahu

is kicking up, you might see locals flying large, two-handed kites. The scenery here is lovely, too, with the Koolau Mountains forming a distant backdrop and Mokolii Island visible offshore.

LANIKAI BEACH, EAST (WINDWARD) OAHU

Tucked away in a quiet residential neighborhood, this beach offers powdery white sand and crystal-clear water but very limited shade. It's worth getting here before dawn, as it's a gorgeous place to catch the sunrise. Unlike at nearby Kailua Beach Park, no food, water, or facilities are available here, so bring whatever you think you will need to enjoy the tranquil setting. Access to this beach is through several narrow pedestrian walkways that you can see from the street, but parking is very limited.

SANDY BEACH PARK, EAST (WINDWARD) OAHU

This south shore, Hawaii Kai–area beach features plenty of room to spread out atop the fine golden sand and enjoy the scenery, including, if the tides are right, a glimpse of the nearby Halona Blowhole. Popular with locals and known for its crashing shorebreak, this beach has lifeguards and facilities. If the waves are rough, though, it's best to retire to the shoreline and watch the activity—which might include kites performing acrobatics in the gusts—from your lounge chair.

WHITE PLAINS BEACH, WEST (LEEWARD) OAHU

A go-to beach for surfing, stand-up paddleboarding, and bodyboarding, White Plains is a favorite among locals (and, often, seals). Not only is it known to be less

crowded than Waikiki, but it also has beautiful azure water and a smooth, sandy bottom. The currents and wind can be strong and unpredictable, but there are lifeguards watching over the swimmers. You'll also find abundant parking, as well as many other amenities.

WAIMEA BAY BEACH PARK, NORTH SHORE

During the summer, the snorkeling is simply magical at this popular, jaw-droppingly beautiful beach. But in winter, surf's up, so be careful if you don't know what you're doing. Major contests are held here as waves frequently reach 20 feet. "The Eddie" surf competition honors big-wave surfer Eddie Aikau, attracting fans from across the Islands, so arrive early in the morning to claim your seat on the dunes.

Oahu's Most Incredible Natural Wonders

WAIMEA BAY AND VALLEY, NORTH SHORE
The scenic and legendary Waimea Bay is famous for powerful, big waves in winter and calm water in summer. Nearby is the lush and expansive Waimea Valley, with exquisite scenery, including waterfalls (there's an admission charge, though).

HALONA BLOWHOLE, EAST (WINDWARD) OAHU
North of the picturesque Hanauma Bay, the Halona Blowhole can be viewed easily from a lookout just off the Kalanianaole Highway. Formed by ancient lava tubes, this blowhole blasts a forceful spray about 30 feet in the air when the tide is right.

MANOA FALLS, HONOLULU
In the lush Manoa Valley, the beautiful and ancient waterfall drops 150 feet into a pool that's surrounded by a tropical rain forest with soaring bamboo, trees, and flowers. It will come as no surprise that the cascade is a popular filming location.

DIAMOND HEAD, HONOLULU
Legendary and majestic, Oahu's breathtaking Diamond Head crater is an iconic symbol of the island. Looming large above Waikiki's coastline, the former military outpost is now a popular place to hike. Panoramic views from the top are truly splendid, but it's a steep climb and always best to go in the early morning to see the sunrise.

KAENA POINT, WEST (LEEWARD) OAHU
Wild and remote, Kaena Point is the westernmost point on Oahu. Featuring picturesque coves and sweeping ocean views, this spot can only be reached by hiking a rocky (and often muddy) trail along the rough coastline that offers extraordinary vistas. It's home to a bird sanctuary and nature reserve. The point has two entrances (Kaena Point State Park and Mokuleia), so if you're feeling inspired, you can trek for about 5 miles round-trip.

HANAUMA BAY, EAST (WINDWARD) OAHU
On the island's southeast coast, Hanauma Bay is considered one of the most popular snorkeling spots here. With brilliant white sand and shallow, calm water, this stunning nature preserve is teeming with many species of colorful tropical fish and marine life. Over the years, it's become increasingly crowded, so visitors are now capped at 1,400 per day. The entrance fee is $25 for adults, and tickets must be booked and paid for in

Diamond Head

advance. (Details are on the Hanauma Bay State Park website: ⊕hanaumabay-statepark.com.)

NUUANU PALI LOOKOUT, EAST (WINDWARD) OAHU

As part of the Koolau mountain range, the renowned Nuuanu Pali Lookout is situated inside of Nuuanu Pali State Park and offers a spectacular panoramic view of Oahu. At nearly 1,000 feet high, this notoriously windy spot offers views far across the island's windward coast and the ocean beyond. It also played a major role in King Kamehameha I's epic victory over the troops of Oahu, with hundreds of warriors driven off the cliff to their deaths.

MAKAPUU POINT, EAST (WINDWARD) OAHU

On the island's southeastern tip, the Makapuu Point lookout is located just off the side of the Kalanianaole Highway. A paved walkway leads to an overlook with a breathtaking panoramic view of Windward Oahu's dramatic sea cliffs and lovely Makapuu Beach Park (or take a short hike to the lighthouse nearby). It's also known as a great spot for whale-watching.

HOOMALUHIA BOTANICAL GARDEN, EAST (WINDWARD) OAHU

This beautiful garden destination, created by the U.S. Army Corps of Engineers, is free to enjoy and is home to tropical trees, plants, and flowers from across the world, all grouped by region.

KOOLAU MOUNTAINS, EAST (WINDWARD) OAHU

Stretching nearly 40 miles, this majestic volcanic mountain formation features an abundance of steep trails that lead to gorgeous waterfalls and streams. The most recognizable section of this mountain range is the cliff that rises to about 2,000 feet on the eastern side.

Flora and Fauna in Hawaii

KUKUI
The kukui, or candlenut, is Hawaii's state tree, and Hawaiians have had many uses for it. Oil was extracted from its nuts and burned as a light source and also rubbed on fishing nets to preserve them. The juice from the husk's fruit was used as a dye. The small kukui blossoms and nuts also have medicinal purposes.

PLUMERIA
Also known as frangipani, this fragrant flower is named after Charles Plumier, the noted French botanist who discovered it in Central America in the late 1600s. Plumeria come in shades of white, yellow, pink, red, and orange. The hearty, plentiful blossoms are frequently used in lei.

HUMPBACK WHALES
Each year, North Pacific humpback whales make the long journey to Hawaii from Alaska. With its warm, protected waters, Hawaii provides the ideal place for the marine mammals to mate and to birth, and to nurse their young. They arrive between November and May, and their presence is an anticipated event. You can see them up close during whale-watching boat tours.

GARDENIA
The gardenia is a favorite for lei makers because of its sweet smell. The plant is native to tropical regions throughout China and Africa, but there are also endemic gardenias in Hawaii. The nanu gardenia is found only in the Islands and has petite white blossoms.

HONU
The *honu*, or Hawaiian green sea turtle, is a magical sight. The graceful reptile is an endangered and protected species in Hawaii. It's easier to encounter *honu* during a snorkeling or scuba-diving excursion, but they occasionally can be spotted basking on beaches.

MONK SEAL

Known as the *ilio holo i ka uaua*, meaning "dog that runs in rough water," monk seals are endemic to Hawaii and critically endangered. The majority of these mammals, which can grow to more than seven feet long, live in the remote, uninhabited Northwestern Hawaiian Islands.

HIBISCUS

In 1923, the Territory of Hawaii passed a law designating hibiscus as Hawaii's official flower. While there are more than 30 introduced species of the large, colorful flowers throughout the Islands, there are five endemic types. The endemic hibiscus has yellow blossoms and is known in Hawaiian as *mao hau hele*, which means the "traveling green tree."

TROPICAL FISH

Approximately 25% of the fish species in the Islands are endemic. Snorkeling in Hawaii is a unique, fun opportunity to see colorful fish found nowhere else on Earth. Interestingly, Hawaii's state fish, the *humuhumunukunukuapuaa*, or reef trigger, is not endemic to the state.

PIKAKE

These small, delicate blossoms are known for their hypnotic, sweet scent. The jasmine flower was introduced from India and was a favorite of Princess Kaiulani. *Pikake*, which is the Hawaiian word for the blossom as well as for a peacock—another favorite of the princess—is the subject of many *mele*, or Hawaiian songs.

NENE GOOSE

Pronounced *nay-nay*, the endemic nene goose (Hawaii's state bird) is one of the world's rarest. A descendant of the Canada goose, it has been bred back from the edge of extinction and reintroduced into the wild. Use caution driving in national and state parks, which they frequent.

What to Eat and Drink in Hawaii

SHAVE ICE
Shave ice is simple in its composition—fluffy ice drizzled in Technicolor syrups. Shave ice traces its roots to Hawaii's plantation past. Japanese laborers would use the machetes from their field work to finely shave ice from large frozen blocks and then pour fruit juice over it.

MUSUBI
Musubi are Hawaii's answer to the perfect snack. Portable, handheld, and salty, *musubi* are a great go-to any time of day. The local comfort food is a slice of fried Spam encased in packed white rice and snugly wrapped with nori, or dried seaweed. Available everywhere, *musubi* are usually just a few dollars.

MAI TAI
When people think of a Hawaiian cocktail, the colorful mai tai often comes to mind. It's the unofficial drink to imbibe at a luau and refreshingly tropical. This potent concoction has a rum base and is traditionally made with orange curaçao, orgeat, fresh-squeezed lime juice, and simple syrup.

HAWAIIAN PLATE
The Hawaiian plate comprises the delicious, traditional foods of Hawaii, all on one heaping plate. You can find these combo meals anywhere, from roadside lunch wagons to five-star restaurants. Get yours with the melt-in-your-mouth shredded kalua pig, pork, or chicken *laulau* (cooked in ti leaves) with *lomi* salmon (diced salmon with tomatoes and onions) on the side and the coconut-milk *haupia* for dessert. Most Hawaiian plates come with the requisite two scoops of white rice. Don't forget to try *poi*, or pounded and cooked taro.

POKE
In Hawaiian, *poke* is a verb that means to slice and cut into pieces. It perfectly describes the technique Hawaiians have used for centuries to prepare poke the dish. The cubed raw fish, most commonly ahi, or tuna, is traditionally tossed with Hawaiian sea salt, *limu kohu* (red seaweed), or *inamona* (crushed kukui nuts). Today, countless varieties of this must-try dish are served in all kinds of restaurants across the Islands. Poke shacks offer no-frills, made-to-order poke.

SAIMIN
This only-in-Hawaii noodle dish is the culinary innovation of Hawaii plantation workers in the late 1800s who created a new comfort food with ingredients and traditions from their home countries.

Poke

MANAPUA

When *kamaaina*, or Hawaii residents, are invited to a potluck, business meeting, or even an impromptu party, you'll inevitably see a box filled with *manapua*. Inside these airy white buns are pockets of sweet *char siu* pork. Head to cities and towns around the Islands, and you'll find restaurants with manapua on their menus, as well as manapua takeout places serving a variety of fillings. There's sweet potato, curry chicken, *lap cheong* (or Chinese sausage)—and even sweet flavors, such as custard and *ube*, a purple yam popular in Filipino desserts.

LOCO MOCO

The traditional version of one of Hawaii's classic comfort-food dishes consists of white rice topped with a hamburger patty and fried eggs and generously blanketed in rich, brown gravy. Cafe 100 in Hilo on the Big Island is renowned as the home of the *loco moco*, but you'll find this popular staple everywhere. It can be eaten any time of day.

KONA COFFEE

In Kona, on the Big Island, coffee reigns supreme. There are roughly 600 coffee farms dotting the west side of the island, each producing flavorful (and quite expensive) coffee grown in the rich, volcanic soil. Kona coffee is typically hand-harvested from August through December.

MALASADA

Malasadas are a beloved treat in Hawaii. The Portuguese pastries are about the size of a baseball and are airy, deep-fried, and dusted with sugar. They are best enjoyed hot and filled with custard; fillings are a Hawaiian variation on the original.

What to Buy in Hawaii

MACADAMIA NUT CANDY
Macadamia nuts are native to Australia, but the gumball-sized nut remains an important crop in Hawaii. It was first introduced in the late 1880s as a windbreak for sugarcane crops. Today, mac nuts are a popular local snack and are especially good baked in cookies or other desserts.

LEI
As a visitor to Hawaii, you may well receive a lei, either a shell, kukui nut, or fragrant flower variety, as a welcome to the Islands. *Kamaaina* (Hawaii residents) mark special occasions by gifting lei.

ALOHA WEAR
Aloha wear in Hawaii has come a long way from the polyester fabrics with too-bright, kitschy patterns (although those still exist). Local designers have been creating dressy, modern aloha attire with softer prints that evoke Island botanicals, heritage, and traditional patterns. Hawaii residents don aloha wear for everything from work to weddings.

LAUHALA
The hala tree is most known for its long, thin leaves and the masterful crafts that are created from them. Lauhala weavers make baskets, hats, mats, jewelry, and more, using intricate traditional patterns and techniques.

JEWELRY
Island-inspired jewelry comes in many styles. Tahitian pearl pendants and earrings are a local favorite, as are delicate, inexpensive shell pieces. The most coveted are Hawaiian heirloom bracelets in gold or silver with one's name enameled in Old English script.

HAWAIIAN COFFEE
Reminisce about your Hawaii getaway each time you brew a cup of aromatic, full-bodied coffee, whether it's from Kona or Kauai. All the main islands grow distinctive coffee. Stores and cafés sell bags of varying sizes, and in some places you can buy direct from a farmer. .

HAWAIIAN HONEY
With its temperate climate and bountiful foliage, Hawaii is ideal for honeybees. The Islands' ecosystem contributes to honeys with robust flavors and textures, including elixirs extracted from the blossoms of the macadamia nut tree, the lehua flower, and the invasive Christmasberry shrub.

KOA WOOD
If you're looking for an heirloom keepsake from the Islands, consider a koa wood product. Grown only in Hawaii, the valuable koa is some of the world's rarest and hardest wood. Hawaiians traditionally made surfboards and canoes from these trees, which today grow only in upland forests.

HAWAIIAN SEA SALT
A long tradition of harvesting salt beds by hand continues today on all the Islands. The salt comes in various colors, including inky black and brick red—the result of the salt reacting and mixing with activated charcoal and *alaea* (volcanic clay). It is renowned by chefs around the state.

UKULELE
In Hawaiian, *ukulele* means "the jumping flea." The small instrument made its way to the Islands in the 1880s via Portuguese immigrants who brought with them the four-string, guitar-like *machete de braga*. It is famous as a solo instrument today, with virtuoso artists like Jake Shimabukuro and Taimane Gardner popularizing the ukulele's versatile sound.

What to Read and Watch

HAWAIIAN MYTHOLOGY BY MARTHA BECKWITH

This exhaustive work of ethnology and folklore was researched and collected by Martha Beckwith over decades and published when she was 69. *Hawaiian Mythology* is a comprehensive look at the Hawaiian ancestral deities and their importance throughout history.

HAWAII'S STORY BY HAWAII'S QUEEN, BY LILIUOKALANI

This poignant book, by Queen Liliuokalani, chronicles the 1893 overthrow of the Hawaiian monarchy and her plea for her people. It's an essential read to understand the political undercurrent and the push for sovereignty that exists in the Islands more than 125 years later.

LETTERS FROM HAWAII BY MARK TWAIN

In 1866, when Samuel Clemens was 31, he sailed from California and spent four months in Hawaii. He eventually mailed 25 letters to the *Sacramento Union* newspaper about his experiences. Along the way, Twain sheds some cultural biases as he visits Kilauea Volcano, meets with Hawaii's newly formed legislators, and examines the sugar trade.

SHOAL OF TIME: A HISTORY OF THE HAWAIIAN ISLANDS BY GAVAN DAWS

Perhaps the most popular book by this best-selling Honolulu author is *Shoal of Time*. Published in 1974, the account of modern Hawaiian history details the colonization of Hawaii and everything that was lost in the process.

MOLOKA'I BY ALAN BRENNERT

The writer's debut novel, set in the 1890s, follows a Hawaiian woman who contracts leprosy as a child and is sent to the remote, quarantined community of Kalaupapa on the island of Molokai, where she then lives. The Southern California–based author was inspired to write the book during his visits to Hawaii.

THE DESCENDANTS

Based on the book by local author Kaui Hart Hemmings, the film adaptation starring George Clooney and directed by Alexander Payne was filmed on Oahu and Kauai. It spotlights a contemporary, upper-class family in Hawaii as they deal with family grief and landholdings in flux.

HAWAII SAYS "ALOHA" BY DON BLANDING

First published in 1928, this volume of enchanting, rhyming verse about Hawaii evokes the rich details about the Islands that mesmerized the author in the 1920s and for the rest of his life. Blanding also illustrated this and many other books and was later named Hawaii's poet laureate.

BLUE HAWAII

The 1961 musical features the hip-shaking songs and moves of Elvis Presley, who plays tour guide Chadwick Gates. Elvis famously sings "Ke Kali Nei Au," or "The Hawaiian Wedding Song," at the iconic and now-shuttered Coco Palms Resort on Kauai. (The resort has remained closed since 1992 following Hurricane Iniki.)

MOANA

The release of *Moana* in 2016 was celebrated by many in Hawaii and the Pacific for showcasing Polynesian culture. The now-beloved animated movie, which tells the story of the demigod Maui, features the voice talents of Aulii Cravalho and Dwayne Johnson. In 2018, *Moana* was re-recorded and distributed in Olelo Hawaii, or the Hawaiian language, with Cravalho reprising her role. It marked the first time a Disney movie was available in Hawaiian.

Kids and Families

CHOOSING A PLACE TO STAY

Resorts: All the big resorts make programs for kids a priority. When booking your room, ask about *keiki* (children's) menus at restaurants, free on-property activities, and pools and water parks designed specifically for the younger set.

In Waikiki, your best bet for kids is the Hilton Hawaiian Village, where there's a large beach and loads of kids' programs. Also good choices: the Alohilani Resort, which has a roster of family-friendly cultural activities, and the Sheraton Waikiki, where the Helumoa Playground features two pools and a water slide.

Condos: You can cook your own food and get twice the space of a hotel room for much less. Be sure to ask about the size of the complex's pool and barbecue availability. For the ultimate family condo experience on Oahu, Marriott's Ko Olina Beach Club is ideal thanks to its sheltered beaches, four pools, barbecues, children's play areas, large kitchens, and an on-site grocery store. In Waikiki, try the Waikiki Shore and Luana Waikiki.

■ TIP➜ **Some hotels and resorts offer free beach towels, chairs, and other amenities. Be sure to check on such things in advance.**

OCEAN ACTIVITIES

On the Beach: In Waikiki, your best beach bets for young children are Kuhio Beach Park and Fort DeRussy Beach Park, both protected from a strong shore break and with a wide stretch of sand, with lifeguards on duty. On the windward side, try Kailua Beach Park, with its shady trees and good bathroom/shower facilities. North Shore beaches are recommended for children only in the summer months, and of these, Waimea Bay, with its wide stretch of sand and good facilities, is best for kids. On the leeward side, Ko Olina's protected coves are great for families with small children.

On the Waves: Waikiki is *the* place for everyone to learn to surf, including kids. Some hotels, including the Royal Hawaiian, the Queen Kapiolani, and the Outrigger Waikiki Beach Resort, offer in-house surf schools. Or, for a less crowded surfing experience, head to Barbers Point.

The Underwater World: Hawaii is a great place to introduce your kids to snorkeling. Even without the mask and snorkel, they'll be able to see colorful fish darting around coral reefs, and they may also spot endangered Hawaiian green sea turtles and dolphins. On Oahu, the quintessential snorkeling experience can be had at Hanauma Bay, where kids can see hundreds of species of fish in protected waters and enjoy a wide stretch of beach. In summer months only, Shark's Cove on the North Shore is an interesting experience for older kids who already have snorkeling basics.

LAND ACTIVITIES

Oahu is fortunate to have the greatest variety of land-based experiences in the Islands. Kids can visit the Honolulu Zoo for twilight tours, explore the undersea world at the Waikiki Aquarium, or husk a coconut at the Polynesian Cultural Center. Hoomaluhia Botanical Garden offers wide-open spaces and a duck pond, while Kualoa Ranch is the place for horseback riding.

AFTER DARK

At night, children get a kick out of a luau, and many of the shows incorporate young audience members. Older kids are more likely to enjoy the handful of more modern luau, incorporating acrobatics, lively music, and fire dancers. Check on the status of Hilton Hawaiian Village's free Friday night fireworks shows, which are especially fun to watch from the beach in Waikiki.

The History of Hawaii

Hawaiian history is long and complex; a brief survey can put into context the ongoing renaissance of native arts and culture.

THE POLYNESIANS

Long before both the Vikings and Christopher Columbus, Polynesian seafarers set out to explore the vast stretches of the open ocean in double-hulled canoes. They didn't just flail around and land here by accident; they understood the deep nuances of celestial navigation and were masters of the craft. From western Polynesia, they traveled back and forth between Samoa, Fiji, Tahiti, the Marquesas, and the Society Isles, settling on the outer reaches of the Pacific, Hawaii, and Easter Island, as early as AD 300. The golden era of Polynesian voyaging peaked around AD 1200, after which the distant Hawaiian Islands were left to develop their own unique cultural practices and subsistence in relative isolation.

The Islands' symbiotic society was deeply intertwined with religion, mythology, science, and artistry. Ruled by an *alii*, or chief, each settlement was nestled in an *ahupuaa*, a pie-shaped land division from the uplands, through the valleys, and down to the shores. Everyone contributed, whether it was by building canoes, catching fish, making tools, or farming land, thereby developing a sustainable society.

A UNITED KINGDOM

When the British explorer Captain James Cook arrived in Kealakekua Bay on the Big Island in 1778, he was greeted by the Hawaiians as a person of important stature. With guns and ammunition purchased from subsequent foreign trading ships, the Big Island chief, Kamehameha the Great, gained a significant advantage over the other *alii* (chiefs). He united Hawaii into one kingdom in 1810,

bringing an end to the frequent interisland battles that dominated Hawaiian life.

Tragically, the new kingdom was beset with troubles. Native religion was abandoned, and *kapu* (laws and regulations) were eventually abolished. The European explorers brought diseases with them, and within a few decades the Native Hawaiian population was decimated.

New laws regarding land ownership and religious practices eroded the underpinnings of pre-contact Hawaii. Each successor to the Hawaiian throne sacrificed more control over the Island kingdom. As Westerners permeated Hawaiian culture, so did social unrest.

MODERN HAWAII

In 1893, the last Hawaiian monarch, Queen Liliuokalani, was overthrown by a group of American and European businesspeople and government officials, aided by an armed militia. This led to the creation of the Republic of Hawaii, and it became a U.S. territory for the next 60 years. The loss of Hawaiian sovereignty and the conditions of annexation have haunted the Hawaiian people since the monarchy was deposed.

Pearl Harbor in Oahu was attacked in 1941, which engaged the United States immediately into World War II. Tourism, from its beginnings in the early 1900s, flourished after the war and naturally inspired rapid real estate development in Waikiki and then elsewhere. In 1959, Hawaii officially became the 50th state.

In the late 1960s and 1970s, the Native Hawaiian community began to celebrate a return to its roots with the revival of traditional hula as a cultural practice, the journeys of the voyaging canoes, and a resurgence of Hawaiian music and language. This movement, called the Hawaiian Renaissance, has influenced life in the Islands ever since.

HAWAIIAN CULTURAL
TRADITIONS HULA, LEI, AND LUAU

HULA: MORE THAN A FOLK DANCE

Hula has been called "the heartbeat of the Hawaiian people" and also "the world's best-known, most misunderstood dance." Both are true. Hula isn't just dance. It is storytelling.

Chanter Edith McKinzie calls it "an extension of a piece of poetry." In its adornments, implements, and customs, hula integrates every important Hawaiian cultural practice: poetry, history, genealogy, craft, plant cultivation, martial arts, religion, protocol. So when 19th-century Christian missionaries sought to eradicate a practice they considered depraved, they threatened more than just a folk dance.

With public performance outlawed and private hula practice discouraged, hula went underground for a generation. The fragile verbal link by which culture was transmitted from teacher to student hung by a thread. Even increasing literacy did not help because hula's practitioners were a secretive and protected circle.

As if that weren't bad enough, vaudeville, Broadway, and Hollywood got hold of the hula, giving it the glitz treatment in an unbroken line from "Oh, How She Could Wicky Wacky Woo" to "Rock-A-Hula Baby." Hula became shorthand for paradise: fragrant flowers, lazy hours. Ironically, this development assured that hundreds of Hawaiians could make a living performing and teaching hula. Many danced 'auana (modern form) in performance; but taught kahiko (traditional), quietly, at home or in hula schools.

Today, decades after the cultural revival known as the Hawaiian Renaissance, language immersion programs have assured a new generation of proficient chanters, songwriters, and translators. Visitors can see more—and more authentic—traditional hula now than at any other time in the last 200 years.

Like the culture of which it is the beating heart, hula has survived.

Lei poo. Head lei. In *kahiko,* greenery only. In auana, flowers.

Face emotes appropriate expression. Dancer should not be a smiling automaton.

Shoulders remain relaxed and still, never hunched, even with arms raised. No bouncing.

Eyes always follow leading hand.

Lei. Hula is rarely performed without a shoulder lei.

Traditional hula skirt is loose fabric, smocked and gathered at the waist.

Arms and hands remain loose, relaxed, below shoulder level— except as required by interpretive movements.

Hip is canted over weight-bearing foot.

Knees are always slightly bent, accentuating hip sway.

Kupee. Ankle bracelet of flowers, shells, or foliage.

In kahiko, feet are flat. In auana, they may be more arched, but not tiptoes or bouncing.

BASIC MOTIONS

Speak or sing

Moon or sun

Grass shack or house

Mountains or heights

Love or caress

At backyard parties, hula is performed in bare feet and street clothes, but in performance, adornments play a key role, as do rhythm-keeping implements such as the *pahu* drum and the *ipu* (gourd).

In hula *kahiko* (traditional style), the usual dress is multiple layers of stiff fabric (often with a pellom lining, which most closely resembles *kapa*, the paperlike bark cloth of the Hawaiians). These wrap tightly around the bosom but flare below the waist to form a skirt. In pre-contact times, dancers wore only kapa skirts. Men traditionally wear loincloths.

Monarchy-period hula is performed in voluminous muumuu or high-necked muslin blouses and gathered skirts. Men wear white or gingham shirts and black pants.

In hula *auana* (modern), dress for women can range from grass skirts and strapless tops to contemporary tea-length dresses. Men generally wear aloha shirts, but sometimes grass skirts over pants or even everyday gear.

SURPRISING HULA FACTS

■ Grass skirts are not traditional; workers from Kiribati (the Gilbert Islands) brought this custom to Hawaii.

■ In olden-day Hawaii, *mele* (songs) for hula were composed for every occasion—name songs for babies, dirges for funerals, welcome songs for visitors, celebrations of favorite pursuits.

■ Hula *mai* is a traditional hula form in praise of a noble's genitals; the power of the *alii* (royalty) to procreate gave mana (spiritual power) to the entire culture.

■ Hula students in old Hawaii adhered to high standards: scrupulous cleanliness, no sex, daily cleansing rituals, certain food prohibitions, and no contact with the dead. They were fined if they broke the rules.

WHERE TO WATCH

If you're interested in "the real thing," there are annual hula festivals on each island. Check the individual island visitors' bureaus websites at ⊕ *www.gohawaii.com*.

If you can't make it to a festival, there are plenty of other hula shows—at most resorts, many lounges, and even at certain shopping centers. Ask your hotel concierge for performance information.

ALL ABOUT LEI

Lei brighten every occasion in Hawaii, from birthdays to bar mitzvahs to baptisms. Creative artisans weave nature's bounty—flowers, ferns, vines, and seeds—into gorgeous creations that convey an array of heartfelt messages: "Welcome," "Congratulations," "Good luck," "Farewell," "Thank you," "I love you." When it's difficult to find the right words, a lei expresses exactly the right sentiment.

WHERE TO BUY THE BEST LEI

Most airports in Hawaii have lei stands where you can buy a fragrant garland upon arrival. Every florist shop in the Islands sells lei; you can also treat yourself to a lei while shopping for provisions at any supermarket or box store. And you'll always find lei sellers at crafts fairs and outdoor festivals.

LEI ETIQUETTE

■ To wear a closed lei, drape it over your shoulders, half in front and half in back. Open lei are worn around the neck, with the ends draped over the front in equal lengths.

■ Pikake, ginger, and other sweet, delicate blossoms are "feminine" lei. Men opt for cigar, crown flower, and ti leaf lei, which are sturdier and don't emit as much fragrance.

■ Lei are always presented with a kiss, a custom that supposedly dates back to World War II when a hula dancer fancied an officer at a U.S.O. show. Taking a dare from members of her troupe, she took off her lei, placed it around his neck, and kissed him on the cheek.

■ You shouldn't wear a lei before you give it to someone else. Hawaiians believe the lei absorbs your mana (spirit); if you give your lei away, you'll be giving away part of your essence.

ORCHID

Growing wild on every continent except Antarctica, orchids—which range in color from yellow to green to purple—comprise the largest family of plants in the world. There are more than 20,000 species of orchids, but only three are native to Hawaii—and they are very rare. The pretty lavender vanda you see hanging by the dozens at local lei stands has probably been imported from Thailand.

MAILE

Maile, an endemic twining vine with a heady aroma, is sacred to Laka, goddess of the hula. In ancient times, dancers wore maile and decorated hula altars with it to honor Laka. Today, "open" maile lei usually are given to men. Instead of ribbon, interwoven lengths of maile are used at dedications of new businesses. The maile is untied, never snipped, for doing so would symbolically "cut" the company's success.

ILIMA

Designated by Hawaii's Territorial Legislature in 1923 as the official flower of the island of Oahu, the golden ilima is so delicate it lasts for just a day. Five to seven hundred blossoms are needed to make one garland. Queen Emma, wife of King Kamehameha IV, preferred ilima over all other lei, which may have led to the incorrect belief that they were reserved only for royalty.

PLUMERIA

This ubiquitous flower is named after Charles Plumier, the noted French botanist who discovered it in Central America in the late 1600s. Plumeria ranks among the most popular lei in Hawaii because it's fragrant, hardy, plentiful, inexpensive, and requires very little care. Although yellow is the most common color, you'll also find plumeria lei in shades of pink, red, orange, and "rainbow" blends.

PIKAKE

Favored for its fragile beauty and sweet scent, pikake was introduced from India. In lieu of pearls, many brides in Hawaii adorn themselves with long, multiple strands of white pikake. Princess Kaiulani enjoyed showing guests her beloved pikake and peacocks at Ainahau, her Waikiki home. Interestingly, pikake is the Hawaiian word for both the bird and the blossom.

KUKUI

The kukui (candlenut) is Hawaii's state tree. Early Hawaiians strung kukui nuts (which are quite oily) together and burned them for light; mixed burned nuts with oil to make an indelible dye; and mashed roasted nuts to consume as a laxative. Kukui nut lei may not have been made until after Western contact, when the Hawaiians saw black beads from Europe and wanted to imitate them.

LUAU: A TASTE OF HAWAII

The best place to sample Hawaiian food is at a backyard luau. Aunts and uncles are cooking, the pig is from a cousin's farm, and the fish is from a brother's boat.

But even locals have to angle for invitations to those rare occasions. So your choice is most likely between a commercial luau and a Hawaiian restaurant.

Some commercial luau are less authentic; they offer little of the traditional diet and are more about umbrella drinks, spectacle, and fun.

For greater culinary authenticity, folksy experiences, and rock-bottom prices, visit a Hawaiian restaurant (most are in anonymous storefronts in residential neighborhoods). Expect rough edges and some effort negotiating the menu.

In either case, much of what is known today as Hawaiian food would be as foreign to a 16th-century Hawaiian as risotto or chow mien. The pre-contact diet was simple and healthy—mainly raw and steamed seafood and vegetables. Early Hawaiians used earth ovens and heated stones to cook seafood, taro, sweet potatoes, and breadfruit and seasoned their food with sea salt and ground kukui nuts. Seaweed, fern shoots, sweet potato vines, coconut, banana, sugarcane, and select greens and roots rounded out the diet.

Successive waves of immigrants added their favorites to the ti leaf–lined table. So it is that foods as disparate as salt salmon and chicken long rice are now Hawaiian—even though there is no salmon in Hawaiian waters and long rice (cellophane noodles) is Chinese.

AT THE LUAU: KALUA PORK

The heart of any luau is the *imu*, the earth oven in which a whole pig is roasted. The preparation of an imu is an arduous affair for most families, who tackle it only once a year or so, for a baby's first birthday or at Thanksgiving, when many Islanders prefer to imu their turkeys. Commercial luau operations have it down to a science, however.

THE ART OF THE STONE
The key to a proper imu is the *pohaku*, the stones. Imu cook by means of long, slow, moist heat released by special stones that can withstand a hot fire without exploding. Many Hawaiian families treasure their imu stones, keeping them in a pile in the backyard and passing them on through generations.

PIT COOKING
The imu makers first dig a pit about the size of a refrigerator, then lay down *kiawe* (mesquite) wood and stones, and build a white-hot fire that is allowed to burn itself out. The ashes are raked away, and the hot stones covered with banana and ti leaves. Well-wrapped in ti or banana leaves and a net of chicken wire, the pig is lowered onto the leaf-covered stones. *Laulau* (leaf-wrapped bundles of meats, fish, and taro leaves) may also be placed inside. Leaves—ti, banana, even ginger—cover the pig followed by wet burlap sacks (to create steam). The whole is topped with a canvas tarp and left to steam for the better part of a day.

OPENING THE IMU
This is the moment everyone waits for: The imu is unwrapped like a giant present and the imu keepers gingerly wrestle out the steaming pig. When it's unwrapped, the meat falls moist and smoky-flavored from the bone, looking just like Southern-style pulled pork, but without the barbecue sauce.

WHICH LUAU?
Most resort hotels have luau on their grounds that include hula, music, and, of course, lots of food and drink. Each island also has at least one "authentic" luau. For lists of the best luau on each island, visit the Hawaii Visitors and Convention Bureau website at ⊕ *www.gohawaii.com*.

MEA AI ONO: GOOD THINGS TO EAT.

LAULAU
Steamed meats, fish, and taro leaf in ti-leaf bundles: fork-tender, a medley of flavors; the taro resembles spinach.

Laulau

LOMI LOMI SALMON
Salt salmon in a piquant salad or relish with onions and tomatoes.

POI
Poi, a paste made of pounded taro root, may be an acquired taste, but it's a must-try during your visit.

Consider: The Hawaiian Adam is descended from *kalo* (taro). Young taro plants are called "keiki" (children). Poi is the first food after mother's milk for many Islanders. Ai, the word for food, is synonymous with poi in many contexts.

Lomi lomi salmon

Not only that, locals love it. "There is no meat that doesn't taste good with poi," the old Hawaiians said.

But you have to know how to eat it: with something rich or powerfully flavored. "It is salt that makes the poi go in," is another adage. When you're served poi, try it with a mouthful of smoky kalua pork or salty lomi lomi salmon. Its slightly sour blandness cleanses the palate. And if you don't like it, smile and say something polite. (And slide that bowl over to a local.)

Poi

E HELE MAI AI! COME AND EAT!

Local-style Hawaiian restaurants tend to be inconveniently located in well-worn storefronts with little or no parking, outfitted with battered tables and clattering Melmac dishes, but they personify aloha, invariably run by local families who welcome tourists who take the trouble to find them.

Many are cash-only operations and combination plates, known as "plate lunch," are a standard feature: one or two entrées, two scoops of steamed rice, one scoop of macaroni salad, and—if the place is really old-style—a tiny portion of coarse Hawaiian salt and some raw onions for relish.

Most serve some foods that aren't, strictly speaking, Hawaiian, but are beloved of kamaaina, such as salt meat with watercress (preserved meat in a tasty broth), or *akubone* (skipjack tuna fried in a tangy vinegar sauce).

Weddings and Honeymoons

There's no question that Hawaii is one of the country's foremost honeymoon destinations, but it's also popular for destination weddings.

THE BIG DAY

Choosing the Perfect Place. You really have two choices to make: the ceremony location and where to have the reception. For the former, Oahu offers beaches, sea-hugging bluffs, gardens, private residences, resort lawns, and, of course, places of worship. As for the reception, there are these same choices, as well as restaurants and even a luau. If you decide to go with the outdoors, make sure to have a backup plan for inclement weather.

Finding a Wedding Planner. If you intend to invite more than an officiant and your betrothed, seriously consider hiring a wedding planner who can help select a location, design the floral scheme, and recommend a florist and photographer. They can also plan the menu and choose a restaurant, caterer, or resort, and suggest Hawaiian traditions to incorporate into your ceremony.

If it's a resort wedding, most properties have on-site wedding coordinators who can provide guidance and one-stop shopping. Resorts also have indoor-outdoor space for ceremonies, private dining areas for any size reception, and stunning on-site photography spots. However, many independent wedding planners around Oahu specialize in certain types of ceremonies. Share your budget, and get a detailed written proposal before you proceed.

Getting Your License. There's no waiting period in Hawaii, no residency or citizenship requirements, and no required blood test or shots. You can apply and pay the fee online; however, both the bride and groom must appear together in person before a marriage-license agent to receive the marriage license at the State Department of Health in Honolulu. You'll need proof of age—the legal age to marry is 18. Upon approval, a marriage license is immediately issued and costs $60. After the ceremony, your officiant—who must be licensed by the Hawaii Department of Health—will mail the marriage certificate to the state, and you'll get your copy about four months later. There's an informative instructional video on the state's official website (⊕ emrs. ehawaii.gov/emrs/public/home.html).

Wedding Attire. In Hawaii, basically anything goes, from long, formal dresses with trains to casual attire—even bathing suits! For men, a pair of solid-color trousers with a nice aloha shirt is appropriate. If you're planning a wedding on the beach, barefoot is the way to go.

Local Customs. The most obvious traditional Hawaiian wedding custom is the lei exchange in which the bride and groom take turns placing a lei around the neck of the other—with a kiss. Bridal lei are usually floral, whereas the groom's is typically made of *maile,* for a green leafy garland that drapes the neck. Brides often also wear a *lei poo*—a circular floral headpiece. Other Hawaiian customs include the blowing of the conch shell, hula, chanting, and Hawaiian music.

THE HONEYMOON

Do you want champagne and strawberries delivered to your room each morning? A breathtaking swimming pool in which to float? A five-star restaurant in which to dine? Then a resort is ideal. A small inn or condominium is also good if you're on a tight budget or don't plan to spend much time in your room. The good news is that Waikiki's accommodations are almost as plentiful as the beaches, and there are many options to ensure your honeymoon is extra-special.

Chapter 2

TRAVEL SMART

Updated by
Tiffany Hill

★ **CAPITAL:**
Honolulu

👥 **POPULATION:**
1,016,508

💬 **LANGUAGE:**
English, Hawaiian

$ **CURRENCY:**
U.S. dollar

☎ **AREA CODE:**
808

⚠ **EMERGENCIES:**
911

🚗 **DRIVING:**
On the right

⚡ **ELECTRICITY:**
120–220 v/60 cycles; plugs
have two or three rectangu-
lar prongs

🕐 **TIME:**
Hawaii-Aleutian Standard
time, five (or six) hours
behind New York

🌐 **WEB RESOURCES:**
www.gohawaii.com
www.hawaii.com
www.hawaii-guide.com

✈ **AIRPORT:**
HNL

KAUAI
○Lihue

NIIHAU

OAHU
✪
HONOLULU

MOLOKAI

LANAI

KAHOOLAWE

MAUI

PACIFIC OCEAN

○Hilo

*BIG
ISLAND*

Know Before You Go

Planning a trip to Oahu? It's better to be prepared. Here are some important pieces of information you should know while making your plans.

THERE ARE SEVERAL AIRPORT TRANSFER OPTIONS

The Daniel K. Inouye International Airport in Honolulu is 20 minutes (60 minutes during rush hour) from Waikiki. Car-rental companies have booths at baggage claim. Shuttle buses then take you to the car-pickup areas.

An inefficient airport taxi system requires you to line up for a wrangler who radios for cars (about $45–$55 to Waikiki). A rideshare via Uber or Lyft is an alternative. Regardless, ask drivers to take Interstate H1, not Nimitz Highway, or your introduction to paradise will be via Honolulu's industrial back side.

The city's reliable bus system ($2.75) makes stops throughout Honolulu and Waikiki. Another option is the Roberts Hawaii shuttle ($21 or $163.90, available as a shared or private ride), which transports you to any hotel in Waikiki.

IT'S BEST TO BOOK RENTAL CARS IN ADVANCE

You can get away with not renting a car if you're staying in Waikiki. For exploring the rest of the island, though, there's no substitute for having your own wheels. To ensure you get a rental car (and the best rates), reserve in advance, especially around holidays and summer breaks.

Avoid renting candy-color convertibles or other flashy cars, and never leave anything valuable inside a vehicle, even if you lock it. Get a portable GPS navigator or make sure your phone has a navigation app, as Oahu's streets can be confusing.

DRIVING ALWAYS TAKES LONGER THAN EXPECTED

Don't let maps fool you. Although the distance between Waikiki and, say, the North Shore is roughly 40 miles, it may take more than an hour to get there, thanks to heavy traffic, construction, and other factors.

Many of Oahu's main roads are a single lane in each direction, with no alternate routes. So if you're stuck behind a slow-moving vehicle, you may have no other choice than to hope it turns soon. Heavy traffic moving toward downtown can begin as early as 6 am, with after-work traffic starting at 3 pm.

OAHU IS EXPENSIVE, BUT THERE ARE WAYS TO SAVE

A vacation to Hawaii doesn't have to break the bank. Online sources, like Groupon or Yelp, offer discounted rates for everything from dinner cruises to massages. Buy your souvenirs at Longs or ABC Stores rather than at shops catering to tourists, and you'll likely get the same type of goods for less money.

You don't need to stay at a pricier waterfront hotel when, in Waikiki, almost all hotels are a short walk to the shore. Access to beaches and most hiking trails on the island is free to the public. For inexpensive fresh fruit and produce, check out weekly farmers' markets and farm stands along the road—they'll often let you try before you buy.

For cheap and quick lunches, consider a food truck. Part of the culinary landscape of Oahu for generations, these lunch wagons—which rove around downtown and other areas—charge less than restaurants. Take advantage of *pau hana* time (happy hour) for cheaper drinks and appetizers at many establishments.

SEEING PEARL HARBOR REQUIRES PLANNING

Consider whether you want to see only the USS *Arizona* Memorial or the USS *Bowfin* and USS *Missouri* as well. You can also visit the nearby Pearl Harbor Aviation Museum on Ford Island. Note, however, that tickets to the USS *Arizona* Memorial are free but must be reserved online in advance for a $1 processing fee. Same-day tickets are not available.

Allow approximately 1 hour and 15 minutes for the USS *Arizona* tour, which includes a 23-minute documentary of the Pearl Harbor attack and a short ferry ride to the memorial itself. Also, allow time for the visitor center, which has two state-of-the-art exhibits that tell the story of the attack on December 7, 1941.

Strict security measures prohibit any sort of bag (purses, backpacks, diaper bags, camera cases—even small ones), although cameras are allowed. Strollers are allowed in the visitor center but not in the theaters or on the shuttle boats. Baggage storage is available for a $5 fee. Also, check ahead on any COVID-19 requirements, and don't forget to bring your ID.

Children under four years of age are not allowed on the USS *Bowfin* for safety reasons, and they may not enjoy the crowds or waiting in line at other sights. Older

kids are likely to find the more experiential, hands-on history of the USS *Bowfin* and USS *Missouri* memorable. The Pearl Harbor Aviation Museum's vintage planes are bonus attractions, if you have the time.

THERE'S MORE TO SEE THAN JUST WAIKIKI

Although Waikiki is a great place to stay, especially for first-time visitors, be sure to leave the hustle and bustle of Oahu's most popular neighborhood and explore the island's other notable areas. Consider, for example, a day trip to the North Shore, home to 10- to 20-foot monster swells in the winter.

Another must-visit neighborhood is Kailua, on Oahu's windward side. Over the last 20 years, it has become a buzzing beach town, complete with hip boutiques as well as restaurants featuring dishes made with locally sourced ingredients.

SAFETY IS A FACTOR WHEN EXPLORING OAHU'S OUTDOORS

Hawaii's natural wonders, while beautiful, can also be perilous if you're not careful. While at the beach, don't turn your back to the ocean; waves can often be unpredictable. It's best to go with a buddy if you're planning to swim, snorkel, or surf. You should also check ahead on hazardous conditions, such as shorebreaks and rip currents. Remember the adage: when in doubt, don't go out.

Since Hawaii is close to the equator, the sun's rays are strong in the Islands, so you should use sunscreen with an SPF of at least 30. Save room in your luggage and protect the environment by buying sunscreen after you arrive. In 2021, the Hawaii State Legislature banned the statewide sale of sunscreen containing reef-harming chemicals. Locally bought products no longer contain oxybenzone and octinoxate, two chemicals proven to cause coral bleaching.

MOSQUITOES CAN REALLY BUG YOU

To protect against mosquitoes, which are most abundant during the summer months, apply repellent containing DEET, and wear a long-sleeve shirt and pants during outdoor activities such as hiking.

IT'S IMPORTANT TO RESPECT LOCAL CULTURE

Hawaii is a unique place with a vibrant, rich culture. Your visit to the Islands will be much more rewarding if you learn about the history and traditions of Hawaii and its peoples. Places such as Bishop Museum and Iolani Palace offer interesting, educational glimpses into Hawaii's storied past.

When you're exploring the outdoors, be mindful of cultural sites, such as the rock wall remains of a temple or Hawaiian petroglyphs. Treat such areas with respect.

Getting Here and Around

A few major landmarks can help you navigate Oahu. The island is made up of three extinct shield volcanoes, which form two mountain ranges: Waianae and Koolau. The Waianae range curves from Kaena State Park, on the island's westernmost point, past Makaha, Waianae, and Nanakuli to Ko Olina on the sunny leeward shore. The extinct craters of Diamond Head and Koko Head are usually visible from anywhere along the island's leeward coast. The jagged Koolau range runs from the island's eastern tip along the windward coast to the famous surfing center on the North Shore.

Air

Flying time to Oahu is about 10 hours from New York, 8 hours from Chicago, and 5 hours from Los Angeles. From the U.S. mainland, Alaska, American, Delta, Hawaiian, Southwest, and United are the primary U.S. carriers to serve Honolulu.

All the major airline carriers serving Hawaii fly direct to Honolulu; some also offer nonstops to Maui, Kauai, and the Big Island, though most flights to the latter two come from the West Coast only. Honolulu International Airport, although open-air and seemingly more casual than most major airports, can be very busy. Allow extra travel time during rush-hour mornings and afternoons.

Plants and plant products are subject to regulation by the Department of Agriculture, both on entering and leaving Hawaii. Upon leaving, you must have your bags x-rayed and tagged at the airport's agricultural inspection station before proceeding to check-in. Pineapples and coconuts with the packer's agricultural inspection stamp pass freely; papayas and certain other fruits must be treated, inspected, and stamped. But most other fruits are banned for export to the U.S. mainland. Flowers pass except for citrus-related flowers, fruits, or parts; jade vine; and mauna loa. Also banned are insects, snails, soil, cotton, cacti, sugarcane, and all berry plants.

Bringing your dog or cat with you is a tricky process and not something to be undertaken lightly. Hawaii is a rabies-free state and requires animals to pass strict quarantine rules, which you can find online at ⊕ *hdoa.hawaii.gov/ai*. Most airlines do not allow pets to travel in the cabin on flights to Hawaii (though Alaska Airlines and Hawaiian Airlines are notable exceptions). If specific pre- and post-arrival requirements are met, most animals qualify for a five-day-or-less quarantine. Masks and proof of vaccination or a negative COVID test are required to visit the animal quarantine facilities.

AIRPORT

The Daniel K. Inouye International Airport (HNL) is roughly 20 minutes (9 miles) west of Waikiki (60 minutes during rush hour) and is served by most of the major domestic and international carriers. To travel to other islands from Honolulu, you can depart from either the interisland terminal or the commuter terminal, located in two separate structures adjacent to the main overseas terminal building. A free Wiki-Wiki shuttle bus operates between terminals.

🚲 Bicycle

Biki Bikeshare Hawaii (⊕ *gobiki.org*) has 1,300 aqua, cruiser-style bicycles at 130 solar-powered stations in the Waikiki and Honolulu corridor. You can unlock a bike from a station using your credit card, without having to sign up for the member pass. A one-way fare costs $4.50 for 30 minutes. There's also a multistop pass for $30, which gets you 300 minutes of riding time. ■TIP➔ **There is a $50 security hold placed on your card when you check out a bike.**

🚌 Bus

Getting around by bus is convenient and affordable on Oahu, particularly in the most heavily touristed areas of Waikiki. Options include Honolulu's municipal transit system, affectionately known as TheBus; the Waikiki Trolleys, brass-trimmed, open-air, hop-on-hop-off vehicles that look like trolleys or large double-decker buses; and brightly painted private buses, some of them free, that shuttle you to such commercial attractions as dinner cruises, shopping centers, and the like.

TheBus is one of the best bargains on Oahu. You can use it to travel around the island or just down Kalakaua Avenue for $2.75. Buses stop in Waikiki every 10–15 minutes to take passengers to nearby shopping areas. Although free transfers have been discontinued, you can purchase a one-day pass for $5.50. Just ask the driver when boarding. Exact change is required, and dollar bills are accepted. Monthly passes cost $70.

The company's website has timetables, route maps, and real-time bus tracking, or you can download the free DaBus2 app for your smartphone. You can call to speak with a representative for route advice, or you can find privately published booklets at most drugstores and other convenience outlets.

The Waikiki Trolley has three lines—each beginning and ending in Waikiki—and dozens of stops that allow you to plan your own itinerary. A one-day pass costs $25 ($5 for the Pink Line) for a single line

and $45 for all lines. Four-day ($65) and seven-day ($75) all-line passes are also available.

The Ocean/Diamond Head Tour (Blue Line) stops at the Duke Kahanamoku statue; along Diamond Head and Kahala; the Halona Blow Hole; Sea Life Park; and Koko Marina. As its name suggests, the Ala Moana Shopping Tour (Pink Line) goes to the Ala Moana Center, a sprawling outdoor mall. The City Arts District Tour (Red Line) travels between Waikiki, Chinatown, and Kakaako and includes stops at the Honolulu Museum of Art, the capitol, Iolani Palace, Punchbowl Crater, and Ala Moana.

🚗 Car

Thanks to public transit, you don't need a car in Waikiki. Elsewhere on the island, though, a car can be invaluable. Avoid the obvious tourist cars—candy-color convertibles, for example—and never leave anything valuable inside, even if you've locked the vehicle. A GPS (either on your smartphone or a separate device) will help guide you through Oahu's some-times-confusing streets.

Reserve in advance to ensure availability (rentals can book up, especially during holidays and summer breaks) and to get the best rates. Also, be prepared to pay for parking; most hotels in Honolulu (and many outside of Honolulu) charge for parking.

Except for one area around Kaena Point, major highways follow Oahu's shoreline and traverse the island at two points. Rush-hour traffic (6:30–9:30 am and 3 or 3:30–6 pm) can be frustrating around Honolulu and the outlying areas. Winter swells also bring heavy traffic to the North Shore, as people hoping to catch

Getting Here and Around

the surfing action clog the two-lane Kamehameha Highway. Parking along many streets is curtailed during these times, and tow-away zones are strictly enforced. Read curbside signs before leaving your vehicle, even at a meter.

Asking for directions will almost always produce a helpful explanation from the locals, but you should be prepared for a Hawaiian term or two. Instead of using compass directions, remember that Hawaii residents refer to places as being either *mauka* (toward the mountains) or *makai* (toward the ocean).

Other directions depend on your location. In Honolulu, for example, people say to "go Diamond Head," which means toward that famous landmark, or to "go *ewa,*" meaning in the opposite direction. A shop on the *mauka*–Diamond Head corner of a street is on the mountain side of the street on the corner closest to Diamond Head. It all makes perfect sense once you get the lay of the land.

CAR RENTALS

Hotel parking garages charge upward of $40 per day, so if you're staying in Waikiki, where you can easily walk or take public transit to many area attractions, consider renting a car only for sightseeing elsewhere on the island. Even though the city bus is a wonderfully affordable way to explore much of Oahu, having your own car gives you flexibility, especially if you're planning lots of stops.

You can rent anything from an econobox and motorcycle to a Ferrari while on Oahu. Rates in Honolulu begin at about $35 a day for an economy car with air-conditioning, automatic transmission, and unlimited mileage. This does not include the airport concession fee, general excise tax, rental-vehicle surcharge, or vehicle-license fee. Note that rates

are sometimes better if you reserve through a rental agency's website. Some rental companies even offer coupons for discounts at various attractions.

It's wise to make reservations far in advance, especially if visiting during peak seasons. When you book, ask about cancellation penalties and drop-off charges, should you plan to pick up the car in one location and return it to another, and request extras, such as GPS and car seats. ■TIP➜ Be sure that a confirmed reservation guarantees you a car. Agencies sometimes overbook, particularly for busy weekends and holiday periods.

In Hawaii you must be 21 years of age to rent a car, and you must have a valid driver's license (which you can use to drive a rental for up to 90 days) and a major credit card. Those under 25 will pay a daily surcharge of around $25. Hawaii's Child Passenger Restraint Law requires that all children under four be in an approved child safety seat in the back seat of a vehicle. Children ages four to seven must be seated in a rear booster seat or child safety seat with a restraint such as a lap and shoulder belt. Car seats and boosters run from $6 to $14 per day.

Allow plenty of time to return your vehicle before your flight home. Traffic in Honolulu is terrible during morning and afternoon rush hours. Give yourself 3½–4 hours prior to departure during these peak times; otherwise, plan on 2½–3 hours.

DRIVING

Driving on Oahu involves traversing a mix of one-way country roads and congested city streets. As in most major cities, traffic in and around Honolulu is bad, especially during rush hour. The H1 highway travels from Kapolei on the west side to Kahala in East Oahu. Weekday rush-hour

Car Rental Resources

Automobile Associations

AAA	☎ 800/222–4357 for roadside assistance	⊕ www.aaa.com
National Automobile Club	☎ 883/622–7377	⊕ www.nacroadservice.com (CA residents only)

Major Agencies

Alamo	☎ 888/233–8749	⊕ www.alamo.com
Avis	☎ 800/633–3469	⊕ www.avis.com
Budget	☎ 800/218–7992	⊕ www.budget.com
Hertz	☎ 800/704–4473	⊕ www.hertz.com
National Car Rental	☎ 884/382–6875	⊕ www.nationalcar.com
Thrifty Car Rental	☎ 800/847–4389	⊕ www.thrifty.com

traffic on the H1 tends to run from 6 to 9 am and again from 3 to 7 pm. During these times, it may take 45 minutes to travel only 10 miles, so plan ahead.

GASOLINE

Gasoline is noticeably more expensive on Oahu than on most of the U.S. mainland.

PARKING

In Honolulu's densest neighborhoods (Chinatown, Kakaako, Ala Moana, Kaimuki, and downtown), parking is often limited and expensive. While there are a variety of parking lots, parking structures, and street parking, you will always have to pay. The same goes for nearly everywhere in Waikiki. Some businesses validate for parking, so it's always good to ask in advance. As you head out west to Kapolei or Haleiwa or northeast to Kailua, parking is easier to come by and often free.

ROAD CONDITIONS

Oahu is relatively easy to navigate. Roads, although their names are often a challenge for the tongue, are usually well marked. Free publications containing helpful maps are found at most hotels throughout Waikiki.

Be mindful of the many one-way streets in Waikiki and the Honolulu neighborhoods of Chinatown, Kakaako, and Kaimuki. Also, watch for the Hawaii Visitors and Convention Bureau's red-caped King Kamehameha signs, which mark major attractions and scenic spots.

ROADSIDE EMERGENCIES

If you have a cell phone, call the roadside assistance number on your car-rental contract or AAA Help. If your car has been broken into or stolen, report it immediately to your rental-car company. If it's an emergency and someone is hurt, call 911.

RULES OF THE ROAD

Hawaii has a strictly enforced mandatory seat-belt law for front- and back-seat passengers. Children under four must be in a car seat (available from car-rental agencies), and children ages four to seven must be seated in a booster seat or child safety seat with a restraint such as a lap and shoulder belt.

Getting Here and Around

Hawaii prohibits texting or talking on the phone (unless you are over 18 and using a hands-free device) while driving. The highway speed limit is usually 55 mph. In-town traffic travels 25–40 mph. Jaywalking is not uncommon, so watch for pedestrians. Unauthorized use of a parking space reserved for persons with disabilities can net you a $250–$500 fine.

Oahu's drivers are generally courteous, and you rarely hear a horn. People will slow down and let you into traffic with a wave of the hand. A friendly wave back is customary. If a driver sticks a hand out the window in a fist with the thumb and pinkie sticking straight out, this is a good thing: it's the *shaka,* the gesture for "hang loose" that's often used to say "thanks."

Cruise

Several major lines offer seasonal cruises to and from the Hawaiian Islands (typically from Los Angeles, San Francisco, or San Diego) with interisland cruise components. But you can also hop aboard a strictly interisland cruise with Norwegian Cruise Line's ship *Pride of America* or Un-Cruise Adventures' smaller yacht.

Ride-Sharing

Both Uber and Lyft operate on Oahu, including in designated locations at the airport. Although you may still want to rent a car while you're on island—especially if you're staying in or visiting the North Shore or towns on the east side of Oahu—ride-shares are good for quick trips and evenings out when you want to avoid parking or you want to imbibe.

Scooter

You might hear them before you see them: the *vroom* of the engine as they zip past traffic. Mopeds and scooters are a common form of transportation in the Islands, both for locals and visitors. They're easier and sometimes cheaper than renting a car, costing around $35 a day or less for multiday rentals. Some companies even rent to people as young as 18. But these freedoms come with a few caveats. Mopeds and scooters aren't allowed on any highways, and renting a scooter requires a valid motorcycle license.

Taxi

Taxis cost $3.10 at the drop of the flag, and each additional mile is $3.60. Taxi and limousine companies can provide a car and driver for half- or full-day island tours, and a number of companies also offer personal guides. Remember, however, the rates are quite steep for these services, running $100 to $200 or more per day.

Essentials

Health and Safety

Hawaii is known not only as the Aloha State, but also as the Health State. The life expectancy here is 81 years, the longest in the nation. Balmy weather makes it easy to remain active year-round, and the low-stress attitude seems to contribute to the general well-being. When visiting the Islands, however, there are a few health issues to keep in mind.

COVID-19

Although COVID-19 brought travel to a virtual standstill for most of 2020 and 2021, vaccinations have made travel possible and safe again. Remaining requirements and restrictions—including those for unvaccinated travelers—can, however, vary from one place (or even business) to the next.

Both the state of Hawaii and the island of Oahu instituted strict vaccination and negative-test requirements. Although many of these protocols were dropped in early 2022, surges could bring them back. Visit ⊕ *hawaiicovid19.com* for the latest information.

Also, in case travel is curtailed abruptly again, consider buying trip insurance. Just be sure to read the fine print: not all travel-insurance policies cover pandemic-related cancellations.

MOSQUITO-BORNE ILLNESSES

The Islands have their share of insects. Most are harmless but annoying—like cockroaches—but dengue fever, a mosquito-borne disease, has been reported on Oahu. For hiking and other outdoor activities, wear long-sleeve shirts and pants, and use mosquito repellent containing DEET. In remote areas, it's a good idea to carry a first aid kit, too.

In damp places, you may encounter the dreaded local centipedes, which are brown and blue and measure up to eight inches long. Their painful sting is similar to those of bees and wasps. When camping, shake out your sleeping bag and check your shoes, as the centipedes like cozy places.

SAFETY PRECAUTIONS

Although Oahu is generally a safe tourist destination, it's still wise to follow the same common-sense safety precautions you would in your own hometown. Rental cars are magnets for break-ins, so don't leave any valuables in the car, not even in a locked trunk. Avoid poorly lighted areas, beach parks, and isolated areas after dark as a precaution. ■TIP➜ **Distribute your cash, credit cards, IDs, and other valuables between a deep front pocket, an inside jacket or vest pocket, and a hidden money pouch. Don't reach for the money pouch once you're in public.**

Hotels

If you like the action and choices of big cities, consider Waikiki, a 24-hour playground with everything from surf to karaoke bars. For an escape from urban life, look to the island's leeward or windward sides or to the North Shore, where the surf culture creates a laid-back atmosphere.

Most of Oahu's major hotels and resorts are in busy Waikiki, where you don't need a car to reach key sights and amenities as public transportation can get you around town as well as around the island. You'll find places to stay along the entire stretches of both Kalakaua and Kuhio Avenues, with smaller and quieter hotels and condos at the eastern end of Waikiki and more business-centric accommodations on the western edge, near the Hawaii Convention Center, Ala Moana Center, and downtown.

Essentials

Leeward Oahu, in the Ko Olina resort area, is about 20 minutes from Honolulu International Airport (40 minutes from Waikiki) and has great golf courses and quiet beaches that make for a relaxing getaway. Note, though, that you'll need a car to explore, and all the resorts in this area charge hefty parking fees.

Other low-key options are on Windward Oahu—home to Turtle Bay, one of the island's premier resorts—or the North Shore. Both have quaint eateries and coffee shops, local boutiques, and some of the island's best beaches.

Hotel reviews have been shortened. For full information, visit Fodors.com.

CONDOS AND VACATION RENTALS

Vacation rentals give you the convenience of staying at a home away from home and getting to know Oahu the way the locals do. You can often save money as well, since you have a kitchen, can cook your meals, and don't pay for hotel parking. Prices, amenities, and locations of vacation homes vary considerably, meaning you should be able to find the perfect getaway.

Properties managed by individual owners can be found in online vacation-rental directories, as well as on the Oahu Visitors Bureau website (⊕ *www.gohawaii. com/islands/oahu*). Don't be surprised to see the same homes advertised on different sites and with different names. Compare companies, as some offer online specials and free nights when booking, and make sure that there will be an on-island point of contact should there be any issues during your stay.

Also ask about the home's licensing as a vacation rental since not all properties advertised carry the necessary license. Technically, rentals of less than 30 days are illegal on Oahu unless the property has a license for short-term vacation rentals or is a hotel with apartment units. The state does take a stand from time to time to enforce vacation rental laws, and you'll have more protection and assurance that you aren't on your own if something goes wrong.

FACILITIES

Assume that all hotel rooms have private baths, phones, and TVs, unless otherwise indicated, but many rentals do not have AC, especially outside of the Waikiki high-rises. Breakfast is noted when it is included in the rate. Most hotels have pools, but many home rentals do not.

PARKING

Most resorts on Oahu charge for parking, even those not in Ko Olina and Waikiki (where virtually all hotels charge for parking), so be sure to ask before you rent a car. Sometimes this is included in the hotel's resort fee, but often it is not.

PRICES

Before you book a room, try calling hotels directly. Sometimes on-property reservationists can get you the best deals, and they usually have the most accurate information about rooms, availability, and hotel amenities. Remember that many reservations centers are not on Oahu.

Hotel prices are the lowest cost of a standard double room in high season.

RESERVATIONS

Always make a reservation. Hotels often fill up, and rooms can be particularly hard to come by at the beginning of festival season in late March or early April as well as in May, when students at the many local colleges graduate.

What It Costs in U.S. Dollars

$	$$	$$$	$$$$
FOR TWO PEOPLE			
Under $180	$180–$260	$261–$340	Over $340

🍸 Nightlife

Oahu is the best of all the Islands for nightlife. The island's few clubs are in Waikiki, but there are bars just about everywhere. On weeknights, it's likely that you'll find the working crowd, still in their business-casual attire, downing chilled beers even before the sun goes down. Though you might call it happy hour, the locals call it *pau hana,* which translates to "done with work." Those who don't have to wake up early in the morning should change into a fresh outfit and start the evening closer to 10 pm.

On the weekends, it's typical to have dinner at a restaurant before hitting the bars at around 9:30. Some barhoppers start as early as 7, but even they usually don't patronize more than two establishments a night because getting from one Oahu nightspot to the next often requires transportation. Happily, cab services are plentiful, and the rideshares Uber and Lyft give Honolulu a San Francisco feel.

The drinking age is 21 on Oahu and throughout Hawaii. Many bars will admit younger people but will not serve them alcohol. By law, all establishments that serve alcoholic beverages must close by 2 am. The only exceptions are a handful in Waikiki with a cabaret license, which can stay open until 4 am. Remember that some establishments may require proof of vaccination before entering.

■ TIP→ Some places have a cover charge of $5–$10, but with many establishments, arriving early means you don't have to pay.

📷 Packing

Outside of a few upscale restaurants that might require a jacket for dinner and golf courses that have collared-shirt or other dress codes, Oahu is casual. Sandals, bathing suits, and comfortable, informal clothing are the norm. The aloha shirt is accepted dress for business and most social occasions. Shorts are acceptable daytime attire, along with a T-shirt or polo shirt.

In summer, synthetic slacks and shirts, although easy to care for, can be uncomfortably warm. If you're visiting in winter or are planning to visit a high-altitude area, bring a sweater or light- to medium-weight jacket. A polar fleece pullover is ideal and makes a great impromptu pillow. Note that there's no need to buy expensive sandals on the Mainland— here, you can get flip-flops (locals call them slippers) for a few dollars and off-brand sandals for $20.

During the pandemic, the Safe Access Oahu program required proof of vaccination to enter many establishments. Although this program ended in early 2022, surges might bring it back, so it doesn't hurt to have proof of vaccination, too. A photo on your phone is fine.

🌐 Passports and Visas

All visitors to the United States require a passport that is valid for six months beyond your expected period of stay.

Except for citizens of Canada and Bermuda, most visitors to the United States

Essentials

NEIGHBORHOOD	LOCAL VIBE	PROS	CONS
Honolulu	Lodging options are limited in downtown Honolulu, but if you want an urban feel, look no farther.	Access to a wide selection of art galleries, boutiques, and restaurants, as well as Chinatown.	No beaches within walking distance. If you're looking to get away from it all, this is not the place.
Waikiki	Lodgings abound in Waikiki, from youth hostels to five-star accommodations. The area is always abuzz with activity, and anything you desire is within walking distance.	You can surf in front of the hotels, wander miles of beach, and explore restaurants and bars.	This is tourist central. Prices are high, and you are not going to get the true Hawaii experience.
East (Windward) Oahu	More in tune with the local experience, this is where you'll find many privately listed (e.g., on Airbnb or VRBO) places and enjoy the lush side of Oahu.	From beautiful vistas to green jungles, this side really captures the tropical paradise most people envision when dreaming of a Hawaii vacation.	The lushness comes at a price—it rains a lot on this side. Also, luxury is not the specialty here; if you want pampering, stay elsewhere.
The North Shore	This is true country living, with one luxurious resort exception. It's bustling in the winter (when the surf is up) and slower-paced in the summer.	Amazing surf and long stretches of sand truly epitomize the beach culture in Hawaii. Historic Haleiwa has enough stores to keep shopaholics busy.	There is no middle ground for accommodations; you're either in backpacker cabanas or $300-a-night suites. There is also zero nightlife, and traffic can be heavy during winter months.
West (Leeward) Oahu	This is the resort side of the rock; there isn't much outside these resorts but plenty on the grounds to keep you occupied for a week.	Ko Olina's lagoons offer the most kid-friendly swimming on the island, and the golf courses are magnificent. Rare is the rainy day out here.	You are isolated from the rest of Oahu, with fewer shopping options or jungle hikes.

must have a visa. If you are from one of the 38 designated members of the Visa Waiver Program, then you only require an ESTA (Electronic System for Travel Authorization) as long as you are staying for 90 days or less.

Note, though, that nationals of Visa-Waiver nations who have traveled to Iran, Iraq, Libya, Somalia, Sudan, Syria, or Yemen no longer qualify for ESTA. Also, if you have been denied a visa to visit the United States, your application for the ESTA program most likely will be denied.

Performing Arts

Oahu has a thriving arts and culture scene, especially in the summer. Check local newspapers, such as the *Honolulu Star-Advertiser* or *MidWeek,* for the latest events. Websites like ⊕ *gohawaii.com* also have listings.

Restaurants

Oahu has undergone a renaissance at both ends of the dining spectrum. Consider budgeting for a meal in at least one pricey restaurant, where chefs such as Roy Yamaguchi, Ed Kenney, Chris Kajioka, or others you've seen on the Food Network and Travel Channel put a sophisticated spin on local foods and flavors. Dishes that take cues from Japan, China, Korea, the Philippines, the United States, and Europe are often filtered through an Island sensibility. Take advantage of the location and order the superb local fish—mahimahi, *opakaka* (Hawaiian pink snapper), ono, and opah.

Spend the rest of your food dollars where budget-conscious locals do: in plate-lunch places and small ethnic eateries, at lunch wagons, or at window-in-the-wall

delis. Snack on a *musubi* (a handheld rice ball wrapped with seaweed and topped with Spam), slurp shave ice with red-bean paste, or order Filipino pork adobo with rice and macaroni salad.

In Waikiki, you can find everything from upscale dining rooms with a view to Japanese noodle shops. By going just a few miles in any direction, you can save money and eat like a local. On Kaimuki's Waialae Avenue, for example, you'll find a coffee shop, a Chinese bakery, an Italian bistro, a dim-sum restaurant, elevated Hawaiian food, Mexican food, and a Hawaii regional-cuisine standout (3660 on the Rise)—all in three blocks and 10 minutes from Waikiki.

Chinatown, 15 minutes in the other direction and easily reached by the Waikiki Trolley, is another dining (and shopping) treasure, not only for Chinese but also for Vietnamese, Filipino, Burmese, and Mexican food. There's even a chic little tea shop. Kakaako, the developing urban area between Waikiki and Chinatown, also offers a mix of local eateries, upscale restaurants, and ethnic takeout.

Although restaurants are fewer outside Honolulu and Waikiki, they tend to be filled with locals and are cheaper and more casual. Thanks to its popular Kailua and Lanikai Beaches, Windward Oahu's dining scene features everything from plate lunches to creative regional offerings. Kapolei, once dominated by Mainland chains and fast-food joints, is now another area with a variety of quality eateries.

Restaurant reviews have been shortened. For full information, visit Fodors. com. Restaurant prices are the average cost of a main course at dinner or, if dinner is not served, at lunch.

Essentials

DISCOUNTS AND DEALS
If you eat early or late, you may be able to take advantage of prix-fixe deals not offered at peak hours. Many upscale restaurants offer great lunch deals with special menus at cut-rate prices designed to give customers a true taste of the place.

PARKING
In Waikiki, downtown Honolulu, or Chinatown, walk, take a cab, or call Lyft or Uber when you are going out for dinner; it can be cheaper and easier than dealing with parking or high valet rates. Elsewhere on Oahu, free or reasonably priced parking is available.

PAYING
Most restaurants take credit cards, but some smaller places do not. It's worth asking. Servers expect a 20% tip at restaurants; some add an automatic gratuity for groups of six or more.

RESERVATIONS AND DRESS
At Honolulu's top upscale restaurants, book your table from home weeks in advance. Otherwise, you can usually reserve when you get into town.

Most top restaurants abide by the dressy casual (i.e., "aloha wear") standard, where dark jeans are acceptable. A select few of Honolulu's nicest spots ask men to wear a jacket.

MEALS AND MEALTIMES
People dine early here—the most sought-after dinner reservations are between 6 and 8. There are a few exceptions: sushi bars and Japanese taverns, a few 24-hour diners, and popular new restaurants. Many island eateries have transitioned their operations to provide more takeout and delivery options.

SMOKING
Smoking is prohibited in enclosed areas open to the public, including restaurants, bars, and clubs.

What It Costs in U.S. Dollars			
$	$$	$$$	$$$$
AT DINNER			
under $17	$17–$26	$27–$35	over $35

Shopping
Savvy shoppers hunt for luxury goods at high-end malls *and* scout tiny boutiques and galleries for items created by local artists and artisans. Honolulu's Chinatown and Kakaako neighborhoods, Kailua on the windward side, and Haleiwa on the North Shore often have the most original merchandise. Some small stores carry imported clothes and gifts—a reminder that, on this island halfway between Asia and the United States, shopping is a multicultural experience.

$ Taxes
A 13.25% tax is added to your hotel bill. A $5-per-day road tax is also assessed on each rental vehicle, plus a $4.50-per-day rental-facility surcharge. Although Hawaii doesn't have a statewide sales tax, 4.7% will be tacked onto goods and services you purchase on Oahu.

Tipping
People who work in the service industry rely on tips, so gratuities are not only common, but expected.

Tipping Guides for Oahu

Bartender	$1–$5 per round of drinks, depending on the number and cost of the drinks
Bellhop	$1–$5 per bag, depending on the level of the hotel
Hotel Concierge	$5 or more, depending on the service
Hotel Doorstaff	$1–$5 for help with bags or hailing a cab
Hotel Maid	$2–$5 each time your room is cleaned
Hotel Room Service Waiter	$1–$2 per delivery, even if a service charge has been added
Restroom Attendants	$1 per vist
Skycap at Airport	$1–$3 per bag checked
Spa Personnel	15%–20% of the cost of your service
Taxi Driver	15%–20% of the fare
Tour Guide	15%–20% of the cost of the tour, per person
Valet Parking Attendant	$2–$5 each time your car is brought to you
Server	20%; nothing additional if a service charge is added to the bill

Visitor Information

Before you go to Hawaii, contact the Oahu Visitors Bureau (OVB) for a free vacation planner and map. The OVB website (⊕ *gohawaii.com/islands/oahu*) has online listings for accommodations, activities, attractions, dining venues, services, transportation, travel professionals, and wedding information. The website also has a calendar of events.

When to Go

Low Season: The fall (September through mid-December) is a slower time for tourism in Oahu. During this period, you can find better rates on just about everything. That beach you want to lounge on will be less crowded, too.

Shoulder Season: Mid-April through June is an in-between time. Because of Hawaii's warm weather, though, this season still attracts plenty of visitors.

High Season: The busiest time is generally from mid-December to March or mid-April, when Hawaii weather is good and temperatures are moderate. Make all reservations well in advance, and don't expect to find deals on accommodations.

WEATHER

In Hawaii, the thermometer generally hovers between the mid-70s to the mid-80s (degrees Fahrenheit). There are essentially just two seasons: summer and winter. Winters, from November through April, are rainier and a bit cooler than the summer months, May through October. But even if it's raining in one part of Oahu, chances are it's dry and sunny on the other coast. Oahu's leeward (western) coast is warmer and more arid than its windward (eastern) side, which is usually cooler and wetter.

Hawaiian Vocabulary

Although an understanding of Hawaiian is by no means required on a trip to the Aloha State, a *malihini*, or newcomer, will find plenty of opportunities to pick up a few of the local words and phrases. Traditional names and expressions are widely used in the Islands. You're likely to read or hear at least a few words each day of your stay.

Simplifying the learning process is the fact that the Hawaiian language contains only seven consonants—*H, K, L, M, N, P, W,* and the silent *'okina,* or glottal stop, written '—plus one or more of the five vowels. All syllables, and therefore all words, end in a vowel. Each vowel, with the exception of a few diphthongized double vowels, such as *au* (pronounced "ow") or *ai* (pronounced "eye"), is pronounced separately. Thus *'Iolani* is four syllables (ee-oh-la-nee), not three (yo-la-nee). Although some Hawaiian words have only vowels, most also contain some consonants, but consonants are never doubled.

Pronunciation is simple. Pronounce *A* "ah" as in *father; E* "ay" as in *weigh; I* "ee" as in *marine; O* "oh" as in *no; U* "oo" as in *true.*

Consonants mirror their English equivalents, with the exception of *W.* When the letter begins any syllable other than the first one in a word, it is usually pronounced as a *V. 'Awa,* the Polynesian drink, is pronounced "ava," *'ewa* is pronounced "eva."

Almost all long Hawaiian words are combinations of shorter words; they are not difficult to pronounce if you segment them. *Kalaniana'ole,* the highway running east from Honolulu, is easily understood as *Kalani ana 'ole.* Apply the standard pronunciation rules—the stress falls on the next-to-last syllable of most two- or three-syllable Hawaiian words—and Kalaniana'ole Highway is as easy to say as Main Street.

Now about that fish. Try *humu-humu nuku-nuku āpu a'a.*

The other unusual element in Hawaiian language is the *kahakō,* or macron, written as a short line (ˉ) placed over a vowel. Like the accent (ˊ) in Spanish, the kahakō puts emphasis on a syllable that would normally not be stressed. The most familiar example is probably *Waikīkī.* With no macrons, the stress would fall on the middle syllable; with only one macron, on the last syllable, the stress would fall on the first and last syllables. Some words become plural with the addition of a macron, often on a syllable that would have been stressed anyway. No Hawaiian word becomes plural with the addition of an *S,* since that letter does not exist in the language.

Note that Hawaiian diacritical marks are not printed in this guide.

PIDGIN

You may hear pidgin, the unofficial language of Hawaii. It is a Creole language, with its own grammar, evolved from the mixture of English, Hawaiian, Japanese, Portuguese, and other languages spoken in 19th-century Hawaii, and it is heard everywhere.

GLOSSARY

What follows is a glossary of some of the most commonly used Hawaiian words. Hawaiian residents appreciate visitors who at least try to pick up the local language.

'a'ā: rough, crumbling lava, contrasting with *pāhoehoe,* which is smooth.

'ae: yes.

aikane: friend.

āina: land.

akamai: smart, clever, possessing savoir faire.

akua: god.

ala: a road, path, or trail.

ali'i: a Hawaiian chief, a member of the chiefly class.

aloha: love, affection, kindness; also a salutation meaning both greetings and farewell.

'ānuenue: rainbow.

'a'ole: no.

'apōpō: tomorrow.

'auwai: a ditch.

auwē: alas, woe is me!

'ehu: a red-haired Hawaiian.

'ewa: in the direction of 'Ewa plantation, west of Honolulu.

hala: the pandanus tree, whose leaves (lau hala) are used to make baskets and plaited mats.

hālau: school.

hale: a house.

hale pule: church, house of worship.

hana: to work.

haole: foreigner. Since the first foreigners were Caucasian, haole now means a Caucasian person.

hapa: a part, sometimes a half; often used as a short form of hapa haole, to mean a person who is part-Caucasian.

hau'oli: to rejoice. Hau'oli Makahiki Hou means Happy New Year. Hau'oli lā hānau means Happy Birthday.

heiau: an outdoor stone platform; an ancient Hawaiian place of worship.

he mea iki or **he mea 'ole:** you're welcome.

holo: to run.

holoholo: to go for a walk, ride, or sail.

holokū: a long Hawaiian dress, somewhat fitted, with a yoke and a train. It was worn at court, and at least one local translates the word as "expensive muumuu."

holomū: a post–World War II cross between a holokū and a mu'umu'u, less fitted than the former but less voluminous than the latter, and having no train.

honi: to kiss; a kiss. A phrase that some tourists may find useful, quoted from a popular hula, is Honi Ka'ua Wikiwiki: Kiss me quick!

honu: turtle.

ho'omalimali: flattery, a deceptive "line," bunk, baloney, hooey.

huhū: angry.

hui: a group, club, or assembly. A church may refer to its congregation as a hui and a social club may be called a hui.

hukilau: a seine; a communal fishing party in which everyone helps to drive the fish into a huge net, pull it in, and divide the catch.

hula: the dance of Hawaii.

iki: little.

ipo: sweetheart. Commonly seen as "ku'uipo," or "my sweetheart."

ka: the. This is the definite article for most singular words; for plural nouns, the definite article is usually nā. Since there is no S in Hawaiian, the article may be your only clue that a noun is plural.

Hawaiian Vocabulary

kahuna: a priest, doctor, or other trained person of old Hawaii, endowed with special professional skills that often included prophecy or other supernatural powers.

kai: the sea, saltwater.

kalo: the taro plant from whose root *poi* (paste) is made.

kamā'aina: literally, a child of the soil; it refers to people who were born in the Islands or have lived there for a long time.

kanaka: originally a man or humanity, it is now used to denote a male Hawaiian or part-Hawaiian, but is occasionally taken as a slur when used by non-Hawaiians. *Kanaka maoli* is used by some Native Hawaiian rights activists to embrace part-Hawaiians as well.

kāne: a man, a husband. If you see this word (or kane) on a door, it's the men's room.

kapa: also called by its Tahitian name, *tapa*, a cloth made of beaten bark and usually dyed and stamped with a repeat design.

kapakahi: crooked, cockeyed, uneven. You've got your hat on *kapakahi*.

kapu: keep out, prohibited. This is the Hawaiian version of the more widely known Tongan word *tabu* (taboo).

kēia lā: today.

keiki: a child; *keikikāne* is a boy, *keikiwahine* a girl.

kōkua: to help, assist. Often seen in signs like "Please *kōkua* and throw away your trash."

kona: the leeward side of the Islands, the direction (south) from which the *kona* wind and *kona* rain come.

kula: upland.

kuleana: a homestead or small plot of ground on which a family has been installed for some generations without necessarily owning it. By extension, *kuleana* is used to denote any area or department in which one has a special interest or prerogative. You'll hear it used this way: "If you want to hire a surfboard, see Moki; that's his *kuleana*."

kupuna: grandparent; elder.

lā: sun.

lamalama: to fish with a torch.

lānai: a porch, a balcony, an outdoor living room.

lani: heaven, the sky.

lau hala: the leaf of the *hala,* or pandanus tree, widely used in handicrafts.

lei: a garland of flowers.

lōlō: feeble-minded, crazy.

luna: a plantation overseer or foreman.

mahalo: thank you.

mahina: moon.

makai: toward the ocean.

mālama: to take care of, preserve, protect

malihini: a newcomer to the Islands.

mana: the spiritual power that the Hawaiians believe inhabits all things and creatures.

manō: shark.

manuahi: free, gratis.

mauka: toward the mountains.

mauna: mountain.

mele: a Hawaiian song or chant, often of epic proportions.

Mele Kalikimaka: Merry Christmas (a transliteration from the English phrase).

Menehune: a Hawaiian pixie. The Menehune were a legendary race of little people who accomplished prodigious work, such as building fishponds and temples in the course of a single night.

moana: the ocean.

mu'umu'u: the voluminous dress in which the missionaries enveloped Hawaiian women. Culturally sensitive locals have embraced the Hawaiian spelling but often shorten the spoken word to "mu'u." Most English dictionaries include the spelling "muumuu."

nani: beautiful.

nui: big.

'ohana: family.

'ono: delicious.

pāhoehoe: smooth, unbroken, satiny lava.

palapala: document, printed matter.

pali: a cliff, precipice.

pānini: prickly pear cactus.

paniolo: a Hawaiian cowboy, a rough transliteration of *español,* the language of the Islands' earliest cowboys.

pau: finished, done.

pilikia: trouble. The Hawaiian word is much more widely used here than its English equivalent.

pū: large conch shell used to trumpet the start of luau and other special events.

puka: a hole.

pule: prayer, blessing. Often performed before a meal or event.

pupule: crazy, like the celebrated Princess Pupule. This word has replaced its English equivalent in local usage.

pu'u: volcanic cinder cone.

tūtū: grandmother

waha: mouth.

wahine: a female, a woman, a wife, and a sign on the ladies' room door; the plural form is *wāhine.*

wai: freshwater, as opposed to saltwater, which is *kai.*

wailele: waterfall.

wikiwiki: to hurry, hurry up (since this is a reduplication of *wiki,* quick, neither *W* is pronounced as a *V*).

Great Itineraries

Highlights of Oahu

From *mauka* (mountains) to *makai* (sea), Oahu is probably the Hawaiian island most likely to please all types of travelers—whether you're an outdoorsy type, a beach bum, a foodie, or a family—and a week should give you enough time to see the highlights. You can either use the bus or take taxis or rideshares while you're in Honolulu, but rent a car to get out on the island and get a true feel for all things Oahu.

DAY 1: WAIKIKI

Given the time difference between Hawaii and the rest of the United States, you'll probably be jet-lagged. Grab coffee and head for a beach: Waikiki, Sans Souci, or Fort DeRussy. You'll see locals on their morning jogs at Kapiolani Park and catching waves at their favorite shore break.

Once caffeinated, hit Kalakaua Avenue on foot, the best way to shop and sightsee. Got kiddos in tow? Try the Waikiki Aquarium or the Honolulu Zoo. Get some refreshments with tea at the Moana Surfrider, the oldest hotel in Waikiki, or mai tais and pupu (hors d'oeuvres) at Duke's Waikiki (a better deal at lunch). In the afternoon, take a surf lesson in the beginner-friendly waves of Waikiki. Finish your day with a seaside dinner.

DAY 2: PEARL HARBOR

Give yourself a whole day for Pearl Harbor. Note that only the USS *Arizona* and the visitor center, which are operated by the National Park Service, are free; the other sights are operated by private entities and charge admission. Also, you must reserve tickets for the USS *Arizona* Memorial online in advance (for a small fee).

After your ferry ride out to the memorial, you can also explore the USS *Bowfin* submarine or take a shuttle to Ford Island and visit the restored USS *Missouri* battleship (the "Mighty Mo") and the Pearl Harbor Aviation Museum. Return to Waikiki for some late-afternoon beach time and a good dinner.

DAY 3: DOWNTOWN HONOLULU AND CHINATOWN

Cab or bus it to downtown Honolulu for a guided tour of the royal residence, Iolani Palace, where you'll get an excellent overview of Hawaii's monarchical era, from the early 1800s through its overthrow in 1893. For more historical highlights, walk between Honolulu Hale (Hawaiian for "house"), Kawaiahao Church, the Hawaiian Mission Houses Historic Site and Archives, the Hawaii State Capitol, Washington Place, the King Kamehameha I statue, and Aliiolani Hale. Several companies offer guided walks of the area.

Continue walking the ½ mile through Honolulu's business district into Chinatown for lunch at one of its eclectic eateries. Browse the shops, art galleries, and cultural sites, like Mauna Kea Marketplace, Chinatown Cultural Plaza, the Izumo Taishakyo Mission, and Kuan Yin Temple.

DAY 4: DIAMOND HEAD AND KAIMUKI

Today you will go the opposite direction from downtown. Tours of Shangri La, the opulent former waterfront home of heiress Doris Duke, with its Islamic art and architecture, book up well in advance, but it's well worth the effort to make an online reservation for a small surcharge. Shuttles to the Kahala home-turned-museum start and end at the Honolulu Museum of Art.

After your tour, grab a to-go lunch from Diamond Head Market & Grill, and enjoy it at the picnic tables at Diamond Head State Monument. Then hike the park's relatively easy 1½-hour, 1.6-mile trail up and down this dormant volcano. Finish the day with dinner in the foodie neighborhood of Kaimuki.

DAY 5: KAILUA AND THE SOUTH SHORE

Head to Windward Oahu for a stop in Kailua, a swim at its quintessential beach, and lunch at Kalapawai Cafe & Deli. Next, drive along the southeastern shore via Waimanalo, and choose your afternoon adventure: 1) do the easy, stroller-friendly hike at Makapuu Point Lighthouse, with great whale-watching views in winter and spring; 2) snorkel at Hanauma Bay State Park, the pristine preserve where you'll have more space to swim with the fish after the morning-to-midday rush; or 3) stop at the Halona Blowhole lookout and the *From Here to Eternity* Halona Beach Cove nearby.

DAY 6: THE NORTH SHORE

The beaches here are home to some of the world's most famous surf breaks. Each winter, surfers from around the

Tips

■ If this is your first visit, stay in Waikiki, which has most of the island's hotels.

■ You don't need a car in Honolulu, but you'll need one to explore farther afield.

■ Don't forget your hat, sunscreen, and good walking shoes any day you head out.

■ Be sure to reserve your free USS *Arizona* Memorial tickets online in advance ($1 charge).

■ Check ahead on any COVID-19 requirements that might be in place at the time of your visit.

globe converge to catch barreling waves of 15 feet or higher. Haleiwa is filled with surf shops, boutiques, and restaurants. Grab lunch from Haleiwa Joe's Seafood Grill or Uncle Bo's Pupu Bar & Grill. Enjoying a frozen treat at Matsumoto's Shave Ice is a sweet way to end the day.

On the Calendar

Local events are a fun way to experience Oahu's diverse culture, and with festivals, parades, concerts, tournaments, and more happening every month across the island, you're sure to find something to please everyone. Remember to check ahead about COVID-19 requirements.

January

Sony Open in Hawaii. The Sony Open in Hawaii is held at the Waialae Country Club in east Honolulu in early to mid-January. Part of the PGA tour, the tournament attracts many of the top players in professional golf. It's also one of the largest charity sports events in the Islands. ☎ *808/523–7888* ⊕ *www. sonyopeninhawaii.com.*

February

Pow! Wow! Hawaii. Watch as dozens of renowned local and international muralists and street artists transform the walls of Kakaako's businesses during this weeklong event, which usually takes place around Valentine's Day. Viewing the dynamic art installations and attending gallery shows and events at the nearby Lana Lane Studios is a fun way to experience this energetic Honolulu neighborhood. ⊕ *powwowworldwide.com/ festivals/hawaii.*

March

King's Runner 10K. This annual race may not be as well recognized as December's Honolulu Marathon, but it's now the largest 10K in Hawaii. Thousands of runners (walkers and strollers are welcome, too) race through a 6.2-mile course that begins in Honolulu, near the Neal S. Blaisdell Center, weaves through Kakaako, and parallels the beautiful beaches of Ala Moana. ⊕ *thehapalua. com/our-events/kings-runner-10k.*

April

Spam Jam. Hawaii loves its Spam, which is spotlighted during this late-April food event. It's a Waikiki block party featuring live entertainment, Spam merchandise, and food booths offering unique snacks, desserts, and more made with the canned meat. ⊕ *spamjamhawaii.com.*

May

Lei Day. This treasured celebration is Hawaii's version of May Day. It takes place every May 1 at Kapiolani Park and includes lei-making demonstrations and contests, hula, crafts, food, and live music.

June

King Kamehameha I Day. The celebration honoring the monarch who united the Hawaiian Kingdom takes place on June 11 with parades and other events throughout the Islands. On Oahu, the parade is held in Waikiki and features floats and traditional *pau* (skirt) riders—namely, women horseback riders draped in lei and wearing ornate, colorful skirts.

July

Ukulele Festival Hawaii. At this beloved annual event, performers *kani ka pila,* or make music, with Hawaii's favorite instrument, the ukulele. Due to the pandemic, the event has been virtual for the past few years, with the many outstanding performances on the festival's YouTube channel. ⊕ *www.ukulelefesthawaii.org/oahu.*

August

Duke's Oceanfest. This weeklong, mid-month festival celebrates waterman Duke Kahanamoku, an Olympian and ambassador of Aloha who loved to swim, surf, and paddle. Surfing and stand-up paddleboarding competitions, outrigger races, and more are held along Waikiki Beach. Some events have been virtual, so check with organizers before heading out. ⊕ *dukesoceanfest.com.*

September

The Aloha Festivals. This quintessential late-September event celebrates the storied, vibrant culture in the Islands. Festivities traditionally include a block party, parade, music, and hula. Like several other large festivals on Oahu, this has pivoted to virtual, with the Royal Court Investiture and other events happening online. Check ahead to see if this has changed. ⊕ *www.alohafestivals.com.*

October

Honolulu Pride. One highlight of Oahu's Pride Month is the Honolulu Pride parade, a day-long, Waikiki event complete with Technicolor floats, live music, and food. ⊕ *hawaiilgbtlegacyfoundation.com/honolulu-pride.*

November

Hawaii Food & Wine Festival. Held over several days at upscale locations across the Islands, this event features notable chefs from Hawaii, the Mainland, and abroad, as well as mixologists and wine producers. You'll eat some of the best foods the Islands have to offer. ⊕ *hawaiifoodandwinefestival.com.*

December

Honolulu City Lights. Celebrate the holidays, Oahu style, throughout December. Honolulu Hale, where the city government is located, is transformed with twinkling lights for virtual and in-person celebrations. Other highlights include dozens of uniquely decorated Christmas trees, Shaka Santa, and Tutu Mele. ⊕ *www.honolulucitylights.org.*

Contacts

Air

AIRPORT Daniel K. Inouye International Airport. (*HNL*). ✉ *300 Rodgers Blvd., Airport Area* ☎ *808/836–6411* ⊕ *airports.hawaii.gov/hnl.*

GROUND TRANSPORTATION Roberts Hawaii. ✉ *Honolulu* ☎ *808/539–9400* ⊕ *www.robertshawaii.com/airport-shuttle.*

MAJOR AIRLINES Alaska Airlines. ☎ *800/252–7522* ⊕ *www.alaskaair. com.* **American Airlines.** ☎ *800/433–7300* ⊕ *www. aa.com.* **Delta Airlines.** ☎ *800/221–1212 for U.S. reservations, 800/241–4141 for international reservations* ⊕ *www.delta. com.* **Hawaiian Airlines.** ☎ *800/367–5320* ⊕ *www. hawaiianairlines.com.* **Southwest.** ☎ *800/435–9792* ⊕ *www.southwest. com.* **United Airlines.** ☎ *800/864–8331 for U.S. reservations* ⊕ *www. united.com.*

LOCAL AIRLINES Mokulele Airlines. ☎ *866/260–7070* ⊕ *www.mokuleleairlines. com.*

Bus

CONTACTS TheBus. ✉ *Honolulu* ⊕ *www.thebus.org.* **Waikiki Trolley.** ✉ *Waikiki Shopping Plaza, 2250 Kalakaua Ave., Honolulu* ⊕ *waikikitrolley.com.*

🚢 Cruise

CONTACTS Norwegian Cruise Line. ☎ *866/234–7350* ⊕ *www.ncl.com.* **Un-Cruise Adventures.** ☎ *888/862–8881* ⊕ *www. uncruise.com.*

🚕 Taxi

CONTACTS TheCAB. ☎ *808/422–2222* ⊕ *www. thecabhawaii.com.* **Carey Honolulu.** ☎ *888/405–1792* ⊕ *www.careyhonolulu. com.* **Charley's Taxi.** ☎ *808/233–3333* ⊕ *www. charleystaxi.com.* **Elite Limousine Service.** ☎ *808/735–2431* ⊕ *www. elitelimohawaii.com.*

🛏 Vacation Rentals

CONTACTS Hawaiian Villa Rentals. ☎ *808/673-6800* ⊕ *www.hawaiianvillarentals.com.* **Private Homes Hawaii.** ☎ *808/896– 9580* ⊕ *www.privatehomeshawaii.com.*

🔘 Visitor Information

CONTACTS Hawaii Tourism Authority. ☎ *800/464–2924 for brochures* ⊕ *www. gohawaii.com.* **Oahu Visitors Bureau.** ☎ *800/464– 2924* ⊕ *www.gohawaii. com/islands/oahu.*

⊕ Websites

CONTACTS Hawaii Beach Safety. ⊕ *hawaiibeachsafety.com.* **Hawaii Department of Land and Natural Resources.** ⊕ *dlnr.hawaii. gov.* **State of Hawaii Portal.** ⊕ *portal.ehawaii.gov and hawaiicovid19.com/travel (for Safe Travels Hawaii information).*

Chapter 3

HONOLULU AND PEARL HARBOR

Updated by Marla Cimini
and Anna Weaver

⊙ Sights	🍴 Restaurants	🛏 Hotels	🛍 Shopping	🍸 Nightlife
★★★★★	★★★★★	★★★★★	★★★★★	★★★★★

WELCOME TO HONOLULU AND PEARL HARBOR

TOP REASONS TO GO

★ **Variety:** The city has something for everyone: beaches, shopping, restaurants, sightseeing, nightlife, and hiking.

★ **History:** Honolulu, like the rest of the island, is saturated in Hawaiian history, from ancient times to the modern day.

★ **Excellent food:** The capital is a melting pot of food and drink and a hub for Hawaii's farm-to-table dining scene.

★ **Great hotels:** A great selection of urban resorts, many on or near the beach, makes it easy to find accommodations that suit your budget.

★ **The great outdoors:** Beaches offer every oceanside activity imaginable, from lounging and swimming to surfing and snorkeling.

1 Waikiki and Diamond Head. Most of Oahu's hotels are in Waikiki, as are shops, restaurants, and that famous beach. Beautiful Diamond Head, a great hiking spot but also a good destination for food, is just to the east.

2 Pearl Harbor. History is preserved and presented at multiple memorials and museums at this still-active naval base.

3 Mapunapuna. What is mostly a warehouse and office area also has some hidden-gem restaurants and shops.

4 Iwilei. Stop in Iwilei for a movie and a number of good restaurants alongside the working harbor and farther inland.

5 Downtown. The business district is bustling during weekdays but dead in the evening. The historic district is easily walkable.

6 Chinatown. Chock-full of history and culture, Chinatown also has some of Honolulu's trendiest bars, restaurants, and boutiques alongside longtime local shops, markets, and restaurants.

7 Kakaako. Completely transformed since the early 2010s, Kakaako is now a great place to shop, eat, and absorb street art.

8 Ala Moana. Come here for the shopping and food at the state's largest mall and enjoy the beachfront park.

9 Makiki Heights. Head up Tantalus for stunning views from *mauka* to *makai* (mountain to ocean).

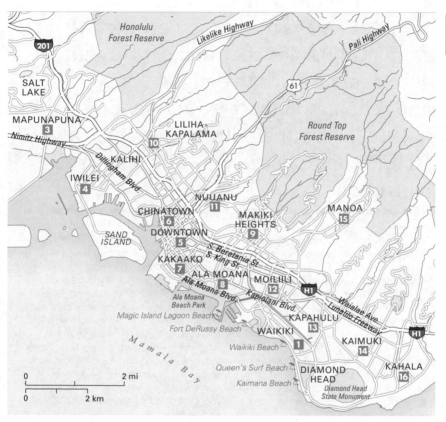

🔟 Kalihi-Liliha-Kapalama. Fabulous food spots popular with locals are the hallmarks of this working-class district.

1️⃣1️⃣ Nuuanu. This largely residential valley is intersected by the Pali Highway.

1️⃣2️⃣ Moiliili. An excellent range of restaurants fall largely along King Street in this neighborhood overlapping with the McCully area.

1️⃣3️⃣ Kapahulu. From Waikiki, head north along Kapahulu Avenue for low-key shops and restaurants.

1️⃣4️⃣ Kaimuki. Kaimuki has emerged as a foodie's paradise in the last decade.

1️⃣5️⃣ Manoa. Home of the largest branch of the University of Hawaii, Manoa is also known for its historic homes.

1️⃣6️⃣ Kahala. This upscale residential area has a beachfront hotel to match and a good-size mall.

As the seat of government, a center of commerce and shipping, and an entertainment and recreation mecca, Honolulu plays many (sometimes conflicting) roles that make it a dynamic, ever-evolving urban delight. Hipsters and scholars, sightseers and foodies, nature lovers and culture vultures can all find their bliss in Hawaii's only true metropolis.

Once there was the broad bay of Mamala and the narrow inlet of Kou, fronting a dusty plain occupied by a few thatched houses and the great Pakaka *heiau* (shrine). Nosing into the narrow passage in 1794, British sea captain William Brown named the port Fair Haven. Later, Hawaiians would call it Honolulu, or "sheltered bay," and it gained further importance in 1804, when King Kamehameha I built a stately compound near the harbor here after reluctantly abandoning his Big Island home to better protect Hawaiian interests.

As shipping traffic increased, the settlement grew into a Western-style town of streets and buildings, tightly clustered around the single freshwater source, Nuuanu Stream. Not until piped water became available in the early 1900s did Honolulu spread across the greening plain, becoming both a city and a county. Two hundred years later, the entire island is, in a sense, Honolulu, which has no official boundaries, extending across flatlands, from Pearl Harbor to Waikiki, and high into the hills.

The main areas of Waikiki, Pearl Harbor, downtown, and Chinatown have the lion's share of the sights, but greater Honolulu's residential neighborhoods also have a lot to offer, including folksy restaurants and takeout places favored by locals. Visits to these areas also afford glimpses of classic Hawaiian homes, from the breezy, double-wing bungalows, with their swooping, Thai-style rooflines, to the tiny, green-and-white, plantation-era houses, with their corrugated tin roofs and window-flanked central doors and porches.

Also common are "Grandma-style" gardens and *ohana* houses, with smaller backyard homes or apartments allowing extended families to live together. In these districts, carports rarely shelter cars but instead serve as rec rooms—beneath the roof, parties are held and neighbors sit to "talk story," and atop it, gallon jars of pickled lemons ferment in the sun.

Planning

Getting Here and Around

AIR

Honolulu's Daniel K. Inouye International Airport (HNL) is Hawaii's busiest, with the most nonstop flights from the mainland United States as well as the majority of the state's international flights.

AIRPORT TRANSFERS

Some hotels have their own pickup and drop-off service, though they may charge a fee, so check when you book accommodations.

Taxi service is available on the center median just outside baggage-claim areas. Look for the yellow-shirted taxi dispatchers, who radio for cabs. The fare to Waikiki runs approximately $40–$45, plus 60¢ per bag and tip, with a maximum of four passengers. An oversize baggage fee may apply. Uber and Lyft also serve the airport.

Another option is to take a private shuttle service, like Roberts Hawaii. The company will greet you at the arrival gate, escort you to baggage claim, and take you to your hotel. Call ahead for the service, which starts at $21 per person one-way.

TheBus, the municipal bus, will take you into Waikiki for only $2.75, but all bags must fit on your lap or under your legs.

CONTACTS Roberts Hawaii. ⊠ *Honolulu* ☎ *808/539–9400* ⊕ *robertshawaii.com.*

BUS

Buses are convenient and affordable, particularly in the most heavily touristed areas of Waikiki. Options include Honolulu's municipal transit system, affectionately known as TheBus, which also travels to and from the airport; the Waikiki Trolleys, brass-trimmed, open-air vehicles that look like trolleys or large double-decker buses; and brightly painted private buses, some of them free, that shuttle you to such commercial attractions as dinner cruises, shopping centers, and the like.

TheBus is one of Oahu's best bargains. You can use it to travel around the island or just down Kalakaua Avenue for $2.75, with buses stopping in Waikiki every 10–15 minutes to take passengers to nearby shopping areas. Exact change (dollar bills are OK) and the system's HOLO cards are accepted. Indeed, you can ride all day for $5.50 using a HOLO card; monthly passes cost $70. Look into downloading the free DaBus2 app for your smartphone.

The hop-on-hop-off Waikiki Trolley has three lines—each beginning and ending in Waikiki—and dozens of stops that allow you to plan your own itinerary. A one-day pass costs $25 ($5 for the Pink Line) for a single line and $45 for all lines. Four-day ($65) and seven-day ($75) all-line passes are also available.

The Ocean/Diamond Head Tour (Blue Line) stops at the Duke Kahanamoku statue, along Diamond Head and Kahala, and at the Halona Blowhole, Sea Life Park, and Koko Marina. As its name suggests, the Ala Moana Shopping Tour (Pink Line) goes to the Ala Moana Center, a sprawling outdoor mall. The City Arts District Tour (Red Line) travels between Waikiki, Chinatown, and Kakaako and includes stops at the Honolulu Museum of Art, the capitol, Iolani Palace, Punchbowl Crater, and Ala Moana.

CONTACTS TheBus. ⊠ *Honolulu* ☎ *808/848–5555* ⊕ *thebus.org.* **Waikiki Trolley.** ⊠ *Honolulu* ☎ *808/465–5543* ⊕ *waikikitrolley.com.*

CAR

If you plan on spending most of your time in Hawaii in Honolulu, it doesn't pay to rent a car for your entire trip, especially if you are staying in Waikiki. Hotels typically charge (a lot) for parking, gas is expensive, and traffic can be heavy, especially during rush hour.

But having a car will make exploring the rest of Oahu easier, so consider renting only for a couple of days. Just be sure to reserve your vehicle as far ahead as possible. Note, too, that the post-pandemic rental-car shortage saw business boom for car-sharing companies like Turo (⊕ turo.com), which help you rent cars from private owners and offer an alternative to the traditional car-rental agencies.

TAXI
In Honolulu, taxis cost $3.10–$3.50 at the drop of the flag, and each additional 1/8-mile is $0.45. Taxi and limousine companies can provide a car and driver for half-day or daylong island tours. Several companies also offer personal guides, though rates for such services can be steep, running $100–$200 or more per day. Uber and Lyft also serve Oahu, including for airport pickups.

Hotels

Most hotels in Honolulu are in Waikiki, with a few downtown and in the Ala Moana area between downtown and Waikiki. Elsewhere on Oahu, accommodations range from quiet and romantic bed-and-breakfasts and cottages to less expensive hotels that are a great value. There are also a few luxury resorts, where you'll truly feel like you're getting away from it all.

Hotel prices are the lowest cost of a standard double room in high season. Hotel reviews have been shortened. For full information, visit Fodors.com.

What It Costs in U.S. Dollars			
$	$$	$$$	$$$$
FOR TWO PEOPLE			
under $180	$180–$260	$261–$340	over $340

Nightlife

Gone are the days when there was nothing to do in Honolulu at night. In fact, many people who arrive on Oahu expecting little more than white-sand beaches are surprised by a nighttime scene so vibrant that it can be hard to pick which DJ to see at which club or which art show opening to attend. Note, though, that after a day on the beach, lingering beneath the swaying palms to watch the sun set over Waikiki, you might want to head back to your hotel and dress up: more and more Honolulu clubs are enforcing a dress code.

Performing Arts

If all-night dancing isn't for you, Oahu also has a thriving arts and culture scene, with community-theater productions, outdoor concerts, film festivals, and chamber-music performances, most of it centered in Honolulu. Major Broadway shows, dance companies, rock stars, and comedians come through the Islands, too. Check local newspapers (and their accompanying websites)—the *Honolulu Star-Advertiser* or *MidWeek*—and *HONO-LULU Magazine* for the latest events.

Restaurants

There's no lack of choices when it comes to dining in Honolulu, where you'll find everything from the haute cuisine of heavy-hitting top-notch chefs to a wide variety of Asian specialties to reliable and inexpensive American favorites.

Restaurant prices are the average cost of a main course at dinner or, if dinner is not served, at lunch. Restaurant reviews have been shortened. For full information, visit Fodors.com.

What It Costs in U.S. Dollars			
$	$$	$$$	$$$$
AT DINNER			
under $17	$17–$26	$27–$35	over $35

Shopping

There are two distinct types of shopping experiences: vast malls with the customary department stores or tiny boutiques with specialty items. That said, three Honolulu malls provide a combination of the standard stores and interesting shops showcasing original paintings and woodwork from local artists and craftsmen.

Although it's easy enough to find designer merchandise and other items you can get back home, with a little effort, you can also find unusual Asian imports. Be sure to scout the malls for the slightly hidden shops, where a sale bin might contain the perfect, and truly unique, souvenir or gift.

In Waikiki, stores open at around 9 or 10 am, and many don't close until 10 or even 11 pm.

Tours

Guided tours are convenient; you don't have to worry about finding a parking spot or getting admission tickets. Most of the tour guides have taken special classes in Hawaiian history and lore, and many are certified by the state of Hawaii. On the other hand, you won't have the freedom to proceed at your own pace, nor will you have the ability to take a detour trip if something else catches your attention.

BUS AND VAN TOURS
Polynesian Adventure
BUS TOURS | This company leads tours of Pearl Harbor and other Oahu sights and also offers a circle-island tour by motor coach, van, or minicoach. ⊠ *Honolulu* ☎ *888/206–4531* ⊕ *polyad.com* ✈ *From $62.*

THEME TOURS
Discover Hawaii Tours
SPECIAL-INTEREST TOURS | In addition to circle-island and other Oahu-based itineraries on motor coaches and minicoaches, this company can also get you from Waikiki to the lava flows of the Big Island or to Maui's Hana Highway and back in one day. ⊠ *Honolulu* ☎ *808/824–3995* ⊕ *discoverhawaiitours.com* ✈ *From $50.*

E Noa Tours
SPECIAL-INTEREST TOURS | This outfitter's certified tour guides conduct circle-island and Pearl Harbor tours, with pickups from Ko Olina and Waikiki. E Noa also owns Waikiki Trolley. ⊠ *Honolulu* ☎ *808/591–2561* ⊕ *enoa.com* ✈ *From $60.*

Waikiki and Diamond Head

Approximately 3 miles east of downtown Honolulu, Waikiki is Oahu's primary resort area. A mix of historic and modern hotels and condos front the sunny 2-mile stretch of beach, and many have clear views of Diamond Head. The area is home to much of the island's dining, nightlife, and shopping—from posh boutiques to hole-in-the-wall eateries to craft booths at Duke's Marketplace.

Waikiki was once a favorite retreat for Hawaiian royalty. In 1901, the Moana Hotel debuted, introducing Waikiki as an international travel destination. The region's fame continued to grow when Duke Kahanamoku helped popularize the sport of surfing, offering lessons to visitors at Waikiki. You can see Duke immortalized in a bronze statue, with a surfboard, on Kuhio Beach.

Today there is a decidedly "urban resort" vibe here. Streets are clean, gardens are manicured, and the sand feels softer than at beaches farther down the coast. At first glance, there isn't much of a local culture—it's mainly tourist crowds—but if you explore the neighborhood, you can still find the relaxed surf-y vibe and friendly "aloha spirit" that has drawn people here for more than a century.

Diamond Head Crater is perhaps Hawaii's most recognizable natural landmark. It got its name from sailors who thought they had found precious gems on its slopes; these later proved to be calcite crystals, a much more common mineral. Hawaiians saw a resemblance in the sharp angle of the crater's seaward slope to the oddly shaped head of the ahi fish and so called it Leahi, though later they Hawaiianized the English name to Kaimana Hila. It is commemorated in a widely known hula—*A ike i ka nani o Kaimana Hila, Kaimana Hila, kau mai i luna* ("We saw the beauty of Diamond Head, Diamond Head set high above").

Sprawling Kapiolani Park lies in the shadow of Diamond Head, which is just beyond the easternmost limits of Waikiki. King David Kalakaua established the park in 1877, naming it after his queen and dedicating it "to the use and enjoyment of the people." In this 500-acre expanse, you can go for a stroll, play all sorts of field sports, enjoy a picnic, see wild animals and tropical fish at the Honolulu Zoo and the Waikiki Aquarium, or hear live music at the Waikiki Shell or the Kapiolani Park Bandstand.

GETTING HERE AND AROUND

Bounded by the Ala Wai Canal on the north and west, the beach on the south, and the Honolulu Zoo to the east, Waikiki is compact and easy to walk around. TheBus runs multiple routes here from the airport and downtown Honolulu. By car, finding Waikiki from H1 can be tricky; look for the Punahou exit for the west

end of Waikiki and the King Street exit for the eastern end.

For those with a Costco card, the cheapest gas on the island is at the three Costco stations. The one in Honolulu is on Arakawa Street, between Dillingham Boulevard and Nimitz Highway; the one in Waipio is at 94-1231 Ka Uka Boulevard; and the one in Kapolei is at 4589 Kapolei Parkway.

 Sights

★ Diamond Head State Monument

STATE/PROVINCIAL PARK | FAMILY | Panoramas from this 760-foot extinct volcanic peak, once used as a military fortification, extend from Waikiki and Honolulu in one direction and out to Koko Head in the other, with surfers and windsurfers scattered like confetti on the cresting waves below. The 360-degree perspective is a great orientation for first-time visitors. On a clear day, look east past Koko Head to glimpse the outlines of the islands of Maui and Molokai.

To enter the park from Waikiki, take Kalakaua Avenue east, turn left at Monsarrat Avenue, head a mile up the hill, and look for a sign on the right. Drive through the tunnel to the inside of the crater. The ¾-mile trail to the top begins at the parking lot. Be aware that the hike up to the crater has numerous stairs to climb; if you aren't in the habit of getting occasional exercise, this might not be for you. At the top, you'll find a somewhat awkward scramble through a tunnel and bunker out into the open air, but the view is worth it.

As you walk, note the color of the vegetation: if the mountain is brown, Honolulu has been without significant rain for a while, but if the trees and undergrowth glow green, you'll know it's the wet season (winter) without looking at a calendar. Winter is when rare Hawaiian marsh plants revive on the floor of the crater. Wear a hat and take bottled

Despite the steep climb, Diamond Head, an extinct volcanic crater on the eastern edge of Waikiki, is one of Honolulu's most popular hiking destinations.

water with you to stay hydrated under the tropical sun as there are no water stations (or any shade) along the hike. Keep an eye on your watch if you're here at day's end: the gates close promptly at 6 pm. ■TIP→ To beat the heat and the crowds, rise early and make the hike before 8 am. ⊠ *Diamond Head Rd. at 18th Ave., Diamond Head* ☎ *808/587–0300* ⊕ *dlnr.hawaii.gov/dsp/parks/oahu/diamond-head-state-monument* 🎫 *$5 per person (non-Hawaii resident), $25 per non-commercial vehicle (cash only).*

Honolulu Zoo

ZOO | FAMILY | The world definitely has bigger and better (and newer) zoos, but this 42-acre facility features well-paved, walkable trails amid a lush garden with tropical flowers. To get a glimpse of the endangered *nene,* the Hawaii state bird, check out the zoo's Kipuka Nene Sanctuary. Other highlights include a Japanese Giant Salamander habitat and an ectotherm complex, which houses a Burmese python, elongated tortoises, and a giant African snail. Though many animals prefer to remain invisible—particularly the big cats—the monkeys and elephants appear to enjoy being seen and are a hoot to watch. It's best to get to the zoo right when it opens because the animals are livelier in the cool of the morning. Children adore the petting zoo, where they can make friends with a llama or stand in the middle of a koi pond.

There's an exceptionally good gift shop. On weekends, the Art on the Zoo Fence, on Monsarrat Avenue on the Diamond Head side outside the zoo, has affordable artwork by local contemporary artists. Metered parking is available all along the *makai* (ocean) side of the park and in the lot next to the zoo—but it can fill up early. TheBus makes stops here along the way to and from Ala Moana Center and Sea Life Park (Routes 8 and 22). ⊠ *151 Kapahulu Ave., Waikiki* ☎ *808/971–7171* ⊕ *www.honoluluzoo.org* 🎫 *$19.*

Kapiolani Park Bandstand

PERFORMANCE VENUE | FAMILY | The Victorian-style Kapiolani Park Bandstand, which was built in the late 1890s, is the park's

Waikiki East and Diamond Head

8th Avenue
7th Avenue
Maunalea Avenue

KAIMUKI

Kilauea Avenue
9th Avenue
10th Avenue
11th Avenue
12th Avenue

Kapaolono Community Park

Wilhelmina Rise
Upper Street
Alohea Avenue
Maunalei Avenue

Francis Street
George Street
Hayden Street

Wela Street
Hinano Street
Edna Street
Makini Street
Kepuhi Street
Kaunaoa Street
Mc Corriston Street
Monsarrat Ave.
Diamond Head Road
Wauke Street

Pakole Street
Makapuu Ave.

Diamond Head State Monument
❶

Diamond Head Road
Kuilei Cliffs Beach Park
Diamond Head Beach Park
Diamond Head Beach Park

G H I

Sights ▼

1 Diamond Head
  State Monument........ H7
2 Honolulu Zoo C4
3 Kapiolani Park
  Bandstand................ C5
4 Waikiki Aquarium....... C6
5 Waikiki Natatorium
  War Memorial............ C6
6 Waikiki Shell............. D5

Restaurants ▼

1 Arancino di Mare........ C3
2 Beachhouse at
  the Moana................ A2
3 Bogart's Café............. F5
4 d.k Steakhouse........... C3
5 Hau Tree C6
6 Herringbone
  Waikiki A1
7 Heyday................... B1
8 Hy's Steak House C2
9 Michel's at the
  Colony Surf C7
10 Morimoto Asia
  Waikiki B3
11 Mugen B3
12 Queensbreak............. C3
13 Side Street Inn
  Kapahulu.................. E1
14 Teddy's
  Bigger Burgers........... C4
15 Tiki's Grill and Bar........ C4

Quick Bites ▼

1 Banán A2
2 Diamond Head Market
  & Grill F4
3 Holey Grail Donuts...... A1
4 South Shore Grill......... F4

Hotels ▼

1 Alohilani Resort
  Waikiki Beach........... B3
2 Aqua Aloha
  Surf Waikiki............. B1
3 Aston at the
  Waikiki Banyan C3
4 Aston Waikiki
  Beach Hotel C4
5 Aston Waikiki
  Beach Tower............ B3
6 Aston Waikiki
  Circle Hotel............. B3
7 Espacio – The
  Jewel of Waikiki B3
8 Hilton Garden Inn
  Waikiki Beach........... B1
9 Hilton Waikiki Beach C2
10 Hotel Renew.............. C3
11 Hyatt Regency Waikiki
  Beach Resort & Spa.... B2
12 Ilima Hotel B1
13 Moana Surfrider,
  A Westin Resort & Spa,
  Waikiki Beach.......... A2
14 Ohana Waikiki East
  by Outrigger............ B2
15 Pacific Monarch........ B2
16 Queen Kapiolani
  Hotel..................... C4
17 Royal Grove Waikiki B2
18 Sheraton
  Princess Kaiulani B2
19 Waikiki Beachcomber
  By Outrigger............. A1
20 Waikiki Beach
  Marriott Resort & Spa... C3
21 Waikiki Sand
  Villa Hotel................ C1

stage for community entertainment and concerts. Founded by King Kamehameha III in 1836, the Royal Hawaiian Band is the nation's only city-sponsored band and performs free concerts at the bandstand as well as at Iolani Palace and the center stage at Ala Moana Center. Visit the band's website for concert dates (⊕ *www.rhb-music.com*), and check event-listing websites and the *Honolulu Star-Advertiser*—Oahu's local newspaper—for information on other coming bandstand attractions. ✉ *2805 Monsarrat Ave., Waikiki* ☎ *808/922–5331.*

Waikiki Aquarium
AQUARIUM | **FAMILY** | This small yet fun attraction harbors more than 3,500 organisms and 500 species of Hawaiian and South Pacific marine life, including an endangered Hawaiian monk seal and a zebra shark. The Living Reef exhibit showcases diverse corals and fascinating reef environments found along Hawaii's shorelines. Check out exhibits on the Northwestern Hawaiian Islands (which explains the formation of the island chain) and Ocean Drifters (about various types of jellyfish). A 60-foot exhibit houses sea horses, sea dragons, and pipefish. A free self-guided mobile audio tour is available via your own smartphone. The aquarium offers activities of interest to adults and children alike, with a focus on the importance of being eco-friendly and keeping our oceans clean. ✉ *2777 Kalakaua Ave., Waikiki* ☎ *808/923–9741* ⊕ *www.waikikiaquarium.org* 💲 *$12.*

Waikiki Shell
PERFORMANCE VENUE | Grab one of the 6,000 "grass seats" (that is, spots on the lawn, though there are actual seats as well) for music under the stars. An eclectic array of musical acts put on concerts at this landmark venue throughout the summer and occasionally during the winter, weather permitting. ■**TIP**➔ **This venue does not allow backpacks or large purses. Check the website for other restrictions.** ✉ *2805 Monsarrat Ave., Waikiki*

☎ *808/768–5400* ⊕ *www.blaisdellcenter. com/venues/waikiki-shell.*

Waikiki Natatorium War Memorial
NOTABLE BUILDING | Although closed to the public, this Beaux Arts–style, 1927 World War I monument, dedicated to the 101 Hawaiian servicemen who lost their lives in battle, stands proudly in Waikiki and is visible from the adjacent Sans Souci/Kaimana Beach. The 100-meter saltwater swimming pool, the training spot for Olympians Johnny Weissmuller and Buster Crabbe and the U.S. Army during World War II, has been closed for decades, as the pool needs repair. Plans to tear down the natatorium were put on hold thanks to efforts by a nonprofit group that continues fighting to save it. With both massive environmental and funding issues, though, the proposed refurbishment remains in flux. ✉ *2777 Kalakaua Ave., Waikiki* ⊕ *natatorium.org.*

Beaches

In 2021, the 2-mile Waikiki Beach—which runs from Hilton Hawaiian Village on one end to Kapiolani Park and Diamond Head on the other—underwent a major sand-replenishment project that added about 20,000 cubic yards to the shoreline. Although it's one contiguous strand, it's as varied as the people who inhabit the Islands. Whether you want to kick back and watch the action from the shade or you want to get out in or on the water, you can find whatever you need here.

If you're staying outside the area and driving to it, park at either end of the beach and walk in. Metered parking is plentiful and affordable ($1 per hour) to the west, at Ala Wai Harbor, and to the east, at Kapiolani Park and the Honolulu Zoo. Resorts also have parking, but the hourly rates are high.

Diamond Head Beach Park

BEACH | You have to do a little hiking to reach this beautiful, remote spot at the base of Diamond Head Crater. Although the beach is just a small, narrow strip of sand with lots of coral in the water, the views from the point are breathtaking, and it's fun to watch the windsurfers skimming along. From the parking area, look for an opening in the wall where an unpaved trail leads down to the beach. Even for the unadventurous, a stop at the lookout point is well worth the time. **Amenities:** parking (no fee); showers. **Best for:** solitude; sunset; surfing; windsurfing. ⊠ *At base of Diamond Head, 3500 Diamond Head Rd., Diamond Head ✛ Park at crest of Diamond Head Rd. and walk down.*

Duke's Beach

BEACH | FAMILY | Named for Hawaii's famous Olympic swimming champion and waterman, Duke Kahanamoku, this hard-packed beach fronting the Hilton Hawaiian Village Waikiki Beach Resort is great for families. It's the only stretch of Waikiki with shade trees on the sand, and its waters are very calm thanks to a rock wall that creates a semiprotected cove. The ocean clarity here is not as good as elsewhere, but this is a small price to pay for peace of mind about youngsters. **Amenities:** food and drink; parking (fee); showers; toilets. **Best for:** sunset; swimming; walking. ⊠ *2005 Kalia Rd., Waikiki.*

★ Fort DeRussy Beach Park

BEACH | FAMILY | A wide, soft, ultra-white shore with gently lapping waves makes this fine beach a family favorite for running-jumping-frolicking fun. Other bonuses include the shaded, grassy grilling area, the sand volleyball courts, and the many aquatic rental options. The beach fronts the Hale Koa Hotel as well as Fort DeRussy. **Amenities:** food and drink; lifeguards; showers; toilets; water sports. **Best for:** swimming; walking. ⊠ *2161 Kalia Rd., Waikiki.*

Outrigger Canoes

If catching a wave on a 10-foot surfboard was a rush, wait until you catch one aboard a 30-foot outrigger canoe! You'll need to paddle a bit, but the captains and beach boys will guide you in and out of the breaks.

Look for the long, skinny boats in front of the Royal Hawaiian Resort, where the family-run, family-friendly **Waikiki Beach Services** (⊕ *www.waikikibeachservices.com*) is one option. A 30-minute experience costs about $35.

Gray's Beach

BEACH | In the 1920s, a little guesthouse called Gray's-by-the-Sea stood on what is now a very narrow strip of sand that's best for walking, admiring the ocean, and imagining a Waikiki of yesteryear. (Note that the tides often put sand space at a premium, so you have to use the elevated concrete walkway most of the time.) You can also enjoy a great view of Diamond Head as well as a mai tai at House Without A Key, a legendary beach restaurant at the Halekulani hotel a few steps away. **Amenities:** food and drink; lifeguards; parking (fee); showers; toilets. **Best for:** walking. ⊠ *2199 Kalia Rd., Waikiki.*

Kahaloa and Ulukou Beaches

BEACH | The "it" spots for the bikini crowd—and just about everyone else—have most of the catamaran charters that sail out to Diamond Head, as well as surfboard and outrigger canoe rentals that make it easy to take advantage of the Canoes surf break. Chair and umbrella rentals are available, and great music and outdoor dancing beckon at the lively Duke's restaurant, where shirt and shoes

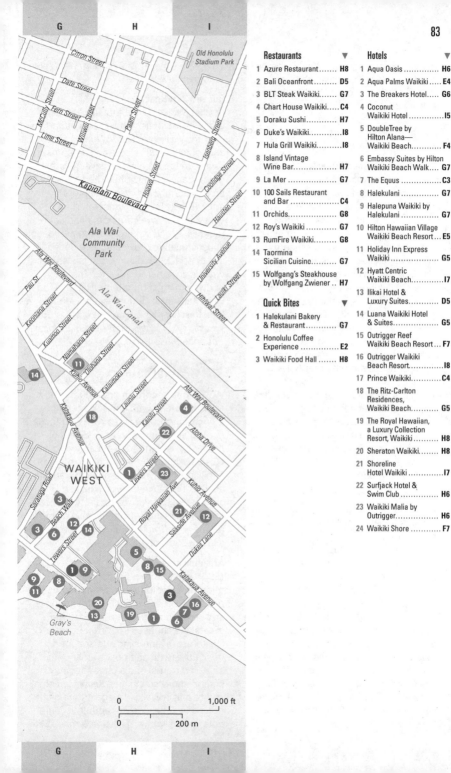

Restaurants ▼

1 Azure Restaurant **H8**
2 Bali Oceanfront **D5**
3 BLT Steak Waikiki **G7**
4 Chart House Waikiki **C4**
5 Doraku Sushi **H7**
6 Duke's Waikiki **I8**
7 Hula Grill Waikiki **I8**
8 Island Vintage
  Wine Bar **H7**
9 La Mer **G7**
10 100 Sails Restaurant
   and Bar **C4**
11 Orchids **G8**
12 Roy's Waikiki **G7**
13 RumFire Waikiki **G8**
14 Taormina
   Sicilian Cuisine **G7**
15 Wolfgang's Steakhouse
   by Wolfgang Zwiener .. **H7**

Quick Bites ▼

1 Halekulani Bakery
  & Restaurant **G7**
2 Honolulu Coffee
  Experience **E2**
3 Waikiki Food Hall **H8**

Hotels ▼

1 Aqua Oasis **H6**
2 Aqua Palms Waikiki **E4**
3 The Breakers Hotel **G6**
4 Coconut
  Waikiki Hotel **I5**
5 DoubleTree by
  Hilton Alana—
  Waikiki Beach **F4**
6 Embassy Suites by Hilton
  Waikiki Beach Walk **G7**
7 The Equus **C3**
8 Halekulani **G7**
9 Halepuna Waikiki by
  Halekulani **G7**
10 Hilton Hawaiian Village
   Waikiki Beach Resort ... **E5**
11 Holiday Inn Express
   Waikiki **G5**
12 Hyatt Centric
   Waikiki Beach **I7**
13 Ilikai Hotel &
   Luxury Suites **D5**
14 Luana Waikiki Hotel
   & Suites **G5**
15 Outrigger Reef
   Waikiki Beach Resort ... **F7**
16 Outrigger Waikiki
   Beach Resort **I8**
17 Prince Waikiki **C4**
18 The Ritz-Carlton
   Residences,
   Waikiki Beach **G5**
19 The Royal Hawaiian,
   a Luxury Collection
   Resort, Waikiki **H8**
20 Sheraton Waikiki **H8**
21 Shoreline
   Hotel Waikiki **I7**
22 Surfjack Hotel &
   Swim Club **H6**
23 Waikiki Malia by
   Outrigger **H6**
24 Waikiki Shore **F7**

not only aren't required, they're discouraged. The Royal Hawaiian Hotel and the Moana Surfrider are both also here. **Amenities:** food and drink; lifeguards; parking (fee); showers; toilets; water sports. **Best for:** partiers; surfing. ⌧ *2259 Kalakaua Ave., Waikiki.*

Kaimana (Sans Souci) Beach

BEACH | FAMILY | Across from the zoo, at the eastern end of Waikiki along what is known as the Gold Coast, this small rectangle of sand is a local-favorite sunning spot for beach lovers of all ages. Although it's usually quieter than the stretches of beach in the heart of town, it's also close to the conveniences of Waikiki. Children can splash safely in its shallow waters, which are protected (for now) by the walls of the historic natatorium, a long-closed, Olympic-size, saltwater swimming arena. Serious swimmers and triathletes also train in the channel beyond the reef here. The Kaimana Beach Hotel and popular Hau Tree lanai restaurant are next door. **Amenities:** lifeguards; parking (fee); showers; toilets. **Best for:** swimming; walking. ⌧ *2776 Kalakaua Ave., Waikiki ✛ Across from Kapiolani Park, between New Otani Kaimana Beach Hotel and Waikiki War Memorial Natatorium.*

Kuhio Beach Park

BEACH | FAMILY | Featuring a bronze statue of Duke Kahanamoku, the father of modern-day surfing, this lively beach is bordered by a landscaped walkway with a few benches and some shade. It's great for strolls and people-watching any time of day. Check out the Kuhio Beach hula mound Tuesday, Thursday, and Saturday at 6:30 (at 6, Nov.–Jan.) for free hula and Hawaiian-music performances and a sunset torch-lighting ceremony. Surf lessons for beginners are available from the beach center every half hour. **Amenities:** food and drink; lifeguards; showers; toilets; water sports. **Best for:** surfing; walking. ⌧ *2461 Kalakaua Ave.,*

Waikiki ✛ Go past Moana Surfrider Hotel to Kapahulu Ave. pier.

Queen's Surf Beach

BEACH | FAMILY | Once the site of Queen Liliuokalani's beach house, this strand near the Waikiki Aquarium draws locals and tourists of all ages—and it seems as if someone is always playing a steel drum. Banyan trees offer shade, the bronze *Surfer on a Wave* sculpture by artist Robert Pashby honors surfing, volleyball nets welcome pros and amateurs alike, and waters that are part of an aquatic reserve provide superb snorkeling opportunities. The beach is also near what is considered the area's premier bodyboarding spot: the break called The Wall. **Amenities:** lifeguards; showers; toilets. **Best for:** swimming; walking. ⌧ *2598 Kalakaua Ave., Waikiki ✛ Across from entrance to Honolulu Zoo.*

🍴 Restaurants

Waikiki has become a great destination for food lovers, with a new generation of innovative chefs and a renewed focus on using local ingredients, indigenous produce, and farm- and ocean-to-table cuisine. Although there are a number of familiar "chain" restaurants and traditional steak houses here, you can also find some solid choices for a variety of meals at all price points—from upscale dining rooms with a view to budget-friendly Japanese noodle shops.

Arancino di Mare

$$$ | ITALIAN | Three locations in town offer fresh seafood, hand-trimmed beef, pastas cooked to order, handmade pizza and bread, homemade desserts, and meats and cheeses imported from Italy. Customer favorites include spaghetti *pescatore* (with shrimp, calamari, mussels, and clams) and a pizza topped with shrimp and Maui onions. **Known for:** small and casual in Waikiki, elegant date-night setting in Kahala; fresh, authentic ingredients; local favorite. ⑤ *Average main: $28*

✉ *Waikiki Beach Marriott Resort, 2552 Kalakaua Ave., Waikiki* ☎ 808/931–6273 ⊕ www.arancino.com.

Azure Restaurant

$$$$ | **MODERN HAWAIIAN** | This legendary indoor-outdoor restaurant has views of Diamond Head and an expansive terrace on the same level as the beach, so you'll feel the calm, island vibes as soon as you arrive. Although it's open for breakfast and lunch, Azure has a much more sophisticated atmosphere in the evening, when you can choose from a selection of small or large plates featuring local seafood, meat, and produce, or you can try the chef's multicourse tasting menu. **Known for:** priceless views and pricey menu; world-class cuisine and excellent service; beautifully presented dishes. ⑤ *Average main: $45* ✉ *Royal Hawaiian Resort, 2259 Kalakaua Ave., Waikiki* ☎ 808/931–7440 ⊕ www.azurewaikiki. com.

Bali Oceanfront

$$$$ | **STEAKHOUSE** | Spacious and sprawling, this many-windowed, multilevel room at Hilton Hawaiian Village takes delightful advantage of its perch above the beach, facing Diamond Head. The wine list is exceptional, and the extensive contemporary menu features seafood, steaks, salads, and chops accented with East–West fusion flavors; desserts are impressive, too. **Known for:** splurge prices; partnerships with local producers for farm-to-table offerings; attentive staff. ⑤ *Average main: $40* ✉ *Hilton Hawaiian Village, 2005 Kalia Rd., Waikiki* ☎ 808/941–2254 ⊕ www.hiltonhawaiian-village.com/bali ⊗ Closed Sun. and Mon. No lunch.

Beachhouse at the Moana

$$$$ | **MODERN HAWAIIAN** | At this elegant, indoor-outdoor restaurant in Waikiki's oldest hotel, try for a table on the veranda, which overlooks the courtyard and a majestic banyan tree. Although it's open all day—and even serves afternoon tea—the Beachhouse is an especially

delightful spot for a sunset dinner, when menu options range from crab cakes and paella to pork chops and steaks. **Known for:** romantic setting; oceanfront dining; gourmet dinners and afternoon tea. ⑤ *Average main: $44* ✉ *Moana Surfrider Hotel, 2365 Kalakaua Ave., Waikiki* ☎ 808/921–4600 ⊕ www.beachhouse-waikiki.com.

BLT Steak Waikiki

$$$$ | **STEAKHOUSE** | One of the swankiest rooms in town is the perfect place for a tête-à-tête, with dark leather booths, polished wooden tables, and local artwork. Sip a raspberry mojito while deciding whether to go surf or turf with the pancetta-dotted lobster Cobb salad, the catch of the day, or one of the many meat dishes. **Known for:** bar menu with excellent burgers and raw oysters; chic cocktails that take the edge off the lofty prices; creative sides like jalapeño mashed potatoes and spicy barbecue Kahuku corn. ⑤ *Average main: $48* ✉ *Trump International Hotel Waikiki Beach Walk, 223 Saratoga Rd., Waikiki* ☎ 808/683–7440 ⊕ www.bltrestaurants.com/location/blt-steak-waikiki ⊗ No lunch.

★ Bogart's Café

$$ | **AMERICAN** | Well established as a local favorite, this unassuming restaurant is situated in a strip mall near Diamond Head and away from the bustle of Waikiki. It's a great spot to grab a bagel or açai bowl in the morning or to linger over a post-sunset dinner—perhaps enjoying seared scallops with cauliflower puree, a pork chop with braised fennel, or one of the pasta dishes, including the chef's signature *cacio e pepe* featuring cheese imported from Italy's Dolomites region. **Known for:** some outdoor seating; a neighborhood staple and local favorite for all-day dining; sophisticated dinner menu. ⑤ *Average main: $22* ✉ *3045 Monsarrat Ave., Waikiki* ☎ 808/739–0999 ⊕ www. bogartscafe.com.

★ Chart House Waikiki

$$$$ | AMERICAN | Enjoy sunset views over the yacht harbor, live music, and signature "Guy-Tai" cocktails at this Waikiki landmark opened in 1969 by surfing legend Joey Cabell. The extensive menu maintains the midcentury notion of fine dining, with oysters Rockefeller, shrimp cocktail, and steaks (including a bison tenderloin from Ted Turner's ranch) alongside poke, macadamia-nut-crusted mahimahi, and the fan-favorite "Joey's ahi mignon." Early birds can take advantage of the "surf break" menu, and there's also a very popular weekend brunch (book in advance). **Known for:** generations of regulars; sought-after tables on the lanai (book well in advance); old-time steak house atmosphere with live music and strong cocktails. ⑤ *Average main: $48* ⊠ *1765 Ala Moana Blvd., Waikiki* 🖀 *808/941–6669* ⊕ *charthousewaikiki. com* ⊗ *No lunch.*

d.k Steakhouse

$$$$ | STEAKHOUSE | D.K. Kodama serves steaks that are free from hormones, antibiotics, and steroids and come straight from Oahu's first dry-aging room. Consider trying the 22-ounce *paniolo* (cowboy) rib eye—dry-aged 30 days on the bone and seasoned with a house-made rub—accompanied by a side of the popular and addictive potatoes au gratin, topped with Maui onions and Parmesan. **Known for:** sunset views from outdoor tables; local flavors, local ownership, and locally sourced produce and select meats; gluten-free and vegan options. ⑤ *Average main: $55* ⊠ *Waikiki Beach Marriott Resort & Spa, 2552 Kalakaua Ave., Waikiki* 🖀 *808/931–6280* ⊕ *dkrestaurants.com/index.php/restaurants/dk* ⊗ *No lunch.*

Doraku Sushi

$$$ | JAPANESE | From entrepreneur Kevin Aoki, son of Benihana founder Rocky Aoki, comes this low-lit, bells-and-whistles, sushi-roll chain (with two additional locations in Hawaii and another in Miami) featuring indoor-outdoor seating, as well as happy hours and a late-night bar scene that keeps the place packed. Newer dishes, such as the sake bomb or stuffed jalepeño rolls, are offered alongside favorites like the tuna *tataki* or the Emperor Roll, a seafood extravaganza of tuna, crab, shrimp, and scallop crusted in *panko* and flash-fried. **Known for:** creative rolls; a buzzing bar scene, with both early and late happy hours; tempura everything, including brownies. ⑤ *Average main: $27* ⊠ *Royal Hawaiian Center, 2233 Kalakaua Ave., Waikiki* 🖀 *808/922–3323* ⊕ *www.dorakusushi.com.*

Duke's Waikiki

$$$ | AMERICAN | FAMILY | Locals often bring Mainland visitors to this open-air restaurant, which has a lively bar and a beachfront setting facing Waikiki's famed Canoes surf break. Named for the father of modern surfing and filled with Duke Kahanamoku memorabilia, this casual spot offers lots of pupus (appetizers), a large salad bar, and crowd-pleasing entrées that include fish, prime rib, and *huli huli* (rotisserie). **Known for:** bar seating usually offers faster service; iconic local spot with great views, a fun bar scene, and a perfect location; Duke's on Sunday is so renowned that musician Henry Kapono wrote a song about it. ⑤ *Average main: $28* ⊠ *Outrigger Waikiki Beach Resort, 2335 Kalakaua Ave., Waikiki* 🖀 *808/922–2268* ⊕ *www.dukeswaikiki. com.*

Hau Tree

$$$ | AMERICAN | Countless anniversaries, birthdays, and other milestones have been celebrated under this lanai restaurant's spectacular *hau* tree, where it's said that even Robert Louis Stevenson found shade as he mused and wrote about Hawaii. Diners are captivated as much by the beach views, spectacular sunsets, and romantic setting as by celebrated chef Chris Kajioka's updated takes on eggs Benedict at breakfast and tuna tartar, scallops, or Kurobuta pork chops

later in the day. **Known for:** an updated menu and attentive service; the romantic beach dining spot folks dream about; spectacular views of the beach by day and the moonlit water by night. $ *Average main: $29 ⊠ The New Otani Kaimana Beach Hotel, 2863 Kalakaua Ave., Waikiki ☎ 808/921–7066 ⊕ www.kaimana.com.*

Herringbone Waikiki
$$$$ | SEAFOOD | Upstairs at International Marketplace and featuring a 2,000-square-foot lanai dining area, casual-chic Herringbone is a lively place for craft cocktails and dinner or weekend brunch. Emphasizing locally sourced seafood, produce, and other ingredients, the menu includes many raw bar options, as well as lobster rolls, king salmon, whole fish, salads, and flatbreads. **Known for:** large outdoor dining space; beef and chicken options for those who don't love seafood; weekend brunch. $ *Average main: $38 ⊠ International Marketplace, 2330 Kalakaua Ave., Waikiki ☎ (808)/797–2435 ⊕ taogroup.com/venues/herringbone-waikiki.*

Heyday
$$$ | AMERICAN | Although it's in the center of Waikiki, this lively outdoor restaurant with a retro, tropical vibe feels a bit tucked away, with a bamboo-lined walkway leading to its entrance and tables set around the pool at the White Sands Hotel. Grab a drink at the whimsical bamboo bar, where a cool crowd sits on wooden swings or bar stools and sips tiki-style cocktails, and peruse the "new continental" menu with a variety of pupus (appetizers) and decadent desserts, as well as such favorites as the B.O.L.T. (bacon, smoked ono salad, lettuce, and tomato) sandwich on a brioche bun or the schnitzel with potato mac salad. **Known for:** swinging seats around the bamboo bar; great food with retro vibe; large and small plates, including vegan options. $ *Average main: $35 ⊠ White Sands Hotel, 431 Nohonani St., Waikiki*

☎ *808/475–6864 ⊕ whitesandshotel.com/eat-drink.*

Hula Grill Waikiki
$$$ | HAWAIIAN | FAMILY | The placid younger sibling of boisterous Duke's, downstairs, resembles an open-air, plantation-period summer home with kitschy decor, stone-flagged floors, warm wood, and floral prints. The food is carefully prepared and familiar—with the occasional intriguing Asian touch—and dishes include steaks, locally caught grilled fish, and a few island-inspired options, such as the Loco Moco and tropical pancakes. **Known for:** nice bar scene for drinks and snacks; spectacular views from the window tables; reliable local dining experience with the right amount of Waikiki kitsch. $ *Average main: $28 ⊠ Outrigger Waikiki Beach Resort, 2335 Kalakaua Ave., Waikiki ☎ 808/923–4852 ⊕ www.hulagrillwaikiki.com.*

Hy's Steak House
$$$$ | STEAKHOUSE | If the Rat Pack reconvened for big steaks and a bigger red, they'd feel right at home at Hy's, which hasn't changed much since it opened in 1976. The formula: prime-grade beef cooked over an open kiawe-wood (mesquite) fire, "old-school" service, a clubby atmosphere, and a wine list recognized for excellence by *Wine Spectator.* **Known for:** desserts flambéed tableside; dark woods, club chairs, banquettes, and that fabulous 1970s feel; a wine list fit for the most persnickety palate. $ *Average main: $60 ⊠ Waikiki Park Heights Hotel, 2440 Kuhio Ave., Waikiki ☎ 808/922–5555 ⊕ hyswaikiki.com ☾ No lunch.*

★ Island Vintage Wine Bar
$$ | WINE BAR | Tucked away on the second floor of the Royal Hawaiian Center, this stylish, sleek, and cozy spot has a selection of more than 40 international wines by the glass—all served via a high-tech vending machine that uses prepaid cards. The food menu is limited, but a few favorites include oversize Wagyu burgers, poke bites with nori chips, and

cheese and charcuterie plates. **Known for:** massive Wagyu burgers; vending-machine wines by the glass; a subdued happy hour. $ *Average main: $25 ☒ Royal Hawaiian Center, 2301 Kalakaua Ave., Bldg. C, Level 2, Waikiki ☏ 808/799–9463 ⊕ www.islandvintagewinebar.com.*

La Mer

$$$$ | **FRENCH** | With spectacular Diamond Head views and an elegant, art deco–tinged interior, La Mer is a romantic, second-floor restaurant, where windows open to the breezes and the sounds of the ocean and Halekulani Hotel's nightly hula show. Three-, four-, or seven-course dinners might feature *kampachi* (amberjack) ceviche with ginger caviar fennel, roasted John Dory with artichokes *barigoule* (braised in white-wine broth), or tomahawk steak (rib eye) with vegetables. **Known for:** classy bar with cocktail and small-bite pairings; it doesn't get more romantic than this; impressive wine list and a sommelier to match. $ *Average main: $160 ☒ Halekulani Hotel, 2199 Kalia Rd., Waikiki ☏ 808/923–2311 ⊕ www.halekulani.com/dining/la-mer ☾ No lunch ⌂ Long-sleeved, collared (or aloha) shirts required for men.*

Michel's at the Colony Surf

$$$$ | **FRENCH** | This romantic restaurant on Waikiki's tranquil Gold Coast features beachside sunset views and traditional French fare. It opened in 1962, and the surroundings reflect this, with lots of wood and stone, bow-tied servers preparing lobster bisque and steak tartare table-side, and a charm that's beloved by old-time locals but sometimes lost on younger diners. **Known for:** a pricey experience and a retro vibe; the sound of the surf and live music most nights; classic French cuisine with some local twists. $ *Average main: $65 ☒ Colony Surf, 2895 Kalakaua Ave., Waikiki ☏ 808/923–6552 ⊕ www.michelshawaii.com ☾ No lunch.*

Morimoto Asia Waikiki

$$$$ | **JAPANESE FUSION** | Iron Chef Masaharu Morimoto serves classics and new fusion favorites at his second-floor restaurant—a sleek space with a lanai, a gorgeous bar, and a dining room designed for entertaining clients or celebrating with friends. Enjoy some Morimoto specialties, including *ishiyaki buri bop* (yellowtail seared tableside with pickled daikon, royal fern, and egg yolk) or spicy black pepper steak, as well as dim sum, sushi, and creative specialty rolls. **Known for:** Asian-fusion menu with enough classics to draw loyalists; attentive service and great food; casual elegance in a lovely spot. $ *Average main: $41 ☒ Alohilani Resort, 2490 Kalakaua Ave., Waikiki ☏ 808/922–0022 ⊕ morimotoasiawaikiki.com.*

Mugen

$$$$ | **ASIAN FUSION** | Food lovers in the know—including the Obamas, who ate here on a recent visit—recognize that chef Jason Yamaguchi's (Roy's nephew) tiny, French-Japanese restaurant offers a truly memorable Waikiki dining experience. Although the perfectly plated dishes on the 11-course tasting menu change seasonally, standouts have included the duck with farro risotto and huckleberry and the veal with persimmon; desserts are incredibly delectable as well. **Known for:** elegant wines and cocktail menu; multicourse tasting menu; exclusive and special experience. $ *Average main: $130 ☒ Espacio The Jewel of Waikiki, 2452 Kalakaua Ave., Waikiki ☏ 808/377–2247 ⊕ www.mugenwaikiki.com.*

100 Sails Restaurant and Bar

$$$$ | **ECLECTIC** | **FAMILY** | The spacious, airy 100 Sails continues the everything-you-can-imagine buffet tradition (with crab legs and prime rib, of course), along with plenty of à la carte small bites, an emphasis on locally sourced ingredients, and a commitment to knock-out presentation. And then there are the views—night after night, the sunsets over the harbor deliver stunning shows of color. **Known for:** high-quality food and a huge selection; international buffet for every meal; views and sunsets to rival those anywhere else in Waikiki. $ *Average main: $60 ⊠ Hawaii Prince Hotel Waikiki, 100 Holomoana St., Waikiki ☎ 808/944–4494 ⊕ www.100sails.com.*

★ Orchids

$$$$ | **SEAFOOD** | Perched along the seawall at historic Gray's Beach, in the luxe Halekulani resort, Orchids is a locus of power breakfasters, ladies who lunch, and those celebrating special occasions at Sunday brunch or dinner. The louvered walls are open to the breezes, sprays of orchids add color, the contemporary international dishes are perfectly prepared, and the wine list is intriguing. **Known for:** a menu with something for just about everyone; island breezes, ocean sounds, and stellar service and food; lovely ocean views and live music at sunset. $ *Average main: $42 ⊠ Halekulani Hotel, 2199 Kalia Rd., Waikiki ☎ 808/923–2311 ⊕ www.halekulani. com/dining/orchids-restaurant 🏛 Collared shirts required for men.*

Queensbreak

$$$ | **AMERICAN** | **FAMILY** | Across from popular Kuhio Beach, and three floors up from busy Waikiki on the pool deck at the Waikiki Beach Marriott Resort & Spa, this laid-back, multilevel, terrace restaurant is a great place to grab a casual bite (fish tacos, poke, Caesar salad, burgers) and a beer, a glass of wine, or a tropical cocktail. In addition to ocean views, you can enjoy happy hour specials and live music. **Known for:** outdoor dining; casual favorites on the menu; live music in the evening. $ *Average main: $35 ⊠ Waikiki Beach Marriott Resort & Spa, 2552 Kalakaua Ave., Waikiki ☎ 808/922–6611 ⊕ www. queensbreak.com.*

Roy's Waikiki

$$$ | **HAWAIIAN** | **FAMILY** | Enjoy a taste of modern Hawaiian cuisine from the chef

Pupu

Entertaining Hawaii-style means having a lot of pupu—the local term for appetizers or hors d'oeuvres— which are often served during *pau hana,*the Islands-style happy hour when locals wind down from the workday and enjoy a couple of drinks. Popular pupu include sushi, tempura, teriyaki chicken or beef skewers, barbecued meat, and the favorite: *poke* (pronounced "po-keh"), or raw fish, seasoned with seaweed, shoyu, and other flavorings.

who started it all, Roy Yamaguchi. Situated in the center of Waikiki, the sprawling, stylish restaurant has been serving innovative pan-Asian dishes since 2007 and remains a fan favorite. **Known for:** indoor and outdoor seating; iconic status; nightly happy hour on the lanai. $ *Average main: $35 ⊠ 226 Lewers St., Waikiki ☎ 808/923–7697 ⊕ www.royyamaguchi. com.*

RumFire Waikiki

$$ | **ASIAN FUSION** | If the perfect sunset happy hour means cocktails, bite-size shareable plates, tropical breezes, ocean sounds, and flaming oversized torches, then "Meet me at Rumfire" should be your motto. Enjoy such dishes as lemon-herb mahimahi, island fish tacos, and "local style" sesame-ahi poke; sip signature concoctions like the RumFire Mai Tai or the Fire Runner, made with spiced rum and tropical juices. **Known for:** hip vibe that attracts young professionals; beachside nightlife scene with great food and cocktails; fabulous location right on the beach. $ *Average main: $25 ⊠ Sheraton Waikiki, 2255 Kalakaua Ave., Waikiki ☎ 808/922–4422 ⊕ www.rumfirewaikiki. com.*

Side Street Inn Kapahulu

$$ | ECLECTIC | FAMILY | The original Hopaka Street pub is famous as the place where celebrity chefs gather after hours; this second Kapahulu Avenue location is also popular and closer to Waikiki. Local-style bar food—salty panfried pork chops with a plastic tub of ketchup, *lup cheong* fried rice, and passion fruit–glazed ribs—is served in huge, shareable portions. **Known for:** sports-bar feel with lots of fried food; portions that can seemingly feed you for a week; popular local spot with a crowd of regulars. $ *Average main: $25* ⊠ *614 Kapahulu Ave., Waikiki* ☎ *808/739–3939* ⊕ *www.sidestreetinn. com* ◔ *No lunch.*

Taormina Sicilian Cuisine

$$$$ | ITALIAN | Honolulu has its share of Italian restaurants, and Taormina, taking its culinary cues from Sicily, is considered one of the best by foodies, locals, and visitors alike. In a sleek, elegant room (there is outdoor seating, but this is one place it's best to dine indoors), you can dine on well-executed classics, from porcini risotto with sautéed foie gras to a breaded veal chop *"alla Taormina"* (the restaurant's take on veal Parmesan). **Known for:** extensive wine list; intimate, quiet respite in bustling Waikiki; authentic Sicilian cuisine. $ *Average main: $36* ⊠ *Waikiki Beach Walk, 227 Lewers St., Waikiki* ☎ *808/926–5050* ⊕ *www.taorminarestaurant.com.*

Teddy's Bigger Burgers

$ | BURGER | Modeled after 1950s diners, this casual spot serves classic, tender, messy burgers—including the Hawaiian teriyaki burger with grilled pineapple and the Kailua with Swiss cheese, mushrooms, and grilled onions—along with turkey and veggie burgers, salads, and chicken breast and fish sandwiches. The fries are crispy, and the shakes rich and sweet. **Known for:** local chain for dependable quick lunches across the island; messy burgers, great fries, and rich milkshakes; diner-style service, with food to go. $ *Average main: $12* ⊠ *Waikiki Grand Hotel, 134 Kapahulu Ave., Waikiki* ☎ *808/926–3444* ⊕ *www.teddysbb.com.*

★ Tiki's Grill and Bar

$$$ | MODERN HAWAIIAN | Tiki's is the kind of fun place people come to Waikiki for: a retro–South Pacific spot with a back-of-the-bar faux volcano, open-air lounge with live local music, indoor-outdoor dining, and a fantastic view of the beach across the street. Chef Ronnie Nasuti turns out beautifully composed plates and puts fresh twists on the super-familiar—like spicy "volcano" chicken wings, watermelon and feta salad, or Thai-style shrimp puttanesca. **Known for:** can get pricey, but a fun experience worthy of a hana hou (encore); surprisingly good food in a made-for-TV setting; Pacific Rim menu inspired by a noted Islands chef. $ *Average main: $32* ⊠ *Aston Waikiki Beach Hotel, 2570 Kalakaua Ave., Waikiki* ☎ *808/923–8454* ⊕ *www.tikisgrill.com.*

Wolfgang's Steakhouse by Wolfgang Zwiener

$$$$ | STEAKHOUSE | The Honolulu outpost of the NY-based original serves good steaks that have been dry-aged on site, as well as classic shrimp cocktails, slabs of Canadian bacon, crab cakes, creamed spinach, broiled jumbo lobster, and the token grilled fish selection. If it sounds like Peter Luger's on the Pacific, then it won't come as a surprise to learn that owner Wolfgang Zwiener was once head waiter at that legendary Brooklyn steak house. **Known for:** surprisingly varied brunch menu (with a killer Bloody Mary); classic NY steak house vibe, food, and attentive service; great location in the heart of Waikiki. $ *Average main: $60* ⊠ *Royal Hawaiian Center, 2201 Kalakaua Ave., Waikiki* ☎ *808/922–3600* ⊕ *www. wolfgangssteakhouse.net.*

Waikiki and Honolulu, looking west to Diamond Head, as seen from above

☕ Coffee and Quick Bites

★ Banán

$ | HAWAIIAN | Follow a narrow beach pathway (between The Cheesecake Factory and Outrigger Waikiki Beach Resort) lined with surfboards to reach this takeout spot specializing in banán, a frozen, vegan-friendly dessert made with local bananas and containing no added sugar. Other snack options include smoothies, smoothie bowls, and ulu (breadfruit) waffles. **Known for:** refreshing snack on a hot day; plant-based frozen desserts; locally owned. $ *Average main: $10* ✉ *2301 Kalakaua Ave., Waikiki* ⊕ *banan.co.*

Diamond Head Market & Grill

$ | AMERICAN | FAMILY | Just five minutes from Waikiki's hotels is chef Kelvin Ro's one-stop food shop—indispensable if you have accommodations with a kitchen or want a quick grab-and-go meal. Join surfers, beachgoers, and Diamond Head hikers at the takeout window to order gourmet sandwiches and plates, such as hand-shaped burgers, portobello mushroom sandwiches, Korean *kalbi* ribs, and grilled ahi with wasabi-ginger sauce, rice, and salad. Selections include sandwiches, bento boxes, and salads. **Known for:** well-priced grab-and-go dinners; excellent desserts and scones; picnic fare for the beach. $ *Average main: $14* ✉ *3158 Monsarrat Ave., Diamond Head* ☎ *808/732-0077* ⊕ *www.diamondheadmarket.com.*

★ Halekulani Bakery & Restaurant

$$ | CONTEMPORARY | Head to this upscale yet casual bakery and restaurant adjacent to the Halepuna hotel lobby for hearty breakfasts, chocolate croissants and fruit tarts, freshly baked bread, and quality coffee, including lattes and cappuccinos. **Known for:** gourmet coffee beverages; delicious French pastries; a great breakfast. $ *Average main: $26* ✉ *Halepuna Waikiki by Halekulani, 2233 Helumoa Rd., Waikiki* ☎ *808/921-7272* ⊕ *www.halekulani.com/dining/halekulani-bakery-restaurant/.*

Malasadas

Malasadas are a contribution of the Portuguese, who came to the Hawaiian Islands to work on the plantations. Roughly translated, the name means "half-cooked," as these deep-fried, heavily sugared treats are said to have been created as a way to use up scraps of rich, buttery egg dough. They are similar to fluffy donuts and are offered in many flavors; some are filled with fruit or cream.

You'll find malasadas at farmers' markets, fairs, and carnivals. In addition, a handful of bakeries specialize in them, including **Leonard's Bakery** (⊠ *933 Kapahulu Ave.*); **Kamehameha Bakery** (⊠ *1284 Kalani St., Unit D-106*); and **Pipeline Bakeshop** (⊠ *3632 Waialae Ave.*). Some Honolulu restaurants serve upscale versions, stuffed with fruit puree. Regardless, eat them fresh and hot or not at all.

Holey Grail Donuts

$ | **BAKERY** | **FAMILY** | Locals love the scrumptious taro-based confections and delightful coffee beverages created by this family-run outfit. Fried in coconut oil, the doughnuts are known for their light texture, splashy colors and designs, and sophisticated flavors with fun names like Island Chocolate, Pineapple Express, Miso Honey, Kale'n It, and Prosperity (with kumquat and poppy seeds). **Known for:** unusual flavors and designs; taro-based doughnuts; locally sourced, fresh ingredients. ⑤ *Average main: $8* ⊠ *325 Seaside Ave., Waikiki* ☎ *808/634-8838* ⊕ *www.holeygraildonuts.com.*

Honolulu Coffee Experience

$ | **CAFÉ** | A massive, antique roaster is the centerpiece of this beautifully appointed, spacious, and airy coffeehouse, the largest and most unique branch of the Waikiki chain, situated near the convention center. There are plenty of options for tea drinkers, too, in addition to pastries, breakfast sandwiches, and açai bowls. **Known for:** lovely spot to relax; high-quality coffee; variety of baked goods. ⑤ *Average main: $12* ⊠ *1800 Kalakaua Ave., Waikiki* ☎ *808/202-2562* ⊕ *www.honolulucoffee.com.*

South Shore Grill

$ | **AMERICAN** | Popular with locals, this counter-service spot is just minutes from Waikiki, on trendy Monsarrat Avenue near the base of Diamond Head. It has something for everyone: generous plate lunches (try the wahoo coated with macadamia-nut pesto and served with a tangy slaw), fish tacos, burritos, burgers, ciabatta-roll sandwiches, and entrée salads. **Known for:** Peanut Butter Temptations for dessert; casual surfer vibe; takeout for the beach. ⑤ *Average main: $14* ⊠ *3114 Monsarrat Ave., Diamond Head* ☎ *808/734-0229* ⊕ *www.southshoregrill.com.*

★ Waikiki Food Hall

$ | **HAWAIIAN** | **FAMILY** | At this bright, lively, upscale food court on the third floor of the Royal Hawaiian Center, you can feast on local and Japanese options ranging from massive, juicy burgers to spicy shrimp tacos to exquisite smoothies topped with colorful, edible designs—all emphasizing the use of fresh, local ingredients. Vendors here include Five Star Shrimp, Milk, JTRRD, Meatally Boys, POTAMA (Pork Tamago Onigiri), Honolulu Burger Co., Surfer's Cafe, and Tap Bar. **Known for:** lots of seating; new and modern; variety of vendors offering upscale options that you can mix and match. ⑤ *Average main: $14* ⊠ *Royal Hawaiian Center, 2201 Kalakaua Ave., Bldg. C, 3rd fl., Waikiki* ✛ *Above the Cheesecake*

Factory ☎ 808/922–2299 for Royal Hawaiian Center ⊕ www.waikikifoodhall.com.

Hotels

A stay in Waikiki puts you in the heart of the action, and though parking can be difficult and pricey, you really don't need a car as there's ready access to the beach, restaurants, activities, and affordable public transportation. To be slightly removed from the main scene, however, opt for accommodations on the *ewa* (western) end of Waikiki.

The hotel selection ranges from super-luxe resorts to small, no-frills places where surfers and beachgoers hang out in the lobby. Room sizes, styles, and configurations can vary tremendously even in the same hotel, so ask questions to ensure that you get an ocean view, say, or have other requirements met. Also inquire about extras: for instance, some hotels—even if they aren't right on the sand—provide their guests with sunblock, towels, chairs, and other beach accessories.

★ Alohilani Resort Waikiki Beach

$$$ | HOTEL | FAMILY | The centerpiece of this modern, stylish high-rise, across the street from the beach in the center of Waikiki, is the lobby's mesmerizing aquarium, filled with nearly 300,000 gallons of seawater and colorful marine life. **Pros:** excellent guest lounge; new and modern, with several on-site restaurants; cutting-edge fitness facilities and spa. **Cons:** you must cross the street for the beach; large hotel that can feel impersonal; resort fee is $48 per day. ⓢ *Rooms from: $275* ⊠ *2490 Kalakaua Ave., Waikiki* ☎ *808/922–1233* ⊕ *www.alohilaniresort. com* ➾ *839 rooms* ◉◎ *No Meals.*

Aqua Aloha Surf Waikiki

$ | HOTEL | FAMILY | This affordable property two blocks from Waikiki Beach appeals to the young (and young at heart) with surfer-chic rooms and suites, a cool blue-and-green color scheme, and lounge chairs throughout. **Pros:** on-site coin-operated laundry; in-room refrigerators and microwaves; pool with sundeck and cabanas. **Cons:** no view and 10-minute walk to beach; no daily housekeeping services; somewhat dated in places. ⓢ *Rooms from: $169* ⊠ *444 Kanekapolei St., Waikiki* ☎ *866/970–4160, 808/954–7410* ⊕ *www.aquaaston.com/hotels/ aqua-aloha-surf-waikiki* ➾ *204 rooms.*

Aqua Oasis

$ | HOTEL | FAMILY | An open-air lobby of Italian marble, a koi pond, hanging egg chairs, and a guava smoothie greet you on arrival at this hideaway a five-minute stroll from Kalakaua Avenue through one of the many public-access ways to the beach. **Pros:** on-site coin-operated laundry; all rooms have lanai; Japanese restaurant adjacent to lobby. **Cons:** $25 per night resort fee and valet parking only; trip to the beach can be a bit of a haul if you're carrying lounge chairs; rooms are slightly dated. ⓢ *Rooms from: $129* ⊠ *320 Lewers St., Waikiki* ☎ *808/923–2300, 866/767–4528, 808/441–7781* ⊕ *www.aquaaston.com/hotels/aqua-oasis* ➾ *96 rooms* ◉◎ *Free Breakfast.*

Aqua Palms Waikiki

$ | HOTEL | FAMILY | The 12-story Aqua Palms was recently revitalized, giving many of its rooms and suites (some with kitchens) energy-efficient air-conditioning and new furnishings, carpeting, drapes, bedding, and lighting fixtures. **Pros:** free coffee and tea in the lobby; recent refurbishments; short walk to park, beach, convention center, and activities. **Cons:** not all rooms have lanai; resort fee is $25 per day; beach access is through the Hilton Hawaiian Village, across the street. ⓢ *Rooms from: $169* ⊠ *1850 Ala Moana Blvd., Waikiki* ☎ *808/954–7424 reservations local number, 866/970–4165 reservations toll-free, 808/947–7256 direct to hotel's front desk* ⊕ *www. aquaaston.com/hotels/aqua-palms-waikiki* ➾ *262 units* ◉◎ *No Meals.*

3

Honolulu and Pearl Harbor WAIKIKI AND DIAMOND HEAD

Aston at the Waikiki Banyan

$$ | RESORT | FAMILY | Families and active travelers love the convenience and action of this hotel, often referred to as "the Banyan," just a block from Waikiki Beach, the aquarium, the zoo, and bustling Kalakaua Avenue. **Pros:** shuttle service around Waikiki; many suites have great views as well as kitchens; fabulous and massive recreation deck for the entire family. **Cons:** sharing hotel with residents; resort fee is $25 per day; suites are individually owned so conditions can vary greatly. *Rooms from: $200 ⊠ 201 Ohua Ave., Waikiki ☎ 808/922–0555, 877/997–6667 toll-free for reservations ⊕ www.astonwaikikibanyan.com ⤴ 876 suites ⦿ No Meals.*

Aston Waikiki Beach Hotel

$$ | HOTEL | FAMILY | A good choice for families, this large, high-rise hotel is directly across the street from a protected stretch of Kuhio Beach and near Kapiolani Park. **Pros:** Coconut Club lounge access for certain rooms/packages; fun for families; great beach access. **Cons:** rooms are dated; resort fee of $42 per day; active lobby area and crowded elevators. *Rooms from: $249 ⊠ 2570 Kalakaua Ave., Waikiki ☎ 808/922–2511 direct to hotel, 877/997–6667 reservations toll-free, 800/877–7666 reservations toll-free ⊕ www.astonwaikikibeach.com ⤴ 645 rooms ⦿ No Meals.*

Aston Waikiki Beach Tower

$$$$ | RESORT | FAMILY | Here, in the center of Waikiki, you get the elegance of a luxury all-suites condominium combined with the intimacy and service of a boutique hotel. **Pros:** a recreation deck with something for everyone; roomy suites with quality amenities; great private lanai and views. **Cons:** space, amenities, and location don't come cheap; you must cross a busy street to the beach; resort fee is $35 per day. *Rooms from: $699 ⊠ 2470 Kalakaua Ave., Waikiki ☎ 808/926–6400, 855/776–1766 toll-free*

⊕ www.astonwaikikibeachtower.com ⤴ 140 suites ⦿ No Meals.

Aston Waikiki Circle Hotel

$$ | HOTEL | Built to resemble a Chinese lantern, this circular, 14-story hotel is a Waikiki landmark, where a charming interior design brings the Pacific inside, beginning at check-in with breezes that flow through an open-air lobby. **Pros:** on-site surfboard lockers and complimentary beach gear; unbeatable location; lanai with a view in every room. **Cons:** resort fee is $25 per day; busy location in Waikiki; small rooms; showers only. *Rooms from: $250 ⊠ 2464 Kalakaua Ave., Waikiki ☎ 808/923–1571, 877/997–6667 toll-free for reservations ⊕ www.astonwaikikicircle.com ⤴ 104 rooms ⦿ No Meals.*

The Breakers Hotel

$ | HOTEL | With a homey atmosphere and a vintage vibe, this small, low-rise complex—two blocks from the beach and close to the Waikiki Beach Walk entertainment, dining, and retail complex—transports its guests back to 1960s-era Hawaii. **Pros:** a throwback to a different era; intimate atmosphere with fabulous poolside courtyard; great location. **Cons:** showers only; parking is extremely limited (but free); a bit worn down and dated. *Rooms from: $170 ⊠ 250 Beach Walk, Waikiki ☎ 808/923–3181, 800/923–7174 toll-free ⊕ www.breakers-hawaii.com ⤴ 63 rooms ⦿ No Meals.*

Coconut Waikiki Hotel

$ | HOTEL | FAMILY | Overlooking the Ala Wai Canal, this reasonably priced boutique hotel has a more residential feel than the typical resort, with a cobblestone driveway, a lobby with rattan furnishings, a small fitness center, and a tiny swimming pool tucked in a backyard. **Pros:** some rooms have two bathrooms; no resort fee if booked directly; good bet for larger groups. **Cons:** area is residential and removed from the action, particularly at night; only valet parking available; walking three blocks to and from the beach on a busy street can be tiresome. $ *Rooms from: $169* ✉ *450 Lewers St., Waikiki* ☎ *866/974–2626 toll-free, 808/923–8828* ⊕ *www.coconutwaikikihotel.com* ⟿ *81 rooms* ❑ *Free Breakfast.*

DoubleTree by Hilton Alana – Waikiki Beach

$$ | **HOTEL** | A convenient location—a 10-minute walk from the Hawaii Convention Center—a professional staff, pleasant public spaces, and a 24-hour business center and small gym draw a global clientele to this reliable chain hotel. **Pros:** heated outdoor pool and 24-hour fitness center; walkable to the beach and Ala Moana mall; walk-in glass showers with oversize rain showerheads. **Cons:** resort fee is $30 per day; little local flavor; a 10-minute walk to the beach. $ *Rooms from: $230* ✉ *1956 Ala Moana Blvd., Waikiki* ☎ *808/941–7275* ⊕ *www. hilton.com/en/hotels/hnlkadt-double-tree-alana-waikiki-beach* ⟿ *317 rooms* ❑ *No Meals.*

Embassy Suites by Hilton Waikiki Beach Walk

$$$ | **RESORT** | **FAMILY** | In a place where space is at a premium, this resort in the heart of Waikiki's Beach Walk dining and shopping area offers families and other groups spacious, one- and two-bedroom suites stylishly decorated in relaxing earth tones with splashes of color. **Pros:** free hot breakfast and happy hour reception daily; no resort fee; spacious and modern rooms. **Cons:** property can seem busy and noisy; lobby feels more like a business hotel; no direct beach access. $ *Rooms from: $319* ✉ *201 Beachwalk St., Waikiki* ☎ *800/362–2779 toll-free, 808/921–2345 direct to hotel* ⊕ *www. embassysuiteswaikiki.com* ⟿ *369 suites* ❑ *Free Breakfast.*

The Equus

$ | **HOTEL** | **FAMILY** | On the *ewa* (western) end of Waikiki, a block from both the Ala Moana Center and Ala Moana Beach Park, this modern, family-owned, boutique hotel has a Hawaiian country theme that pays tribute to Hawaii's polo-playing history. **Pros:** nicely furnished rooms; casual and fun atmosphere; attentive staff. **Cons:** resort fee is $25 a day; must cross a major road to reach the beach; busy, hectic area. $ *Rooms from: $160* ✉ *1696 Ala Moana Blvd., Waikiki* ☎ *808/949–0061* ⊕ *www.equushotel. com* ⟿ *67 rooms* ❑ *No Meals.*

Espacio – The Jewel of Waikiki

$$$$ | **HOTEL** | As its name suggests, this is one of the most luxurious hotel experiences in Hawaii, with nine designer suites, each occupying an entire floor and featuring smart-home technology, a large private lanai with a hot tub, two or three bedrooms, a gourmet kitchen, and spacious bathrooms with saunas. **Pros:** highest level of service; incredible ocean views; height of opulence and luxury. **Cons:** exceptionally expensive; across the street from the beach; swimming pool is shared and on the small side. $ *Rooms from: $3000* ✉ *2452 Kalakaua Ave., Waikiki* ☎ *855/945–4089 toll-free, 808/377–2246 direct to hotel* ⊕ *www. espaciowaikiki.com* ⟿ *9 rooms* ❑ *Free Breakfast.*

★ Halekulani

$$$$ | **RESORT** | Its name translates to the "house befitting heaven," and this beachfront haven does, indeed, seem like a slice of heaven thanks to impeccable service and spacious guest rooms that are artfully appointed with marble and wood, neutral color schemes, modern furniture, updated technology, and bathrooms that have oversize soaking tubs as well as showers. **Pros:** heavenly interior and exterior spaces; award-winning spa and wonderful bars and restaurants; no resort fee. **Cons:** narrow beachfront with little room for sunbathing; lofty room rates; might feel a bit formal for Waikiki. $ *Rooms from: $500* ✉ *2199 Kalia Rd., Waikiki* ☎ *808/923–2311 direct to hotel, 800/367–2343 reservations toll-free* ⊕ *www.halekulani.com* ⟿ *453 rooms* ❑ *No Meals.*

★ Halepuna Waikiki by Halekulani

$$$$ | HOTEL | This high-rise boutique property offers the same outstanding service and attention to detail as its elegant sister hotel, the Halekulani, but without the beachfront location and higher prices. **Pros:** no resort fee; fresh, modern, and well appointed; great access to Waikiki Beach and Beach Walk shopping and dining. **Cons:** swimming pool can get busy; rooms can be small; no direct beach access. ⑤ *Rooms from: $366* ✉ *2233 Helumoa Rd., Waikiki* ☎ *808/921–7272 direct to hotel, 800/422–0450 reservations toll-free* ⊕ *www.halepuna.com* ⌁ *297 rooms* ⦿ *No Meals.*

Hilton Garden Inn Waikiki Beach

$$ | HOTEL | FAMILY | Most of the rooms at this expansive, midrange, chain hotel in the heart of Waikiki have a lanai with seating and feature a partial ocean or a Waikiki city view. **Pros:** no resort fee; near International Marketplace's shops and restaurants; rooftop pool. **Cons:** two-block walk to the beach; valet-only parking; the large resort can feel impersonal. ⑤ *Rooms from: $200* ✉ *2330 Kuhio Ave., Waikiki* ☎ *808/892–1820* ⊕ *www.hilton. com/en/hotels/hnlkugi-hilton-garden-inn-waikiki-beach* ⌁ *623 rooms* ⦿ *No Meals.*

Hilton Hawaiian Village Waikiki Beach Resort

$$$ | RESORT | FAMILY | Location, location, location: this five-tower mega-resort sprawls over 22 acres on Waikiki's widest stretch of beach, with the greenery of neighboring Fort DeRussy creating a buffer zone between it and central Waikiki's high-rise lineup. **Pros:** activities and amenities can keep you and the kids busy for weeks; stellar spa and fitness center; a large variety of room options. **Cons:** resort fee is $50 per day; parking is expensive ($49 per day for self-parking); size of property can be overwhelming. ⑤ *Rooms from: $325* ✉ *2005 Kalia Rd., Waikiki* ☎ *808/949–4321, 800/774–1500 toll-free* ⊕ *www.hiltonhawaiianvillage. com* ⌁ *4499 rooms* ⦿ *No Meals.*

Hilton Waikiki Beach

$$ | HOTEL | On the Diamond Head end of Waikiki and two blocks from Kuhio Beach, this 37-story high-rise is great for travelers who want to be near the action but not right in it. **Pros:** pleasant, comfortable public spaces; central location; every room has a lanai. **Cons:** older property that shows some wear; $45 a day (valet only parking); resort fee is $30 per day. ⑤ *Rooms from: $225* ✉ *2500 Kuhio Ave., Waikiki* ☎ *808/922–0811 direct to hotel, 888/370–0980 toll-free* ⊕ *www. hiltonwaikikibeach.com* ⌁ *609 rooms* ⦿ *No Meals.*

★ Holiday Inn Express Waikiki

$ | HOTEL | FAMILY | Thanks to wallet-friendly rates and unexpected perks, this 44-story chain hotel—with compact but stylish and smartly equipped and configured rooms—bustles, so its speedy elevators are often full. **Pros:** select rooms have great views; free breakfast with large selection; modern conveniences abound. **Cons:** three-block walk to the beach; busy hotel and lobby can feel crowded; resort fee is $25 per day. ⑤ *Rooms from: $179* ✉ *2058 Kuhio Ave., Waikiki* ☎ *877/859–5095 toll-free for reservations, 808/947–2828 direct to hotel* ⊕ *www.ihg.com* ⌁ *596 rooms* ⦿ *Free Breakfast.*

Hotel Renew

$ | HOTEL | Just a block from Waikiki Beach, this stylish boutique hotel focuses on wellness and renewal, making it a calm alternative to the big, bustling resorts that dominate the area. **Pros:** close to zoo, aquarium, and beach; free beach supplies, including towels, chairs, umbrellas, and snorkel gear; personalized, upscale service. **Cons:** rooms do not have lanai; daily amenity fee of $25; no pool. ⑤ *Rooms from: $165* ✉ *129 Paoakalani Ave., Waikiki* ☎ *808/687–7700, 877/997–6667 toll-free* ⊕ *www.hotelrenew.com* ⌁ *72 rooms* ⦿ *No Meals.*

Hyatt Centric Waikiki Beach

$$ | HOTEL | Modern and stylish, with an urban beach vibe, the Hyatt Centric has a friendly staff, rooms in several sizes and configurations, and a sprawling, seventh-floor lobby with a breakfast café and lovely outdoor pool area. **Pros:** lovely pool deck; fresh, modern, and right in the middle of Waikiki; spacious rooms and bathrooms. **Cons:** not on the beach; rooms don't have lanai; resort fee is $33 per day. ⑤ *Rooms from: $215* ✉ *349 Seaside Ave., Waikiki* ☎ *808/237–1234* ⊕ *www.hyatt.com* ↗ *230 rooms* ⍭ *No Meals.*

Hyatt Regency Waikiki Beach Resort & Spa

$$$ | RESORT | FAMILY | There's no other resort between the ocean and this high-rise hotel, which is across the street from Kuhio Beach and features a lively, atrium-style lobby with three levels of shopping (including a farmers' market on Tuesday and Thursday afternoons), a two-story waterfall, gardens, and free live evening entertainment. **Pros:** beach chairs and towels for guests; on-site spa and many shopping and dining options; spacious rooms with soaring windows and lanai. **Cons:** resort fee is $45 per day; on-site pool is quite small; in a very busy and crowded part of Waikiki. ⑤ *Rooms from: $300* ✉ *2424 Kalakaua Ave., Waikiki* ☎ *808/923–1234 direct to hotel, 800/633–7313 toll-free for reservations* ⊕ *www.hyattregencywaikiki.com* ↗ *1230 rooms* ⍭ *No Meals.*

Ilikai Hotel & Luxury Suites

$$$ | RESORT | FAMILY | At Waikiki's *ewa* (western) edge, overlooking Ala Wai Harbor and a five-minute walk from Ala Moana Beach Park, this high-rise resort is a Honolulu landmark—Jack Lord's character, Steve McGarrett, appears on a lanai here in the opening of the original *Hawaii Five-O* TV series. **Pros:** spacious rooms with kitchens; sunset views from most ewa-side rooms; removed from some of the bustle yet still close to everything. **Cons:** despite renovations, it still shows its age; five-minute walk to the beach; resort fee is $25 per day. ⑤ *Rooms from: $300* ✉ *1777 Ala Moana Blvd., Waikiki* ☎ *808/954–7417, 866/536–7973 toll-free* ⊕ *www.ilikaihotel.com* ↗ *779 rooms* ⍭ *No Meals.*

Ilima Hotel

$ | HOTEL | FAMILY | Tucked away on a residential side street near Waikiki's Ala Wai Canal, this locally owned, 17-story, condo-style hotel is a throwback to old Waikiki, offering large units that are ideal for families. **Pros:** friendly and helpful service; free parking (first-come, first-served); spacious rooms with separate bedrooms and kitchens. **Cons:** no ocean views; resort fee is $29 per day; furnishings are dated (though renovations are planned). ⑤ *Rooms from: $160* ✉ *445 Nohonani St., Waikiki* ☎ *808/923–1877, 800/801–9366* ⊕ *www.ilima.com* ↗ *98 units* ⍭ *No Meals.*

Luana Waikiki Hotel & Suites

$$ | HOTEL | FAMILY | If you like Hawaiiana and appreciate a bit of kitsch, this welcoming hotel with both rooms and condo units is a great option. **Pros:** on-site coin-operated laundry facilities; free yoga and folding bicycles; sundeck with pool and barbecue grills. **Cons:** pool is small; resort fee is $25 per day; no direct beach access. ⑤ *Rooms from: $225* ✉ *2045 Kalakaua Ave., Waikiki* ☎ *808/955–6000 direct to hotel, 855/747–0755 toll-free* ⊕ *www.aquaaston.com/hotels/luana-waikiki-hotel-and-suites* ↗ *225 units* ⍭ *No Meals.*

Moana Surfrider, A Westin Resort & Spa, Waikiki Beach

$$$$ | RESORT | Waikiki's oldest hotel is still a wedding and honeymoon favorite, with a sweeping main staircase and Victorian furnishings in its historic (and expensive) Moana Wing and more contemporary rooms in its 1950s-era Diamond Head Tower and refurbished Surfrider Tower, where oceanfront suites have two separate lanai—one for sunrise and another for sunset. **Pros:** can't beat the

Hotel Cultural Programs

In 2022, the state launched its Malama Hawaii program, which encourages visitors to learn about and care for the land and to seek authentic Island experiences. As part of this program, some hotels are offering special packages and voluntourism opportunities. Be sure to ask about them when booking.

In addition to lei-making and hula-dancing lessons, you can learn how to strum a ukulele, listen to Grammy Award–winning Hawaiian musicians, watch a revered master *kumu* (teacher) share the art of ancient hula and chant, chat with a marine biologist about Hawaii's endangered species, learn about the island's sustainability efforts, or get a lesson in the Hawaiian language or in the art of canoe making.

location; elegant, historic property; lovely beach bar that often features live music. **Cons:** expensive parking ($35 per day for self-parking across the street); resort fee is $42 per day; you'll likely dodge bridal parties in the lobby. $ *Rooms from: $479* ✉ *2365 Kalakaua Ave., Waikiki* ☎ *808/922–3111, 866/716–8112 toll-free* ⊕ *www.moana-surfrider.com* ⇆ *791 rooms* ❚❂❚ *No Meals.*

Ohana Waikiki East by Outrigger

$$ | HOTEL | FAMILY | If you want to be in central Waikiki and don't want to pay beachfront lodging prices, consider the Ohana Waikiki East, which is a mere two blocks from the beach and within walking distance of shopping, restaurants, and nightlife. **Pros:** spacious accommodations; reasonable rates close to the beach; in the middle of the Waikiki action. **Cons:** resort fee is $25 per day and parking fee is $35 per night; an older property with signs of wear and tear; very basic public spaces. $ *Rooms from: $259* ✉ *150 Kai-ulani Ave., Waikiki* ☎ *808/922–5353 direct to hotel, 866/956–4262 toll-free* ⊕ *www. outrigger.com/hotels-resorts/hawaii/oahu/ ohana-waikiki-east-by-outrigger* ⇆ *441 rooms* ❚❂❚ *No Meals.*

Outrigger Reef Waikiki Beach Resort

$$$ | HOTEL | FAMILY | A prime location and aloha spirit keep guests returning to the Outrigger Reef, where rooms were renovated and the beach was widened in 2021, with 23 new rooms, a beachfront restaurant, and a luxury guest lounge added in 2022. **Pros:** attentive staff; on the beach; direct access to Waikiki Beach Walk. **Cons:** resort fee is $40 per day; views from nonoceanfront rooms are uninspiring; pool is not beachfront. $ *Rooms from: $319* ✉ *2169 Kalia Rd., Waikiki* ☎ *808/923–3111 direct to hotel, 866/956–4262 toll-free, 800/688–7444* ⊕ *www.outriggerreef-onthebeach.com* ⇆ *669 rooms* ❚❂❚ *No Meals.*

Outrigger Waikiki Beach Resort

$$$$ | RESORT | FAMILY | Outrigger's star property sits on one of the finest sections of Waikiki Beach, a location that—along with an array of cultural and dining options and great live-music and bar scenes—make it a favorite. **Pros:** excellent lounge that's worth splurging on an upgrade to access; the best beach bar in Waikiki; on-site activities and amenities (including a spa) abound. **Cons:** rooms are dated; resort fee is $40 per day; a busy property (often used as a pedestrian throughway to the beach).

Rooms from: $450 ✉ *2335 Kalakaua Ave., Waikiki* ☎ *808/923–0711, 808/956–4262, 800/442–7304 toll-free* ⊕ *www.outriggerwaikikihotel.com* ⇨ *525 rooms* ❙⦿❙ *No Meals.*

Pacific Monarch

$$ | HOTEL | FAMILY | One block from the western end of Waikiki Beach, this 34-story condominium resort offers sweeping views of Waikiki and the Pacific Ocean, especially from its rooftop deck, complete with a small pool, hot tub, and sauna. **Pros:** all rooms have lanai; fantastic views; hospitality lounge. **Cons:** older property with the wear to show for it; resort fee is $25 per day; stairs to the pool deck are fairly steep and dark and may be difficult for some. ⑤ *Rooms from: $185* ✉ *2427 Kuhio Ave., Waikiki* ☎ *808/923–9805* ⊕ *www.pacificmonarch.com* ⇨ *216 rooms* ❙⦿❙ *No Meals.*

Prince Waikiki

$$$$ | HOTEL | The sleek, modern Prince—which looks to Asia both in its high-style decor and such pampering touches as the traditional *oshiburi* (chilled hand towel) for refreshment upon check-in—has luxury oceanfront rooms and suites overlooking the Ala Wai Boat Harbor at Waikiki's *ewa* (western) edge. **Pros:** parking included; fantastic views from all rooms; no resort fee. **Cons:** rooms don't have lanai; no beach access; busy property. ⑤ *Rooms from: $400* ✉ *100 Holomoana St., Waikiki* ☎ *888/977–4623 toll-free for reservations, 808/956–1111 direct to hotel* ⊕ *www.princewaikiki.com* ⇨ *563 rooms* ❙⦿❙ *No Meals.*

Queen Kapiolani Hotel

$$$ | HOTEL | With a contemporary look combined with a retro nod to the 1970s, the Queen Kapiolani Hotel is a short walk from the beach and is known for its stunning, unobstructed views of Diamond Head—a fabulous backdrop for its expansive pool deck. **Pros:** large collection of museum-quality art; incredible Diamond Head views; beach gear available at valet

desk. **Cons:** noise from pool bar can be bothersome; bathrooms are small and a bit dated; resort fee is $40 per day. ⑤ *Rooms from: $280* ✉ *150 Kapahulu Ave., Waikiki* ☎ *808/650–7841* ⊕ *www.queenkapiolani.com* ⇨ *315 rooms* ❙⦿❙ *No Meals.*

The Ritz-Carlton Residences, Waikiki Beach

$$$$ | HOTEL | The only Ritz-Carlton on Oahu welcomes well-heeled guests from across the globe with its signature elegance and impeccable service. **Pros:** pampering service and pools with views; very private; luxuriously appointed accommodations. **Cons:** families can sometimes overrun the facilities; pricey, particularly given distance from beach; not close to the beach. ⑤ *Rooms from: $679* ✉ *383 Kalaimoku St., Waikiki* ☎ *808/922–8111* ⊕ *www.ritzcarlton.com* ⇨ *552 units* ❙⦿❙ *No Meals.*

Royal Grove Waikiki

$ | HOTEL | This pink, six-story hotel feels like a throwback to the days of boarding houses—when rooms were outfitted for function, not style, and served with simple hospitality at a price that didn't break the bank. **Pros:** a bit of local flavor; very economical Waikiki option; no resort fee. **Cons:** no on-site parking and minimum stays during busy seasons; rooms and property are very dated; no air-conditioning in some rooms. ⑤ *Rooms from: $150* ✉ *151 Uluniu Ave., Waikiki* ☎ *808/923–7691* ⊕ *www.royalgrovehotel.com* ⇨ *87 rooms* ❙⦿❙ *No Meals.*

★ The Royal Hawaiian, a Luxury Collection Resort, Waikiki

$$$$ | RESORT | There's nothing like the iconic "Pink Palace of the Pacific," which is on 14 acres of prime Waikiki Beach and which has held fast to the luxury and grandeur that first defined it in the 1930s, when it became a favorite of the rich and famous. **Pros:** luxury in a prime location; can't beat it for history; mai tais and sunsets are amazing. **Cons:** very small swimming pool; high-traffic driveway entrance in center of Waikiki; resort fee is $42 per day. $ *Rooms from: $525* ✉ *2259 Kalakaua Ave., Waikiki* ☎ *808/923–7311, 866/716–8110 toll-free* ⊕ *www.royal-hawaiian.com* ⤳ *528 rooms* ⦿ *No Meals.*

Sheraton Princess Kaiulani

$$ | HOTEL | FAMILY | The Princess Kaiulani sits across the street from the regal Moana Surfrider, without some of the more elaborate amenities (such as a spa or a kid's club), but with rates that are considerably kinder to the wallet. **Pros:** great value for the location; in the heart of everything in Waikiki, with the beach right across the street; beach service with chairs, towels, fruit, and water available. **Cons:** resort fee is $37 per day; self parking is $42 per night; lobby area can feel like Grand Central Station. $ *Rooms from: $259* ✉ *120 Kaiulani Ave., Waikiki* ☎ *808/922–5811, 866/716–8109 toll-free* ⊕ *www.princess-kaiulani.com* ⤳ *1040 rooms* ⦿ *No Meals.*

★ Sheraton Waikiki

$$$$ | HOTEL | FAMILY | Towering over its neighbors along the beachfront, this big, busy hotel offers stunning views from most of its modern rooms, which have been updated in neutral shades with splashes of color. **Pros:** swimming pools often ranked among the Islands' best; fresh, modern guest rooms; variety of on-site activities and dining options. **Cons:** room sizes and views vary; resort fee is $42 per day; busy atmosphere clashes with laid-back Hawaiian style. $ *Rooms from: $455* ✉ *2255 Kalakaua Ave., Waikiki* ☎ *808/922–4422, 866/716–8109 toll-free for reservations* ⊕ *www.sheraton-waikiki. com* ⤳ *1636 rooms* ⦿ *No Meals.*

Shoreline Hotel Waikiki

$$$$ | HOTEL | Situated on bustling Seaside Avenue, this 14-story, 1970s-era property has been transformed into an urban-chic boutique hotel with both island and retro touches that playfully blend 20th-century style with modern necessities. **Pros:** hipster decor a refreshing break from

Looking for a Private Beach?

Oahu's oldest hotels—the Royal Hawaiian Hotel and Moana Surfrider—are also the only hotels in Waikiki with property lines that extend into the sand. They have created private roped-off beach areas with lounge chairs and umbrellas that can be accessed only by hotel guests for a fee. The areas are adjacent to the hotel properties at the top of the beach and usually require reservations during the busy season.

old-style Hawaiiana; great location in the middle of Waikiki; resort fee waived if you book direct. **Cons:** pool is accessed via two flights of stairs; rooms are inconsistently sized and equipped; if splashy colors aren't your thing, skip it. $ *Rooms from: $359* ✉ *342 Seaside Ave., Waikiki* ☎ *808/931–2444, 855/931–2444 toll-free* ⊕ *www.shorelinehotelwaikiki.com* ⤳ *135 rooms* ⦿ *No Meals.*

Surfjack Hotel & Swim Club

$$$ | HOTEL | A surfing vibe and authentic, whimsical Hawaiian touches throughout (the lobby, for instance, evokes the living room of the interior designer's grandmother) set this hip boutique property apart from other modernized midcentury digs. **Pros:** Ed Kenney restaurant on site; hipster, urban-chic vibe that works; retro, locally designed decor. **Cons:** rooms can be inconsistent; far from the beach; resort fee is $25 per day. $ *Rooms from: $300* ✉ *412 Lewers St., Waikiki* ☎ *808/923–8882* ⊕ *www.surfjack.com* ⤳ *112 rooms* ⦿ *No Meals.*

Waikiki Beachcomber by Outrigger

$$ | HOTEL | FAMILY | Almost directly across from the Royal Hawaiian Center and next to International Market Place, the

Beachcomber is a well-situated high-rise hotel for families as well as those looking for a boutique feel in the heart of the action. **Pros:** lovely pool area; great beach views from some rooms; renovated and stylish. **Cons:** resort fee is $35 per day; not beachfront; very busy area in the thick of Waikiki action. ⑤ *Rooms from: $260* ✉ *2300 Kalakaua Ave., Waikiki* ☎ *808/922–4646, 877/418–0711* ⊕ *www. waikikibeachcomber.com* ⊅ *496 rooms* ⊙ *No Meals.*

Waikiki Beach Marriott Resort & Spa

$$$$ | RESORT | FAMILY | Set on 5 acres across from Kuhio Beach and close to Kapiolani Park, the Honolulu Zoo, and the Waikiki Aquarium, this flagship Marriott offers daily activities for children and adults and has an expansive pool deck with ocean views, several pools, plenty of cabanas and lounge chairs, and the Queensbreak restaurant. **Pros:** central location in Waikiki; massive pool deck; lots of airy, tropical public spaces. **Cons:** resort fee is $37 per day; self-parking is $45 per day; large impersonal hotel, requires lots of walking. ⑤ *Rooms from: $350* ✉ *2552 Kalakaua Ave., Waikiki* ☎ *808/922–6611, 800/367–5370 toll-free* ⊕ *www.marriottwaikiki.com* ⊅ *1310 rooms* ⊙ *No Meals.*

Waikiki Malia by Outrigger

$$ | HOTEL | Guests who return to this older property year after year appreciate its proximity to restaurants and shops and its easygoing "come as you are" vibe. **Pros:** on-site coin-operated laundry facilities; convenient location; good value for the basics. **Cons:** resort fee of $22 per day; property shows its age in places; no views and small pool. ⑤ *Rooms from: $205* ✉ *2211 Kuhio Ave., Waikiki* ☎ *808/923–7621 direct to hotel, 866/956–4262 toll-free* ⊕ *www.outrigger. com/hotels-resorts/hawaii/oahu/waiki-ki-malia-by-outrigger* ⊅ *332 rooms* ⊙ *No Meals.*

Condo Comforts

The local **Foodland** grocery-store chain has two locations near Waikiki, one in Market City in Kaimuki (✉ 2939 Harding Ave., ☎ 808/734–6303) and the other in the Ala Moana Center (✉ 1450 Ala Moana Blvd., ☎ 808/949–5044).

The popular ABC convenience stores have many locations. In addition to beach supplies, apparel, and just about everything else, some also sell foodstuffs, made-to-order meals, and alcoholic beverages.

Waikiki Sand Villa Hotel

$ | HOTEL | FAMILY | This family-run property offers economical rates and proximity to the beach, restaurants, and shops—all just three blocks away. **Pros:** no resort fee; recently refreshed rooms; pool and foot spa great for lounging. **Cons:** street noise from Ala Wai can get loud; 10-minute walk to the beach; noise from the bar might annoy some. ⑤ *Rooms from: $165* ✉ *2375 Ala Wai Blvd., Waikiki* ☎ *808/922–4744, 800/247–1903 toll-free* ⊕ *www.waikikisandvillahotel.com* ⊅ *214 rooms* ⊙ *No Meals.*

Waikiki Shore

$$ | HOTEL | FAMILY | Nestled between Fort DeRussy Beach Park and the Outrigger Reef Resort, the only condo hotel directly on Waikiki Beach is beloved by some for its spaciousness and by others for its quieter, western-end location. **Pros:** units available in different sizes; right on the beach; great views from spacious private lanai. **Cons:** two management companies rent here, so ask questions when booking; extra cleaning fee can be hefty; some units are dated and amenities in them vary. ⑤ *Rooms from: $230* ✉ *2161*

Kalia Rd., Waikiki ☎ 808/952–4500 Castle reservations, 808/922–3871 Outrigger reservations local, 800/688–7444 Outrigger reservations toll-free ⊕ www.castleresorts.com ⤳ 168 suites ⏇ No Meals.

Nightlife

BARS

★ Duke's Waikiki

BARS | Making the most of its spot on Waikiki Beach, Duke's is a bustling destination featuring live music everyday. This laid-back bar-and-grill's surf theme pays homage to Duke Kahanamoku, who popularized the sport in the early 1900s. Contemporary Hawaiian musicians like Henry Kapono and the Maunalua group have performed here, as have nationally known musicians like Jimmy Buffett. It's not unusual for surfers to leave their boards outside to step in for a casual drink after a long day on the waves. The cocktail menu is filled with Island-style drinks: try a sunset sour or coconut mojito while watching the Waikiki waves. ⊠ Outrigger Waikiki, 2335 Kalakaua Ave., Suite 116, Waikiki ☎ 808/922–2268 ⊕ www.dukeswaikiki.com.

Genius Lounge Sake Bar & Grill

BARS | Removed from the tourist traps along Kalakaua Avenue, the Genius Lounge is tucked away on the third floor of a former apartment building on Lewers Street. The extensive drink menu offers beer and wine, cocktails, homemade sangria, and, of course, sake. Locally inspired dishes are also available. Though small, the space is open to the outdoors and furnished with dark woods and lit by candles, making for an intimate setting for small gatherings and Friday-night dates. The crowd is mostly Asian visitors and transplants, but a daily happy hour (6–8 pm) lures office workers and pre-club prowlers. ⊠ 346 Lewers St., 3rd fl., Waikiki ☎ 808/626–5362 ⊕ www.geniusloungehawaii.com.

Hideout

BARS | Located at the Laylow Hotel, one of Waikiki's newer properties, this mini-oasis has a firepit, tiki torches, comfy couches, and palm trees swaying overhead. Although there's a full food menu, it's best to come here for expertly mixed cocktails or mocktails and some pupu—perhaps the poke tacos or the pork belly Brussels sprouts. A daily happy hour from 4:30 to 6:30 pm makes things easier on the wallet. ⊠ Laylow Hotel, 2299 Kuhio Ave., Waikiki ☎ 808/628–3060 ⊕ www.hideoutwaikiki.com.

★ Lewers Lounge

BARS | Set back from the main entrance of the Halekulani hotel and decked out with dramatic drapes and cozy banquettes, Lewers Lounge is a great place for cocktails, both classic and contemporary. Standouts include Chocolate Dreams (made with Van Gogh Dutch Chocolate Vodka) and the Lost Passion (tequila, Cointreau, and fresh juices topped with champagne). Enjoy your libation with great nightly live jazz and tempting desserts, such as the hotel's famous coconut cake. ⊠ Halekulani Hotel, 2199 Kalia Rd., Waikiki ☎ 808/923–2311 ⊕ www.halekulani.com/dining/lewers-lounge.

Lulu's Waikiki

BARS | Even if you're not a surfer, you'll love this place's retro vibe and unobstructed second-floor view of Waikiki Beach. The open-air setting, casual dining menu, and tropical drinks are all you need to help you settle into your vacation. The venue transforms from a nice spot for breakfast, lunch, or dinner (happy hour is 3 to 5 pm) into a bustling, high-energy club with live music lasting into the wee hours. ⊠ Park Shore Waikiki Hotel, 2586 Kalakaua Ave., Waikiki ☎ 808/926–5222 ⊕ www.luluswaikiki.com.

★ Mai Tai Bar at the Royal Hawaiian

BARS | The bartenders here sure know how to mix up a killer mai tai. This is, after all, the establishment that first made the famous drink in the Islands. The pink umbrella–shaded tables at the outdoor bar are front-row seating for sunsets and also have an unobstructed view of Diamond Head. It's an ideal spot to soak in the island vibes just steps from the sand. Contemporary Hawaiian musicians hold jam sessions on stage nightly, and small bites are also available. ⊠ *Royal Hawaiian Hotel, 2259 Kalakaua Ave., Waikiki* ☎ *808/923–7311* ⊕ *www. royal-hawaiian.com/dining-overview/ mai-tai-bar.*

★ Maui Brewing Co.

BARS | The craft beers produced by this Lahaina-based company are Island favorites, and a visit to this brewpub adjacent to the Beachcomber hotel's lobby means you don't have to island hop to sample its offerings at the source. Ask about limited-release drafts to imbibe the brand's hidden gems, or order a flight of freshly brewed beers. Maui Brewing strives to source local ingredients for its beer and its food, and the menu here includes a poke bowl made with locally caught tuna, a kale salad that incorporates Waianae-based Naked Cow Dairy feta, and a Brewmaster pizza featuring Honolulu-based Kukui sausage. ⊠ *Waikiki Beachcomber by Outrigger, 2300 Kalakaua Ave., 2nd fl., Waikiki* ☎ *808/843–2739* ⊕ *www.mbcrestaurants.com/waikiki.*

RumFire

BARS | Locals and visitors head here for the convivial atmosphere, the trendy decor, and the million-dollar view of Waikiki Beach and Diamond Head. Come early to get a seat for happy hour (3–5 pm daily). If you're feeling peckish, there's a menu of tasty, Asian-influenced small plates. RumFire also features original cocktails, signature shots, and daily live music. On Friday and Saturday nights, the bar gets even livelier once local DJs start spinning. ⊠ *Sheraton Waikiki, 2255 Kalakaua Ave., Waikiki* ☎ *808/922–4422* ⊕ *www.rumfirewaikiki.com.*

Mai Tais

Hard to believe, but the cocktail known all over the world as the mai tai has been around for more than 50 years. Although the recipe has changed slightly over time, the original formula, created by bar owner Victor J. "Trader Vic" Bergeron, included 2 ounces of 17-year-old J. Wray & Nephew rum over shaved ice, ½ ounce of DeKuyper orange curaçao, ¼ ounce of Trader Vic's rock-candy syrup, ½ ounce of orgeat syrup, and the juice of one fresh lime. Done the right way, this tropical drink still lives up to the name "mai tai!," meaning "out of this world!"

Tiki's Grill & Bar

BARS | Tiki torches light the way to this fun restaurant and bar overlooking Kuhio Beach. A mix of locals and visitors heads here for happy hour and, later, to enjoy its kitschy cool, casual vibe. There's great nightly entertainment featuring contemporary Hawaiian musicians playing lively and popular cover tunes. The drinks menu is extensive and (not surprisingly) tiki-focused. Don't leave without sipping on the Lava Flow (rum, coconut milk, pineapple juice, strawberry puree) or noshing on coconut shrimp, ahi poke, or macadamia-crusted fish of the day. And if you love the tiki vibe, you can purchase an array of whimsical merchandise, including the colorful tiki mugs. If you're here during the holidays, ask the host about the "Christmas bar." ⊠ *Aston Waikiki Beach Hotel, 2570 Kalakaua Ave., Waikiki* ☎ *808/923–8454* ⊕ *www.tikisgrill. com.*

Waiolu Ocean Cuisine

BARS | Hawaiian bars should have two things: stellar views of the sunset over the ocean and equally stellar mai tais. This lounge has both, as well as nightly live music, ranging from contemporary to Hawaiian, Thursday through Sunday. Come either for sunset or for the late-night happy hour, but it's best to reserve a table: seats are scarce once the music starts at 6:30 pm, and an attractive crowd starts showing up around 8. ⊠ *Trump International Hotel, 223 Saratoga Rd., Waikiki* ☎ *808/683–7456* ⊕ *www. trumphotels.com/waikiki.*

Wang Chung's Karaoke Bar
BARS | Dubbed the "Friendliest Bar in Waikiki," a visit to this charming karaoke joint is a must on any trip to the island. The positive vibe comes from owner Dan Chang, who personally welcomes his guests to this LGBTQ-friendly establishment. The bar is in the lobby of the Stay Hotel and has a full kitchen cranking out Asian- and Latin-inspired dishes. It's known for a lively late-night crowd and innovative cocktails. The list of karaoke songs is extensive, and the place gets jammed, so arrive early if you really want to add your name to the list and sing a song. ⊠ *Stay Hotel Waikiki, 2424 Koa Ave., Waikiki* ☎ *808/201–6369* ⊕ *www. wangchungs.com.*

CLUBS
Hula's Bar and Lei Stand
DANCE CLUBS | Hawaii's oldest and best-known gay-friendly nightspot offers panoramic views of Diamond Head by day and high-energy club music by night. Check out the all-day happy hour, which starts at 10 am. There's an abundance of drink specials on weekends and discounted pitchers of beer and cocktails on Sunday. Food options include nachos, tacos, pork sliders, and more. Celebrity patrons have included Elton John, Adam Lambert, and Dolly Parton. ⊠ *Waikiki Grand Hotel, 134 Kapahulu Ave., 2nd fl., Waikiki* ☎ *808/923–0669* ⊕ *www.hulas.com.*

Sky Waikiki Raw & Bar
LIVE MUSIC | This bar 19 stories above the city offers nearly 360-degree bird's-eye views of Diamond Head, the Waikiki beaches, and the classic coral Royal Hawaiian hotel. It's also one of the best spots to take in a Waikiki sunset. Be sure to order the popular SkyTai cocktail as you enjoy the views. There are also happy hour drink specials daily and a limited menu featuring fresh seafood. The indoor club, where resident DJs spin on Friday and Saturday nights, exudes contemporary-LA chic. ⊠ *Waikiki Trade Center, 2270 Kalakaua Ave., Waikiki* ☎ *808/979–7590* ⊕ *www.skywaikiki.com.*

🎭 Performing Arts

DINNER CRUISES AND SHOWS
Magic of Polynesia
MAGIC | **FAMILY** | Hawaii's top illusionist, John Hirokawa, displays mystifying sleight of hand in this highly entertaining show, which incorporates contemporary hula and Islands music into its acts. It's held in the Waikiki Beachcomber by Outrigger's showroom, and reservations are required for dinner (nightly at 5:45) and the show (at 7). Menu choices range from ginger-sesame–glazed chicken to a deluxe steak-and-lobster combo. Walk-ins are permitted if you just want the entertainment. The box office is open daily from noon to 9 pm. ⊠ *Waikiki Beachcomber by Outrigger, 2300 Kalakaua Ave., Waikiki* ☎ *808/971–4321* ⊕ *www. waikikibeachcomber.com/things-to-do/ the-magic-of-polynesia-show.*

FILM
Sunset on the Beach
FILM | **FAMILY** | It's like watching a movie at the drive-in, minus the car and the speaker box. Bring a blanket and arrive early to find a good spot on the sand to enjoy live entertainment, food from top local restaurants, and a movie on a 30-foot screen. Held three to four times each year at Queen's Surf across from the Honolulu Zoo, Sunset on the Beach is a favorite event for both locals and visitors. If the weather is blustery, beware of flying sand. ⊠ *Queen's Surf Beach, Kalakaua Ave., Waikiki* ⊕ *www. sunsetonthebeach.net* 🎟 *Free.*

LUAU

The luau is an experience that everyone, both local and tourist, should have. It's an exciting way to capture the "aloha spirit" and learn a bit about island culture. Today's luau offer traditional foods and entertainment, but they often incorporate fun, contemporary flair as well. With many, you can watch the roasted pig being carried out of its *imu*, a hole in the ground used for cooking food with heated stones.

Luau prices average around $150 per person, and several are held around the island, including a few are in Waikiki. Reservations—and a camera—are a must.

Royal Hawaiian Luau: Aha'aina

FOLK/TRADITIONAL DANCE | FAMILY | With a beachfront location in the middle of Waikiki, the Royal Hawaiian's Aha'aina luau is an exceptional, upscale event with hula, fire dancing, live music, Hawaiian-inspired and luau-favorite dishes, and more. Options range from "standard dinner and show" to "premium dinner and show." The three-hour event is held two nights a week (Monday and Thursday); be sure to reserve in advance during the high season. ⊠ *The Royal Hawaiian, a Luxury Collection Resort, 2259 Kalakaua Ave., Waikiki* ☎ *808/921–4600* ⊕ *www. royal-hawaiianluau.com* ☒ *From $200.*

Waikiki Starlight Luau

FOLK/TRADITIONAL DANCE | FAMILY | This Waikiki luau is done spectacularly on the rooftop of Hilton Hawaiian Village. There isn't an *imu* ceremony, but the live entertainment is top-notch, and the views are unparalleled. Prices vary depending on your age and where you want to sit. The event also includes dinner with traditional specialties, games, and cultural activities, such as hula lessons and conch blowing. It's held Sunday–Thursday at 5 pm. ⊠ *Hilton Hawaiian Village, 2005 Kalia Rd., Waikiki* ☎ *808/941–5828* ⊕ *www. hiltonhawaiianvillage.com.*

MUSIC

★ Blue Note Hawaii

MUSIC | Music lovers adore this intimate venue, which draws local and national acts throughout the year. Acoustics are fantastic, and seating is at tables, all with excellent views. The atmosphere is sophisticated, and the food here is excellent, too, with small and large plates offered. It's worthwhile to find out who's performing while you're in town so you can purchase tickets in advance, since the more popular acts sell out quickly. This 300-seat room is centrally located (at the Outrigger resort), so you can grab a drink at Duke's before or after the show. ⊠ *Outrigger Waikiki Beach Resort, 2335 Kalakaua Ave., Waikiki* ☎ *808/777–4890* ⊕ *www.bluenotehawaii. com* ☒ *From $35.*

Honolulu Zoo Concerts

CONCERTS | FAMILY | Since the early 1980s, the Honolulu Zoo Society has sponsored hour-long evening concerts branded the "Wildest Show in Town." They're held at 6 pm on Wednesday, June–August. Listen to local legends play everything from Hawaiian to jazz to Latin music. Take a brisk walk through the zoo, or join in the family activities. This is an alcohol-free event, and there's food for those who haven't brought their own picnic supplies. Gates open at 4:35. ■ TIP➜ This is one of the best deals in town. ⊠ *Honolulu Zoo, 151 Kapahulu Ave., Waikiki* ☎ *808/971–7171* ⊕ *www.honoluluzoo.org* ☒ *From $11.*

THEATER

Hawaii can be an expensive gig for touring shows and music acts that depend on major theatrical sets. Not many manage to stop here, and those that do sell out fast. Oahu has developed several excellent local community theater companies, which present first-rate, though not professional, entertainment all year long. (Anyone who attends is always surprised to learn that the Honolulu Theatre for Youth is the only professional troupe in the state.) Community support for these groups is strong.

Diamond Head Theatre

THEATER | As Hawaii's oldest performing arts center (and the third-oldest community theater in the United States), this venue offers a little of everything: musicals, dramas, and experimental productions. ⊠ *520 Makapuu Ave., Diamond Head* ☎ *808/733–0274* ⊕ *www.diamondheadtheatre.com* ⊿ *From $15.*

Shopping

Waikiki's hotels and malls or other shopping centers all have notable shops, and the abundance of name-brand and specialty items will be energizing or overwhelming, depending on your sensibilities.

Clothing, jewelry, and handbags from Europe's top designers sit next to Hawaii's ABC Stores, a chain of convenience stores that sells groceries as well as souvenirs. Now more than ever, it's possible to find interesting, locally produced items and independent stores in Waikiki, but you must be willing to search beyond the expensive purses and the tacky wooden tikis to find innovation and quality.

Larger shopping centers (including the Royal Hawaiian Center) may offer some type of parking validation with purchase, so be sure to check or ask in advance.

CLOTHING

Blue Ginger

MIXED CLOTHING | FAMILY | This little shop offers a great selection of Hawaii-made items for adults and children. Look for brightly colored, beach-casual clothing, bags, jewelry, and accessories in soft cotton and rayon aloha prints. ⊠ *227 Lewers St., Waikiki* ☎ *808/924–7900* ⊕ *www.blueginger.com.*

Newt at the Royal

HATS & GLOVES | Newt is known for high-quality, handwoven Panama hats and tropical sportswear for men and women. ⊠ *The Royal Hawaiian Hotel, 2259 Kalakaua Ave., Waikiki* ☎ *808/923–4332* ⊕ *www.newtattheroyal.com.*

Oiwi Ocean Gear

MIXED CLOTHING | Featuring stylish, high-quality activewear especially for ocean, paddling, and beach enthusiasts, this locally owned shop was founded in 1999 in the nearby beach town of Kailua. Its original designs are created in-house and showcase the ocean, nature, and unique images of Hawaiian culture. Items, many of which contain sun protection (UPF apparel), include shirts, rash guards, board shorts, surf leggings, hats, accessories, and more. ⊠ *Royal Hawaiian Shopping Center, Waikiki* ⊕ *www.oiwioceangear.com.*

Waikiki Beachboy Store

SWIMWEAR | FAMILY | Tucked away in the Royal Hawaiian's lobby, this tiny shop is a great place to pick up a memento of your surf lesson. It's filled with a variety of high-quality Waikiki Beach Services gear, including the best-selling logo rash guards and T-shirts of the type worn by their beachboys and surf instructors. There's also a selection of locally designed bathing suits from Pualani Hawaii, swimwear from the Colombian brand Maaji, accessories, sunscreen, and original artwork. ⊠ *Royal Hawaiian Resort, 2259 Kalakaua Ave., Shop 9, Waikiki* ☎ *808/922–2223* ⊕ *www.waikikibeachservices.com/ waikiki-beach-boy-store.*

FOOD

★ Honolulu Cookie Company

FOOD | To really impress those back home, pick up a box of locally baked, gourmet cookies. Choose from dozens of delicious flavors of premium shortbread delights with a wide variety of sizes, all designed for travel. In addition to the location in the Royal Hawaiian Center, there are a number of these stores in Waikiki, so you probably won't be able to avoid them—even if you try. ⊠ *Royal*

Hawaiian Center, 2233 Kalakaua Ave., Waikiki ☎ 808/931–8937 ⊕ www.honolulucookie.com.

GALLERIES
Tabora Gallery Waikiki
ART GALLERIES | Pieces by a number of local and international artists are featured here, including original paintings; limited-edition prints; works in wood, metal, glass, ceramic, and acrylic; and handcrafted jewelry. There's another branch on Oahu, in the town of Haleiwa, and you'll also find locations on other Islands. ✉ International Marketplace, 2330 Kalakaua Ave., 2nd floor, Waikiki ☎ 8080/779–4339 ⊕ taboragallery.com.

Wyland Galleries
ART GALLERIES | In addition to exhibiting the beautiful and inspiring work of the world-famous marine life artist Wyland, this expansive art gallery showcases works by a number of other artists, both lesser-known and highly acclaimed. There are also locations in the Oahu town of Haleiwa and on other Islands. ✉ 226 Lewers St., Waikiki ☎ 808/924–1322 ⊕ www.wyland.com/galleries.

GIFTS
★ Aloha Collection
HANDBAGS | Located in the Moana Surfrider hotel, the flagship store of this innovative company is filled with colorful, lightweight, "splash-proof" bags of all sizes, shapes, and styles—from tiny zippered travel pouches to eye-catching beach bags to oversize totes. The company continually offers new patterns and styles, so bag lovers will always find a unique beach- and/or travel-friendly option. ✉ Moana Surfrider, 2369 Kalakaua Ave., Diamond Head Wing Shop #1, Waikiki ⊕ aloha-collection.com.

★ House of Mana Up
SOUVENIRS | Mana Up is a groundbreaking organization that promotes Hawaii-based entrepreneurs and shares their unique products with consumers. Its large retail store in the Royal Hawaiian Center not only showcases innovative, locally made items but also shares the stories of the makers behind them. It's fun to browse for gourmet chocolate, edible coffee bars, art, sustainable food wrappers, surf-inspired clothing, extra-comfy flip-flops (called slippers in Hawaii), children's books, and much more. All the profits are used to support these small businesses. ✉ Royal Hawaiian Center, 2201 Kalakaua Ave., Space A108 (1st fl.), Waikiki ☎ 808/425–4028 ⊕ www.manauphawaii.com.

★ Keep it Simple
GENERAL STORE | Founded by local entrepreneurs Jillian Corn and Hunter Long (who is also a professional skateboarder), Keep it Simple strives to promote a healthier planet by selling high-quality, natural, organic, and/or vegan items with minimal (or zero) packaging. Look for unique beauty and bath products and accessories, as well as items for the kitchen and elsewhere in the home. ✉ Waikiki Beach Walk, 240 Lewers St., Waikiki ☎ 808/744–3115 ⊕ www.keepitsimplezerowaste.com.

JEWELRY
Na Hoku Gallery
JEWELRY & WATCHES | Like its larger sibling in the Ala Moana Center, this designer and island-lifestyle jewelry store sells Tahitian pearls and ocean- and marine-theme jewelry. ✉ Outrigger Waikiki, 2335 Kalakaua Ave., Waikiki ☎ 808/922–0556 ⊕ www.nahoku.com.

Philip Rickard
JEWELRY & WATCHES | This famed jeweler creates heirloom-quality Hawaiian pieces in platinum and different shades of gold that feature traditional scrolling patterns, enameled names, and inlays. Items from the outfit's Wedding Collection are often sought by celebrities. ✉ International Market Place, 2330 Kalakaua Ave., Level 1, Banyan Court, #105, Waikiki ☎ 808/924–7972 ⊕ www.philiprickard.com.

SHOPPING CENTERS
★ Royal Hawaiian Center

MALL | This three-block-long center has more than 110 establishments, including an Apple Store and ABC Stores, as well as local gems, such as Oiwi Ocean Gear, Mana Up, Fighting Eel, Honolulu Cookie Company, Koi Honolulu, Hawaiian Island Arts, Island Soap & Candleworks, and Royal Hawaiian Quilts. In addition to a number of restaurants, you can dine at the Waikiki Food Hall. Complimentary cultural classes, a theater, and nightly outdoor entertainment round out the offerings. Note for drivers: the center offers free parking for three hours with validation at shops and restaurants. ⊠ 2201 Kalakaua Ave., Waikiki ☎ 808/922–0588 ⊕ www.royalhawaiiancenter.com.

2100 Kalakaua

MALL | The ultimate destination for designer shopping in Hawaii is this elegant town house–style center, where shops include Chanel, Coach, Tiffany & Co., Yves Saint Laurent, Bottega Veneta, Gucci, Hugo Boss, Miu Miu, and Moncler. ⊠ 2100 Kalakaua Ave., Waikiki ☎ 808/922–2246 ⊕ www.luxuryrow.com.

Waikiki Beach Walk

MALL | This open-air mall at the west end of Kalakaua Avenue and next to the Royal Hawaiian Center contains 70 locally owned stores and restaurants. Get reasonably priced, fashionable resort wear at Mahina, find unique pieces by local artists at Under the Koa Tree, or buy local delicacies from the Poke Bar. Of course, you can pick up T-shirts, bathing suits, and casual beach attire here, too. The mall also features free local entertainment on its outdoor fountain stage at least once a week. ⊠ 226 Lewers St., Waikiki ☎ 808/931–3591 ⊕ www.waikikibeachwalk.com.

Activities

SPAS

Excellent day and resort spas can be found throughout Oahu, primarily in the resorts of Waikiki. Individual treatments and day packages offer a wide choice of rejuvenating therapies, some of which are unique to the Islands. Try the popular *lomilomi* massage with kukui-nut oil (*lomi* meaning to rub, knead, and massage using palms, forearms, fingers, knuckles, elbows, knees, feet, even sticks). Add heated *pohaku* (stones) placed on the back to relieve sore muscles, or choose a facial using natural ingredients such as coconut, mango, papaya, ti leaf, Hawaiian honey, or ginger. Many full-service spas offer private couples' treatment rooms, fitness suites, yoga, and hydrotherapy pools.

Abhasa Spa

SPAS | Organic skin and body treatments are the highlights at this spa tucked away in the Royal Hawaiian Hotel's coconut grove. Vegetarian-lifestyle spa therapies, color-light therapy, and a facial fusing invigorating *lomilomi* technique with *pohaku* are all available. You can have your treatment in any of Abhasa's eight indoor rooms or in one of its three garden cabanas. ⊠ Royal Hawaiian Hotel, 2259 Kalakaua Ave., Waikiki ☎ 808/922–8200 ⊕ www.abhasa.com.

Mandara Spa at Hilton Hawaiian Village Beach Resort & Spa

SPAS | From its perch in the Kalia Tower, this outpost of the chain that originated in Bali overlooks the mountains, ocean, and downtown Honolulu. Hawaiian ingredients and traditional techniques are included in an array of services. Relieve achy muscles with a Thai poultice massage, perhaps with a reflexology or Balinese body polish add-on. This is one of the largest spas in Honolulu, with 25 treatment rooms, spa suites for couples, individual relaxation lounges with wet and dry saunas for men and women,

Jacuzzis, traditional Japanese showers, a private infinity pool, fitness facilities, a salon, and a boutique. The delicately scented, candlelit foyer can fill up quickly with robe-clad conventioneers, so be sure to make a reservation. ⊠ *Hilton Hawaiian Village Beach Resort & Spa, 2005 Kalia Rd., 3rd and 4th fl., Kalia Tower, Waikiki* ☎ *808/945–7721* ⊕ *www.mandaraspa.com.*

Na Hoola Spa at the Hyatt Regency Waikiki Resort & Spa

SPAS | The 16 rooms of Waikiki's premier resort spa are on two floors of the Hyatt on Kalakaua Avenue. Arrive early for your treatment to enjoy the serene, postcard-perfect beach views. You can choose from more than 15 different types of massages, including those for couples, and many of the treatments for body, face, and hair feature Hawaiian healing plants—noni, kukui, awa, and kalo. This spa also has various day packages that last three to six hours. The small exercise room, however, is for use by hotel guests only. ⊠ *Hyatt Regency Waikiki Resort & Spa, 2424 Kalakaua Ave., Waikiki* ☎ *808/923–1234, 808/237–6330 for reservations* ⊕ *www.hyatt.com/en-US/spas/Na-HoOla-Spa/home.*

Royal Kaila Spa

SPAS | The Marriott's spa, which faces Waikiki Beach, uses nature-based Aveda products to incorporate healing plant essences in its massage, facial, and body treatments. Linger with a cup of tea between treatments, and gaze through 75-foot-high windows at the activity outside. Lush Hawaiian foliage, sleek Balinese teak furnishings, and a mist of ylang-ylang and nutmeg in the air encourage relaxation. ⊠ *Waikiki Beach Marriott Resort & Spa, 2552 Kalakaua Ave., Waikiki* ☎ *808/369–8088* ⊕ *www.royalkaila-spa.com.*

SpaHalekulani

SPAS | Massages and body and facial therapies at this intimate, tranquil spa are influenced by the traditions of Pacific Island cultures. Try the Samoan Nonu, which uses warm stones and healing nonu gel to relieve muscle tension. The exclusive line of bath and body products is scented by maile, lavender orchid, or coconut passion. Facilities are specific to your treatment and may include a Japanese *furo* bath or a steam shower. ⊠ *Halekulani Hotel, 2199 Kalia Rd., Waikiki* ☎ *808/931–5322* ⊕ *www.halekulani.com/living/spahalekulani.*

Pearl Harbor

Approximately 9 miles west of downtown Honolulu, beyond Honolulu International Airport.

On December 7, 1941, the Japanese bombed Pearl Harbor. It was the catalyst for the United States' entrance into World War II. On that fateful day, more than 2,000 people died, and a dozen ships were sunk. Here, at what is still a key Pacific naval base, the attack is remembered every day by thousands of visitors. In recent years, the memorial has also been the site of reconciliation ceremonies involving Pearl Harbor veterans from both sides.

There are five distinct sights in Pearl Harbor, but only two are part of the Pearl Harbor National Memorial, with the others privately operated. Make reservations for the national park portion.

 ## Sights

Battleship *Missouri* Memorial

MILITARY SIGHT | **FAMILY** | The Japanese signed their Terms of Surrender after World War II on the deck of the USS *Missouri*, which was commissioned in 1944 and was the last American battleship ever built. To begin your visit of the fully restored vessel, pick up tickets online or at the Pearl Harbor Visitor Center. Then board a shuttle bus for the eight-minute ride to Ford Island and the teak decks and towering superstructure of the "Mighty Mo." Join a guided tour to learn more about the *Missouri*'s long and dramatic history. Near the entrance are a gift shop, a lunch wagon, and a shave ice stand. ⊠ *Ford Island, 63 Cowpens St., Pearl Harbor* ✢ *You cannot drive directly to the USS Missouri; you must take a shuttle bus from Pearl Harbor Visitor Center* ☎ *808/455–1600* ⊕ *ussmissouri. org* ⊠ *From $34.99* ☉ *Closed Sun.–Tues.*

Pacific Fleet Submarine Museum

MILITARY SIGHT | FAMILY | The USS *Bowfin* claimed to have sunk 44 enemy ships during World War II and now serves as the centerpiece of the new and expanded Pacific Fleet Submarine Museum, which opened in 2021 after a $20 million renovation. Aboard the so-called Pearl Harbor Avenger, compartments are fitted out as though "Sparky" was away from the radio room just for a moment and "Cooky" might be right back to his pots and pans. Admission to the privately operated museum includes an audio tour. For safety reasons, children under four are not allowed aboard the submarine, though they can visit the museum. ⊠ *11 Arizona Memorial Pl., Pearl Harbor* ☎ *808/423–1341* ⊕ *www.bowfin.org* ⊠ *$21.99* ☞ *Tickets available in advance or on arrival.*

Pearl Harbor Aviation Museum

HISTORY MUSEUM | FAMILY | This Ford Island museum documents the history of aviation in the Pacific during World War II and is housed in seaplane hangars 37 and 79, which survived the Japanese attack on Pearl Harbor on December 7, 1941. The numerous interesting, and sometimes interactive, displays include the plane flown by President George H. W. Bush. You can purchase tickets online ahead of time, at the Pearl Harbor Visitor Center, or at the museum itself after you get off the shuttle bus that departs for the museum and the USS *Missouri* from the visitor center. ⊠ *Ford Island, 319 Lexington Blvd., Pearl Harbor* ✢ *Access is only via the shuttle bus to Ford Island from the Pearl Harbor Visitor Center* ☎ *808/441–1000* ⊕ *pearlharboraviationmuseum.org* ⊠ *$25.99.*

★ Pearl Harbor National Memorial

NATIONAL PARK | FAMILY | Pearl Harbor is still a working military base as well as Oahu's most visited attraction, consisting of five distinct destinations. Managed by the National Park Service, the Pearl Harbor Visitor Center and USS *Arizona* Memorial make up the national memorial, where exhibits tell the story not only of the devastating Japanese attack on Pearl Harbor on December 7, 1941, but also of the wartime internment of Japanese Americans, World War II battles in the Aleutian Islands, and the occupation of Japan after the war. The history continues at three, privately operated sights: the Pacific Fleet Submarine Museum (whose centerpiece is the USS *Bowfin)*, the Battleship *Missouri* Memorial, and the Pearl Harbor Aviation Museum.

A valid, government-issued, photo ID is required to enter the base. You can walk to the visitor center or the submarine museum from the parking lot, but access to the USS *Arizona* requires a ferry ride (and ticket reservations via ⊕ *www. recreation.gov*), and access to other sites, including the USS *Missouri* and the aviation museum, requires a shuttle bus trip.

With the exception of the visitor center, no bags of any kind—not even small purses—are allowed at any of the sights, though cameras, cell phones, and wallets can be hand-carried. A bag check is available. Children under four can visit the submarine museum but, for safety reasons, are not allowed on the USS *Bowfin* itself. ⊠ *Pearl Harbor Visitor Center, 1 Arizona Memorial Pl., Pearl Harbor* ☎ *808/422–3399, 877/444–6777*

Continued on page 117

USS *West Virginia* (BB48), 7 December 1941

PEARL HARBOR

December 7, 1941. Every American then alive recalls exactly what they were doing when the news broke that the Japanese had bombed Pearl Harbor, the catalyst that brought the United States into World War II.

Although it was clear by late 1941 that war with Japan was inevitable, no one in authority seemed to have expected the attack to come in just this way, at just this time. So when the Japanese bombers swept through a gap in Oahu's Koolau Mountains in the hazy light of morning, they found the bulk of America's Pacific fleet right where they hoped it would be: docked like giant stepping stones across the calm waters of the bay named for the pearl oysters that once prospered there. More than 2,000 people died that day, including 49 civilians. A dozen ships were sunk.

And on the nearby air bases, virtually every American military aircraft was destroyed or damaged. The attack was a stunning success, but it lit a fire under America, which went to war with "Remember Pearl Harbor" as its battle cry. Here, in what is still a key Pacific naval base, the attack is remembered every day by thousands of visitors, including many curious Japanese, who for years heard little World War II history in their own country. In recent years, the memorial has been the site of reconciliation ceremonies involving Pearl Harbor veterans from both sides.

GETTING AROUND

Pearl Harbor is both a working military base and the most-visited Oahu attraction. Five distinct destinations share a parking lot and are linked by footpath, shuttle, and ferry.

The visitor center is accessible from the parking lot. The USS *Arizona* Memorial itself is in the middle of the harbor; get tickets for the ferry ride online ahead of time. The Pacific Fleet Submarine Museum/USS *Bowfin* are also reachable from the parking lot. The USS *Missouri* is docked at Ford Island, a restricted area of the naval base. Vehicular access is prohibited. To get there, take a shuttle bus from the station near the *Bowfin*.

ARIZONA MEMORIAL

Snugged up tight in a row of seven battleships off Ford Island, the USS *Arizona* took a direct hit that December morning, exploded, and rests still on the shallow bottom where she settled.

The swooping, stark-white memorial, which straddles the wreck of the USS *Arizona*, was designed to represent both the depths of the low-spirited, early days of the war, and the uplift of victory.

A visit here begins at the Pearl Harbor Visitor Center, which recently underwent a $58 million renovation. High definition projectors and interactive exhibits were installed, and the building was modernized. From the visitor center, a ferry takes you to the memorial itself, and shuttles access the USS *Oklahoma*.

A somber, contemplative mood descends upon visitors during the ferry ride to the *Arizona*; this is a place where 1,177 crewmen lost their lives. Gaze at the names of the dead carved into the wall of white marble. Scatter flowers (but no lei—the string is bad for the fish). Salute the flag. Remember Pearl Harbor.

☎ 808/422-3399
⊕ www.nps.gov/perl

USS *MISSOURI* (BB63)

BATTLESHIP *MISSOURI* MEMORIAL

Together with the *Arizona* Memorial, the *Missouri's* presence in Pearl Harbor perfectly bookends America's WWII experience, which began December 7, 1941, and ended on the "Mighty Mo's" starboard deck with the signing of the Terms of Surrender.

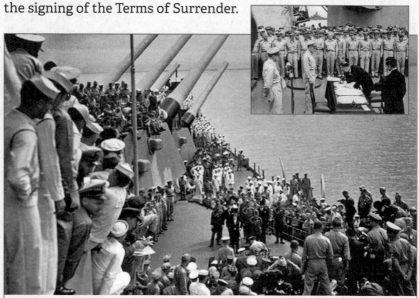

Surrender of Japan, USS *Missouri,* 2 September 1945

In the parking area behind the Pacific Fleet Submarine Museum, board a shuttle for an eight-minute ride to Ford Island and the teak decks and towering superstructure of the *Missouri*. The largest battleship ever built, the *Missouri* famously hosted the final act of WWII, the signing of the Terms of Surrender. The commission that governs this floating museum has surrounded it with WWII-style buildings, among them a lunch wagon, a shaved ice stand, and a souvenir shop.

■TIP➔ **Definitely hook up with a tour guide (no additional charge) or audio tour—these add a great deal to the experience.**

The *Missouri* is all about numbers: 209 feet tall, six 239,000-pound guns, capable of firing up to 23 miles away. Absorb these during the tour, then stop to take advantage of the view from the decks. The Mo is a work in progress, with only a handful of her hundreds of spaces open to view.

☎ *808/455-1600* or *877/644-4896*
⊕ *www.ussmissouri.org*

USS *BOWFIN* (SS287)

PACIFIC FLEET SUBMARINE MUSEUM & PARK

Launched one year to the day after the Pearl Harbor attack, the USS *Bowfin* reportedly sank 44 enemy ships during WWII and now serves as the centerpiece of a museum honoring all submariners.

Although the *Bowfin* no less than the *Arizona* Memorial commemorates the lost, the mood here is lighter. Perhaps it's the childlike scale of the boat, a metal tube just 16 feet in diameter, packed with ladders, hatches, and other obstacles, like the naval version of a jungle gym. Perhaps it's the World War II-era music that plays in the covered patio. Or it might be the museum's touching displays—the penciled sailor's journal, the Vargas girlie posters. Aboard the boat nicknamed "Pearl Harbor Avenger," compartments are fitted out as though "Sparky" was away from the radio room just for a moment, and "Cooky" might be right back to his pots and pans. The museum includes many artifacts to spark family conversations, among them a vintage dive suit that looks too big for Shaquille O'Neal.

A caution: The *Bowfin* could be hazardous for very young children; no one under four allowed.

☎ *808/423–1341*
🌐 *www.bowfin.org*

PEARL HARBOR AVIATION MUSEUM

This museum opened on December 7, 2006, as as a tribute to aviation in the Pacific. Located on Ford Island in Hangars 37 and 79, actual seaplane hangars that survived the Pearl Harbor attack, the museum is made up of a theater where a short film on Pearl Harbor kicks off the tour, an education center, a shop, and a restaurant. Exhibits—many of which are interactive and involve sound effects— include an authentic Japanese Zero in a diorama setting, vintage aircraft, and the chance to play the role of a World War II pilot using one of six flight simulators. Various aircrafts are employed to narrate the great battles: the Doolittle Raid on Japan, the Battle of Midway, Guadalcanal, and so on. The actual Stearman N2S-3 in which President George H. W. Bush soloed is housed in Hangar 79.

☎ *808/441–1000*
🌐 *www.pearlharboraviationmuseum.org*

PLAN YOUR PEARL HARBOR DAY LIKE A MILITARY CAMPAIGN

DIRECTIONS

Take H–1 west from Waikiki to Exit 15A and follow signs. Or take TheBus route 20 or 47 from Waikiki. Beware high-priced private shuttles. It's a 30-minute drive from Waikiki.

WHAT TO BRING

You must present a valid, government-issued, photo ID.

It's best to travel light. No bags (even small purses) are allowed, so plan to carry cameras and stash cell phones and other items in pockets or to check bags at the visitor center ($5). Lines for this can be long, so allow plenty of time, particularly if you have timed-entry memorial tickets.

All you really need, though, are comfortable walking shoes, a light jacket, sunglasses, and sunscreen. One final note: Leave nothing in your car; theft is a problem despite security patrols.

HOURS

Visitor center hours are 7 am to 5 pm daily. Most attractions don't open till 8 am, and some close at 4. Note, too, that last entry is often an hour before closing.

TICKETS

Arizona: Free. $7.99 for museum audio tours; $1 per-person ticket reservation fee.

Aviation: $25.99 adults, $14.99 children; from $10.70 for flight simulator.

Missouri: $34.99 adults, $17.49 children.

Bowfin: $21.99 adults, $12.99 children. Children under 4 may go into the museum but not aboard the *Bowfin*.

Passport to Pearl Harbor: 1-day access to all ships and exhibits; $89.99 adults (ages 13+), $44.95 children, $1 per-person reservation fee (buy at ⊕ *recreation.gov*).

KIDS

This might be the day to enroll younger kids in the hotel children's program. Preschoolers chafe at long waits, and attractions involve some hazards for toddlers. Older kids enjoy the *Bowfin* and *Missouri*, especially.

MAKING THE MOST OF YOUR TIME

You could see the highlights in half a day, but it would be rushed, so plan on a full day. **Timed tickets for the USS *Arizona* Memorial can be reserved up to two months in advance.** Same-day, first-come, first-served tickets are no longer sold.

SUGGESTED READING

Pearl Harbor and the USS Arizona Memorial, by Richard Wisniewski. 76-page magazine-size quick history.

Bowfin, by Edwin P. Hoyt. Dramatic story of undersea adventure.

The Last Battleship, by Scott C. S. Stone. Story of the Mighty Mo.

timed ticket reservations ⊕ www.nps. gov/perl ✉ Visitor center and USS Arizona Memorial free (aside from $1 ticket reservation fee); fees for other sites ⚲ Reservations required to access USS Arizona Memorial.

★ Pearl Harbor Visitor Center

VISITOR CENTER | The gateway to the Pearl Harbor National Memorial and the starting point for visitors to this historic site has interpretive exhibits in two separate galleries (*Road to War* and *Attack*) that feature photographs and personal memorabilia from World War II veterans. There are also other exhibits, a bookstore, and a Remembrance Circle, where you can learn about the people who lost their lives on December 7, 1941. Survivors are sometimes on hand to give their personal accounts and answer questions. The visitor center is also where you start your tour of the USS *Arizona* Memorial if you have reserved the requisite timed-entry ticket (⊕ www.recreation.gov; $1 reservation fee). ✉ Pearl Harbor National Memorial, 1 Arizona Memorial Pl., Pearl Harbor ☎ 808/954–8759, 866/332–1941 toll-free ⊕ nps.gov/perl ✉ Free (timed-entry ticket fee $1).

★ USS *Arizona* Memorial

NATIONAL PARK | FAMILY | The USS *Arizona*, which was destroyed by a Japanese bomber on December 7, 1941, lies precisely where she sank. You must reserve your free tickets (⊕ www.recreation. gov) ahead of time to ensure access to the memorial. When your tour starts, you watch a short documentary film, then board the ferry to the memorial. At the site, you may scatter flowers in memory of the dead (but no lei—the string is bad for the fish). ✉ Pearl Harbor National Memorial, Pearl Harbor ☎ 808/422–3399 ⊕ nps.gov/perl ✉ Free (advanced reservation timed-entry tickets $1); audio tours and other features cost extra.

Mapunapuna

Mapunapuna is an area filled with factories and offices surrounding the airport. Tucked amid car dealerships, a Kaiser Permanente medical center, and warehouses are fast-food joints, a Chinese restaurant, local plate-lunch places, and Mitch's, a somewhat undiscovered gem of a sushi spot.

🍴 Restaurants

Mitch's Fish Market & Sushi Bar

$$$$ | SUSHI | This microscopic sushi bar is an adjunct of a wholesale seafood market. The fish, air-freighted from around the world, is ultra-fresh, well-cut (into huge pieces—to the regret of those who follow the one-bite rule), and prepared for the serious sushi lover. **Known for:** otoro (fattiest part of tuna); hole-in-the-wall atmosphere; BYOB. Ⓢ *Average main: $60* ✉ 524 Ohohia St., near Honolulu International Airport, Mapunapuna ☎ 808/837–7774 ⊕ mitchssushi.com.

Iwilei

Before the arrival of Captain Cook, Iwilei was a network of fishponds. After his arrival, it became home to a prison, railway depot, and houses of ill repute. (When the red-light district was shut down in 1916, one prostitute hopped a ship to Pago Pago. Also onboard was Somerset Maugham, who immortalized her as Sadie Thompson in his short story "Rain.")

Today, the primary reason to visit this industrial zone is the Dole Cannery shopping complex, which also has a multiplex. The shopping center really was a pineapple cannery before its conversion; almost any local of a certain age has tales of summer jobs there.

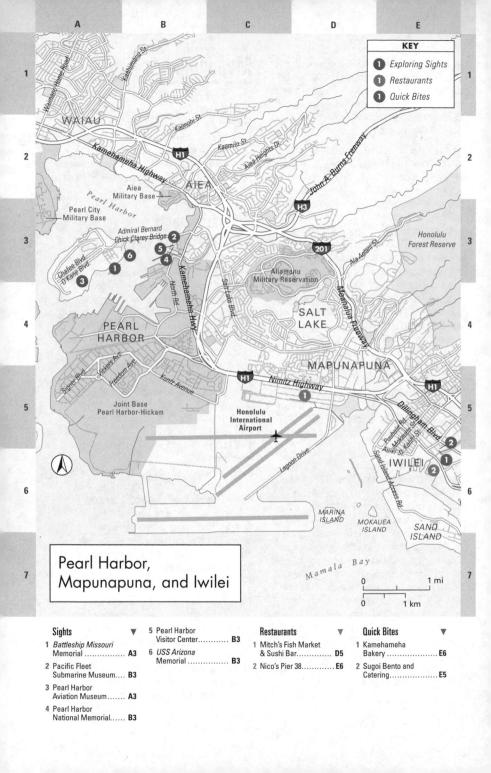

KEY

1 *Exploring Sights*
1 *Restaurants*
1 *Quick Bites*

Pearl Harbor, Mapunapuna, and Iwilei

0 _____ 1 mi
0 _____ 1 km

Sights ▼

1 *Battleship Missouri*
  Memorial **A3**
2 Pacific Fleet
  Submarine Museum.... **B3**
3 Pearl Harbor
  Aviation Museum....... **A3**
4 Pearl Harbor
  National Memorial...... **B3**
5 Pearl Harbor
  Visitor Center............ **B3**
6 *USS Arizona*
  Memorial **B3**

Restaurants ▼

1 Mitch's Fish Market
  & Sushi Bar.............. **D5**
2 Nico's Pier 38............ **E6**

Quick Bites ▼

1 Kamehameha
  Bakery **E6**
2 Sugoi Bento and
  Catering.................. **E5**

🍴 Restaurants

★ Nico's Pier 38

$$ | **SEAFOOD** | **FAMILY** | Lyonnaise chef Nico Chaiz's harborside restaurant is steps from the Honolulu Fish Auction, which explains his "line-to-plate" concept—super-fresh fish dishes at a reasonable price. But he lets his French flag fly in dishes like steak *frites* and bouillabaisse, too. **Known for:** lunch at the bar with a cold beer; pan-seared ahi steak crusted in toasted seaweed and sesame seeds; excellent double cheeseburger. ⑤ *Average main: $21* ☒ *1129 N. Nimitz Hwy., Pier 38, Iwilei* ☎ *808/540–1377* ⊕ *www. nicospier38.com.*

☕ Coffee and Quick Bites

Kamehameha Bakery

$ | **BAKERY** | **FAMILY** | This well-established bakery offers both old-school classics and newer treats, some of which have become cult favorites. You'll salivate as you stare at the cases filled with inexpensive pastries, doughnuts, cookies, and breads. **Known for:** opens early (before dawn) and sells out of many things by midmorning; variety of malasadas; friendly service. ⑤ *Average main: $1* ☒ *City Square Shopping Center, 1284 Kalani St., Unit D106, Iwilei* ☎ *808/845–5831* ⊕ *kamehamehabakeryhi.net.*

Sugoi Bento and Catering

$ | **MODERN HAWAIIAN** | This breakfast-and-lunch spot located in a strip mall was among the first of a new wave of plate-lunch places to take particular care with quality and nutrition, offering brown rice and green salad as options instead of the usual white rice and mayo-loaded mac salad. Sweet-and-spicy garlic chicken and *mochiko* (rice-batter-dipped and fried) chicken, adapted from traditional Japanese dishes, are specialties that bring locals back again and again. **Known for:** ample parking; local favorites; grab-and-go for the beach. ⑤ *Average main: $11* ☒ *City Square Shopping Center, 1286*

Kalani St., Suite B-106, Iwilei ☎ *808/841–7984* ⊕ *sugoihawaii.com* ☯ *No dinner. Closed Sun.*

🛍 Shopping

GIFTS
Indich Collection

HOUSEWARES | Bring home some aloha you can sink your bare feet into. Designs from this exclusive Hawaiian rug collection depict Hawaiian petroglyphs, banana leaves, heliconia, and other tropical plants or scenery. ☒ *550 Ward Ave., Kakaako* ☎ *808/596–7333* ⊕ *indichcollection.com.*

Downtown

Throughout downtown, which is about 6 miles east of Honolulu International Airport, the city's past and present are delightfully intertwined, as evidenced by the architecture. Postmodern glass-and-steel office buildings look down on the Aloha Tower, built in 1926 and, until the early 1960s, the tallest structure in Honolulu.

You'll also find history in the cut-stone, turn-of-the-20th-century storefronts on Merchant Street; the gracious, white-columned, American-Georgian manor that was the home of the Islands' last queen; the jewel-box palace occupied by the monarchy before it was overthrown; the Spanish-inspired stucco and tile-roofed Territorial Era government buildings; and the 21st-century glass pyramid of the First Hawaiian Bank Building.

GETTING HERE AND AROUND

To reach downtown Honolulu from Waikiki by car, take Ala Moana Boulevard to Alakea Street, and turn right; three blocks up on the right, between South King and Hotel Streets, there's a municipal parking lot in Alii Place. There are also public lots in buildings along Alakea, Smith, Beretania, and Bethel Streets (Chinatown

Shangri La

The marriage of heiress Doris Duke to a much older man when she was 23 didn't last. But their around-the-world honeymoon did leave her with two lasting loves: Islamic art and architecture, which she first encountered on that journey; and Hawaii, where the honeymooners made an extended stay while Doris learned to surf and befriended Islanders unimpressed by her wealth.

Today, visitors to her beloved Oahu home—where she spent most winters—can share both loves by touring her estate. The sought-after tours are coordinated by and begin at the Honolulu Museum of Art in downtown Honolulu. A short van ride then takes small groups to the house itself, on the far side of Diamond Head.

■ TIP→ For more information, see the listing in the East (Windward) Oahu chapter.

Gateway on Bethel Street is a good choice). The best parking downtown, however, is metered street parking along Punchbowl Street—when you can find it.

Another option is to take the highly popular and convenient TheBus to the Aloha Tower Marketplace, or you can take a trolley from Waikiki.

Sights

Hawaiian Mission Houses Historic Site and Archives

HISTORY MUSEUM | The determined Hawaii missionaries arrived in 1820, gaining royal favor and influencing a wide array of Islands life. Their descendants became leaders in government, business, and education. Here you can learn about their influence and walk through their original dwellings, including Hawaii's oldest Western-style wooden structure, a white-frame house that was prefabricated in New England and shipped around the Horn. A *hale pili* (traditional Hawaiian dwelling) sits nearby. Be sure to sign up for one of the hourly guided tours: docents not only paint an excellent picture of what mission life was like, but they also take you to areas of the museum you wouldn't otherwise be able to see. Special Hawaiian, architectural,

and history tours are also offered on certain days. Rotating displays showcase such arts as Hawaiian quilting, portraits, and even toys, and a rich archival library is also open to the public. ✉ *553 S. King St., Downtown* ☎ *808/447–3910* ⊕ *missionhouses.org* ✉ *$12* ✆ *Closed Sun., Mon., Wed., Thurs.*

Hawaii State Capitol

GOVERNMENT BUILDING | The capitol's architecture is richly symbolic: the columns resemble palm trees, the legislative chambers are shaped like volcanic cinder cones, and the central court is open to the sky, representing Hawaii's open society. Replicas of the Hawaii state seal, each weighing 7,500 pounds, hang above both its entrances. The building, which in 1969 replaced Iolani Palace as the seat of government, is surrounded by reflecting pools, just as the Islands are embraced by water. A pair of statues, often draped in lei, flank the building: one of the beloved Queen Liliuokalani and the other of the sainted Father Damien de Veuster, famous for helping Molokai's Hansen's disease (leprosy) patients. ✉ *415 S. Beretania St., Downtown* ☎ *808/586–0221* ⊕ *www.capitol.hawaii.gov* ✉ *Free* ✆ *Closed weekends.*

Take a guided tour of Iolani Palace, America's only royal residence, built in 1882.

Hawaii State Library

LIBRARY | This beautifully renovated main library was built in 1913. Its Samuel Manaiakalani Kamakau Room, on the first floor in the *mauka* (Hawaiian for "mountain") courtyard, houses an extensive Hawaii and Pacific book collection and pays tribute to Kamakau, a missionary student whose 19th-century writings in English offer rare and vital insight into traditional Hawaiian culture. ⊠ *478 S. King St., Downtown* ☎ *808/586–3500* ⊕ *librarieshawaii.org* 🖼 *Free* ☼ *Closed Sun. and Wed.*

Honolulu Hale

GOVERNMENT BUILDING | This Mediterranean Renaissance–style building was constructed in 1929 and serves as the center of government for the City and County of Honolulu. Stroll through the shady, open-ceiling lobby with exhibits of local artists. During the winter holiday season, the Hale (Hawaiian for "house") becomes the focal point for the annual Honolulu City Lights, a display of lighting and playful holiday scenes spread around the campus, including the famous, gigantic Shaka Santa and Tute Mele. The mayor's office keeps a calendar of upcoming events. ⊠ *530 S. King St., Downtown* ☎ *808/768–4385 for general city info* ⊕ *honolulu.gov/visitors* 🖼 *Free* ☼ *Closed weekends.*

★ Honolulu Museum of Art

ART MUSEUM | Originally built around the collection of a Honolulu matron who donated much of her estate to the museum, the Honolulu Academy of Arts is housed in a maze of courtyards, cloistered walkways, and quiet, low-ceiling spaces. There's an impressive permanent collection that includes the third-largest assembly of Hiroshige's ukiyo-e Japanese prints in the country (donated by author James Michener); Italian Renaissance paintings; and American and European art by Monet, van Gogh, and Whistler, among many others. The newer Luce Pavilion complex, nicely incorporated into the more traditional architecture of the museum, has a traveling-exhibit gallery, a Hawaiian gallery, an excellent café,

KEY

- **1** Exploring Sights
- **1** Restaurants
- **1** Quick Bites
- **1** Hotels

A   B   C   D   E   F

CHINATOWN

DOWNTOWN

KAKAAKO

Kakaako
Waterfront Park

Ala Moana
Regional Park

Nimitz Hwy

Nimitz Hwy

North Beretania St

North King St

Aala Street

Maunakea St

South Vineyard Blvd

Nuuanu Avenue

Pali Highway

Nuuanu Avenue

S. School St.

Nuuanu Avenue

Pali Highway

Prospect Street

Iolani Avenue

Queen Emma Street

Smith St.

Bethel St.

Bishop Street

Merchant Street

Queen Street

Alakea Street

Richards Street

Punchbowl Street

South Beretania St.

South King Street

Kinau Street

Lauhala St.

Lisbon St.

Tintana St.

Ward Avenue

Victoria St.

Kapiolani Blvd

Ala Moana Boulevard

South Street

Auahi Street

Coral Street

Cooke Street

Pohukaina St.

Keawe St.

Ohe St.

Koula St.

Ilalo Street

Ahui Street

Queen Street

Ward Avenue

Kamakee Street

Queen Street

Kawaiahao Street

Halekauwila Street

Iianiwai Street

Kamani Street

Ala Moana Boulevard

Auahi Street

0   1,000 ft

0   200 m

Downtown, Chinatown, Kakaako, and Ala Moana

Sights ▼

1 Foster Botanical Garden **D1**
2 Hawaiian Mission Houses Historic Site and Archives **D5**
3 Hawaii State Capitol.... **D4**
4 Hawaii State Library.... **D4**
5 Hawaii Theatre........... **C3**
6 Honolulu Hale **D4**
7 Honolulu Museum of Art **F5**
8 Iolani Palace **D4**
9 Izumo Taishakyo Mission of Hawaii **C1**
10 Kamehameha I Statue **C4**
11 Kawaiahao Church..... **D5**
12 Kuan Yin Temple **C1**
13 Maunakea Marketplace............ **B2**
14 Nuuanu Avenue......... **B3**
15 Oahu Market **B2**
16 POW! WOW! Hawaii Murals **C7**
17 Washington Place **D3**

Restaurants ▼

1 Akasaka.................. **I8**
2 Bac Nam................. **G6**
3 Chef Chai **F7**
4 Fête....................... **C3**
5 53 By The Sea........... **C8**
6 Highway Inn Kakaako...**C6**
7 Honolulu Museum of Art Café **F4**
8 Legend Seafood Restaurant................**C2**
9 Little Village Noodle House............**C2**
10 Livestock Tavern........ **B3**
11 Mariposa **H8**
12 Merriman's Honolulu....**E8**
13 Moku Kitchen **C6**
14 MW Restaurant........... **I8**
15 PAI Honolulu **B3**
16 Panya **F8**
17 Pho To Chau Restaurant............... **B2**
18 The Pig and the Lady... **B2**
19 Scratch Kitchen.......... **F8**
20 Senia **B3**
21 Tangö Contemporary Cafe **F8**
22 Terry's Place............. **C2**
23 Yanagi Sushi............. **E6**

Quick Bites ▼

1 Hank's Haute Dogs **C6**
2 Local Joe **B3**
3 Lucky Belly.............. **B2**
4 Mei Sum Dim Sum **C2**

Hotels ▼

1 Ala Moana Hotel..........**I8**
2 Aston at the Executive Centre Hotel..............**C3**

Punchbowl Crater

ALA MOANA

Ala Moana Regional Park

and a gift shop. The Doris Duke Theatre screens art films. This is also the jumping-off point for tours of Doris Duke's striking estate, which is now the Shangri La Museum of Islamic Art, Culture, and Design. If you wish to visit, you should reserve tickets well in advance. ✉ 900 S. Beretania St., Downtown ☎ 808/532–8700 ⊕ honolulumuseum.org ⊠ $20 ⊘ Closed Mon.–Wed.

★ Iolani Palace

CASTLE/PALACE | America's only official royal residence, on the site of an earlier palace, was completed in 1882. It contains the thrones of King Kalakaua and his successor (and sister) Queen Liliuokalani. Bucking the stereotype of simple island life, the palace had electric lights even before the White House. Downstairs galleries showcase the royal jewelry, as well as a kitchen and offices that have been restored to the glory of the monarchy. The palace gift shop and ticket office are now in what was formerly the Iolani Barracks, built to house the Royal Guard. The palace has self-guided audio tours and guided tours. ■**TIP**➡ **Guided tours are only available in the mornings, and it's best to make reservations a few days in advance.** ✉ 364 S. King St., Downtown ☎ 808/522–0822 ⊕ www.iolanipalace. org ⊠ $30 guided tour, $25 audio tour ⊘ Closed Sun. (except for monthly Kamaaina Sun.).

Kamehameha I Statue

PUBLIC ART | Honoring the Big Island chieftain who united all the warring Hawaiian Islands into one kingdom at the turn of the 18th century, this statue, which stands with one arm outstretched in welcome, is one of two cast in Paris by American sculptor T. R. Gould. The original statue, lost at sea and replaced by this one, was eventually salvaged and is now in Kapaau, on the Big Island, near the king's birthplace. Each year on the king's birthday (June 11), the more famous copy is draped in fresh lei that

reach lengths of 18 feet and longer. A parade proceeds past the statue, and Hawaiian civic clubs, women in hats and impressive long holoku dresses, and men in sashes and cummerbunds honor the leader, whose name means "The One Set Apart." ✉ 417 S. King St., outside Aliiolani Hale, Downtown ⊕ www.goha-waii.com/islands/oahu/regions/honolulu/king-kamehameha-statue.

Kawaiahao Church

CHURCH | Fancifully called Hawaii's Westminster Abbey, this historic house of worship witnessed the coronations, weddings, and funerals of generations of Hawaiian royalty. Each of the building's 14,000 coral blocks was quarried from reefs offshore at depths of more than 20 feet and transported to this site. Interior woodwork was created from the forests of the Koolau Mountains. The upper gallery displays paintings of the royal families. The graves of missionaries and of King Lunalilo are adjacent. Services in English, with songs and prayers in Hawaiian, are held each Sunday. An all-Hawaiian service is held at 5 pm on the second and fourth Sunday of the month (Kawaiahao's affiliation is United Church of Christ). Although there are no guided tours, you can look around the church at no cost. ✉ 957 Punchbowl St., at King St., Downtown ☎ 808/469–3000 ⊕ kawaiahao.org ⊠ Free.

Washington Place

HISTORIC HOME | This white-column mansion was built by sea captain John Dominis, whose son married Liliuokalani, the woman who became the Islands' last queen. Deposed by American-backed forces, the queen returned to the home—which is in sight of the royal palace—where she lived until her death. From 1922 to 2002, it was home to Hawaii's sitting governors. The nonprofit Washington Place Foundation now operates the gracious estate, which is open for one public tour on Thursday

only. ✉ *320 S. Beretania St., Downtown*
☎ *808/586–0248* ⊕ *washingtonplace.*
hawaii.gov ✉ *Donations accepted*
⊗ *Closed Fri.–Wed.*

 Restaurants

Honolulu Museum of Art Café

$$ | **AMERICAN** | The Honolulu Museum of
Art's cool courtyards and galleries filled
with works by masters from Monet to
Hokusai are well worth a visit, and, after-
ward, so is this popular lunch restaurant.
The open-air café is flanked by a burbling
water feature and 8-foot-tall ceramic
"dumplings" by artist Jun Kaneko—a
tranquil setting in which to eat your salad
or sandwich, shaded by a 75-year-old
monkeypod tree. **Known for:** nice spot for
Sunday brunch; piadina pesto-caprese
flatbread sandwich; limited but beautiful-
ly prepared menu of soups, salads, sand-
wiches, and mains. $ *Average main: $18*
✉ *Honolulu Museum of Art, 900 S. Bere-*
tania St., Downtown ☎ *808/532–8734*
⊕ *honolulumuseum.org/cafe* ⊗ *Closed*
Mon.–Wed. No dinner.

PAI Honolulu

$$$ | **MODERN AMERICAN** | Michelin star–
restaurant chef Kevin Lee and his general
manager wife, Justine, are at the helm
of the innovative, upscale Pai (short for
ho'opai, meaning "to encourage" in
Hawaiian). The tantalizing and surprising
fusion cuisine is served in a modern,
arched dining room and patio tucked into
the atrium of the Harbor Court condo
building. **Known for:** attention to detail in
each dish; homemade breads; superb
cocktails and wine pairings. $ *Average*
main: $30 ✉ *Harbor Court, 55 Merchant*
St., Suite 110, Downtown ☎ *808/744–*
2531 ⊕ *www.paihonolulu.com* ⊗ *Closed*
Mon. and Tues. No lunch.

Yanagi Sushi

$$$ | **JAPANESE** | One of relatively few
restaurants to serve a complete menu
until 2 am (until 10 pm on Sunday) offers

not only sushi and sashimi around a
small bar, but also *teishoku* (combination
menus), tempura, stews, and cook-it-
yourself shabu-shabu. The fish can be
depended on for freshness and variety.
Known for: local favorite; late-night happy
hour; baked crabmeat volcano roll, spicy
shrimp tempura roll, live abalone sashimi.
$ *Average main: $28* ✉ *762 Kapiolani*
Blvd., Downtown ☎ *808/597–1525*
⊕ *www.yanagisushi-hawaii.com.*

 Hotels

Aston at the Executive Centre Hotel

$$ | **HOTEL** | Downtown Honolulu's only
hotel is an all-suites high-rise in the
center of the business district, within
walking distance of the historic Capitol District, museums, and Honolulu's
Chinatown, and a 10-minute drive from
Honolulu International Airport. **Pros:** good
spot for overnighting before or after a
cruise; discounted passes to nearby 24
Hour Fitness; close to many attractions.
Cons: parking is very expensive; suites
are individually owned, so quality of
room can vary; no beach within walking
distance. $ *Rooms from: $260* ✉ *1088*
Bishop St., Downtown ☎ *808/539–3000,*
855/945–4090 toll-free reservations
⊕ *www.aquaaston.com/hotels/*
aston-at-the-executive-centre-hotel ⤳ *90*
suites ⦿ *No Meals.*

 Nightlife

BARS

★ Bar Leather Apron

BARS | This intimate, James Beard Award–
nominated cocktail spot, oddly situated
in the mezzanine of an office building,
seats only six at the bar along with a
few other tables. So you'll want to make
reservations to enjoy bespoke cocktails that utilize only the finest liquors
and ingredients. Owners Tom Park and
Justin Park (no relation) have cultivated
a reputation for their E Ho'o Pau Mai Tai

made with a 5-year-old, raisin-infused El Dorado rum and another 12-year-old El Dorado rum, as well as coconut water syrup, spiced orgeat, ohia blossom honey, lime, vanilla, and absinthe—all served with a kiawe wood–smoke presentation. ✉ *Topa Financial Center, 745 Fort St., Mezzanine Level, Suite 127A, Downtown* ☎ *808/524–0808* ⊕ *www.barleather-apron.com* ⊗ *Closed Sun. and Mon.*

Murphy's Bar & Grill

PUBS | On the edge of Chinatown and the financial district, this bar has served drinks to such locals and visitors as King Kalakaua and Robert Louis Stevenson since the late 1800s. The kind of Irish pub you would find in Boston, Murphy's offers a break from all the tropical, fruit-garnished drinks found in Waikiki, and it's definitely the place to be on St. Patrick's Day. Friendly bartenders and waitstaff serve Guinness on tap, pub food favorites, and Irish specialties like corned beef and cabbage and shepherd's pie. If you time it right, you can try their incredible homemade pies, which are served only on Friday and quickly sell out. ✉ *2 Merchant St., Downtown* ☎ *808/531–0422* ⊕ *www.murphyshawaii. com.*

🎭 Performing Arts

DINNER CRUISES AND SHOWS

Most dinner cruises depart either from the piers adjacent to the Aloha Tower Marketplace in downtown Honolulu or from Kewalo Basin Harbor, near Ala Moana Beach Park, and head along the coast toward Diamond Head. There's usually a buffet-style dinner with local flavor, dancing, drinks, a sensational sunset, and even potential whale spotting between December to April. Some cruises offer discounts for online reservations. Most major credit cards are accepted. In all cases, reservations are essential.

Buying Flowers and Fruit 🛍️

You can bring home fresh pineapple, papaya, or coconut to share with friends and family. Orchids will also brighten your home and remind you of your trip to the Islands. By law, all fresh fruit and plant products must be inspected by the Department of Agriculture before export. Ask at the shop about agricultural rules so a surprise confiscation doesn't spoil your departure. Shipping to your home usually is best.

Atlantis Cruises

CONCERTS | The sleekly high-tech *Majestic,* designed to sail smoothly in rough waters, powers farther along Waikiki's coastline than its competitors. Enjoy seasonal whale-watching trips between January and March during the day or year-round sunset cocktail and dinner cruises aboard the 400-passenger boat. (Atlantis is also known for its submarine tours off Waikiki.) The boat's dining room is elegantly laid out, and the standard Hawaiian buffet fare perfectly accompanies the tropical cocktails, Champagne, beer, or guava juice. Most passengers are honeymooners and those celebrating anniversaries and birthdays—or even the occasional proposal—and this, plus the Hawaiian music, makes the atmosphere festive. For the best view of Waikiki and the sunset, head to the top deck. ✉ *1 Aloha Tower Rd., Pier 6, Downtown* ☎ *808/973–9800, 800/381–0237* ⊕ *majestichawaii.com* 🎟 *From $65.*

Star of Honolulu Cruises

CONCERTS | The celebrated 1,500-passenger *Star of Honolulu* offers four sunset dinner-cruise packages, from a roast beef buffet and Polynesian show to a romantic, seven-course, fine-dining excursion with live jazz. The company also runs whale-watching and special holiday cruises. ⊠ *Aloha Tower Marketplace, 1 Aloha Tower Dr., Pier 8, Downtown* ☎ *808/983–7730* ⊕ *starofhonolulu.com* 🎫 *From $99.*

MUSIC

Chamber Music Hawaii

MUSIC | This group, consisting of four ensembles, has been around for decades and performs at the Honolulu Museum of Art's Doris Duke Theatre (⊠ *901 S. Beretania St., Honolulu*), the Paliku Theatre at Windward Community College (⊠ *45-720 Keaahala Rd., Kaneohe*), the University of Hawaii's West Oahu Library (⊠ *1001 Farrington Hwy., Kapolei*), and other locations around the island. The season runs from fall through spring. ⊠ *Downtown* ☎ *808/722–0172* ⊕ *chambermusichawaii. org.*

Hawaii Opera Theatre

OPERA | Locals refer to it as "HOT," probably because the Hawaii Opera Theatre has been turning the opera-challenged into opera lovers since 1961. All operas are sung in their original language, with a projected English translation. ⊠ *Neal S. Blaisdell Center Concert Hall, 777 Ward Ave., Honolulu* ☎ *808/596–7372 main office, 800/836–7372 toll-free* ⊕ *hawaii-opera.org.*

THEATER

Hawaii can be an expensive gig for touring shows and music acts that depend on major theatrical sets. Not many manage to stop here, and those that do sell out fast. Oahu has developed several excellent local community theater companies, which present first-rate, though not professional, entertainment all year long. (Anyone who attends is always surprised to learn that the Honolulu Theatre for Youth is the only professional troupe in the state.) Community support for these groups is strong.

★ Honolulu Theatre for Youth

THEATER | FAMILY | This group stages delightful productions, with creative props and engaging stories, August through May. Founded in 1955, it's one of the oldest children's theaters in the country (it's the only professional troupe in Hawaii), offering drama-education programs as well as school and family performances. ⊠ *Tenney Theatre, 229 Queen Emma Sq., Downtown* ☎ *808/839–9885* ⊕ *www.htyweb.org.*

Kumu Kahua Theatre

THEATER | Focusing on plays written by local playwrights about Island life and Hawaiian experiences, this troupe stages five or six productions a year in an intimate, 100-seat auditorium. ⊠ *46 Merchant St., Downtown* ☎ *808/536–4441* ⊕ *www.kumukahua.org.*

🛍 Shopping

The downtown shopping scene, like that in neighboring Chinatown, is ever changing. Focus on the small galleries—which have helped foster the area's arts and culture renaissance—and the burgeoning array of hip, home-decor stores tucked between ethnic restaurants.

Chinatown

Chinatown's original business district was made up of dry-goods and produce merchants, tailors and dressmakers, barbers and herbalists. The meat, fish, and produce stalls remain, but the mix is heavier now on gift and curio stores, lei stands, jewelry shops, and bakeries, with a smattering of noodle makers and travel agents and dozens of restaurants.

The name "Chinatown" here has always been a misnomer. Though three-quarters of Oahu's Chinese lived closely packed in these 25 acres in the late 1800s, even then the neighborhood was half Japanese. Today you hear Vietnamese and

Tagalog as often as Mandarin and Cantonese, and there are voices of Japan, Singapore, Malaysia, Korea, Thailand, Samoa, and the Marshall Islands, as well.

Perhaps a more accurate name is the one used by early Chinese: *Wah Fau* (Chinese port), signifying a landing and jumping-off place. As soon as they finished their plantation contracts, Chinese laborers hurried into the city to start businesses here. It's a launching point for today's immigrants, too: Southeast Asian shops almost outnumber Chinese establishments; stalls carry Filipino specialties like winged beans and goat meat; and you'll find Japanese, Cambodian, Laotian, Thai, and Korean cuisine and goods for sale.

In the half century after the first Chinese laborers arrived in Hawaii in 1852, China-town was a link to home for the all-male cadre of workers who planned to return to China rich and respected. Merchants not only sold supplies, they held mail, loaned money, wrote letters, translated documents, sent remittances to families, served meals, offered rough bunkhouse accommodations, and were the center for news, gossip, and socializing.

Although much happened to China-town in the 20th century—beginning in January 1900, when almost the entire neighborhood was burned to the ground to halt the spread of bubonic plague—it remains a bustling, crowded, noisy, and odiferous place bent primarily on buying and selling and sublimely oblivious to its status as a National Historic District or encroaching gentrification.

GETTING HERE AND AROUND

Chinatown occupies 15 blocks immediately north of downtown Honolulu—it's flat, compact, and very walkable. Street parking can be hard to find depending on the time and day of the week. There are many paid municipal and private parking lots with varying rates.

■ TIP→ Bring cash to use at the ethnic markets, eateries, stores, and vendor stalls that don't accept credit cards or have a minimum spending amount to use one.

 Sights

Foster Botanical Garden

GARDEN | Some of the trees in this botanical garden, which opened in 1931, date from 1853, when Queen Kalama allowed a young German doctor to lease a portion of her land. More than 150 years later, you can see these trees and countless others along with bromeliads, orchids, and other tropical plants, some of which are rare or endangered. Look out in particular for the cannonball tree and the redwood-size quipo tree. A docent-led tour is available every day at 10:30 am (call for reservations). ⊠ *180 N. Vineyard Blvd., Chinatown* ☎ *808/768–7135 for daily guided tours reservations* ⊕ *www.honolulu.gov/parks/hbg/honolulu-botani-cal-gardens* ⊴ *$5.*

Hawaii Theatre

PERFORMANCE VENUE | Opened in 1922, this theater earned rave reviews for its neoclassical design, with Corinthian columns, marble statues, and plush carpeting and drapery. The so-called Pride of the Pacific was rescued from demolition in the early 1980s, underwent a $30-million renovation, and is now listed on both the State and National Registers of Historic Places. The 1,400-seat venue hosts concerts, theatrical productions, dance performances, and film screenings. Guided tours of the theater end with a miniconcert on the historic orchestral pipe organ and can be booked through the box office. If you're interested in the first Tuesday of the month tours at 11 am, call a few days ahead to reserve. ⊠ *1130 Bethel St., Chinatown* ☎ *808/528–0506* ⊕ *www.hawaiitheatre.com* ⊴ *$10 for tour.*

Izumo Taishakyo Mission of Hawaii

RELIGIOUS BUILDING | From Chinatown Cultural Plaza, cross a stone bridge to the Izumo Taishakyo Mission of Hawaii to visit the shrine established in 1906. It honors Okuninushi-no-Mikoto, a *kami* (god) who is believed in Shinto tradition to bring good fortune if properly courted (and thanked afterward). ⊠ *215 N. Kukui St., Chinatown ✢ At the canal* ☎ *808/538–7778* ⊕ *izumotaishahawaii. com.*

Kuan Yin Temple

TEMPLE | A couple of blocks *mauka* (toward the mountains) from Chinatown is the oldest Buddhist temple in the Islands. Mistakenly called a goddess by some, Kuan Yin, also known as Kannon, is a bodhisattva—one who chose to remain on Earth doing good even after achieving enlightenment. Transformed from a male into a female figure centuries ago, she is credited with being particularly sympathetic to women. You will see representations of her all over the Islands: holding a lotus flower (beauty from the mud of human frailty), as at the temple; pouring out a pitcher of oil (like mercy flowing); or as a sort of Madonna with a child. Visitors are permitted but should be mindful that this is a practicing place of worship. ⊠ *170 N. Vineyard Blvd., Chinatown ✢ Park at Foster Botanical Gardens.*

Maunakea Marketplace

MARKET | **FAMILY** | On the corner of Maunakea and Hotel Streets is this busy plaza surrounded by shops and an air-conditioned indoor market and food court where you can buy fresh seafood and seasonal local produce or chow down on banana *lumpia* (spring rolls) and fruit smoothies or bubble tea (juices and flavored teas with tapioca balls inside). It gets packed during Chinese Lunar New Year. ⊠ *1120 Maunakea St., Chinatown* ⊕ *geyserholdings.com/maunakea.*

Nuuanu Avenue

STREET | **FAMILY** | Both Chinatown's main *mauka–makai* drag and Bethel Street, which runs parallel, are lined with art galleries, restaurants, tattoo parlors, bars and pubs, an antiques auctioneer, dress shops, one small theater/exhibition space (The ARTS at Marks Garage), and one historic stage (the Hawaii Theatre). You can also take in the unique early 1900s architecture of the buildings. ⊠ *Nuuanu Ave., Chinatown.*

Oahu Market

MARKET | **FAMILY** | In this tenant-owned market founded in 1904, you'll find a taste of old-style Chinatown, where you might spot a whole butchered pig, head intact, on display, and where glassy-eyed fish of every size and hue lie forlornly on ice. Bizarre magenta dragonfruit, ready-to-eat *char siu* (Cantonese barbecued pork) and pork belly, and bins brimming with produce add to the color. You'll find some of the cheapest Oahu prices on fruits and vegetables in this and other Chinatown markets. ⊠ *N. King St., Chinatown ✢ At Kekaulike St.*

🍴 Restaurants

Fête

$$ | **AMERICAN** | At lunch, regulars pack into this tiny, brick-walled space for the burgers and specials; at dinner, they come for the pasta and locally sourced seafood dishes or the to-die-for twice-fried Kauai chicken with grits and collard greens. Here, you'll probably get cozy with the table next to you as wait staffers glide between tables with full trays and great attitudes. **Known for:** craft cocktails and extensive drink menu; Brooklyn-meets-Hawaii menu; great pau hana (happy hour) menu. ⑤ *Average main: $25* ⊠ *2 N. Hotel St., Chinatown* ☎ *808/369–1390* ⊕ *fetehawaii.com* ◷ *Closed Sun.*

Legend Seafood Restaurant

$ | CHINESE | At this large Chinatown institution, the dim sum cart ladies stop at your table and show you their Hong Kong–style fare. If you come for breakfast dim sum, arrive before 9 am, especially on weekends, if you want to hear yourself think. **Known for:** easy parking in the cultural plaza parking lot; still-warm custard tarts; dim sum, reasonably priced by the dish. $ *Average main: $13* ⊠ *Chinese Cultural Plaza, 100 N. Beretania St., Suite 108, Chinatown* ✣ *In the Chinatown Cultural Plaza* ☎ *808/532–1868* ⊕ *www. legendseafoodhonolulu.com.*

★ Little Village Noodle House

$$ | CHINESE | Unassuming and budget-friendly, Little Village is so popular with locals that it expanded to the space next door. Considered some of the best Chinese food on Oahu, the extensive Pan-Asian menu is filled with crowd-pleasers like honey-walnut shrimp and crispy orange chicken. ■**TIP→ Two hours of free parking are available in the lot immediately to the right of the restaurant (if you can nab a space). Known for:** BYOB; something for everyone on the menu; fun interior design with village decor. $ *Average main: $18* ⊠ *1113 Smith St., Chinatown* ☎ *808/545–3008* ⊕ *littlevillagehawaii.com* ◷ *Closed Tues. No lunch Mon., Wed., and Thurs.*

Livestock Tavern

$$ | MODERN AMERICAN | Livestock Tavern scores big with its seasonal offerings of comfort foods and craft cocktails and its cowboy-minimalist decor. Although meat, including some of the best burgers in town, commands the menu, offerings like *burrata*, creative salads, sandwiches, and fish round out the possibilities. **Known for:** fresh-cut fries; lively bar scene; go-to lunch spot. $ *Average main: $20* ⊠ *49 N. Hotel St., Chinatown* ☎ *808/537–2577* ⊕ *livestocktavern.com.*

Pho To Chau Restaurant

$ | VIETNAMESE | Those people lined up on River Street know where to go for bowls of steaming pho (Vietnamese beef noodle soup) with all the best trimmings. This hole-in-the-wall storefront was the go-to pho spot long before hipsters and foodies found Chinatown. **Known for:** large pho can be easily shared; no-frills service and sometimes a wait for food once seated; old-school, 1970s decor. $ *Average main: $10* ⊠ *1007 River St., Chinatown* ☎ *808/533–4549* ▤ *No credit cards* ◷ *No dinner* ⌲ *Cash only.*

★ The Pig and the Lady

$$ | ASIAN | Chef Andrew Le's casual noodle house attracts downtown office workers by day and becomes a creative contemporary restaurant at night, pulling in serious chowhounds. Drawing on both his Vietnamese heritage and multicultural island flavors, the talented, playful Le is a wizard with spice and acid, turning out dishes of layered flavor. **Known for:** Hanoi-style egg coffee; bahn mi sandwiches at lunch and pho all day; homemade soft-serve custards and sorbets, including unexpected flavors. $ *Average main: $20* ⊠ *83 N. King St., Chinatown* ☎ *808/585–8255* ⊕ *thepigandthelady.com* ◷ *Closed Sun. and Mon.*

★ Senia

$$$ | MODERN AMERICAN | Every item on the modern American menu at this small, sophisticated, James Beard Award–nominee is carefully concocted and artfully plated. You can order à la carte or indulge in the pricey tasting menu at the Chef's Counter; dessert is a must thanks to pastry chef Mimi Mendoza's delectable works of art. **Known for:** Senia cookie made with peanut butter, toffee, and Valrhona chocolate; charred cabbage that looks like a mossy rock but mesmerizes the tastebuds; sophisticated cocktails and an encyclopedic wine menu. $ *Average main: $30* ⊠ *75 N. King St., Chinatown* ✣ *Between The Pig & The Lady and Smith & Kings* ☎ *808/200–5412*

⊕ *restaurantsenia.com* ⊘ *Closed Sun. and Mon. No lunch.*

Terry's Place

$$ | BISTRO | This country-style European bistro is in a quiet courtyard next to its sister wine shop. Owner Terry Kakazu brings her wine expertise to the menu of classic, elevated comfort food. **Known for:** great place for groups and celebrations; small plates to share; extensive wine list. ⑤ *Average main: $25* ✉ *31 N. Pauahi St., Chinatown* ☎ *808/533–4277* ⊕ *terrys. place* ⊘ *Closed Sun. and Mon. No lunch.*

Coffee and Quick Bites

Local Joe

$ | CAFÉ | Local Joe is a great spot to stop for coffee and a light bite before or after your explorations in the Aloha Tower, Chinatown, downtown, and historic Honolulu. The coffee shop roasts its own beans and has a latte art "printer" that leaves detailed designs on your drink. **Known for:** delicious coffee; nice presentations; convenient location. ⑤ *Average main: $7* ✉ *110 Marin St., Chinatown* ☎ *808/536–7700* ⊕ *www.localjoehi.com* ⊘ *Closed Sun.*. Honolulu Roasters

Lucky Belly

$$ | ASIAN | A hip local crowd sips cocktails and slurps huge bowls of noodles with a modern twist at this popular fusion ramen bar known for its savory broth and its trendy small plates, such as pork belly buns and oxtail dumplings. The service here is unpretentious and attentive if you eat in, but you can also order your food to go, and late-night hours make it a great stop after shows at the Hawaii Theatre or when dinner elsewhere didn't quite do the trick. **Known for:** "Belly Bowl" with smoked bacon, sausage, and pork belly; steaming hot pot dishes; small but unique cocktail menu. ⑤ *Average main: $17* ✉ *50 N. Hotel St., Chinatown* ☎ *808/531–1888* ⊕ *luckybellyhi.com* ⊘ *Closed Sun. No lunch.*

Mei Sum Dim Sum

$ | CHINESE | In contrast to the sprawling, noisy halls where dim sum is generally served, Mei Sum is compact, shiny, and bright—it's also favored by locals who work in the area. Be ready to guess and point at the color photos of dim sum favorites or the items on the carts as they come by, or ask fellow diners for suggestions. **Known for:** dim sum made fresh daily; deep-fried garlic eggplant; house special garlic rice. ⑤ *Average main: $11* ✉ *1170 Nuuanu Ave., Suite 102, Chinatown* ⊹ *Next to post office* ☎ *808/531–3268* ⊕ *www.meisumdim-sum.com.*

Nightlife

BARS

Encore Saloon

BARS | Although this bar serves good Mexican-inspired food (try the pork carnitas burrito), it's best known for its impressive drinks menu featuring more than 50 varieties of tequila and mezcal. You can also get wine and canned beer. ✉ *10 N. Hotel St., Chinatown* ☎ *808/367–1656* ⊕ *www.encoresaloon. com* ⊘ *Closed Sun.*

J. Dolan's

BARS | The drinks and rotating beers on tap at this Irish, *Cheers*-like bar are reasonably priced by Honolulu standards, and its menu of New York–style pizzas, both classic and inventive, is a crowd-pleaser, too. ✉ *1147 Bethel St., Chinatown* ☎ *808/537–4992* ⊕ *jdolans. com.*

The Manifest

BARS | With exposed red brick, big skylights, and rotating exhibitions of work by local photographers and painters, The Manifest has an artist's loft feel to it. It's a café by day and a cocktail bar and night club by night, so it serves a good cup of Joe as well as quality cocktails. ✉ *32 N. Hotel St., Chinatown* ⊕ *www.manifesthawaii.com* ⊘ *Closed Sun.*

The Tchin Tchin! Bar

BARS | This chill bar gets its name from the Chinese expression "qing, qing" (which means "please please"), often used as a toast; soldiers returning from the Chinese Opium Wars introduced it in France and throughout Europe. With an extensive wine menu—by the glass and the bottle—plus a selection of single malt bourbon, whiskey, and scotch, it's an ideal spot for a drink or tapas-style food. The bar's rooftop lanai is the best place to sit, romantically lit with string lights and featuring a large living wall flourishing with ferns. ⊠ *39 N. Hotel St., Chinatown* ☎ *808/528–1888* ⊕ *thetchintchinbar.com* ⊘ *Closed Sun. and Mon.*

👜 Shopping

Shopping in Chinatown, with its typical mix of the tacky and the unique, is a bustling cultural experience not to be missed. Tucked amid the produce stands are boutiques selling reasonably priced Asian silk clothing, curio shops with everything from porcelain statues to woks to Mao shoes, and exotic apothecaries filled with glass jars of mysterious herbs.

Visit the Chinatown Cultural Plaza for fine-quality jade and the New Hong Kong Market for fresh fruit, crack seed (a popular dried-fruit snack), and boxed or tinned delicacies with indecipherable names. Look for newer, hipper clothing, jewelry, books, art, and collectibles in stores along Nuuanu and Pauahi.

Chinatown is also Honolulu's lei center, with shops strung along Beretania and Maunakea (locals all have their favorites where they're greeted by name). In spring, look for gardenia nosegays wrapped in ti leaves.

Pauahi Street

OTHER SPECIALTY STORE | Along Pauahi Street, between the cross streets of Smith and Bethel, are several hip and trendy stores, coffee shops, and restaurants. Roberta Oaks sells modern aloha wear for men, women, and children. There's also a location of Fighting Eel, with its fashionable local clothing and accessories. BAS Bookshop has a well-curated selection of art and design books from around the world, along with pottery, clothes, and other small items. A branch of Morning Glass Coffee shares an open hallway with the music-centric EP Bar. Native Books at Arts & Letters, Valia Honolulu, Ginger13, and The ARTS at Marks Garage are among the other offerings in this area. ⊠ *Pauahi Street, Chinatown.*

Place

HOUSEWARES | Owner and interior designer Mary Philpotts McGrath creates a Hawaiian sense of place at this design studio/workshop known for its well-curated assemblage of sophisticated home items in all price ranges. You'll find a global collection of fine lighting, furniture, and textiles, as well as works by local artists and artisans. ⊠ *54 S. School St., #100, Chinatown* ☎ *808/275–3075* ⊕ *www. placehawaii.com.*

Kakaako

This 600-acre section of Honolulu between the Ala Moana Center and downtown is in the process of a redevelopment plan that began in 2012. It's definitely a neighborhood in transition, with everything from ramshackle mechanic shops to the University of Hawaii's medical school.

Its old warehouses and mom-and-pop storefronts are gradually being replaced by luxury condos, trendy restaurants, local boutiques, and big-box retailers like T. J. Maxx. New happenings, such as the Honolulu Night Market pop-up shopping event, are also taking root.

You won't soon forget the eye-popping murals the POW! WOW! collective has painted on the buildings in the redeveloping Kakaako neighborhood.

Sights

POW! WOW! Hawaii Murals

PUBLIC ART | The POW! WOW! Worldwide art collective was founded in Hawaii in 2010 and has spread to nearly 20 cities around the world. Its most visible Oahu endeavor is a multiblock area where colorful, eclectic, and innovative murals are painted on once-derelict looking warehouses and other buildings. Every year around Valentine's Day, artists from all over come to refresh existing murals and add new ones. The event wraps up with a big food, art, and entertainment festival centered at the SALT at Our Kakaako complex, but you can grab a bite and take in the unique street art here at any time of the year. ⊠ *Kakaako* ✛ *Murals are centered on Cooke, Auahi, and Pohukaina Sts.* ☎ *808/223–7462* ⊕ *www. powwowworldwide.com/murals/hawaii.*

Restaurants

53 By The Sea

$$$$ | **CONTEMPORARY** | Housed in a McVilla aimed at attracting a Japanese wedding clientele, this restaurant serves contemporary Continental food that focuses primarily on beautifully plated, well-prepared standards—albeit with a million-dollar view of Honolulu. Perched at the water's edge, with famed surf break Point Panic offshore, 53 By The Sea uses its setting to great advantage—the crescent-shape dining room faces the sea, so even if you're not at a table nestled against the floor-to-ceiling windows, you have a fine view. **Known for:** on-site wedding chapel in case the mood strikes; odd villa decor that somehow works; free valet parking. ⑤ *Average main: $50* ⊠ *53 Ahui St., Kakaako* ☎ *808/536–5353* ⊕ *53bythesea.com.*

Highway Inn Kakaako

$ | **MODERN HAWAIIAN** | **FAMILY** | Highway Inn serves what it does best: local favorites like Kalbi ribs, *kalua* (roasted in an underground oven) pork sliders, beef stew, and old-fashioned hamburger steaks. This is also a great spot to try poi (the pudding-like dish made of pounded taro). **Known for:** signature combo plates; Kakaako location is in SALT complex; relatively close to the cruise terminal. ⑤ *Average main: $16* ✉ *680 Ala Moana Blvd., Kakaako* ☎ *808/954–4955* ⊕ *www.myhighwayinn.com.*

Merriman's Honolulu

$$$ | **BISTRO** | This is fine dining without the fussiness, where cordial, well-trained servers present your "Bag O' Biscuits" or smoking oysters on the half shelf with equal aplomb and know all the details of each menu item. The large Hawaiian-French bistro has floor-to-ceiling windows and native wood accents throughout, and chef-owner Peter Merriman focuses on farm-to-table food, using Oahu-sourced ingredients as much as possible. **Known for:** Waialua chocolate purse (a take on molten lava cake); lobster potpie; tableside poke. ⑤ *Average main: $35* ✉ *1108 Auahi St., Suite 170, Kakaako* ☎ *808/215–0022* ⊕ *merrimanshawaii.com.*

Moku Kitchen

$$ | **HAWAIIAN** | **FAMILY** | In the hip SALT complex, Moku appeals to both foodies and families with authentic farm-to-table cuisine and a laid-back, urban setting. It's one of legendary chef Peter Merriman's restaurants and focuses on upcountry farm fare cooked in the on-site rotisserie; pizzas, salads, and sandwiches; and craft cocktails. **Known for:** live music; happy hour; impressive list of craft cocktails, wine, and beer, including the signature monkeypod mai tai. ⑤ *Average main: $20* ✉ *SALT at Our Kakaako, 660 Ala Moana Blvd., Kakaako* ☎ *808/591–6658* ⊕ *www.mokukitchen.com.*

Tangö Contemporary Cafe

$$ | **ECLECTIC** | On the ground floor of a glass-sheathed condominium, Tangö's spare contemporary setting stays humming through breakfast, lunch, and dinner. Finnish chef Göran Streng honors his heritage a bit with unfussy dishes such as gravlax with crispy skin, but the menu is, by and large, "general bistro," running from bouillabaisse to herb-crusted rack of lamb, with some Asian nods. **Known for:** attentive staff; Hamakua mushroom risotto; loco moco (unlike any you'll have elsewhere). ⑤ *Average main: $25* ✉ *Hokua Bldg., 1288 Ala Moana Blvd., Kakaako* ☎ *808/593–7288* ⊕ *tangocafehawaii.com* ☾ *No dinner Sun.*

Coffee and Quick Bites

Hank's Haute Dogs

$ | **HOT DOG** | **FAMILY** | Owner Hank Adaniya's idea of a hot dog involves things like a duck and foie gras sausage with truffle mustard and stone fruit compote. Originally a true hole-in-the-wall, the gentrified Hank's is still a tiny spot where you can go classic with the Chicago Dog, made with the traditional fixings (including neon-green relish), or gourmet with the butter-seared lobster sausage topped with garlic-relish aioli. **Known for:** part of Kakaako's SALT area; 11 varieties of dogs daily, plus another 5 or so daily specials; fries, truffle fries, and onion rings to die for. ⑤ *Average main: $9* ✉ *324 Coral St., Kakaako* ☎ *808/532–4265* ⊕ *www.hankshautedogs.com* ☞ *Remember to get parking validated.*

Nightlife

BARS

Aloha Beer

BREWPUBS | At this cool brewpub, you order everything at the counter and then grab a seat in either the industrial indoor taproom or the casual outdoor area. The HI Brau Room upstairs, which has its own speakeasy-style entrance, is definitely worth checking out for unique cocktails, too. With 12 beers on draft, including the Hop Lei IPA, Waimanalo Farmhouse, Froot Loops, and Portlock

Porter, you can find something to your taste. If you're hungry, there's also pretty good food—snacking boards, hearty sandwiches, small plates, and steak frites. ⊠ *700 Queen St., Kakaako* ☎ *808/544–1605* ⊕ *www.alohabeer.com.*

★ **Bevy Bar**

BARS | Tucked at the end of a row of new boutiques, Bevy is urban, modern, and furnished with upcycled materials (its benches are upholstered in denim jeans, and its tabletops feature flattened wine boxes). Locals in the know come for artisan cocktails created by owner and master mixologist Christian Self, who deftly concocts libations with obscure ingredients and complex flavors. Look for live music on some nights. ⊠ *675 Auahi St., Kakaako* ☎ *808/594–7445* ⊕ *bevyhawaii.com* ◔ *Closed Mon.*

★ **Honolulu Beerworks**

BREWPUBS | Oahu's brewing scene has erupted in Kakaako's industrial neighborhood, and one brewpub in particular has led the charge: Honolulu Beerworks. In a converted warehouse, owners Geoff and Charmayne Seideman and their crew brew nine beers—in addition to limited releases—such as the Pia Mahiai Saison (made with local oranges, other citrus, and Big Island honey) or the rich South Shore Stout. When you need some *ono grinds* (delicious food) to go along with your local brew, order the bar's ahi dip. It's a regular spot for many locals, particularly on the weekends. You might just make new friends sitting at one of the bar's long picnic tables, made from reclaimed wood. ⊠ *328 Cooke St., Kakaako* ☎ *808/589–2337* ⊕ *www.honolulubeerworks.com* ◔ *Closed Mon.*

★ **Waikiki Brewing Company**

BREWPUBS | This company not only brews its own quality craft beer but also serves delicious food. This is its second location—the original is in Waikiki at 1945 Kalakaua Avenue—and it always offers nine beers on tap, including the Skinny Jeans IPA and the Hana Hou Hefe, to

which orange peel and strawberry puree are added before fermentation. You can also buy six-packs at the bar to go. Here, the chef smokes meat in house using local kiawe wood, resulting in tender and flavorful beef brisket, pulled pork, chicken, and bratwurst. Accompanying barbecue sauces are made with Waikiki Brewing beer. ⊠ *831 Queen St., Kakaako* ☎ *808/591–0387* ⊕ *waikikibrewing.com.*

Performing Arts

DANCE
Ballet Hawaii

BALLET | Established in 1976, Ballet Hawaii is a local company that's active throughout the year. Its annual, Hawaii-theme *The Nutcracker,* usually held at the nearby Blaisdell Concert Hall (⊠ *777 Ward Ave.*), is a local holiday tradition. Other shows take place at the Hawaii Theatre (⊠ *1130 Bethel St.*) in Chinatown and elsewhere. ⊠ *777 S. Hotel St., Suite 101, Kakaako* ☎ *808/521–8600* ⊕ *ballethawaii.org.*

MUSIC
Hawaii Symphony Orchestra

MUSIC | The Hawaii Symphony Orchestra is the latest incarnation of the now-defunct, century-old Honolulu Symphony, with a mission to bring international talent to Hawaiian audiences of all ages. The orchestra performs at the Neal Blaisdell Concert Hall and the Waikiki Shell. Ticket prices vary. ⊠ *Honolulu* ☎ *808/380–7784* ⊕ *www.myhso.org.*

🛍 Shopping

CLOTHING
Anne Namba Designs

MIXED CLOTHING | This designer combines the beauty of classic kimonos with contemporary styles to make unique pieces for career and evening. In addition to women's apparel, she designs a men's line. ⊠ *324 Kamani St., Kakaako* ☎ *808/589–1135* ⊕ *www.annenamba.com.*

HOME DECOR

fishcake

OTHER SPECIALTY STORE | A place to find unusual art, this gallery hosts changing exhibitions and events showcasing works by designers and artists from near and far. It also carries small and large home items you won't find anywhere else in Honolulu, offers interior design services, and has a café featuring a rotation of pop-up coffee and tea spots. ⊠ *307 Kamani St., Suite C, Kakaako* ☎ *808/800–6151* ⊕ *www.fishcake.us* ⊗ *Closed Mon.*

SPORTING GOODS

Boca Hawaii

SPORTING GOODS | This triathlon shop near the Bike Factory offers training gear and bike rentals, aerial yoga and capoeira classes, and nutritional products. ■**TIP→ Inquire directly about the latest schedule of classes at the store, which is owned and operated by top athletes.** ⊠ *330 Cooke St., Kakaako* ☎ *808/591–9839* ⊕ *bocahawaii.com.*

Ala Moana

Ala Moana abuts Waikiki to the east (stopping at the Ala Wai Canal) and King Street to the north. Kakaako, Kewalo Basin Harbor, and the Blaisdell Center complex roughly mark its western edge. Probably its most notable attraction is the sprawling Ala Moana Center, jam-packed with almost any store you could wish for.

 Beaches

Honolulu proper only has one beach: Ala Moana. Popular with locals, it hosts everything from Dragon Boat competitions to the Lantern Floating Ceremony.

★ **Ala Moana Regional Park** (*Ala Moana Beach Park*)

BEACH | FAMILY | A protective reef makes Ala Moana essentially a ½-mile-wide saltwater swimming pool. Very smooth sand and no waves create a haven for families and stand-up paddleboarders. After Waikiki, this is the most popular beach among visitors, and the free parking area can fill up quickly on sunny weekends. On the Waikiki side is a peninsula called Magic Island, with shady trees and paved sidewalks ideal for jogging. Ala Moana Regional Park also has playing fields, tennis courts, and a couple of small ponds for sailing toy boats. The beach is for everyone, but only in the daytime; after dark, it's a high-crime area, with many unhoused people. **Amenities:** food and drink; lifeguards; parking (free); showers; toilets. **Best for:** swimming; walking. ⊠ *1201 Ala Moana Blvd., Ala Moana* ⊕ *www.honolulu.gov/parks.*

🍴 Restaurants

Akasaka

$$ | JAPANESE | Step inside this tiny sushi bar, tucked amid the strip clubs behind the Ala Moana Hotel, and you'll swear you're in an out-of-the-way Edo neighborhood. Don't be deterred by its dodgy neighbors or its reputation for inconsistent service—this is where locals come when they want the real deal, and you'll be greeted with a cheerful "*Iraishaimase!*" (Welcome!) before sitting at a diminutive table or perching at the small sushi bar. **Known for:** spicy tuna roll; no pretense, nothing fancy; popular local spot for late-night food. ⑤ *Average main: $21* ⊠ *1646 B Kona St., Suite B, Ala Moana* ☎ *808/942–4466* ⊕ *www.akasakahawaii.com* ⊗ *No lunch on Sun.*

Bac Nam

$ | VIETNAMESE | Tam and Kimmy Huynh's menu ranges far beyond the usual pho and *bun* (cold noodle dishes) found at many Vietnamese restaurants. This welcoming, no-frills, hole-in-the-wall spot, which locals swear by, features lamb curry, tapioca dumplings, head-on tamarind shrimp, and other dishes that hail from both North and South Vietnam. **Known for:** excellent crabmeat curry soup;

spring and summer rolls; limited free parking behind the restaurant. $ *Average main: $12* ✉ *1117 S. King St., Ala Moana* ☎ *808/597–8201* ⊙ *Closed Sun.*

Chef Chai

$$$ | FUSION | This contemporary dining room in a condo building across from the Blaisdell Center is the go-to spot before and after plays or concerts. The creative starters and seafood and meat entrées on the eclectic, global-fusion menu are healthier than the norm as they don't rely on butter or cream, with dishes like lobster bisque thickened instead with squash puree. **Known for:** excellent desserts; early-bird and prix-fixe menu options that will leave you stuffed; ahi tartare with avocado mousse in miniwaffle cones. $ *Average main: $30* ✉ *Pacifica Honolulu, 1009 Kapiolani Blvd., Ala Moana* ☎ *808/585–0011* ⊕ *chefchai. com* ⊙ *Closed Mon. and Tues.*

Mariposa

$$$ | HAWAIIAN | Yes, the popovers and the wee cups of bouillon are available at lunch, but in every other regard, the menu at this Neiman Marcus restaurant departs from the classic model, incorporating a clear sense of Pacific place. The breezy, open-air veranda, with a view of Ala Moana Regional Park, the twirling ceiling fans, and the life-size hula-girl murals say "Hawaii." It's still a spot for ladies who lunch, but it also welcomes a more casual crowd. **Known for:** lovely Hawaii-style interiors; extensive cocktail menu; corn chowder. $ *Average main: $35* ✉ *Neiman Marcus, Ala Moana Center, 1450 Ala Moana Blvd., Ala Moana* ☎ *808/951–3420* ⊕ *neimanmarcushawaii. com/Restaurants/Mariposa.htm.*

★ MW Restaurant

$$$ | HAWAIIAN | The "M" and "W" team of husband-and-wife chefs Michelle Karr-Ueko and Wade Ueko combine their collective experience (20 years alongside chef Alan Wong, a side step to the famed French Laundry, and some serious kitchen time at comfort food icon Zippy's) to create a uniquely local menu with a decidedly upscale twist. Michelle's flair for sweets has resulted in a dessert menu as long as the main one, including tropical fruit creamsicle brûlée, an MW candy bar, and the frozen lilikoi soufflé. **Known for:** excellent fish dishes; scrumptious desserts (save room); nice craft cocktails. $ *Average main: $35* ✉ *888 Kapiolani Blvd., Suite 201, Ala Moana* ☎ *808/955–6505* ⊕ *www.mwrestaurant. com.*

Panya

$$ | ECLECTIC | Run by Hong Kong–born sisters Alice and Annie Yeung, this easy-breezy café is known for its pastries, desserts, and happy hours but also offers crowd-pleasing, contemporary fare, both American (salads, sandwiches, pastas) and Asian (Thai-style steak salad, Japanese-style fried chicken, Singaporean seafood *laksa*). Dine inside for the air-conditioning and disco vibe, or choose a spot on the covered lanai. **Known for:** Japanese cheesecake; French-style pastries and cakes; eclectic and extensive menu. $ *Average main: $18* ✉ *1288 Ala Moana Blvd., Kakaako* ☎ *808/946–6388* ⊕ *www. panyabistro.com* ⊙ *Closed Mon.*

Scratch Kitchen

$$ | MODERN AMERICAN | Tucked into the chic South Shore Market in Kakaako's Ward Village, Scratch Kitchen has hipster decor, an open kitchen, and creative comfort food. It's popular for breakfast and brunch and has both small plates and generous entrées on its dinner menu. **Known for:** large portions; milk 'n' cereal pancakes; spicy (and good) chicken and waffles. $ *Average main: $18* ✉ *South Shore Market at Ward Village, 1170 Auahi St., Kakaako* ⊹ *Enter on side of building, along Queen St.* ☎ *808/589–1669* ⊕ *www.scratch-hawaii.com.*

Inexpensive Local Souvenirs

Hawaii can be an expensive place. If you're shopping for souvenirs or gifts, consider the following relatively affordable items, which are sold all over the island.

Locally published, Hawaii-themed books for children and adults can be found at places like **Na Mea Hawaii/Native Books** in Ward Village/Chinatown and **BookEnds** in Kailua.

Just when you thought peanut butter couldn't get any better, someone added coconut to it and made it even more delicious. The coconut peanut butter from **North Shore Goodies** makes a great gift.

If you are a fan of plate lunches, **Rainbow Drive-In** has T-shirts with regular orders—"All rice," "Gravy all over," "Boneless"—printed on them. They come packed in an emblematic plate-lunch box.

Relive your memories of tea on the veranda by purchasing Island Essence Tea at **Moana Surfrider.**

Harvested from a salt farm on Molokai, **Hawaii Traditional Gourmet Sea Salts** come in a variety of flavors, including black lava, red alaea clay, and classic. They're colored to match their flavor, so they are beautiful as well as tasty.

Foodland makes insulated cooler bags that are decorated with uniquely local designs that go beyond tropical flowers and coconuts. Look for the pidgin or poke designs. The Hawaii-themed reuseable totes at **Whole Foods** are also very popular.

Made with all-natural, island ingredients, like kukui-nut oil and local flowers and herbs, even seaweed, indigenous bar soap is available online or in stores like **Blue Hawaii Lifestyle.**

Hotels

Ala Moana Hotel

$$$ | HOTEL | A decent value in a pricey hotel market, location is the hallmark of this property, which is connected to Oahu's largest mall, the Ala Moana Center, by a pedestrian ramp and is just a 10-minute walk from Waikiki, a 2-minute stroll from Ala Moana Beach Park, and a block from the convention center. **Pros:** very convenient location; great value (and no resort fee); refreshed pool deck, lobby, and a new Starbucks. **Cons:** expensive parking; smaller and older rooms in Kona Tower; outside the heartbeat of Waikiki. ⑤ *Rooms from: $269* ⊠ *410 Atkinson Dr., Ala Moana* ☎ *808/955–4811, 866/488–1396* ⊕ *www.alamoanahotelhonolulu. com* *1100 rooms* ⑩ *No Meals.*

Nightlife

BARS
Mai Tai's

BARS | After a long day of shopping at the Ala Moana Center, the fourth-floor Mai Tai's is the perfect spot to relax. What you will find is live entertainment and happy hour specials for both food and drink. What you won't find is a cover charge or a dress code. To avoid waiting in line, arrive before 9 pm. ⊠ *Ala Moana Center, 1450 Ala Moana Blvd., Ala Moana* ⊕ *instagram.com/maitaisalamoana.*

Shopping

Getting to the Ala Moana shopping area from Waikiki is quick and inexpensive thanks to TheBus and the Waikiki Trolley.

BOOKS

★ Na Mea Hawaii

BOOKS | In addition to Island-style clothing for adults and children, Hawaiian cultural items, and unusual artwork, such as Nii-hau-shell necklaces, this boutique's book selection covers Hawaiian history and language and includes children's books set in the Islands. Na Mea also has classes on Hawaiian language, culture, and history. ⊠ *Ward Village, 1200 Ala Moana Blvd., Suite 270, Ala Moana* ☎ *808/596–8885* ⊕ *www.nameahawaii.com.*

CLOTHING

Reyn Spooner

MIXED CLOTHING | This is a good place to buy the aloha-print fashions residents wear. Look for the limited-edition Christmas shirt, a collector's item manufactured each holiday season. Reyn Spooner has seven locations statewide and offers styles for men and children and, sometimes, limited-edition women's wear. ⊠ *Ala Moana Shopping Center, 1450 Ala Moana Blvd., Shop 2247, Ala Moana* ☎ *808/949–5929* ⊕ *www.reynspooner. com.*

CRAFTS

Na Hoku

JEWELRY & WATCHES | If you look at the wrists of *kamaaina* (local) women, you might see Hawaiian heirloom bracelets fashioned in either gold or silver and engraved in a number of Islands-inspired designs. Na Hoku sells these and other traditional Hawaiian jewelry along with an array of modern Island-influenced designs that capture the heart of the Hawaiian lifestyle in all its elegant diversity. There are a number of Na Hoku locations on Oahu, as well as on the other Islands and the Mainland. ⊠ *Ala Moana Center, 1450 Ala Moana Blvd., Shop 2006, Ala Moana* ☎ *808/946–2100* ⊕ *www.nahoku.com.*

Koa Keepsakes

Items handcrafted from native Hawaiian wood make beautiful gifts. Koa and milo have a distinct color and grain. The scarcity of koa forests makes the wood extremely valuable. That's why you'll notice a large price gap between koa-wood-veneer products and the real thing.

FOOD

Honolulu Cookie Company

FOOD | Hugely popular with Islands residents and visitors, these pineapple-shaped shortbread cookies, half-dipped in milk or dark chocolate, come in an assortment of flavors from macadamia nut to mango and lilikoi. Made locally in Kalihi, these gourmet cookies are sold in boxes and tins of varying sizes at a number of locations in Ala Moana and Waikiki. ⊠ *Ala Moana Shopping Center, 1450 Ala Moana Blvd., Ala Moana* ☎ *808/945–0787* ⊕ *www.honolulucookie.com.*

Longs Drugs

FOOD | Try Longs at the Ala Moana Center (or one of its many other outposts) to stock up on chocolate-covered macadamia nuts, candies, cookies, Islands tea, and 100% Kona coffee—at reasonable prices—to carry home. ⊠ *Ala Moana Shopping Center, 1450 Ala Moana Blvd., 2nd level, Ala Moana* ☎ *808/941–4010* ⊕ *longs.staradvertiser.com.*

GIFTS

Blue Hawaii Lifestyle

SOUVENIRS | The Ala Moana store carries a large selection of locally made products, including soaps, honey, tea, salt, chocolates, art, and CDs. Every item is carefully selected from various Hawaiian companies, artisans, and farms—from the salt fields of Molokai to the lavender farms of Maui to the single-estate chocolate of Oahu's North Shore. An in-store café serves healthy smoothies, panini, tea, and espresso. ✉ *Ala Moana Shopping Center, 1450 Ala Moana Blvd., Shop 2312, Ala Moana* ☎ *808/949–0808* ⊕ *www.bluehawaiilifestyle.com.*

SHOPPING CENTERS
Ala Moana Shopping Center
MALL | FAMILY | The world's largest open-air shopping mall is a five-minute bus ride from Waikiki. More than 350 stores and 160 dining options (including multiple food courts) make up this 50-acre complex, which is a unique mix of national and international chains as well as smaller, locally owned shops and eateries—and everything in between. The newer Lanai @ Ala Moana Center is worth stopping at for a range of casual dining options in one spot. More than 30 luxury boutiques in residence include Gucci, Louis Vuitton, and Christian Dior. All of Hawaii's major department stores are here, including the state's only Neiman Marcus and Nordstrom, plus Macy's, Target, and Bloomingdale's. ✉ *1450 Ala Moana Blvd., Ala Moana* ☎ *808/955–9517* ⊕ *www.alamoanacenter.com.*

Ward Village
SHOPPING CENTER | FAMILY | Heading west from Waikiki toward downtown Honolulu, you'll run into a section of town with five distinct shopping-complex areas; there are more than 135 specialty shops and 40 eateries here. The Ward Entertainment Center features 16 movie screens, including a state-of-the-art, 3D, big-screen auditorium, and all theaters have reclining chairs and access to an extended food menu and alcoholic beverages for those of age. The South Shore Market is a contemporary collection of local shops and restaurants, plus T. J. Maxx and Nordstrom Rack. For distinctive Hawaiian gifts, such as locally made muumuus, koa-wood products, and Niihau shell necklaces, visit Martin & MacArthur and Na Mea Hawaii. Over at the Ward Gateway Center, the Ohana Hale Marketplace is worth a stop to visit 140 local small

businesses, including food stalls, apparel and accessories shops, and gift and craft stands. You can hop on TheBus or take a trolley from Waikiki. There's also free parking around the entire Ward Village, though sometimes you have to circle for awhile to find a spot. Valet parking is also available. ✉ *1050-1200 Ala Moana Blvd., Ala Moana* ☎ *808/591–8411* ⊕ *www.wardvillage.com/shopping.*

Activities

SPAS
Hoala Salon and Spa
SPAS | This Aveda concept spa has everything from Vichy showers to hydrotherapy rooms to customized aromatherapy. They'll even touch up your makeup for free before you leave. ✉ *Ala Moana Shopping Center, 3rd fl., 1450 Ala Moana Blvd., Ala Moana* ☎ *808/947–6141* ⊕ *www.hoalasalonspa.com.*

Makiki Heights

Makiki is home to the more unassuming neighborhood where former president Barack Obama grew up. Highlights include the exclusive Punahou School he attended and the notable Central Union Church, as well as the Tantalus area overlook.

Sights

The Liljestrand House
HISTORIC HOME | Art, architecture, and history buffs will enjoy the 90-minute tours of the mid-century modern Liljestrand House. Perched high on Tantalus Drive, with a spectacular view to match, this once-private home was built by famous Hawaii architect Vladimir Ossipoff. You'll learn about his "tropical modernism" building techniques, about the home's local art, and about Betty Liljestrand's dedication to creating the perfect, functional family home in collaboration with

Oahu's Best Shave Ice

Islands-style shave ice (never *shaved ice*—it's a pidgin thing) is said to have been born when neighborhood kids hung around the icehouse, waiting to pounce on the shavings from large blocks of ice, carved with ultrasharp Japanese planes that created an exceptionally fine-textured granita.

In the 1920s, according to the historian for syrup manufacturer Malolo Beverages & Supplies, Chinese vendors developed sweet fruit concentrates to pour over the ice.

The evolution continued with mom-and-pop shops adding their own touches, such as hiding a nugget of Japanese sweet bean paste in the center, placing a small scoop of ice cream at the bottom, and adding *li hing mui* powder (a Chinese seasoning used on preserved fruits).

There's nothing better on a sticky, hot day. Not all of Oahu's best shave ice is in Honolulu, but these two are:

Waiola. This spot is known for its finely shaved ice, wide variety of flavors, and, more recently, its regular appearances in the reboot of *Hawaii Five-0*. In real life, the service is a bit surly, and the prices are slightly higher than elsewhere, but it's close to Waikiki. ⊠ *525 Kapahulu Ave., Kapahulu.*

Uncle Clay's House of Pure Aloha. In a strip mall in the residential neighborhood of Aina Haina, Uncle Clay's (HOPA) is a happy place. It specializes in all-natural syrups, homemade from cane sugar and locally sourced fruits, and even offers a flavor called "kalespin"—a combination of kale and spinach. ⊠ *Aina Haina Shopping Center, 820 W. Hind Dr., Aina Haina (right off Kalanianaole Hwy.)*

Ossipoff. ⊠ *3300 Tantalus Dr., Makiki Heights* ☎ *808/537–3116* ⊕ *www.lil-jestrandhouse.org* ⓢ *$40* ☞ *No children under 10.*

Tantalus and Round Top Drive

SCENIC DRIVE | **FAMILY** | A few minutes and a world away from Waikiki and Honolulu, this scenic drive shaded by vine-draped trees has frequent pullouts with views of Diamond Head and the *ewa* side of Honolulu. It's a nice change of pace from urban life below. At Puu Ualakaa State Wayside (Tantalus), stop to see the sweeping view from Manoa Valley to Honolulu.

To start the drive, go to the Punchbowl cemetery (National Memorial Cemetery of the Pacific), and follow Tantalus Drive uphill. You'll spot wild chickens, darting mongoose (the squirrels of Hawaii), and

maybe the occasional wild boar along the road as you drive. ⊠ *3200 Round Top Dr., Makiki Heights* ⊕ *dlnr.hawaii.gov/dsp/parks/oahu/puu-ualakaa-state-wayside.*

☕ Coffee and Quick Bites

Honolulu Burger Company

$ | **BURGER** | **FAMILY** | Owner Ken Takahashi retired as a nightclub impresario on the Big Island to become a real-life burger king. This modest spot is the home of the locavore burger, made with range-fed beef, Manoa lettuce, tomatoes, and a wide range of toppings, all island-grown—and you can taste the difference. **Known for:** a presence at local farmers' markets or elsewhere in its own food truck; Miso Kutie Burger topped with red miso glaze and Japanese cucumber slices; Blue Hawaii Burger with blue

The Bishop Museum is Hawaii's state historical museum and the repository for the royal artifacts of the last surviving direct descendant of King Kamehameha the Great.

cheese and bacon. $ *Average main: $13* ✉ *1295 S. Beretania St., Makiki Heights* ☎ *808/626–5202* ⊕ *honoluluburgerco. com* ⊗ *Closed Mon.*

Kalihi-Liliha-Kapalama

North of downtown Honolulu, just off H1, is the tightly packed neighborhood of Kalihi. It's home to large industrial pockets but also the stellar Bishop Museum and great local eateries, like Mitsu-Ken.

Liliha-Kapalama (that latter is sometimes referred to as just "Palama") is the sliver of land that runs from ocean to mountain (known as an *ahupuaa* in Hawaiian). It's presided over by famed Kamehameha Schools, which from its hillside perch looks down on a warren of modest homes and shops.

👁 Sights

★ Bishop Museum

SCIENCE MUSEUM | FAMILY | Founded in 1889 by Charles R. Bishop as a memorial to his wife, Princess Bernice Pauahi Bishop, the museum began as a repository for the royal possessions of this last direct descendant of King Kamehameha the Great. Today, it's the state's designated history and culture museum. Its five exhibit halls contain almost 25 million items that tell the history of the Hawaiian Islands and their Pacific neighbors.

Gain understanding of the entire region in the Pacific Hall, and learn about the culture of the Islands through state-of-the-art and often-interactive displays in the Hawaiian Hall. Spectacular artifacts—lustrous feather capes, bone fishhooks, the skeleton of a giant sperm whale, photography and crafts displays, and a well-preserved grass house—are displayed inside a three-story, 19th-century, Victorian-style gallery. The building alone, with its huge turrets and immense stone walls, is worth seeing.

In the 16,500-square-foot science adventure wing, it's hard to miss the three-story simulated volcano where regular "lava melts" take place to the delight of younger (and young at heart) visitors. Also check out the planetarium, daily tours, *lauhala*-weaving and science demonstrations, special exhibits, the Shop Pacifica, and the Bishop Museum Café, which serves *ono* (delicious) Hawaiian food by local restaurant Highway Inn. ⊠ *1525 Bernice St., Kalihi* ☎ *808/847–3511* ⊕ *www. bishopmuseum.org* ⊠ *$25 (parking $5).*

Restaurants

Mitsu-Ken

$ | **HAWAIIAN** | The garlic chicken may haunt your dreams, so it's worth the trek to a downscale neighborhood to find this unprepossessing joint. Line up, order the plate lunch with rice and salad, and sink your teeth into the profoundly garlicky masterpiece drizzled with a sweet glaze. **Known for:** limited hours (just 7 am to noon); delicious breakfast bentos; cash only. ⑤ *Average main: $9* ⊠ *2300 N. King St., Kapalama* ☎ *808/848–5573* ⊕ *instagram.com/mitsukenokazu* ⊟ *No credit cards* ⊗ *Closed Sun.–Tues. No dinner.*

Nuuanu

Immediately *mauka* of Kalihi, off the Pali Highway, are a renowned resting place and a carefully preserved home where royal families retreated during the doldrums of summer. Nuuanu Pali was the sight of a famous battle that was key to King Kamehameha I's success in uniting all the Hawaiian Islands under his rule and becoming the Islands' first monarch. Nuuanu Valley is known for its lush, quiet beauty and has several notable cemeteries, churches, and embassies.

Sights

National Memorial Cemetery of the Pacific

CEMETERY | Nestled in the bowl of Puowaina, or Punchbowl Crater, this 112-acre cemetery is the final resting place for more than 50,000 U.S. war veterans and family members and is a solemn reminder of their sacrifice. Among those buried here is Ernie Pyle, the famed World War II correspondent who was killed by a Japanese sniper on Ie Shima, an island off the northwest coast of Okinawa. Intricate stone maps provide a visual military-history lesson. Puowaina, formed 75,000–100,000 years ago during a period of secondary volcanic activity, translates as "Hill of Sacrifice." Historians believe this site once served as an altar where ancient Hawaiians offered sacrifices to their gods.

■ **TIP→ The entrance to the cemetery has unfettered views of Waikiki and Honolulu—perhaps the finest on Oahu.** ⊠ *2177 Puowaina Dr., Nuuanu* ☎ *808/532–3720* ⊕ *www.cem.va.gov/cems/nchp/nmcp. asp* ⊠ *Free.*

Queen Emma Summer Palace

HISTORIC HOME | Queen Emma, King Kamehameha IV's wife, used this small but stately New England–style home in Nuuanu Valley as a retreat from the rigors of court life in hot and dusty Honolulu during the mid- to late 1800s. Guided tours highlight the residence's royal history and its eclectic mix of European, Victorian, and Hawaiian furnishings, most of which are original to the home. There are excellent examples of feather-covered kahilis, *umeke* (bowls), and koa-wood furniture. Visitors also learn how Queen Emma established what is today the largest private hospital in Hawaii, opened a school for girls, and ran as a widow for the throne, losing to King Kalakaua. A short drive away, you can visit the Royal Mausoleum State Monument, where she, her husband, and their son, Albert, who died at age 4, are buried beside

Greater Honolulu

Sights ▼

1 Bishop Museum **B3**
2 Dolphin Quest at
  The Kahala Hotel & Resort ,,..... **I8**
3 The Liljestrand House **F4**
4 Lyon Arboretum.................... **H3**
5 National Memorial Cemetery
  of the Pacific **D5**
6 Queen Emma Summer Palace **E3**
7 Tantalus and Round Top
  Drive............................... **G3**

Restaurants ▼

1 Chiang Mai Thai Cuisine........... **F6**
2 Hoku's.............................. **J8**
3 Imanas Tei **F6**
4 Izakaya Nonbei **G7**
5 Kapa Hale........................... **I7**
6 Koku Head Cafe.................... **H7**
7 Mitsu-Ken **B3**
8 Mud Hen Water.................... **H7**
9 Sasabune Hawaii................... **E6**
10 The Surfing Pig Hawaii........... **H7**
11 3660 on the Rise.................. **H7**
12 Tokkuri Tei **G7**
13 Waioli Kitchen & Bake Shop **G4**

Quick Bites ▼

1 Fukuya Delicatessen **F6**
2 Honolulu Burger Company **E6**
3 Leonard's Bakery **G7**
4 Waiola Shave Ice.................. **F6**

Hotels ▼

1 The Kahala Hotel & Resort **J8**

Pali Highway

61

Round Top
Forest Reserve

University Ave.

Dole St.

Waialae Ave.

Harding Ave.

Lunalilo Freeway

Pahoa Ave.

Palolo Ave.

10th Ave.

18th Ave.

KAIMUKI

12th Ave.

16th Ave.

Kilauea Ave.

Alohea Ave.

Campbell Ave.

errat Ave.

H1

72

KAHALA

Kahala
Beach

Kahala Ave.

Diamond Head
State Monument

DIAMOND
HEAD

Diamond Head Rd.

BLACK POINT

DIAMOND
HEAD

Diamond Head
Beach

many other Hawaiian royals. Guided tours are offered Tuesday through Saturday by appointment. ✉ *2913 Pali Hwy., Nuuanu* ☎ *808/595–3167* ⊕ *www.daughtersofhawaii.org* ✉ *$14* ⊗ *Closed Sun. and Mon.*

Moiliili

Packed into the neighborhood of Moiliili, about 3 miles from Waikiki, are flower and lei shops, restaurants, and little stores selling Hawaiian and Asian goodies. Most places of interest are along King Street, between Isenberg Street and Waialae Avenue.

Restaurants

Chiang Mai Thai Cuisine
$$ | THAI | Long beloved for its northern Thai classics, such as spicy curries and stir-fries and sticky rice in woven-grass baskets, made using family recipes, Chiang Mai is a short cab ride from Waikiki. Some dishes, like the signature barbecue Cornish game hen with lemongrass and spices, show how acculturation can create interesting pairings. **Known for:** local business-lunch favorite; spring rolls and Chiang Mai wings; limited parking in a small lot in back. ⑤ *Average main: $25* ✉ *2239 S. King St., Moiliili* ☎ *808/941–1151* ⊕ *www.chiangmairestaurant.com* ⊗ *No lunch weekends.*

Imanas Tei
$$$ | JAPANESE | *Nihonjin* (Japanese nationals) and locals flock to this tucked-away, bamboo-ceilinged restaurant for its tasteful, simple decor and equally tasteful—and perfect—sushi, sashimi, *nabe* (hot pots prepared at the table), and grilled dishes. You assemble your meal dish by dish, and the cost can add up if you aren't careful. **Known for:** traditional izakaya experience; simple food that some feel is better than in Japan; long waits. ⑤ *Average main: $30* ✉ *2626 S. King St., Moiliili* ☎ *808/941–2626* ⊕ *imanastei.com* ⊗ *Closed Sun. No lunch.*

Sasabune Hawaii
$$$$ | JAPANESE | Try to get a coveted seat at the counter, and prepare for an unforgettable sushi experience—if you behave, as chef Seiji Kumagawa prefers that diners eat *omakase*-style, letting him sending out his favorite courses (generally two pieces of sushi or six to eight slices of sashimi), each priced individually and each served with instructions ("please, no *shoyu* on this one" or "one piece, one bite"). People who've defied Kumagawa have been kicked out of the restaurant midmeal. **Known for:** no phone calls allowed in the restaurant; one of Honolulu's top sushi spots; fast service. ⑤ *Average main: $150* ✉ *1417 S. King St., Moiliili* ☎ *808/947–3800* ⊕ *sasabuneh.com* ⊗ *Closed Sun. and Mon. Lunch is takeout only.*

☕ Coffee and Quick Bites

Fukuya Delicatessen
$ | JAPANESE | Get a taste of local Japanese culture at this family operation on the main thoroughfare in Moiliili, a mile or so *mauka* out of Waikiki. Open since 1939, the delicatessen offers take-out breakfasts and lunches, Japanese snacks, noodle dishes, and confections—and it's a local favorite for catering, from parties to funeral gatherings. **Known for:** kid-friendly menu; nori-wrapped chicken; mochi tray, offering samples of everything. ⑤ *Average main: $8* ✉ *2710 S. King St., Moiliili* ☎ *808/946–2073* ⊕ *fukuyadeli.com* ⊗ *Closed Mon. and Tues. No dinner.*

🛍 Shopping

Although considered separate from the University of Hawaii's Manoa campus and in need of updating in places, Moiliili has a distinct college-town feel. A look past the tired exteriors reveals a haven of shops that have a loyal community following.

poke, which is everything locals dream about; Japanese food that delivers time and again; salmon skin salad. $ *Average main: $40* ✉ *449 Kapahulu Ave., #201, Kapahulu* ☎ *808/732–6480* ⊕ *www.tokkuritei-hawaii.com* ☯ *No lunch Sun.*

☕ Coffee and Quick Bites

Leonard's Bakery

$ | **BAKERY** | Whether you spell it *malasada* or *malassada,* when you're in Hawaii, you must try these deep-fried, holeless Portuguese doughnuts. Leonard's Bakery is the most famous of all the island establishments making them and was the first island bakery to commercialize their production. **Known for:** small parking lot and long lines; original and various filled malasadas; pão doce (Portuguese sweet bread). $ *Average main: $2* ✉ *933 Kaphalulu Ave., Kapahulu* ☎ *808/737–5591* ⊕ *leonardshawaii.com.*

Waiola Shave Ice

$ | **CAFÉ** | **FAMILY** | Longtime local favorite Waiola Shave Ice, known for its supersoft and powdery shave ice (or snow cone) and wide variety of flavors, became nationally known through regular appearances on the reboot of the *Hawaii Five-0* TV show. It's a fast-moving line, so know your order when you get to the window. **Known for:** slightly brusk service; a large menu allowing for lots of customization; excellent example of a Hawaii classic. $ *Average main: $4* ✉ *3113 Mokihana St., Kapahulu* ☎ *808/949–2269* ⊕ *facebook.com/WaiolaShaveIce.*

🛍 Shopping

Kapahulu, like many older neighborhoods, should not be judged at first glance. It begins at the Diamond Head end of Waikiki and continues up to the H1 freeway and is full of variety; shops and restaurants are located primarily on Kapahulu Avenue.

Take Home a Taste of Oahu

You don't necessarily have to buy a whole pineapple to enjoy Hawaii's fruit flavors back home. Tropical fruit jams are easy to pack and don't spoil. Coffee from Kona or Waialua (right here on Oahu) is another option. There are also dried-food products such as saimin, haupia mixes, and teriyaki barbecue sauce. All kinds of cookies are available, as well as exotic teas, drink mixes, and pancake syrups. And don't forget the macadamia nuts and bottles of locally distilled liquor or handcrafted island beer.

CLOTHING

Bailey's Antiques & Aloha Shirts

ANTIQUES & COLLECTIBLES | Vintage aloha shirts are the specialty at this kitschy store. Prices range from $3.99 to several hundred dollars for the 15,000 shirts in stock. Thousands of them are used; others are creations by top designers. The tight space and musty smell are part of the thrift-shop atmosphere. ■**TIP→** Antiques hunters can also buy old-fashioned postcards, glassware, Hawaiian LPs, authentic military clothing, funky hats, and denim jeans from the 1950s. ✉ *517 Kapahulu Ave., Kapahulu* ☎ *808/734–7628* ⊕ *www.alohashirts.com* ☯ *Closed Sun. and Mon.*

SPORTING GOODS

Island Paddler

SPORTING GOODS | Fashionable beach clothing and bags, bathing suits, hats, and rash guards supplement a huge selection of paddling accessories. ■**TIP→ Check out the wooden decorative paddles: they become works of art when mounted on the wall at home.** ✉ *716 Kapahulu Ave., Kapahulu* ☎ *808/737–4854* ⊕ *www.islandpaddlerhawaii.com.*

The Punchbowl, yet another extinct volcanic crater, is home to the National Memorial Cemetery of the Pacific, the largest military cemetery in Hawaii.

JEWELRY
Maui Divers Design Center

JEWELRY & WATCHES | For a look into the harvesting and design of coral and black pearl jewelry, visit this shop and take a free tour at its adjacent factory near the Ala Moana Shopping Center. ■ **TIP→ Avoid the "Pick a Pearl" option at their other kiosk locations unless you're prepared to be upsold on a jewelry setting or two for the pearls "found" in your shells.** ✉ *1520 Liona St., Moiliili* ☎ *808/946–2929* ⊕ *www.mauidivers.com* ⊘ *Closed Sat. and Sun.*

Kapahulu

Walk just a few minutes from the eastern end of Waikiki, and you'll find yourself in this very local main drag of restaurants, bars, and shops, where Bailey's Antiques and Aloha Shirts is the place for rare, wearable collectibles, and Leonard's Bakery is the place for *malasadas* (Portuguese deep-fried doughnuts rolled in sugar).

Restaurants

Izakaya Nonbei

$$$ | JAPANESE | Teruaki Mori designed this pub, one of the most traditional of Honolulu's izakayas, to make you feel that you're in a northern inn during winter in his native Japan. Dishes not to miss include *aji tataki* (seared, vinegar-marinated jack mackerel topped with ginger); *karei karaage* (delicate deep-fried flounder); fried *gobo* (burdock) chips; and crab, avocado, and bacon salad. **Known for:** long waits (reservations strongly recommended); great happy hour and late-night spot; tiny spot with a huge menu. ⑤ *Average main: $30* ✉ *3108 Olu St., Kapahulu* ☎ *808/734–5573* ⊕ *www.izakayanonbei. com* ⊘ *Closed Mon.*

Tokkuri Tei

$$$$ | JAPANESE | The playful atmosphere at this local favorite belies the quality of the food created by chef Hideaki "Santa" Miyoshi. Best to just say "*omakase, kudasai*" ("chef's choice, please"), and he'll order for you. **Known for:** ahi tartare

Island Triathlon & Bike

SPORTING GOODS | This source for bikes, sports bathing suits, water bottles, and active clothing also rents bicycles and organizes group rides around Honolulu. ✉ *3297 Campbell Ave., Kapahulu* ☎ *808/342–5138* ⊕ *www.itbhawaii.com.*

Snorkel Bob's

SPORTING GOODS | The chain, popular throughout the Islands, sells or rents gear—including fins, snorkels, wet suits, and beach chairs—and schedules ocean activities with other suppliers. It's also a good place to seek advice about the best snorkeling beaches and conditions, which vary considerably with the seasons. ✉ *700 Kapahulu Ave., Kapahulu* ☎ *808/735–7944* ⊕ *snorkelbob.com.*

Kaimuki

Ten minutes beyond Kapahulu, this commercial thoroughfare runs through a neighborhood that, despite ongoing development, still has a good number of cool old Craftsman bungalows. Kaimuki has also become a food mecca, rivaled only by Chinatown, with perhaps Oahu's most diverse concentration of eateries. If you want to discover the island's culinary trends, this is the place to do it.

🍴 Restaurants

★ Koko Head Cafe

$ | **MODERN HAWAIIAN** | When Lee Anne Wong, best known as a competitor on the first season of Bravo's *Top Chef,* moved to the Islands, foodies waited with bated breath for this, her first restaurant. It's a lively yet laid-back café, where she took the concept of breakfast and flipped it, creating innovative dishes like Elvis's Revenge, a peanut butter and banana tempura sandwich with candied bacon, and her signature dumplings, which change daily. **Known for:** crazy busy weekends; cornflake french toast; creative cocktail menu. ⑤ *Average main: $15* ✉ *1145c 12th Ave., Kaimuki* ☎ *808/732–8920* ⊕ *kokoheadcafe.com* ⊘ *No dinner.*

Mud Hen Water

$$ | **HAWAIIAN** | The name of this restaurant is the English translation of *w aialae* (meaning a gathering spot around a watering hole). Renowned chef Ed Kenney explores modern interpretations of the Hawaiian foods he remembers from his childhood with an ever-changing locavore menu. **Known for:** sorbetto and gelato; small plates and snacks; beet poke. ⑤ *Average main: $17* ✉ *3452 Waialae Ave., Kaimuki* ☎ *808/737–6000* ⊕ *www.mudhenwater.com* ⊘ *Closed Mon. Brunch Sun. only.*

The Surfing Pig Hawaii

$$$ | **BARBECUE** | This fancier sibling of the island's four Kono's barbecue spots focuses on Americana-tinged-with-Hawaiian food and drink served in a small, lofted eatery with a surfer-industrial vibe. Heaping portions of juicy smoked and grilled meats are the specialty, but the menu also has several great fish appetizers and entrées. **Known for:** a strong neighborhood brunch option; old-fashioned with bacon-infused bourbon, bacon garnish, and "smoking" cloche presentation; pork, beef, and porchetta slider trio. ⑤ *Average main: $30* ✉ *3605 Waialae Ave., Kaimuki* ☎ *808/744–1992* ⊕ *thesurfingpighawaii.com.*

3660 on the Rise

$$$$ | **MODERN HAWAIIAN** | Named for its address on Honolulu's premier Waialae Avenue, this restaurant brought fresh dining to Kaimuki when it opened in 1992, inspiring a neighborhood dining renaissance. Loyalists swear by the steaks, the crab cakes, and the signature dish, ahi *katsu* wrapped in *nori* (seaweed) and deep-fried, with a wasabi-ginger butter sauce. **Known for:** somewhat dated interior; special-occasion restaurant; good desserts. ⑤ *Average main: $40* ✉ *3660 Waialae Ave., Kaimuki* ☎ *808/737–1177* ⊕ *3660ontherise.com* ⊘ *Closed Mon. No lunch.*

Nightlife

BARS
BREW'd Craft Pub

BREWPUBS | The Kaimuki night scene got a bit livelier in 2014 with the arrival of this pub, which, after all, stays open until 2 am. It's a small place—you have to squeeze between nearby patrons to get to and from your table—but the wait staff is friendly and knowledgeable about the 150-plus beer menu. BREW'd also offers better versions of standard pub fare than you'll find at some places in town, including a good braised beef poutine. ⊠ *3441 Waialae Ave., Suite A, Kaimuki ✛ Corner of 9th and Waialae Aves.* ☎ *808/732–2337* ⊕ *www.brewdcraftpub.com.*

Shopping

FLOWERS AND PLANTS
Kawamoto Orchid Nursery

FLORIST | Kawamoto grows all flowers on its 3½-acre orchid farm near downtown Honolulu. Their specialty is the cattleya, a favorite for Mother's Day, but they also grow hundreds of hybrids. The nursery now does the bulk of its business online, and they have decades of experience shipping temperamental orchids to the Mainland. ⊠ *Kawamoto Orchid Nursery, 2630 Waiomao Rd., Kaimuki* ☎ *808/732–5808* ⊕ *kawamotoorchids.com* ☉ *Closed Sun.*

SPORTING GOODS
Downing Hawaii

SPORTING GOODS | Look for old-style Birdwell surf trunks here, along with popular labels, such as Quiksilver, Roxy, Dakine, and Billabong, which supplement Downing's own line of surf wear and surfboards. ⊠ *3021 Waialae Ave., Kaimuki* ☎ *808/737–9696* ⊕ *www.downingsurf.com* ☉ *Closed Sun.*

Manoa

Manoa is probably best known as the home of the University of Hawaii's main campus. The surrounding area is chock-full of interesting coffee shops, restaurants, and stores supported by the collegiate and professorial crowd. History and beauty linger around verdant Manoa Valley at places like the Manoa Chinese Cemetery, Manoa Falls, and Lyon Arboretum. Manoa Valley Theatre puts on top-notch community productions year-round.

⊙ Sights

Lyon Arboretum

GARDEN | Tucked all the way back in Manoa Valley, this is a gem of an arboretum operated by the University of Hawaii. Hike to a waterfall, or sit and enjoy beautiful views of the valley while having a picnic. You'll also see an ethnobotanical garden, a Hawaiian *hale* (house) and garden, and one of the largest palm collections anywhere—all within a parklike setting. Its educational mission means there are often regular talks and walks, plus classes on lei-making, lauhala weaving, Hawaiian medicinal arts, and more, which you can take for an additional fee. ⊠ *3860 Manoa Rd., Manoa* ☎ *808/988–0456* ⊕ *manoa.hawaii.edu/lyon* ⊠ *Suggested donation of $10* ☉ *Closed Sat. and Sun.* ⚲ *Reservations required.*

🍴 Restaurants

★ **Waioli Kitchen & Bake Shop**

$ | AMERICAN | Dating from 1922, this historic café surrounded by the verdant Manoa Valley landscape is part of the Hawaii Salvation Army headquarters and has been independently operated by Ross and Stefanie Anderson since late 2018. A short menu of simple, delicious breakfast and lunch items are ordered at the counter and delivered to your chosen table, either inside the cozy, multiroom bungalow or on the covered lanai. **Known for:** honey and salt produced on the property and a burgeoning garden; braised short rib loco moco; assorted homemade pastries, scones, muffins, breads, jams, and jellies. $ *Average main: $10* ✉ *Salvation Army Headquarters, 2950 Manoa Rd., Manoa* ☎ *808/744–1619* ⊕ *waiolikitchen.com* ☉ *Closed Mon. and Tues. No dinner.*

🎭 Performing Arts

THEATER
Kennedy Theatre

THEATER | Eclectic programs—everything from Hawaiian language to musical theater to Bollywood—are offered at this space on the Manoa campus of the University of Hawaii. The theater, which opened in 1963, was designed by internationally renowned architect I. M. Pei. ✉ *1770 East-West Rd., Manoa* ☎ *808/956–7655 Box Office* ⊕ *manoa. hawaii.edu/liveonstage.*

Manoa Valley Theatre

THEATER | Wonderful performances grace this intimate community theater in lush Manoa Valley. ✉ *2833 E. Manoa Rd., Manoa* ☎ *808/988–6131* ⊕ *www.manoavalleytheatre.com.*

Kahala

Oahu's wealthiest neighborhood has streets lined with multimillion-dollar homes. Lanes at intervals along tree-lined Kahala Avenue provide public access to Kahala's quiet, narrow coastal beaches offering views of Koko Head. Kahala Mall includes restaurants, a movie theater, and a Whole Foods grocery store. Kahala is also the home of the private Waialae Country Club, where the golf course hosts the Sony Open PGA tournament in January.

⊙ Sights

Dolphin Quest at The Kahala Hotel & Resort

OTHER ATTRACTION | FAMILY | This worldwide dolphin-encounter group has an Oahu location in The Kahala Hotel & Resort, where trained Atlantic bottlenose dolphins hold court in their outdoor lagoon adjacent to the pool area. Activities with the creatures go on throughout the day and can be watched from lanai, walkways, and even some rooms. Programs include kid-specific sessions where children can feed and interact with dolphins, fish, and other aquatic animals, as well as various interactive offerings for teens and adults. ✉ *The Kahala Hotel & Resort, 5000 Kahala Ave., Kahala* ☎ *808/739–8918* ⊕ *dolphinquest.com/oahu-hawaii* ✆ *From $155* ⚠ *Advanced reservations highly recommended.*

🍴 Restaurants

Hoku's

$$$$ | ASIAN FUSION | Everything about Hoku's speaks of quality and sophistication: the wall of windows with their beach views, the avant-garde cutlery and dinnerware, the solicitous staff, and the carefully constructed Euro-Pacific cuisine. The tasting menus frequently change, focusing even more on seasonal cuisine made with fresh, local ingredients (including herbs from the hotel's on-site herb garden). **Known for:** setting and service that can outshine the food; relaxed elegance in the grande dame of Hawaii's social scene; panoramic views from every table. $ *Average main: $110* ✉ *The Kahala Hotel & Resort, 5000 Kahala Ave., Kahala* ☎ *808/739–8760* ⊕ *www.hokuskahala.com* ☉ *No lunch. Tasting or set menus only.*

★ **Kapa Hale**

$$$ | HAWAIIAN | Putting a playful and creative spin on Hawaii regional cuisine, Kapa Hale has elegantly presented, upscale, fusion cuisine and cocktails by a local-boy

chef. Menu items are changed seasonally and sourced locally with fun, wordplay names for different dishes. **Known for:** hip interior; modern local cuisine; creative drink menu. $ *Average main: $30* ✉ *4614 Kilauea Ave., Suite 102, Kahala* ☎ *808/888–2060* ⊕ *www.kapahale.com* ☾ *Closed Mon. Brunch Sat. and Sun. only. No lunch on weekends.*

Hotels

★ The Kahala Hotel & Resort

$$$$ | **RESORT** | **FAMILY** | Hidden away in the upscale residential neighborhood of Kahala (on the other side of Diamond Head from Waikiki), this elegant oceanfront hotel with top-notch service, one of Hawaii's very first luxury resorts, has hosted celebrities, princesses, the Dalai Lama, and nearly every president since Lyndon Johnson. **Pros:** heavenly spa; away from hectic Waikiki; top-notch Hoku's restaurant. **Cons:** small pool; in a residential neighborhood, so not much to do within walking distance of hotel; far from Waikiki. $ *Rooms from: $495* ✉ *5000 Kahala Ave., Kahala* ☎ *808/739–8888, 800/367–2525 toll-free* ⊕ *www.kahalaresort.com* ⤴ *338 rooms* ❈ *No Meals.*

Shopping

Upscale Kahala, near the slopes of Diamond Head and a 10-minute drive from Waikiki, has a shopping mall and some gift stores.

ART GALLERIES
Nohea Gallery

ART GALLERIES | This gallery represents hundreds of artisans who specialize in koa furniture, bowls, and boxes, as well as art glass and ceramics. Original paintings and prints—all with an Islands theme—add to the selection. The store also carries unique handmade Hawaiian jewelry starting under $20 with ti leaf, maile, and coconut-weave designs.

Home items like locally made kitchen towels and Tutu Nene hand-sewn native Hawaiian ducks make great souvenirs. A second Nohea Gallery location is in the Hyatt Regency Waikiki. ✉ *Kahala Mall, 4211 Waialae Ave., Kahala* ☎ *808/762–7407* ⊕ *noheagallery.com.*

SHOPPING CENTERS
Kahala Mall

MALL | **FAMILY** | This indoor mall has more than 100 stores and restaurants, with a mix of national retailers and not-to-be-missed, homegrown boutiques, clothing stores, and galleries. You can also browse local foods and products at Whole Foods. For post-shopping entertainment, see what's playing at the Kahala Theatres, where you'll also find a full kitchen and bar. ✉ *4211 Waialae Ave., Kahala* ☎ *808/732–7736* ⊕ *www.kahalamall-center.com.*

Activities

SPAS
The Kahala Spa

SPAS | Escape the hustle and bustle of metro Honolulu at the elegant yet homey Kahala property favored by celebrities and dignitaries. The two-story spa suites have wooden floors, handmade Hawaiian quilts, Kohler infinity-edged whirlpool tubs, private vanity areas, and private gardens where you can relax with a green tea extract infused with various fruits. Custom treatments merge Hawaiian, Asian, and traditional therapies. Romance packages are also available. ✉ *The Kahala Hotel & Resort, 5000 Kahala Ave., Kahala* ☎ *808/739–8938* ⊕ *www.kahalaresort.com.*

Chapter 4

WEST (LEEWARD) AND CENTRAL OAHU

Updated by
Cheryl Crabtree

4

👁 Sights	🍴 Restaurants	🛏 Hotels	👜 Shopping	🍸 Nightlife
★★★☆☆	★★★☆☆	★★★★★	★★★☆☆	★★★☆☆

WELCOME TO WEST (LEEWARD) AND CENTRAL OAHU

TOP REASONS TO GO

★ **Gorgeous beaches:** From Pokai Bay and surf mecca Makaha to Yokohama Bay, the leeward side of the island affords excellent opportunities to ditch tourist droves and connect with real Hawaiians who live and play along a mostly undeveloped shoreline.

★ **Ko Olina:** A privately owned development on the southwest corner of Oahu, Ko Olina offers the region's best options for dining, nightlife, and golf, as well as one of the island's best luau.

★ **Shopping:** Head to Central Oahu for discounted traditional island souvenirs in premium outlets and big-box stores—where it's easier to find parking.

★ **Blast to the past:** Visit Hawaii's Plantation Village and Dole Pineapple Plantation to learn about Oahu's commercial farming roots.

★ **Oahu's best sunsets:** The west-facing leeward side of the island is an ideal place to watch the sun dip into the Pacific at the end of the day.

Leeward and Central Oahu generally refer to the regions west and north of Pearl Harbor. Heading west from Honolulu, the H1 freeway leads to Oahu's "second city," Kapolei. From there, Farrington Highway continues west and north to the Ko Olina resorts and the Hawaiian communities of Nanakuli and Waianae, and then on to the beach and the end of the road at Keawaula, aka Yokohama Bay. Central Oahu occupies the fertile central valley, home to plantations, farms, military installations, and working-class towns like Wahiawa, as well as predominately residential communities, such as Ewa Beach, Mililani, and Waipio.

Oahu's commercial and residential future is expected to center here in the coming decades, and this area will expand and evolve more than any other region on the island. The central plateau in particular is meant to be a sustainable farming hub to ensure abundant fresh food supplies no matter what happens in the rest of the world.

Phase one of the HART (Honolulu Authority for Rapid Transportation) rail project runs for 10 miles between the Aloha Stadium and Kapolei, with trains making it easier to reach West Oahu attractions.

1 Kapolei. Hawaii's "second city" is a newish development meant to ease the burden of the congested Honolulu area and boost the future of the state.

2 Ko Olina. Protected lagoons and myriad lodging, dining, and activity options attract thousands of visitors to this privately owned community.

3 Waianae. Many native Hawaiians live in and around Waianae, a modest town that anchors the leeward side of the island.

4 Wahiawa. A small but busy town in the heart of Central Oahu, Wahiawa serves as an important center for military personnel and workers at nearby farms and the Dole Plantation.

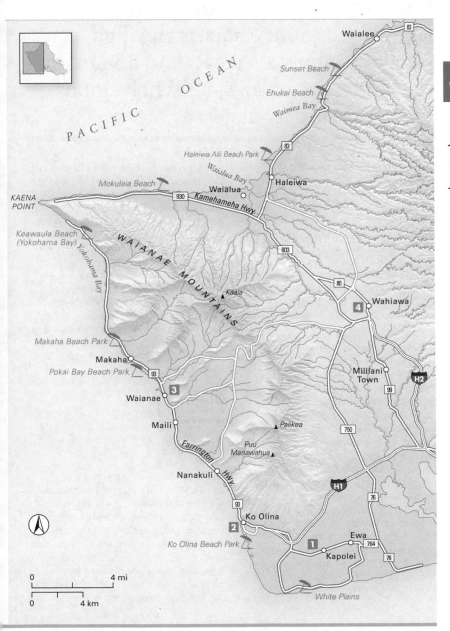

PACIFIC OCEAN

Waialee

Sunset Beach

Ehukai Beach

Waimea Bay

Haleiwa Alii Beach Park

Waialua Bay

Mokuleia Beach

KAENA POINT

Keawaula Beach (Yokohama Bay)

Yokohama Bay

WAIANAE MOUNTAINS

Kaala

Makaha Beach Park

Makaha

Pokai Bay Beach Park

Waianae

Maili

Palikea

Puu Manawahua

Farrington Hwy.

Nanakuli

Ko Olina

Ko Olina Beach Park

White Plains

Kapolei

Ewa

Milifani Town

Wahiawa

Waialua   Kamehameha Hwy.

Haleiwa

930

83

83

803

80

4

H2

99

H1

750

76

76

764

93

93

93

1

2

3

0   4 mi

0   4 km

The rugged Waianae Range of mountains bisects the leeward side of the island from the central plateau. The queen of the range, Mount Kaala, is the highest peak on Oahu (4,003 feet) and dominates the landscape on all sides when clouds fail to obscure its majesty.

The mountains shield the western slopes from trade winds and heavy rain that falls to the north and east. The western side thus appears drier, and its beaches are known for their pristine white sands and crystal clear waters that are excellent for snorkeling and diving. This geography (combined with flows from the western slopes of the parallel eastern Koolau Range) also results in abundant water flows to the fertile central valley plains— where much of Oahu's delectable bounty originates.

The region's eastern portion edges Pearl Harbor and includes the Aloha Stadium, Hawaii's Plantation Village, the Wet 'n' Wild Hawaii water park, and Waikele Premium Outlets near Waipio. Kapolei, Oahu's burgeoning "second city," lies due west of Pearl Harbor. It is a planned community, where, for years, the government has been trying to attract enough jobs to lighten inbound traffic to downtown Honolulu. A major mall and community center, Ka Makana Alii, opened here in 2017 to serve an expected influx of shoppers in the ensuing decades. Ko Oli- na—a lively, privately owned community centered on a golf course, several major resorts, and four man-made lagoons— occupies the island's southwestern tip.

Some locals avoid Leeward and Central Oahu because of traffic that tends to bot- tleneck at the intersection of the H1, H2, and H3 freeways. But those who time their travels to avoid the traffic find great rewards throughout the region, especially the chance to explore the gorgeous and remote west coast beaches, including the far-flung Hawaiian communities of Nanakuli and Waianae and the end of the road at Keawaula, aka Yokohama Bay. A visit to Ko Hana Distillers and a walk through the Dole Plantation's 3-acre maze (the world's largest) near Wahiawa are well worth including in any Central Oahu excursion itinerary.

Planning

Beaches

The North Shore may be known as "country," but the west side is truly the rural area on Oahu. There are commuters from this side to Honolulu, but many are born, live, and die over here with scarcely a trip to town. For the most part, there's little hostility toward outsiders, but occasional problems have flared up— generally on the order of car break-ins, not violence—mostly due to drug abuse, which has ravaged the fringes of the island. In short, lock your car when you stop to take in the breathtaking views, don't bring valuables, and enjoy the amazing beaches.

The beaches on the west side are expansive and empty. Most Oahu residents and tourists don't make it to this side simply because of the drive; in traffic it can take almost 90 minutes to make it to Kaena Point from downtown Honolulu. But you'll be hard-pressed to find a better sunset anywhere.

Getting Here and Around

AIRPORT TRANSFERS
Roberts Hawaii
Roberts Hawaii runs shuttle services from Daniel K. Inouye International Airport to Ko Olina. Fares are $34 each way. ☎ 808/539–9400 ⊕ www.airportshuttle-hawaii.com.

BUS
It might be possible to rely on public transportation if you are staying at one of the Ko Olina hotels. TheBus routes C and 40 run up and down the west side. Route 52 travels from the Ala Moana Center in Honolulu to Wahiawa and Haleiwa on the North Shore; the trip takes about 1¼ hours to Wahiawa and about 1½ hours to Haleiwa.

CAR
It's relatively easy to get to West Oahu, which begins at folksy Waipahu and continues past Makakilo and Kapolei on H1 and Highway 93, Farrington Highway. It takes about a half hour to reach Ko Olina from Waikiki, but rush hour traffic can create delays.

A couple of cautions as you head to the leeward side: Highway 93 is a narrow, winding, two-lane road, notorious for accidents. There's an abrupt transition from an expansive freeway to a two-lane highway at Kapolei, and by the time you reach Nanakuli, it's a country road, so

slow down. Also be aware of congestion between Ko Olina and Waianae during commuter hours.

TAXI
If you don't rent a car, rideshares like Uber or Lyft are the most popular option in the region between Honolulu and Ko Olina. Roberts Hawaii also offers transportation to Waikele Premium Outlets and to Ko Olina.

Hotels

The full-service Ko Olina resorts and vacation rentals are your best options in this area, which doesn't have many short-term accommodations at all apart from basic motels. But be sure to factor in the hefty parking and resort fees when comparing with lodgings elsewhere on the island.

PRICES
Hotel prices are the lowest cost of a standard double room in high season. Hotel reviews have been shortened. For full information, visit Fodors.com.

What It Costs in U.S. Dollars			
$	$$	$$$	$$$$
FOR TWO PEOPLE			
under $180	$180–$260	$261–$340	over $340

Restaurants

Dining opportunities abound at the Four Seasons Resort Oahu, Aulani, and Marriott's Beach Vacation Club within the Ko Olina community. The fear of traffic congestion on the freeways prevents some locals and visitors from driving here for dinner, but many come for lunch and happy hours, as well as to mark special occasions with a fancy meal and west-side sunset experience.

PRICES

Restaurant prices are the average cost of a main course at dinner or, if dinner is not served, at lunch. Restaurant reviews have been shortened. For full information, visit Fodors.com.

What It Costs in U.S. Dollars			
$	$$	$$$	$$$$
AT DINNER			
under $17	$17–$26	$27–$35	over $35

Safety

Car break-ins and beach thefts are common on the leeward side, so keep all your belongings in sight, and never leave anything in your car.

Kapolei

22 miles west of downtown Honolulu.

The planned community of Kapolei, where, for years, the government has been trying to attract enough jobs to lighten inbound traffic to downtown Honolulu, is often called Oahu's "second city." It occupies much of 1800s business mogul James Campbell's 41,000-acre Ewa plain estate, which once cultivated vast tracts of sugarcane and pineapple.

The first phases broke ground starting in the 1980s. Today, it is a thriving community with government centers, industrial parks, big-box malls, businesses small and large, and the West Oahu campus of the University of Hawaii. The Ko Olina complex to the west is officially part of the district and has a Kapolei zip code.

GETTING HERE AND AROUND

From downtown Honolulu, you can get to Kapolei in 30 minutes by car. Note, though, that traffic can double or triple the driving time.

When the HART (Honolulu Authority for Rapid Transportation) trains begin to run in late 2022, riders will be able to travel between the Aloha Stadium and East Kapolei, about a 42-minute trip, including stops. Four stations include park-and-ride lots.

 Sights

Hawaii's Plantation Village

HISTORY MUSEUM | **FAMILY** | Starting in the 1800s, immigrants seeking work on the sugar plantations came to the Islands like so many waves against the shore. At this museum 30 minutes from downtown Honolulu (without traffic), visit authentically furnished buildings, original and replicated, that re-create and pay tribute to the plantation era. See a Chinese social hall; a Japanese shrine, sumo ring, and saimin stand; a dental office; and historic homes. The village is open for guided tours only. ⊠ *Waipahu Cultural Gardens Park, 94-695 Waipahu St., Waipahu* ☎ *808/677–0110* ⊕ *hawaiiplantationvillage.org* ⊠ *$15* ☾ *Closed Sun.*

 Beaches

★ White Plains Beach

BEACH | **FAMILY** | Concealed from the public eye for many years as part of the former Barbers Point Naval Air Station, this beach is reminiscent of Waikiki but without the condos and the crowds. It is a long, sloping stretch with numerous surf breaks, but it is also mild enough at the shore for older children to play freely. It has views of Pearl Harbor and, over that, Diamond Head. Although the sand lives up to its name, the real impact of this beach comes from its history as part of a military property for the better part of a century. Expansive parking, great restroom facilities, and numerous tree-covered barbecue areas make it a great day-trip spot. As a bonus, a Hawaiian monk seal takes up residence here several months out of the year (seals are rare in the Islands). **Amenities:** lifeguards; parking (no fee); showers; toilets. **Best for:** surfing; swimming. ⊠ *Essex Rd. and Tripoli Rd., Kapolei* ⊕ *Take Makakilo Exit off H1 West, then turn left. Follow it into base gates, make left. Blue signs lead to beach.*

🛍 Shopping

SHOPPING CENTERS

Aloha Stadium Swap Meet & Marketplace

MARKET | This thrice-weekly outdoor bazaar attracts hundreds of vendors and even more bargain hunters. Every Hawaiian souvenir imaginable can be found here, from coral shell necklaces to bikinis, as well as a variety of ethnic wares, from Chinese brocaded dresses to Japanese pottery. There are also ethnic foods, silk flowers, and luggage in aloha floral prints. That said, be prepared to wade through the usual sprinkling of used and counterfeit goods to find value. Wear comfortable shoes, use sunscreen, and bring bottled water. The flea market takes place in the Aloha Stadium parking lot Wednesday and Saturday 8–3 and Sunday 6:30–3. Admission is $1 per person ages 12 and up.

You can take either Uber or Lyft from your hotel. You might also ask your hotel concierge about shared shuttle services. For a cheaper but slower ride, take TheBus. The new Honolulu Rail trains will connect the Aloha Stadium with Kapolei when they start running (currently scheduled for late 2022). So you could shop at the swap meet and hop on the train to Ka Makana Alii to

treasure-hunt even longer—all without a car! ⊠ *Aloha Stadium, 99-500 Salt Lake Blvd., Aiea* ☎ *808/486–6704* ⊕ *alohastadium.hawaii.gov/aloha-stadium-swap-meet-marketplace.*

Ka Makana Alii — The Center for West Oahu

MALL | This mall lures patrons with easy access from the H1 freeway, abundant free parking, and several island ware–focused stores, including Noeau, with an array of locally designed, handcrafted items. The adjacent Honolulu Rail station is scheduled to open in late 2022. ⊠ *91-5431 Kapolei Pkwy., Kapolei* ☎ *808/628–4800* ⊕ *www.kamakanaalii.com.*

Waikele Premium Outlets

MALL | Armani Exchange, Calvin Klein, Coach, and Saks Fifth Avenue outlets anchor this discount destination of around 50 stores. ⊠ *94-790 Lumiaina St., Waipahu* ☎ *808/676–5656* ⊕ *www.premiumoutlets.com/outlet/waikele.*

Ko Olina

5 miles west of Kapolei, 25 miles west of downtown Honolulu.

For centuries, Hawaiian nobility rejuvenated at this pristine enclave on the island's southwestern edge. Today, Ko Olina is a major visitor hub, part of a decades-long master plan to attract jobs to the leeward side. The privately owned, 642-acre complex is a community unto itself, with one guarded public entrance/exit off Farrington Highway. It includes a golf course, three natural lagoons, a series of four man-made lagoons, three major resorts (each with a range of restaurants, shops, and activities), 4½ miles of walking paths, and a shopping area with additional restaurants and cafés. It's also home to the famed Paradise Cove Luau.

West (Leeward) and Central Oahu

PACIFIC OCEAN

KAENA POINT

Yokohama Bay

WAIANAE MOUNTAINS

Kaala

Makaha Valley

Makaha Beach Park
Papaoneone Beach
Makaha
Pokai Bay Beach Park
Waianae

Maili

Farrington Hwy.

Nanakuli

Kahe Point Beach Park
(Electric Beach)
Kahe

Ko Olina Beach
Ko Olina

Kapolei

Palikea

Puu Manawahua

Kunia Camp

Mililani Town

Wahiawa

Waipahu

Ewa

Ewa Beach

White Plains Beach

Waialee
Sunset Beach
Sunset Beach
Ehukai Beach
Waimea Bay
Haleiwa Alii Beach Park
Waialua Bay
Haleiwa
Mokuleia Beach
Waialua
Kamehameha Hwy.

0   4 mi
0   4 km

KEY
1 Exploring Sights
1 Restaurants
1 Hotels

Sights ▼
1 Dole Plantation............ **E3**
2 Hawaii's
    Plantation Village **E6**
3 Kahumana Farm **C5**
4 Ko Hana Distillers....... **D5**
5 Kukaniloko Birthstones
    State Monument......... **E4**
6 Wet 'n' Wild Hawaii **D7**

Restaurants ▼
1 The Beach House
    by 604 .... **B5**
2 Coquito's
    Latin Cuisine............. **B5**
3 Countryside Cafe **B5**
4 Makahiki—The Bounty
    of the Islands............. **C7**
5 Mina's Fish House **C7**
6 Monkeypod by
    Merriman Ko Olina **C7**
7 Noe........................ **C7**
8 Roy's Ko Olina **C7**

Hotels ▼
1 Aulani, A Disney Resort
    & Spa...................... **C7**
2 Four Seasons Resort
    Oahu at Ko Olina......... **C7**
3 Marriott's Ko Olina
    Beach Club **C7**

The Lanikuhonua Nature Preserve, with its pristine beach, edges the north end of the complex. The shoreline is public, but most of the 11-acre site belongs to the Lanikuhonua Cultural Institute, a nonprofit that preserves and promotes Hawaiian culture.

The lagoons are open to the public, but public parking is limited (first-come, first-served, sunrise to sunset). Come before 10 am to nab one of the prized spots. If you do manage to find a space, plan to walk at least a short bit to the lagoons along public access paths. Even resort guests pay hefty fees to park on site.

GETTING HERE AND AROUND
You can get to Ko Olina in 45 minutes from downtown Honolulu by car unless traffic is heavy, in which case it might take well over an hour.

Sights

Wet 'n' Wild Hawaii
WATER PARK | FAMILY | This 29-acre family attraction has waterslides, water cannons, and waterfalls. ⊠ *400 Farrington Hwy., Ko Olina* ✛ *Off H1 at Exit 1* ☎ *808/674–9283* ⊕ *www.wetnwildhawaii. com* 🎫 *$60, parking $10 per car.*

Beaches

Kahe Point Beach Park (Electric Beach)
BEACH | Directly across from the electricity plant—hence the name—Electric Beach (also known as Kahe Point) is a haven for tropical fish, making it a great snorkeling spot. The expulsion of hot water from the plant raises the temperature of the ocean, attracting Hawaiian green sea turtles, spotted moray eels, and spinner dolphins. Although the visibility is not always the best, the crowds are often small (though growing), and the fish are guaranteed. It's best to wear reef shoes here because of the sharp rocks.

Unfortunately, there can be a strong current, so it's not very kid-friendly. This is also a great place to stop for a picnic and admire the views. **Amenities:** parking (no fee); showers; toilets. **Best for:** snorkeling; sunset. ⊠ *Farrington Hwy., Ko Olina* ✛ *1 mile west of Ko Olina Resort.*

★ **Ko Olina Beach**
BEACH | FAMILY | This is the best spot on the island if you have small kids. The resort area commissioned a series of four man-made lagoons, but, as it has to provide public beach access, you are the winner. Huge rock walls protect the lagoons, making them perfect spots for the kids to get their first taste of the ocean without getting bowled over. The large expanses of seashore grass and hala trees that surround the semicircle beaches are made-to-order for nap time. A 1½-mile jogging track connects the lagoons. Due to its appeal for *keiki* (children), Ko Olina is popular, and the parking lot fills up quickly when school is out and on weekends, so try to get here before 10 am. The biggest parking lot is at the farthest lagoon from the entrance. There are actually three resorts here: Aulani (the Disney resort), Four Seasons Resort Oahu, and the Marriot's Ko Olina Beach Club (which has a time-share section as well). **Amenities:** food and drink; parking (no fee); showers; toilets. **Best for:** sunset; swimming; walking. ⊠ *92 Aliinui Dr., 23 miles west of Honolulu, Ko Olina* ✛ *Take Ko Olina exit off H1 West and proceed to guard shack.*

🍴 Restaurants

Makahiki — The Bounty of the Islands
$$$$ | HAWAIIAN | FAMILY | The buffet restaurant at Disney's Aulani resort offers a wide variety of locally produced items, as well as familiar dishes from stateside and the rest of the world. You'll find sustainable Hawaiian seafood, Asian selections, familiar grilled meats and

Ko Olina, a planned resort community on the island's southwestern shore, is the biggest tourist area on Leeward Oahu.

vegetables, and a kids' menu; an à la carte menu is also available. ■TIP→ Arrive early for dinner and have a drink at the adjacent Olelo Room, where the staff are fluent in Hawaiian; you can get a language lesson along with your libation. **Known for:** popular Disney character breakfasts (which book up weeks in advance); true reflection of Hawaii; wide array of food to please every member of the family. ⑤ *Average main: $65* ✉ *Aulani, a Disney Resort & Spa, 92-1185 Aliinui Dr., Ko Olina* ☎ *808/674–6200* ⊕ *www.disneyaulani. com/dining/table-service/makahiki-buffet* ⊘ *No lunch.*

★ Mina's Fish House

$$$$ | SEAFOOD | Michael Mina, a James Beard Award winner, designed an exceptional line-to-table menu that celebrates the local catch and matches the panoramic views from indoor and lanai oceanfront tables. This might be the only restaurant in Hawaii (or the world) to have an on-site "fish sommelier," who guides you through the mind-boggling array of cooking techniques, flavorings, and portions—from fillet to whole fish— and helps you choose the best matches for your particular palate. **Known for:** daily happy hour; charbroiled Hawaiian seafood tower; Kona lobster dishes. ⑤ *Average main: $51* ✉ *Four Seasons Oahu Ko Olina Resort, 92-1001 Olani St., Ko Olina* ☎ *808/679–0079* ⊕ *www.michaelmina. net* ⊘ *No lunch weekdays.*

Monkeypod by Merriman Ko Olina

$$$ | HAWAIIAN | Local farm-to-table guru Peter Merriman is known throughout Hawaii for his inventive and popular restaurants, and this one captures his creativity and locally inspired food mantra perfectly. Local slack-key guitar music and the gentle buzz of diners kicking back make this a nice stop for a leisurely lunch—that could easily slide into happy hour. **Known for:** life-changing strawberry cream pie; lobster deviled eggs and fresh fish tacos; indoor–outdoor setting.

$ Average main: $28 ⊠ Ko Olina Resort, 92-1048 Olani St., Ko Olina ☎ 808/380–4086 ⊕ www.monkeypodkitchen.com.

Noe

$$$$ | **ITALIAN** | Classic dishes from southern Italy's Amalfi Coast dominate the menu at this sleek Four Seasons restaurant, with seating indoors, in various intimate and more social spaces, and outdoors overlooking a nature preserve. Locals come to celebrate special occasions, while guests from throughout the Ko Olina community come to feast on homemade pastas—especially the signature tagliatelle with truffle pesto and mushrooms—and multiple dishes that showcase Kona lobster. **Known for:** weekend brunch; four-course tasting menu; extensive Italian wine list. $ Average main: $49 ⊠ Four Seasons Oahu at Ko Olina, 92-1001 Olani St., Ko Olina ☎ 808/679–3347 ⊕ www.fourseasons.com/oahu/dining/restaurants/noe ⊗ No lunch weekdays.

Roy's Ko Olina

$$$$ | **HAWAIIAN** | The Ko Olina outpost of Roy's famed restaurant chain overlooks the 18th hole of the Ko Olina Golf Course and reflects a distinct west-side vibe, as most of the friendly staff come from this side of the island and exude an authentic "aloha" spirit. Dine on Roy's Hawaii-Asia-Europe fusion signature dishes and the chef's west side–influenced creations out on the patio or in the iconic wood-beam-and-concrete interior. **Known for:** scenic golf course views; braised short ribs and other Roy's signature dishes; great getaway from Ko Olina resort crowds. $ Average main: $44 ⊠ Ko Olina Golf Club, 92-1220 Aliinui Dr., Kapolei ☎ 808/676–7697 ⊕ www.royyamaguchi.com.

Hotels

★ Aulani, A Disney Resort & Spa

$$$$ | **RESORT** | **FAMILY** | Disney's first property in Hawaii melds the Disney magic with breathtaking vistas, white sandy beaches, and sunsets that even Mickey stops to watch. **Pros:** Painted Sky: HI Style Studio makeovers for kids; tons to do on-site; family-friendly done right. **Cons:** areas and events can get really busy; Disney character breakfasts require advance reservation (book far in advance); a long way from Waikiki. $ Rooms from: $549 ⊠ 92-1185 Aliinui Dr., Kapolei ☎ 714/520–7001, 808/674–6200, 866/443–4763 ⊕ www.disneyaulani.com ⇌ 832 rooms ⏐O⏐ No Meals.

★ Four Seasons Resort Oahu at Ko Olina

$$$$ | **RESORT** | At the first Four Seasons on the island, nearly every room or suite in the 17-story hotel offers floor-to-ceiling windows and a private lanai, all with an ocean view. **Pros:** luxurious and exclusive; secluded, even in the Ko Olina complex; amenities and options abound. **Cons:** luxury doesn't come cheap; it doesn't always measure up to other Four Seasons; an hour from Waikiki. $ Rooms from: $775 ⊠ 92-1001 Olani St., in the Ko Olina complex, Ko Olina ☎ 808/679–0079, 844/387–0308 ⊕ www.fourseasons.com/oahu ⇌ 371 rooms ⏐O⏐ No Meals.

Marriott's Ko Olina Beach Club

$$$$ | **RESORT** | **FAMILY** | Though primarily a time-share property, the Marriott here also offers nightly rentals, which range from hotel-style standard guest rooms to expansive and elegantly appointed one- or two-bedroom guest villa apartments, all within Ko Olina's 642-acre gated community. **Pros:** resort area offers entertainment, shopping, and dining options beyond the property; suites are beautifully decorated and have ample space for families; nice views. **Cons:** the

coast beyond Ko Olina is rural without a lot for visitors to do; rooms and suites vary, so ask when booking; an hour to Honolulu and Waikiki. $ *Rooms from: $660* ✉ *92-161 Waipahe Pl., Ko Olina* ☎ *808/679–4700, 800/845–5279* ⊕ *www. marriott.com* ⤸ *544 units* ❘❍❘ *No Meals.*

Performing Arts

Paradise Cove Luau

FOLK/TRADITIONAL DANCE | FAMILY | At one of the largest events on Oahu, you can stroll, drink in hand, through an authentic village, learn traditional arts and crafts, and play local games. The lively stage show includes a fire-knife dancer, singing emcee, and both traditional and contemporary hula and other Polynesian dances. A finale dance features participation from the audience. Admission includes the buffet, activities, and the show. You pay extra for table service, box seating, and shuttle transport to and from Waikiki—the stunning sunsets are free. It starts daily at 5. ✉ *92-1089 Alii Nui Dr., Ko Olina* ☎ *808/842–5911* ⊕ *www.paradisecove. com* ⤸ *$125.*

⚡ Activities

SPAS

Laniwai — A Disney Spa

SPAS | At this spa, every staff member—or "cast member," as they call themselves—is extensively trained in Hawaiian culture and history to ensure they are projecting the right *mana,* or energy, in their work. To begin each treatment, you select a special *pohaku* (lava rock) with words of intent, then cast it into a reflective pool. Choose from about 150 spa therapies, and indulge in Kula Wai, the only outdoor hydrotherapy garden on Oahu—with private vitality pools, a reflexology path, six different "rain" showers, whirlpool jet spas, and more. ✉ *Aulani, A Disney Resort & Spa, 92-1185 Aliinui Dr., Ko Olina* ☎ *808/674–6300* ⊕ *www. disneyaulani.com/spa-fitness/.*

Waianae

9 miles north of Ko Olina.

Waianae refers to both the town and the western (leeward) shores of Oahu, from Ko Olina up to Yokohama Bay and the end of the road near Kaena Point. It's mostly rural, without tourist traps and few restaurants apart from fast-food outlets, tiny cafés, and hole-in-the-wall poke shacks. Still, the Waianae coast is well worth a day trip, mostly to experience an area where "real" Hawaiians, descendants of natives who populated the coast centuries before the *haoles* arrived, live and play. The beaches boast crystal clear water. Turtles and dolphins swim near the shores, and when surf's up, Oahu's finest shredders show up to have fun and wow the watchers on the sand.

GETTING HERE AND AROUND

Waianae is about 15 or 20 minutes north of Ko Olina by car along Highway 93.

Sights

Kahumana Farm

FARM/RANCH | FAMILY | Stop by one of the largest organic farms on Oahu to learn about Hawaii's natural and cultural environment from dedicated community members. Tours of the 31-acre property, tucked between mountains in the scenic Lualualei Valley, take place on Thursday at 4:30 and include exotic-fruit tastings, farm-animal feedings, and crop harvesting. If you can't join a tour, try to pick up local merchandise at the gift shop, whose proceeds benefit the nonprofit organization's programs that serve unhoused families, people with disabilities, and food-challenged youth. ✉ *86-660 Lualualei Homestead Rd., Waianae* ☎ *808/696–2655* ⊕ *www.kahumana. org* ⤸ *Farm tours $40* ⚓ *Reservations essential.*

In the summer, when the surf is calm, Makaha is a great snorkeling destination; in the winter, it's a popular surfing spot, especially for locals.

Beaches

Makaha Beach Park

BEACH | FAMILY | This beach provides a slice of local life that most visitors don't see. Families string up tarps for the day, fire up hibachis, set up lawn chairs, get out the fishing gear, and strum ukulele while they "talk story" (chat). Legendary waterman Buffalo Keaulana can be found in the shade of the palms playing with his grandkids and spinning yarns of yesteryear. In these waters, Buffalo not only invented some of the most outrageous methods of surfing, but also raised his world-champion son, Rusty. He also made Makaha the home of the world's first international surf meet in 1954, and it still hosts his Big Board Surfing Classic. With its long, slow-building waves, it's a great spot to try out longboarding. The swimming is generally decent in summer, but avoid the big winter waves. The only parking is along the highway, but

it's free. **Amenities:** lifeguards; showers; toilets. **Best for:** surfing; swimming. ⊠ *84-450 Farrington Hwy., Waianae* ✛ *Go 32 miles west of Honolulu on the H1, then exit onto Farrington Hwy. The beach will be on your left.*

Papaoneone Beach

BEACH | You may have to do a little exploring to find Papaoneone Beach, which is tucked behind three condos. Park on the street, and then duck through an easy-to-spot hole in the fence to reach this extremely wide, sloping beach that always seems to be empty. The waters are that eerie blue found only on the west side. Waves can get high here (it faces the same direction as the famed Makaha Beach), but, for the most part, the shore break makes for great easy rides on your bodyboard or belly. The only downside is that, with the exception of a shower, all facilities are for the condos at the adjacent Beach Lovers Hawaii, so it's just you and the big blue. **Amenities:** showers. **Best for:** solitude; swimming. ✉ *84-946 Farrington Hwy., Waianae* ✛ *In Makaha, across from Jade St.*

Pokai Bay Beach Park

BEACH | FAMILY | This gorgeous swimming and snorkeling beach is protected by a long breakwater left over from a now-defunct boat harbor. The entire length is sand, and a reef creates smallish waves perfect for novice surfers. **Amenities:** parking (no fee); showers; toilets. **Best for:** snorkeling; swimming. ✉ *85-027 Waianae Valley Rd., Waianae* ✛ *Off Farrington Hwy.*

Yokohama Bay

BEACH | FAMILY | You'll be one of the few outsiders at this Waianae coast beach at the very end of the road. If it weren't for the little strip of paved road, it would feel like a deserted isle: no stores, no houses, just a huge sloping stretch of beach and some of the darkest-blue water off the island. Locals come here to fish and swim in waters calm enough for children in summer. Early morning brings with it spinner dolphins by the dozens just offshore. Although Makua Beach up the road is the best spot to see these animals, it's not nearly as beautiful and sandy as "Yokes." **Amenities:** lifeguards; parking (no fee); showers; toilets. **Best for:** solitude; sunset; swimming. ✉ *81-780 Farrington Hwy., Waianae* ✛ *About 7 miles north of Makaha.*

Restaurants

The Beach House by 604

$$ | HAWAIIAN | Housed in a former officer's dining hall right on the west-facing beach at Pokai Bay, the hip, casual, younger sibling of Pearl Harbor's Restaurant 604 is a great place to stop for a bite before or after a surf session at Makaha or a day trip up the west side to Yokohama Bay. The island-inspired menu focuses on comfort foods and includes everything from poke, burgers, fries, and pizza to traditional island plates with fish and rice. **Known for:** live music Thursday–Sunday; excellent sunset-viewing spot; lively happy hour. $ *Average main: $22* ✉ *85-010 Army St., Waianae* ☎ *808/725-2589* ⊕ *www.beachhouse604.com.*

Coquito's Latin Cuisine

$$ | LATIN AMERICAN | A humble, family-run restaurant in a tiny roadside shack, Coquito's serves an eclectic array of traditional Puerto Rican and Latin American dishes, from *arroz con gandules* (rice with peas) and shrimp mofongo to *pastel borricúa* (ground green-banana masa stuffed with pork), Colombian empanadas, and Argentinian flank steak with chimichurri sauce. Order takeout for a picnic at a beach park, or dine in the small outdoor patio (no alcohol sold here, so you need to BYOB). **Known for:** Cuban sandwiches; various desserts, including tres leches cake and Puerto Rican flancocho, flan de coco, and tembleque; nearly everything prepared in-house. $ *Average main: $18* ✉ *85-773 Farrington Hwy., Waianae* ☎ *808/888-4082* ⊕ *www.facebook.com/coquitoslatincuisinerest* ☽ *Closed Sun. and Mon.*

Countryside Cafe

$ | HAWAIIAN | FAMILY | Escape the tourist traps and rub elbows with locals at this small, busy breakfast–brunch café, with outdoor porch seating and ocean views (come early or order takeout, as it closes early afternoon). Island favorites dominate the menu, including corned beef hash *loco moco* and *lilikoi* (passionfruit) pancakes for breakfast and garlic shrimp with mushrooms, fish tacos, and *kalbi* ribs for lunch. **Known for:** friendly service; island-style eggs Benedict, pancakes, and French toast; fresh ingredients, large portions. $ *Average main: $15* ✉ *87-70 Farrington Hwy. #104, Waianae* ☎ *808/888-5448* ⊕ *www.countrysidecafe808.net.*

Wahiawa

Approximately 20 miles northeast of Ko Olina, 20 miles north of downtown Honolulu.

Oahu's central plain is a patchwork of old towns and new residential developments, military bases, farms, ranches, and shopping malls, with a few noteworthy attractions and historic sites scattered about. Central Oahu encompasses the Moanalua Valley, residential Pearl City and Mililani, and the old plantation town of Wahiawa, on the uplands halfway to the North Shore.

James Dole first planted pineapples in the central plateau in the early 1900s, and the Dole Pineapple Plantation fields still border the northern limits of Wahiawa, a small town with a heavy military and working-class vibe. Lake Wilson (Wahiawa Reservoir) surrounds three sides of the town, and Highway 99 crosses two bridges (and several stoplights) to pass through.

Wahiawa is the commercial hub for several military bases, including Schofield Barracks, Wheeler Army Airfield, and the U.S. Naval Computer and Telecommunications Area Master Station Pacific. The main drag—a five-block stretch of Highway 99 where traffic often slows to a snail's pace—was once a fast-food mecca but in recent years has given birth to a handful of decent cafés and restaurants.

GETTING HERE AND AROUND

For Central Oahu, all sights are most easily reached by either the H1 or the H2 freeway. Highway 99 goes through Schofield Barracks. Highway 80 goes through the town of Wahiawa.

Sights

Dole Plantation

COLLEGE | FAMILY | Pineapple plantation days are nearly defunct in Hawaii, but you can still celebrate the state's famous golden fruit at this promotional center with exhibits, a huge gift shop, a snack concession, educational displays, and one of the world's largest mazes. Take the self-guided Garden Tour, or hop aboard the Pineapple Express for a 20-minute train tour to learn a bit about life on a pineapple plantation. Kids love the more than 3-acre Pineapple Garden Maze, made up of 14,000 tropical plants and trees. If you do nothing else, stop by the cafeteria in the back for a delicious pineapple soft-serve Dole Whip. This is about a 40-minute drive from Waikiki, a suitable stop on the way to or from the North Shore. ⊠ *64-1550 Kamehameha Hwy., Wahiawa* ☎ *808/621–8408* ⊕ *www. doleplantation.com* ✉ *Plantation free, Pineapple Express $12, maze $9, garden tour $8.*

★ Ko Hana Distillers

DISTILLERY | Polynesians brought sugarcane to Hawaii more than 1,000 years ago, long before plantations were established on the Islands in the 1800s. Ko Hana grows 34 varieties of heirloom sugarcane and harvests it all by hand, then presses and distills the juice to make small-batch pure-cane rums. Stop by the tasting room at the farm in rural Kunia near Wahiawa, in the heart of the central valley for tastings. Standouts include Koho, a barrel-aged rum, and Kokoleka, made with pure cacao and raw honey. Sign up in advance for tours, which happen daily every hour until 4 pm and include a side-by-side tasting of white and barrel-aged rums. For a more in-depth experience, reserve a spot on a farm tour (Thursday morning at 10) and sample canes as well as rums. ⊠ *92-1770*

Kunia Rd., Kunia ☎ *808/649–0830*
⊕ *www.kohanarum.com/home* ✉ *Tasting*
$10, tour and tasting $25, farm tours $45.

Kukaniloko Birthstones State Monument
HISTORIC SIGHT | In the cool uplands of
Wahiawa is haunting Kukaniloko, where
noble chieftesses went to give birth to
high-ranking children. One of the most
significant cultural sites on the island, the
lava-rock stones here were believed to
possess the power to ease labor pains.
The site is marked by approximately 180
stones covering about a half acre. It's a
40- to 45-minute drive from Waikiki. ⊠ *Ka-*
mehameha Hwy. and Whitmore Ave.,
Wahiawa ✛ *The north side of Wahiawa*
town.

Chapter 5

NORTH SHORE

Updated by
Cheryl Crabtree

👁 Sights	🍴 Restaurants	🛏 Hotels	🛍 Shopping	🍸 Nightlife
★★★★★	★★★☆☆	★★★★☆	★★★☆☆	★☆☆☆☆

WELCOME TO NORTH SHORE

TOP REASONS TO GO

★ **Scenes of old Hawaii:** The wild, relatively undeveloped North Shore looks and feels more like the Oahu that existed centuries ago. Walk along bluff top and valley trails to discover ancient sites, and swim and fish in the crystal clear waters that sustained ancient communities.

★ **Farm-fresh bounty:** Oahu natives refer to the North Shore as the "country"—the source of much of the island's produce and seafood.

★ **World-famous beaches and waves:** Banzai Pipeline, Sunset Beach, Waimea Bay—in winter they are the hallowed waters of surfing's greatest breaks. In summer, the glorious beaches provide the perfect setting for snorkeling and marine wildlife spotting.

★ **Laid-back vibe:** The North Shore is the antithesis of Waikiki. You won't find any high-rises or freeways here; outside of touristy Haleiwa, it's just miles of scenic coastline and country roads.

The main North Shore towns include Haleiwa (the hub), neighboring Waialua, Pupukea (just north of Waimea Bay), and the Kahuku district, which stretches from Kawela Bay and Kuilima/ Turtle Bay to the small town of Kahuku.

1 Waialua. Life here once revolved around a sugar mill, but now it's a tranquil, mostly residential community that anchors the remote, uncrowded northwestern stretches of Oahu.

2 Haleiwa. The North Shore's touristy commercial hub reflects an early 1900s plantation-era vibe.

3 Pupukea. This is global surf culture's center of the universe, in the heart of a 7-mile stretch of the world's best breaks.

4 Kahuku. The easternmost North Shore district is home to legendary Turtle Bay Resort, famed shrimp shacks, and family-owned farms.

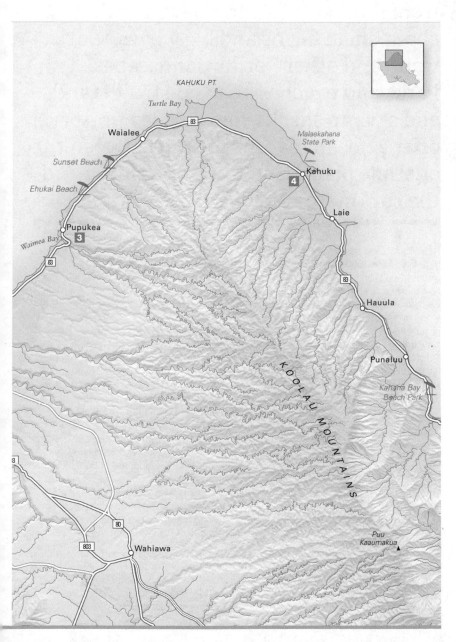

KAHUKU PT.

Turtle Bay

Waialee

Sunset Beach

Ehukai Beach

Pupukea
3

Waimea Bay

83

83

Malaekahana
State Park

Kahuku
4

Laie

83

Hauula

Punaluu

Kahana Bay
Beach Park

KOOLAU MOUNTAINS

Puu
Kaaumakua

80

803

Wahiawa

3

An hour from town and a world away in atmosphere, Oahu's North Shore, roughly from Kahuku Point to Kaena Point, is about small farms and big waves, tourist traps, and otherworldly landscapes. Parks and beaches, roadside fruit stands and shrimp shacks, and a valley preserve offer a dozen reasons to stop between the onetime plantation town of Kahuku and the surf mecca of Haleiwa.

Haleiwa has had many lives, from resort getaway in the 1900s to plantation town through the 20th century to its life today as a surfer and tourist magnet. Beyond Haleiwa is the tiny village of Waialua; a string of beach parks; an airfield where gliders, hang gliders, and parachutists play; and, at the end of the road, Kaena Point State Park, which offers a brisk hike, striking views, and whale-watching in season.

Pack wisely for a day's North Shore excursion: swim and snorkel gear, light jacket and hat (the weather is mercurial, especially in winter), sunscreen and sunglasses, bottled water and snacks, towels and a picnic blanket, and both sandals and closed-toe shoes for hiking. A small cooler is nice; you may want to pick up some fruit or fresh corn. As always, leave valuables in the hotel safe, and lock the car whenever you park.

Planning

Beaches

"North Shore, where the waves are mean, just like a washing machine," sing the Kaau Crater Boys about this legendary side of the island. And in winter, they are absolutely right. At times, the waves overtake the road, stranding tourists and locals alike. When the surf is up, there are signs on the beach telling you how far to stay back so that you aren't swept out to sea. The most prestigious big-wave contest in the world, the "Eddie" (Eddie Aikau Big-Wave Invitational), is held at Waimea Bay on waves the size of a five- or six-story building. The Triple Crown of Surfing roams across three North Shore beaches in the winter months.

That all changes come summer, when this tiger turns into a kitten, with water smooth enough to water-ski on and ideal for snorkeling. The fierce Banzai Pipeline surf break becomes a great dive area, allowing you to explore the coral heads that, in winter, have claimed so many lives on the ultrashallow but big, hollow tubes created here. Even with the monster surf at a dull roar, this is still a time for caution: lifeguards are scarce, and currents don't subside just because the waves do.

That said, it's a place like no other on Earth and must be explored. From the turtles at Mokuleia to the tunnels at Shark's Cove, you could spend your whole trip on this side of Oahu and not be disappointed. A drive to the North Shore takes about an hour from Waikiki, but allot a full day to explore the beaches and Haleiwa, which, though burgeoning, retains a surf-town charm.

Getting Here and Around

AIR
Daniel K. Inouye International Airport in Honolulu is the island's only airport, so it's also the gateway to the North Shore, despite the 45-minute drive (more with traffic).

AIRPORT TRANSFERS
North Shore Transport provides shuttle transportation to and from Honolulu International Airport, transfers to other hotels and resorts, and shuttles to nearby towns and activities. Airport transfers start at $166 per person.

Roberts Hawaii's Airport Transport Service takes passengers from Daniel K. Inouye International Airport to Turtle Bay. Prices start at $103 person (based on two-person minimum, otherwise individual passengers are $206).

CONTACTS North Shore Transport. ⊠ Haleiwa ☎ 808/225–0522 ⊕ northshoretransport.com. **Roberts Hawaii.** ⊠ Honolulu ☎ 808/539–9400 ⊕ www.robertshawaii.com/airport-shuttle/oahu.

BUS
TheBus provides frequent daily service to the North Shore and is a practical way to get around, as parking is limited and fills quickly, especially in Haleiwa and at popular surf breaks. Nevertheless, bags must fit under your seat or on your lap, so TheBus is not an option if you have large checked bags and want to travel from the airport. (Surfboards aren't allowed either.)

Route 60 travels from Honolulu to Kaneohe and up the windward side to Turtle Bay, Pupukea, and Haleiwa and back. Route 52 transports riders from the Ala Moana Center to Haleiwa, traversing Central Oahu.

CAR
From Waikiki, the quickest route to the North Shore is H1 west to H2 north, and then the Kamehameha Highway past Wahiawa. You'll hit Haleiwa in just under an hour. The windward route (H1 east, H3, Likelike or Pali Highway, through the mountains, or Kamehameha Highway north) takes at least 90 minutes to Haleiwa, but the drive is far prettier.

TAXI
Taxis are very expensive and hard to find, but the rideshares Uber and Lyft have become popular options in recent years, especially for rides to and within the Haleiwa area. Most visitors who come up from Honolulu for day trips without a car sign up with a tour company.

Hotels

North Shore accommodation options are extremely limited compared to Honolulu and the southern shores of Oahu. Turtle Bay Resort is the only major hotel in the area, and the adjacent Kuilima condos provide legal short-term rentals. County of Honolulu law requires a 30-day minimum for most other vacation rental properties on the North Shore; currently, short-term rentals are legal only at condo complexes within 3,000 feet of a resort.

PRICES

Hotel prices are the lowest cost of a standard double room in high season. Hotel reviews have been shortened. For full information, visit Fodors.com.

What It Costs in U.S. Dollars

$	$$	$$$	$$$$
FOR TWO PEOPLE			
under $180	$180–$260	$261–$340	over $340

Restaurants

Most North Shore eateries cluster in the town of Haleiwa and at the Turtle Bay resort, which has options that range from casual poolside bars to the upscale Alaia restaurant. No North Shore trek is complete without a stop at a shrimp shack or truck and a slice of pie at Ted's Bakery. The classic shacks and food trucks are found mostly on the south side of Haleiwa and at the famed hub in Kahuku, at the North Shore's eastern limits, though some trucks travel to North Shore beaches and surf breaks during busy seasons.

PRICES

Restaurant prices are the average cost of a main course at dinner or, if dinner is not served, at lunch. Restaurant reviews have been shortened. For full information visit Fodors.com.

What It Costs in U.S. Dollars

$	$$	$$$	$$$$
AT DINNER			
under $17	$17–$26	$27–$35	over $35

Waialua

30 miles northwest of Honolulu.

A tranquil, multicultural burg with sleepy residential areas, uncrowded beach parks, and small mom-and-pop businesses, Wailua provides refuge from neighboring (and often tourist-choked) Haleiwa. In the 1900s, the Waialua Sugar Company attracted workers from around the world, and their descendants continue to live and work here. The former sugar operation buildings now hold a General Store and eclectic, trendy shops, art studios, maker spaces for surfboard shapers and other craftspeople, and a coffee mill. Waialua is also the gateway to a wild and scenic coastline that includes Mokuleia Beach Park, Kaena Point State Park, and Kawaihapai Airfield (formerly known as Dillingham Airfield), where gliders and parachutists launch and land.

GETTING HERE AND AROUND

Waialua, which is just west of Haleiwa, is about a 45-minute drive from Honolulu via the H2 and Highway 99 or Highway 803 through Central Oahu. TheBus Route 52 travels between Honolulu and Haleiwa, and Route 521 connects Haleiwa and Waialua.

Sights

Kaena Point State Park

STATE/PROVINCIAL PARK | FAMILY | The name means "the heat," and, indeed, this windy, barren coast lacks both shade and fresh water (or any man-made amenities). Pack water, wear sturdy closed-toe shoes, don sunscreen and a hat, and lock the car. The hike is along a rutted dirt road, mostly flat and nearly 3 miles long (one-way), ending at a rocky, sandy headland. It is here that Hawaiians believed the souls of the dead met with their family gods and, if judged worthy to enter the afterlife, leapt off into eternal darkness at Leina Kauhane, just south of the point.

North Shore

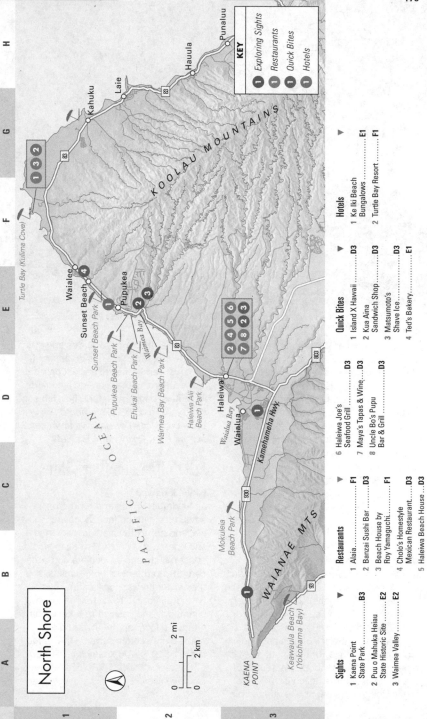

KEY

- ① Exploring Sights
- ① Restaurants
- ① Quick Bites
- ① Hotels

KOOLAU MOUNTAINS

WAIANAE MTS

KAENA POINT

OCEAN

PACIFIC

Turtle Bay (Kuilima Cove)

Mokuleia Beach Park

Keawaula Beach (Yokohama Bay)

Waimea Bay

Waialua Bay

Pupukea Beach Park

Ehukai Beach Park

Waimea Bay Beach Park

Haleiwa Alii Beach Park

Sunset Beach Park

Kamehameha Hwy

Punaluu
Hauula
Laie
Kahuku
Waialee
Sunset Beach
Pupukea
Haleiwa
Waialua

2 mi
2 km

▶ **Sights**

1 Kaena Point
  State Park..............**B3**
2 Puu o Mahuka Heiau
  State Historic Site......**E2**
3 Waimea Valley..........**E2**

▶ **Restaurants**

1 Alaia....................**F1**
2 Banzai Sushi Bar........**D3**
3 Beach House by
  Roy Yamaguchi..........**F1**
4 Cholo's Homestyle
  Mexican Restaurant.....**D3**
5 Haleiwa Beach House ...**D3**
6 Haleiwa Joe's
  Seafood Grill...........**D3**
7 Maya's Tapas & Wine....**D3**
8 Uncle Bo's Pupu
  Bar & Grill.............**D3**

▶ **Quick Bites**

1 Island X Hawaii.........**D3**
2 Kua Aina
  Sandwich Shop..........**D3**
3 Matsumoto's
  Shave Ice..............**D3**
4 Ted's Bakery............**E1**

▶ **Hotels**

1 Ke Iki Beach
  Bungalows.............**E1**
2 Turtle Bay Resort......**F1**

Kaena Point is remote and barren, but it's a beautiful place of religious significance for ancient Hawaiians, who believed it was where the souls of the dead departed for the afterlife.

In summer and at low tide, the small coves offer bountiful shelling; in winter, don't venture near the water. Rare native plants dot the landscape, and seabirds like the Laysan albatross nest here. If you're lucky, you might spot seals sunbathing on the rocks. From November through March, watch for humpbacks spouting and breaching. Binoculars and a camera are highly recommended. ⊠ *69-385 Farrington Hwy., Waialua* ⊕ *dlnr.hawaii.gov/dsp/parks/oahu/ kaena-point-state-park.*

Beaches

Mokuleia Beach Park

BEACH | There is a reason why the producers of the TV show *Lost* chose this beach for their set: it's on the island's remote, northwest point and about 10 miles from the closest store or public restroom. Its beauty is in its lack of facilities and isolation—all the joy of being stranded on a deserted island without the trauma of the plane crash. The beach is wide and white, the waters bright blue (but a little choppy) and full of sea turtles and other marine life. Mokuleia is a great secret find; just remember to pack supplies and use caution, as there are no lifeguards. **Amenities:** parking (no fee). **Best for:** sunset, walking. ⊠ *68-67 Farrington Hwy., Waialua* ⊹ *West of Haleiwa town center, across from Dillingham Airfield.*

☕ Coffee and Quick Bites

Island X Hawaii

$ | **HAWAIIAN** | Recharge for more adventure with coffee, chocolate, shave ice, and boba drinks at family-owned and operated Island X Hawaii, in an old sugar mill garage. Chocolate and coffee come from the neighboring fields, and the owner crafts the all-natural syrups with organically grown mango, papaya, pineapple, and passionfruit. **Known for:** intriguing location; fresh ingredients; made-from-scratch syrups. **$** *Average main: $5* ⊠ *67-106 Kealohanui St., Unit C-1, Waialua* ☎ *808/637–2624* ⊕ *www. islandxhawaii.com.*

🛍 Shopping

GIFTS

Island X Hawaii

SOUVENIRS | This eclectic store in a section of the Old Waialua Sugar Mill carries gifts, clothes, and local food items—especially coffee and chocolate that is produced in Waialua. You can get a short unofficial tour of the coffee and cacao mill and roasting area just outside (this includes samples of coffee, cacao beans, and chocolate). ⊠ *Waialua Sugar Mill, 67-106 Kealohanui St., Waialua* ☎ *808/637–2624* ⊕ *www.islandxhawaii. com.*

North Shore Soap Factory

SOUVENIRS | Housed in a converted silo in the historic Old Waialua Sugar Mill, this is a working factory where you can watch the soap as it's made. The soaps are all natural and use as many local ingredients as possible. The factory also sells lotions and essential oils, gift sets, and T-shirts. ⊠ *Waialua Sugar Mill, 67-106 Kealohanui St., Waialua* ☎ *808/637–8400* ⊕ *north-shoresoapfactory.com.*

Haleiwa

3 miles northeast of Waialua, 30 miles northwest of Honolulu.

The North Shore's shopping, dining, and surf-culture hub has preserved its historic plantation-era roots and melded it with a laid-back 1960s-era vibe. The town sits amid a picture-perfect setting on Waialua Bay, where the Anahulu River empties into the harbor.

In the 1920s, Waialua had a posh hotel at the end of a railroad line (both long gone). During the '60s, hippies congregated here, followed by surfers from around the world. Today, the streets of historic Haleiwa Town reflect a fun mix of old and new, with charming general stores and contemporary boutiques, galleries, and eateries.

Haleiwa Alii Beach Park and Haleiwa Beach Park border the bay and provide endless opportunities for water sports and other activities. Be sure to stop in at Liliuokalani Protestant Church, founded by missionaries in the 1830s. It's fronted by a large, stone archway built in 1910 and covered with night-blooming cereus. Also check out the historic Rainbow Bridge, whose distinctive double arches appear in many local works of art.

GETTING HERE AND AROUND

Haleiwa is about a 45-minute drive from Honolulu via the H2 and Highway 99 through Central Oahu. TheBus Route 52 transports passengers between Honolulu and Haleiwa via Central Oahu, and Route 60 travels around the windward side of the island, from Haleiwa to Kahuku and south to Kaneohe and Honolulu.

🏖 Beaches

★ Haleiwa Alii Beach Park

BEACH | FAMILY | The winter waves are impressive here, but in summer, the ocean is like a lake, ideal for family swimming. The beach itself is big and tends to be full of locals. Its broad lawn off the highway is often the site of volleyball and Frisbee games, family barbecues, and art festivals and carnivals. This beach is also the opening break for the Triple Crown of Surfing. **Amenities:** lifeguards; parking (no fee); showers; toilets. **Best for:** surfing; swimming. ⊠ *66-167 Haleiwa Rd., Haleiwa* ✛ *North of Haleiwa town center and past harbor.*

🍽 Restaurants

Banzai Sushi Bar

$$$ | JAPANESE FUSION | An array of authentic Japanese dishes made with Hawaiian seafood and fresh, seasonal, mostly organic North Shore veggies and fruits attracts locals and visitors alike to this hip yet family-friendly sushi house. The extensive menu includes classic sashimi and tempura, off-the-wall sushi rolls,

Wagyu beef, broiled fish entrées, and various vegetarian and gluten-free options. **Known for:** some traditional Japanese seating; full bar with good selection of Japanese whiskeys and sakes; unusual rolls using macadamia nuts and island spices. $ *Average main: $28* ⊠ *North Shore Marketplace, 66-246 Kamehameha Hwy., Suite B, Haleiwa* ☎ *808/637–4404* ⊕ *banzaisushibarhawaii.com* ☯ *Closed Mon.*

Cholo's Homestyle Mexican Restaurant
$$ | **MEXICAN** | **FAMILY** | There are only a couple of North Shore institutions that are considered gathering places—Foodland (the great grocery store) is one, and Cholo's is the other. Festively done up with Mexican tchotchkes, it serves decent rice-and-beans plates of Mexican standards (steak fajitas, burritos, enchiladas) at affordable prices. **Known for:** fresh mango margaritas; excellent ahi tacos; lively happy hour. $ *Average main: $18* ⊠ *North Shore Marketplace, 66-250 Kamehameha Hwy., Haleiwa* ☎ *808/637–3059* ⊕ *www.cholos.mx.*

Haleiwa Beach House
$$ | **AMERICAN** | **FAMILY** | One of the newer restaurants on the North Shore takes full advantage of its epic water views. The menu is chock full of surf-and-turf options, from juicy burgers to grilled steaks, blackened fish to red Thai curry with lobster and shrimp. **Known for:** solid, reliable beef, seafood, salads, and kids options; craft beers on draft and a nice wine list; view and setting that can't be beat. $ *Average main: $26* ⊠ *62-540 Kamehameha Hwy., Haleiwa* ☎ *808/637–3435* ⊕ *www.haleiwabeachhouse.com.*

Haleiwa Joe's Seafood Grill
$$$ | **AMERICAN** | After the long drive to the North Shore, watching the boats and surfers come and go from the harbor while you enjoy a mai tai on Haleiwa Joe's open-air lanai may be just what you need. This casual little joint, just past the Rainbow Bridge, rarely changes (to some, that might feel dated, but regulars appreciate the familiarity); a more upscale Kaneohe location overlooks the lush Haiku Gardens. **Known for:** good daily fish specials; reliable food with a nice harbor setting; crunchy coconut shrimp. $ *Average main: $29* ⊠ *66-011 Kamehameha Hwy., Haleiwa* ☎ *808/637–8005* ⊕ *www.haleiwajoes.com.*

Maya's Tapas & Wine
$$$ | **TAPAS** | A cozy, romantic space with a slightly sophisticated (for the North Shore) vibe, Maya's serves up classic Spanish and Mediterranean dishes with island twists. Here, seafood paella is made with local line-caught fish and shrimp, a burger showcases Kunoa beef, and hand-tossed flatbreads come with roasted local veggies and macadamia nut pesto. **Known for:** popular happy hour and Sunday brunch; craft cocktails and sangria; savory paella and other specials. $ *Average main: $28* ⊠ *66-250 Kamehameha Hwy., Unit D-101, Haleiwa* ☎ *808/200–2964* ⊕ *www.mayastapasandwine.com* ☯ *Closed Mon. No dinner Sun.*

Uncle Bo's Pupu Bar & Grill
$$$ | **HAWAIIAN** | **FAMILY** | One of the North Shore's liveliest eateries is set in a casual, contemporary space. It serves Hawaiian-style fare—from poke bowls and fresh wild-caught moonfish to nachos with ham and *kalua* pig on wonton chips—as well as pasta dishes, pizza, soups, and salads. **Known for:** indoor-outdoor seating; in the heart of town; something for everyone. $ *Average main: $27* ⊠ *66-111 Kamehameha Hwy., #101, Haleiwa* ☎ *808/797–9649* ⊕ *www.unclebosrestaurant.com.*

☕ Coffee and Quick Bites

Kua Aina Sandwich Shop

$ | **BURGER** | **FAMILY** | This North Shore spot has gone from funky burger shack (it first opened in 1975) to institution, with crowds of tourists and locals standing in line to order the large, hand-formed burgers heaped with bacon, cheese, and pineapple. Frankly, there are better burgers to be had around the island, but this place commands a truly loyal following. **Known for:** decent burgers and fries; a pilgrimage stop on the North Shore surf circuit; tourists by the busload. ⑤ *Average main: $13* ✉ *66-160 Kamehameha Hwy., Haleiwa* ☎ *808/637–6067* ⊕ *kua-ainahawaii.com.*

Matsumoto's Shave Ice

$ | **CAFÉ** | **FAMILY** | For a real slice of Haleiwa life, stop at family-run Matsumoto's Shave Ice for cool treats that are available in every flavor imaginable. For something different, order a shave ice with adzuki beans—the red beans are boiled until soft, mixed with sugar, and then placed in the cone with the ice on top. **Known for:** homemade adzuki beans; one of the most popular shave ice spots on Oahu; the Matsumoto with lemon, pineapple, and coconut syrup. ⑤ *Average main: $4* ✉ *66-111 Kamehameha Hwy., Suite 605, Haleiwa* ☎ *808/637–4827* ⊕ *www.matsumotoshaveice.com.*

Hotels

Ke Iki Beach Bungalows

$$$ | **RESORT** | **FAMILY** | At this 1½-acre, sloped, beachfront lot with six duplex bungalows, you can choose from studios and one- or two-bedroom units—outfitted with breezy beach-house furnishings, individual grills, hammocks, and picnic tables—and enjoy access to a 200-foot strand of sugary white-sand beach running between the North Shore's famous Waimea Bay and Ehukai Beach (Banzai Pipeline). **Pros:** steps to the beach and bike path to Sunset Beach and Waimea Bay; outdoor showers, meditation area, and beachfront seating for nightly stargazing; popular with families for reunions and weddings. **Cons:** some bungalows close to highway noise; high surf in winter months; a bit far from restaurants and shopping. ⑤ *Rooms from: $295* ✉ *59-579 Ke Iki Rd., Haleiwa* ☎ *808/638–8829, 866/638–8229* ⊕ *www.keikibeach.com* 🛏 *12 units* ⦿*❙ No Meals.*

🛍 Shopping

The North Shore has no major malls, but it does have a couple of open-air shopping complexes and numerous shops and makeshift stands—some on the side of the road, others a bit more hidden where you'll find one-of-a-kind treasures. Eclectic shops are the best place to score skin-care products made on the North Shore, Hawaiian music CDs, sea glass and shell mobiles, coffee grown in the Islands, and clothing items unavailable elsewhere.

Be sure to chat with the owners in each shop. North Shore residents are an animated, friendly bunch, with multiple talents. Stop in for coffee and a shopkeeper might reveal a little about his or her passion for creating distinguished pieces of artwork.

SHOPPING CENTERS

Haleiwa Store Lots

MALL | **FAMILY** | The most notable tenant here is the legendary Matsumoto's Shave Ice. (You'll know it by the long line of people.) The shiny, open-air complex is also home to the locally owned Haleiwa Fruit Stand and the casual beach-chic boutique Guava Shop, as well as surf photographer Clark Little's art gallery. ✉ *66-111 Kamehameha Hwy., Haleiwa* ⊕ *www.haleiwastorelots.com.*

North Shore Marketplace

MALL | FAMILY | While playing on the North Shore, check out this open-air plaza that includes a number of art galleries, as well as clothing, gelato, and jewelry stores. And don't miss the Silver Moon Emporium for eclectic Islands fashions. People drive out of their way for the Coffee Gallery or for happy hour at Cholo's Home-style Mexican Restaurant or Maya's Tapas and Wine. ⊠ *66-250 Kamehameha Hwy., Haleiwa* ☎ *808/637–4416* ⊕ *northshore-marketplacehawaii.com.*

CLOTHING

The Growing Keiki

CHILDREN'S CLOTHING | FAMILY | Frequent visitors return to this store year after year for a fresh supply of unique, locally made, Hawaiian-style clothing for youngsters. ⊠ *66-051 Kamehameha Hwy., Haleiwa* ☎ *808/637–4544* ⊕ *www.facebook.com/TheGrowingKeiki.*

★ Silver Moon Emporium

WOMEN'S CLOTHING | The small boutique carries everything from Brighton jewelry and European designer wear to fashionable T-shirts, shoes, and handbags. Expect attentive and personalized yet casual service. The stock changes frequently, and there's always something wonderful on sale. No matter what your taste, you'll find something for everyday wear or special occasions. ⊠ *North Shore Marketplace, 66-250 Kamehameha Hwy., Haleiwa* ☎ *808/637–7710.*

FOOD

Tropical Fruits Distributors of Hawaii

FOOD | Avoid the hassle of airport inspections. This company specializes in packing inspected pineapple and papaya and will deliver to your hotel and to the airport check-in counter. It also ships to elsewhere in the United States as well as to Canada. Think about ordering online. ⊠ *Dole Plantation, 64-1550 Kamehameha Hwy., Haleiwa* ☎ *800/697–9100* ⊕ *www.dolefruithawaii.com.*

SPORTING GOODS

Surf N Sea

SPORTING GOODS | FAMILY | This water-sports store has everything you need for an active vacation under one roof. Purchase rash guards, swimwear, T-shirts, footwear, hats, and shorts. Book scuba-diving tours and lessons and rent kayaks, snorkeling or scuba gear, spears for free diving, surfboards, stand-up paddleboards, and bodyboards. Experienced surfing instructors will take beginners to the small breaks on the North Shore beaches, with their notoriously huge (winter) or flat (summer) waves. Warning to fishing enthusiasts: a fishing pole is the one ocean apparatus this shop doesn't carry. ⊠ *62-595 Kamehameha Hwy., Haleiwa* ☎ *800/899–7873* ⊕ *www.surfnsea.com.*

Pupukea

6 miles northeast of Haleiwa.

Pupukea is a tiny village that anchors the Seven Mile Miracle—the legendary stretch of North Shore coast that faithfully serves up some of the world's best barrels and perfectly shaped waves every winter. It's also home to Foodland, the only grocery store between Kahuku/Laie and Haleiwa, which means you're likely to rub elbows in the checkout line with seasoned professional surfers and visiting celebrities, along with slipper-clad locals.

Across the street are Shark's Cove and Three Tables, both excellent snorkeling and scuba sites when the winter swells abate. The Banzai Pipeline and Sunset Beach are just a mile up the road. Drive up the hill behind Foodland to explore the sacred Puu o Mahuka Heiau, the largest shrine on the island.

While Waimea Bay is known for its big winter waves and surf culture, the Waimea Valley is an area of great historical significance. It's also known for its botanical specimens, including big tropical trees.

👁 Sights

Puu o Mahuka Heiau State Historic Site
RUINS | Worth a stop for its spectacular views from a bluff high above the ocean overlooking Waimea Bay, this sacred spot spans 2 acres and is the largest *heiau* (place of worship) on the island. At one time it was used as a *heiau luakini*, or a temple for human sacrifices. It's now on the National Register of Historic Places. Turn up the road at the Pupukea Foodland and follow it to the site. ✉ *Pupukea Rd., ½ mile north of Waimea Bay, Pupukea* ✛ *From Rte. 83, turn right on Pupukea Rd. and drive 1 mile uphill* ⊕ *dlnr.hawaii.gov/dsp/parks/oahu/puu-o-mahuka-heiau-state-historic-site.*

★ Waimea Valley
GARDEN | FAMILY | Waimea may get lots of press for the giant winter waves in the bay, but the valley itself is a newsmaker and an ecological treasure in its own right, with a local nonprofit working to conserve and restore its natural habitat. Follow the Kamananui Stream up the valley through the 1,875 acres of gardens. The botanical collections here have more than 5,000 species of tropical flora, including a superb gathering of native Hawaiian and international plants. It's the best place on the island to see native species, such as the endangered Hawaiian moorhen.

You can also see the restored Hale o Lono *heiau* (shrine) along with other ancient archaeological sites; evidence suggests that the area was an important spiritual center. Daily activities include botanical walking tours and cultural tours. At the back of the valley, Waihi Falls plunges 45 feet into a swimming pond. ■ TIP➔ **Bring your board shorts—a swim is the perfect way to end your hike, although the pond can get crowded. Be sure to bring mosquito repellent, too; it can get buggy.** ✉ *59-864 Kamehameha Hwy., Pupukea* ☎ *808/638–7766* ⊕ *www.waimeavalley. net* 🎫 *$20.*

🏖 Beaches

Ehukai Beach Park

BEACH | What sets Ehukai apart is the view of the famous Banzai Pipeline. Here the winter waves curl into magnificent tubes, making it an experienced wave-rider's dream. It's also an inexperienced swimmer's nightmare. Spring and summer waves, on the other hand, are more accommodating to the average person, and there's good snorkeling. Except when the surf contests are happening, there's no reason to stay on the central strip. Travel in either direction from the center, and the conditions remain the same but the population thins out, leaving you with a magnificent stretch of sand all to yourself. **Amenities:** lifeguards; parking (no fee); showers; toilets. **Best for:** snorkeling; surfing. ⊠ *59-337 Ke Nui Rd., Pupukea ✛ 1 mile north of Foodland at Pupukea.*

★Pupukea Beach Park (*Shark's Cove*)

BEACH | Surrounded by shade trees, Pupukea Beach Park is pounded by surf in the winter months but offers great diving and snorkeling in summer (March through October). Its cavernous lava tubes and tunnels are great for both novice and experienced snorkelers and divers, though it's imperative that you wear reef shoes at all times since there are a lot of sharp rocks. Sharp rocks also mean that this beach isn't the best for little ones. Some dive-tour companies offer round-trip transportation from Waikiki. Equipment rentals and dining options are nearby. **Amenities:** parking (no fee); showers; toilets. **Best for:** diving; snorkeling; swimming. ⊠ *Pupukea ✛ 3½ miles north of Haleiwa, across street from Foodland.*

★Sunset Beach Park

BEACH | The beach is broad, the sand is soft, the summer waves are gentle—making for good snorkeling—and the winter surf is crashing. Many love searching this shore for the puka shells that adorn the necklaces you see everywhere. **Amenities:** lifeguards; parking (no fee); showers; toilets. **Best for:** snorkeling; sunset; surfing. ⊠ *59-144 Kamehameha Hwy., Pupukea ✛ 1 mile north of Ehukai Beach Park.*

★Waimea Bay Beach Park

BEACH | Made popular in that old Beach Boys song "Surfin' U.S.A.," this is a slice of big-wave (25 to 30 feet) heaven in winter. Summer is the time to swim and snorkel in the calm waters. The shore break is great for novice bodysurfers. Due to the beach's popularity, its postage-stamp parking lot is often full, but it's also possible to park along the side of the road and walk in. **Amenities:** lifeguards; parking (no fee); showers; toilets. **Best for:** snorkeling; surfing; swimming. ⊠ *61-31 Kamehameha Hwy., Pupukea ✛ Across from Waimea Valley, 3 miles north of Haleiwa.*

☕ Coffee and Quick Bites

Ted's Bakery

$ | AMERICAN | FAMILY | Sunburned tourists and salty surfers rub shoulders in their quest for Ted's famous chocolate *haupia* cream pie (layered coconut and dark chocolate puddings topped with whipped cream) and hearty plates—like garlic shrimp, gravy-drenched hamburger steak, and mahimahi. Parking spots and the umbrella-shaded tables are at a premium, so be prepared to grab and go; if you can't get enough of that haupia goodness, Foodland and other grocery chains typically stock a selection of the famous pies as well. **Known for:** plate lunches; Ted's pies, which seem to show up at every Oahu potluck; reliable all-day dining. ⑤ *Average main: $14* ⊠ *59-024 Kamehameha Hwy., Pupukea* ☎ *808/638–8207* ⊕ *www.tedsbakery. com.*

Shrimp Shacks

No drive to the North Shore is complete without a shrimp stop. Stands dot Kamehameha Highway from Kahaluu to Kahuku. For about $12, you can get a shrimp plate lunch or a snack of chilled shrimp with cocktail sauce, served from a rough hut or converted van (many permanently parked) with picnic-table seating.

The shrimp-shack phenomenon began with a lost lease and determined restaurateurs. In 1994, when Giovanni and Connie Aragona couldn't renew the lease on their Haleiwa deli, they began hawking their best-selling dish—an Italian-style scampi preparation involving lemon, butter, and lots of garlic—from a truck alongside the road. About the same time, aquaculture was gaining a foothold in nearby Kahuku, with farmers raising sweet, white shrimp and huge, orange-whiskered prawns in shallow freshwater ponds. The ready supply and the

success of the first shrimp truck led to many imitators.

Although it's changed hands, that first business lives on as **Giovanni's Original Shrimp Truck**, parked in Kahuku town. Signature dishes include the garlic shrimp and a spicy shrimp sauté, both worth a stop.

But there's plenty of competition: at least a dozen stands, trucks, or stalls are operating at any given time, with varying menus (and quality).

Not all that shrimp comes fresh from the ponds; much of it is imported. The only way you can be sure you're buying local, farm-raised shrimp is if the shrimp is still kicking. **Romy's Kahuku Prawns and Shrimp Hut** (Kamehameha Highway, near Kahuku) is an arm of one of the longest-running aquaculture farms in the area; it sells live shrimp and prawns and farm-raised fish along with excellent plate lunches.

Kahuku

Kawela Bay is 5½ miles northeast of Pupukea, Kahuku is about 9 miles northeast of Pupukea.

The Kahuku district, which stretches from Kahuku town to Kawela Bay, includes Kahuku Point, the northernmost point on Oahu. The area is best known for fresh fruits and veggies from local farms (watch for stands along the highway), shrimp shacks, and exceptional high school football stars who go on to play at top-tier colleges and in the NFL.

Kahuku town has a collection of brand-name stores and tiny mom-and-pop

shops amid modest residential neighborhoods filled with longtime island residents. Multimillion-dollar homes line the shores of the gated Kawela Bay community, but there's public beach access off Kamehameha Highway at Kawela Camp. Park on the side of the road, and walk about ¼ mile along a trail to get there.

Beaches

Turtle Bay (*Kuilima Cove*)
BEACH | FAMILY | Now known more for its namesake resort than its magnificent beach at Kuilima Cove, Turtle Bay is mostly passed over on the way to the better-known beaches of Sunset and

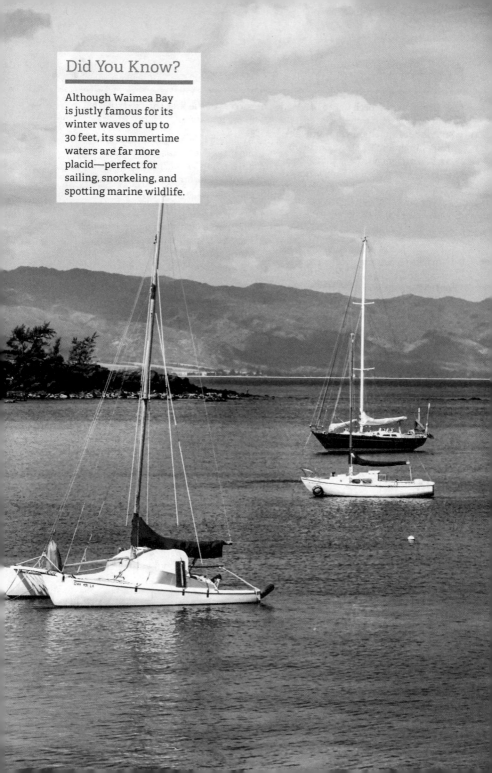

Did You Know?

Although Waimea Bay is justly famous for its winter waves of up to 30 feet, its summertime waters are far more placid—perfect for sailing, snorkeling, and spotting marine wildlife.

Waimea. But for those with average swimming capabilities, this is a good place to be. The crescent-shaped stretch is protected by a huge sea wall, so you can see and hear the fury of the northern swell while blissfully floating in cool, calm waters. The convenience of this spot is also hard to pass up—there is a concession selling sandwiches and sunblock right on the beach. The resort has free parking for beach guests. **Amenities:** food and drink; parking (no fee); showers; toilets. **Best for:** sunset; swimming. ⊠ *57-20 Kuilima Dr., 4 miles north of Kahuku, Kahuku* ⊹ *Turn into Turtle Bay Resort and follow signs to public parking lot and beach access spots.*

🍴 Restaurants

Alaia
$$$$ | HAWAIIAN | The menus at Turtle Bay Resort's signature restaurant—a casual but chic open-air space overlooking Turtle Bay and the Seven Mile Miracle—showcase Hawaiian comfort food with a modern, upscale twist, including braised *kalbi* short ribs, roast chicken with macadamia nut mole, and Salanova lettuce. About 95% of the fresh produce, from lettuce, tomatoes, and breadfruit to apple bananas and kitchen herbs, comes from the 100-acre organic farm across the road and is grown in partnership with longtime local farmers. **Known for:** braised short ribs; sweeping ocean views; special-occasion dinners. ⑤ *Average main: $45* ⊠ *Turtle Bay Resort, 57-091 Kamehameha Hwy., Kahuku* ☎ *866/475–2569* ⊕ *www.turtlebayresort.com/dining/alaia* ☺ *No lunch.*

Beach House by Roy Yamaguchi
$$$$ | MODERN HAWAIIAN | Loyalists of Roy Yamaguchi's celebrated spots in Hawaii Kai and Waikiki are thrilled to find his North Shore outpost—a rustic, beam-and-concrete-floor pavilion literally on the sand at Turtle Bay. All the favorites are served at this more beach-casual spot, from the miso deep-water black cod to the beef short ribs, along with a more casual lunch menu. **Known for:** special-occasion celebrations; casual, romantic setting right on the beach; fresh North Shore ingredients. ⑤ *Average main: $42* ⊠ *Turtle Bay Resort, 57-091 Kamehameha Hwy., Kahuku* ☎ *808/293–0801* ⊕ *www.royyamaguchi. com/beach-house-by-roy-yamaguchi.*

🛏 Hotels

★ Turtle Bay Resort
$$$$ | RESORT | FAMILY | Sprawling over nearly 1,300 acres of natural landscape on the edge of Kuilima Point in Kahuku, this resort has spacious guest rooms (averaging nearly 500 square feet) with lanai that showcase stunning peninsula views. **Pros:** fabulous open public spaces in a secluded area of Oahu; beautiful spa; excellent location for exploring the North Shore. **Cons:** hefty resort fee; 24/7 resort living isn't for everyone; very remote—even Haleiwa is a 20-minute drive. ⑤ *Rooms from: $759* ⊠ *57-091 Kamehameha Hwy., Kahuku* ☎ *808/293–6000, 800/203–3650, 866/827–5321 for reservations* ⊕ *www.turtlebayresort.com* ⊷ *452 rooms* ⦵ *No Meals.*

🍸 Nightlife

★ Off the Lip
COCKTAIL LOUNGES | West-oriented views (particularly stellar at sunset), creative cocktails incorporating fresh fruit and herbs from neighboring farms, homemade syrups and spirits, and live entertainment most nights draw locals and visitors alike to this classy, surf-themed lobby bar at Turtle Bay Resort. It's also the only nightlife choice on the North Shore east of Haleiwa, and night crawlers should know that the bar usually stops serving by 10 pm. ⊠ *57-091 Kamehameha Hwy., Kahuku* ☎ *866/475–2569* ⊕ *www.turtlebayresort.com/dining/lip.*

Shopping

Kuilima Farm Stand

MARKET | FAMILY | Turtle Bay Resort purchased 468 acres of prime North Shore agricultural land near the entrance to the resort and created an organic farm to supply fresh ingredients to its restaurants, as well as to support 34 sustainably farmed community garden plots. A farm stand with multiple stalls shares the bounty with locals and visitors. Pull off the highway to pick up sustainably grown pineapple, papaya, corn, and other fruits and veggies, plus locally made souvenirs. The stand is open daily 9 to 5. ⊠ *57-146 Kamehameha Hwy., Kahuku* ✛ *Mauka side of highway, across from Kawela Bay* ☎ *808/628–7400* ⊕ *kuilimafarm.com.*

Activities

SPAS

Nalu Spa at Turtle Bay

SPAS | Luxuriate at the ocean's edge in this lovely spa at Turtle Bay Resort. Try one of the signature treatments, including a coconut-lava shell massage or a ginger-lime sugar scrub followed by a coconut-argan oil infusion. There are private spa suites, an outdoor treatment cabana that overlooks the surf, and a lounge area and juice bar. Spa guests may also join fitness classes for a fee. ⊠ *Turtle Bay Resort, 57-091 Kamehameha Hwy., Kahuku* ☎ *808/447–6868* ⊕ *www.turtlebayresort.com/wellness/ spa.*

Chapter 6

EAST (WINDWARD) OAHU

6

Updated by
Anna Weaver

⊙ Sights	🍴 Restaurants	🛏 Hotels	🛍 Shopping	🍸 Nightlife
★★★★☆	★★★☆☆	★☆☆☆☆	★★☆☆☆	★☆☆☆☆

WELCOME TO EAST (WINDWARD) OAHU

TOP REASONS TO GO

★ **Beautiful beaches:** Although Oahu's windward side is known more for windsurfing than swimming, there are still some gorgeous beaches with magnificent views.

★ **Stunning emerald-green cliffs:** These are the kinds of dramatic backdrops that you see in movies.

★ **Fewer crowds:** Windward Oahu is primarily residential, so it just doesn't get the crowds of areas like Waikiki (or even Haleiwa).

★ **Local life:** If you want to see how Oahu locals really live, then make for the windward side, including some of the small villages that are still around.

★ **Polynesian Cultural Center:** The best Polynesian cultural experience on the island is here.

Locals refer to the east side of Oahu as the windward side because of the east-to-west trade winds that carried sailing ships to the Islands in years gone by and that still keep Hawaii cooler and lower in humidity than other Polynesian islands in the South Pacific. Because this side of the island sees much more frequent— often daily—showers, it is cooler and greener than the leeward side, where most hotels are found. A day trip to the windward side feels like a visit to another island with its slower pace, fewer crowds, and drop-dead gorgeous scenery.

1 Hawaii Kai. This strip mall–filled suburb on the southeast shore is a great place to stop for picnic supplies or lunch before heading to Hanauma Bay or beginning your cliff-hugging drive to the windward side.

2 Waimanalo. Nestled between the Koolau Mountains and a spectacular beach with turquoise-blue waters, this small village is where many Native Hawaiian families live.

3 Kailua. With two of Oahu's top beaches and filled with upscale boutiques and great restaurants, Kailua is popular with locals and visitors alike.

4 Kaneohe. The sprawling suburb is the largest of Oahu's windward villages. It's next to the stunning Koolaus, which means restaurants and sights that include a backdrop of incredible scenery.

5 Kaaawa. So small you may well pass right through it before realizing you're there, Kaaawa's claim to fame is as the next-door neighbor to popular Kualoa Ranch.

6 Laie. Most folks trek to the windward side's northernmost village to spend a day and evening at the Polynesian Cultural Center.

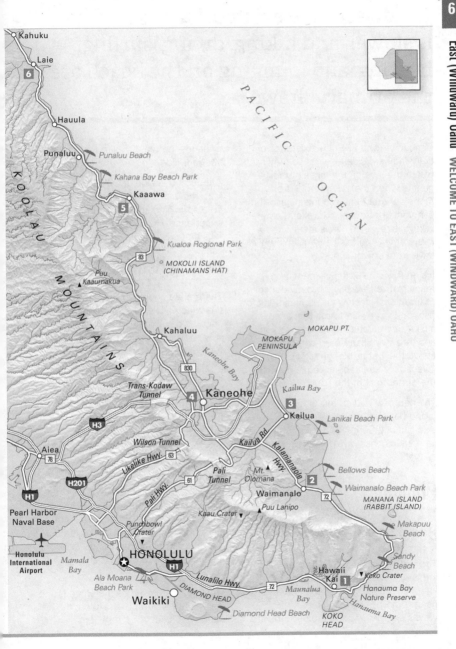

Kahuku

Laie

6

Hauula

Punaluu — Punaluu Beach

Kahana Bay Beach Park

Kaaawa

5

PACIFIC OCEAN

Kualoa Regional Park

83

MOKOLII ISLAND
(CHINAMANS HAT)

KOOLAU MOUNTAINS

Puu
Kaaumakua

Kahaluu

Kaneohe Bay

MOKAPU
PENINSULA

MOKAPU PT.

830

Trans-Koolaw
Tunnel

4 Kaneohe

Kailua Bay

3 Kailua

Lanikai Beach Park

H3

Wilson Tunnel

Kailua Rd.

Aiea

78

Likelike Hwy.

63

61

Pali
Tunnel

Mt.
Olomana

Kalanianaole Hwy.

Bellows Beach

2

Waimanalo Beach Park

H201

Pali Hwy.

Waimanalo

72

MANANA ISLAND
(RABBIT ISLAND)

H1

Pearl Harbor
Naval Base

Punchbowl
Crater

Kaau Crater

Puu Lanipo

Makapuu
Beach

Honolulu
International
Airport

Mamala
Bay

HONOLULU

H1

Ala Moana
Beach Park

Lunalilo Hwy.

72

Hawaii
Kai

1

Sandy
Beach

Koko Crater

Hanauma Bay
Nature Preserve

Waikiki

DIAMOND HEAD

Maunalua
Bay

Diamond Head Beach

KOKO
HEAD

Hanauma Bay

Looking at Honolulu's topsy-turvy urban sprawl, you would never suspect the windward side existed. Here the pace is slower, and hiking, diving, surfing, boating, and lounging on the beach are the primary draws.

Oahuans like to keep the existence of the windward side a secret so they can watch the awe on the faces of their guests when the car emerges from tunnels through the mountains and the panorama of turquoise bays and emerald valleys is revealed. Jaws literally drop. Every time. And this just a 15-minute drive from downtown.

It's on this side of the island where many Native Hawaiians live. Evidence of traditional lifestyles is abundant in old fishponds, rock platforms that once were altars, taro patches still being worked, and throw-net fishermen posed stock-still above the water (though today, they're invariably wearing polarized sunglasses, the better to spot the fish).

The natural world on this side of the island beckons. But a visit to the Polynesian Cultural Center and poking through little shops and wayside stores are musts as well.

Planning

Beaches

The windward side is ideal for sunbathing, swimming, and windsurfing or kiteboarding, or for the more intrepid, hang gliding. For the most part, the waves are mellow, and the bottoms are all sand—perfect if you're traveling with younger kids.

Although this side of Oahu gets more rain, the vistas are so beautiful that a little sprinkling shouldn't dampen your experience. Plus, it benefits the waterfalls that cascade down the Koolaus.

Getting Here and Around

There are a couple of ways to reach the windward side. One possibility is to spend a day hugging the coast all the way to Laie, home of the Polynesian Cultural Center. First, head east on the H1 past Diamond Head until it becomes Kalanianaole Highway. Look for Kamehameha Highway upon reaching Kaneohe, and follow this two-lane road all the way to the North Shore.

Another option that's just as spectacular but much more direct is taking the H1 to either the Pali Highway, the Likelike Highway, or the H3 across the mountains and through the tunnels to Kaneohe and beyond. Although the Pali Highway affords the opportunity to take in the view from its namesake lookout, the H3 offers the most breathtakingly beautiful arrival to this side of the island.

CAR

Though TheBus serves the entire island, you'll need a car to fully explore the windward side.

Hotels

Regulations severely limiting bed-and-breakfast and short-term vacation rentals on Oahu were adopted in 2019, largely driven by residents of the windward side. This translates into a scarcity of lodging options, but those you'll find are embedded within windward communities rather than tourist enclaves.

PRICES

Hotel prices are the lowest cost of a standard double room in high season. Hotel reviews have been shortened. For full information, visit Fodors.com.

What It Costs in U.S. Dollars			
$	$$	$$$	$$$$
FOR TWO PEOPLE			
under $180	$180–$260	$261–$340	over $340

Restaurants

Many folks on the windward side never travel to "town" (Honolulu) in search of great dining options. Join the locals for fine-dining in Hawaii Kai, locally brewed beer, fresh fish and Hawaii regional cuisine in Kailua, and shave ice or Mediterranean-inspired pupu in a local neighborhood.

PRICES

Restaurant prices are the average cost of a main course at dinner or, if dinner is not served, at lunch. Restaurant reviews have been shortened. For full information, visit Fodors.com.

What It Costs in U.S. Dollars			
$	$$	$$$	$$$$
AT DINNER			
under $17	$17–$26	$27–$35	over $35

Hawaii Kai

Approximately 10 miles southeast of Waikiki.

Driving southeast from Waikiki on busy, four-lane Kalanianaole Highway, you'll pass a dozen bedroom communities tucked into the valleys at the foot of the Koolau Range, with fleeting glimpses of the ocean from a couple of pocket parks. Suddenly, civilization falls away, the road narrows to two lanes, and you enter the rugged coastline of Koko Head and Ka Iwi.

This is a cruel coastline: dry, windswept, and with rocky shores and untamed waves that are notoriously treacherous. While walking its beaches, do not turn your back on the ocean, don't venture close to wet areas where high waves occasionally reach, and be sure to heed warning signs.

At this point, you're passing through Koko Head Regional Park. On your right is the bulging remnant of a pair of volcanic craters that the Hawaiians called Kawaihoa, known today as Koko Head. To the left is Koko Crater and an area of the park that includes a hiking trail, a dryland botanical garden, a firing range, and a riding stable. Ahead is a sinuous shoreline with scenic pullouts and beaches to explore.

Named the Ka Iwi Coast (*iwi,* "ee-vee," are bones—sacred to Hawaiians and full of symbolism) for the channel just offshore, this area was once home to a ranch and small fishing enclave that were destroyed by a tidal wave in the 1940s.

GETTING HERE AND AROUND

Driving straight from Waikiki to Makapuu Point takes from a half to a full hour, depending on traffic. There isn't a huge number of sights per se in this corner of Oahu, so a couple of hours should be plenty of exploring time, unless you make a lengthy stop at a particular point.

Sights

★ Halona Blowhole

VIEWPOINT | Below a scenic turnout along the Koko Head shoreline, this oft-photographed lava tube sucks the ocean in and spits it out. Don't get too close, as conditions can get dangerous. ■TIP→ **Look to your right to see the tiny beach below that was used to film the wave-washed love scene in *From Here to Eternity*.**

In winter, this is a good spot to watch whales at play. Offshore, the island of Molokai calls like a distant siren, and, every once in a while, Lanai is visible in blue silhouette. Take your valuables with you, and lock your car, because this popular scenic location is a hot spot for petty thieves. ⊠ *Kalanianaole Hwy., Hawaii Kai* ✣ *1 mile east of Hanauma Bay*.

Koko Crater Botanical Garden

GARDEN | If you've visited any of Oahu's other botanical gardens, this one will stand in stark contrast. Inside the tallest tuff cone on Oahu, in one of the hottest and driest areas on the island, Koko Crater Botanical Garden showcases dryland species of plants, including baobab trees, cacti, plumeria, and bougainvillea. ■TIP→ **Bring plenty of water, sunscreen, and a hat. Though it's close to Oahu's more lush windward side, this is a scorching spot.** ⊠ *7491 Kokonani St., Hawaii Kai* ✣ *Entrance at end of Kokonani St.* ☎ *808/768–7135* ⊕ *honolulu.gov/parks/hbg.html* ⊠ *Free*.

Lanai Lookout

VIEWPOINT | A little more than a ½ mile past Hanauma Bay as you head toward Makapuu Point, you'll see a turnout on the ocean side with some fine views of the coastline. In winter, you'll have an opportunity to see storm-generated waves crashing against lava cliffs. This is also a popular place for winter whale-watching, so bring your binoculars, some sunscreen, and a picnic lunch, and join the small crowd scanning for telltale white spouts of water only a few hundred yards away. On clear days, you should be able to see the islands of Molokai and Lanai off in the distance, hence the name. ⊠ *Kalanianaole Hwy., Hawaii Kai* ✣ *Just past Hanauma Bay*.

★ Shangri La Museum of Islamic Art, Culture & Design

HISTORIC HOME | In 1936, heiress Doris Duke bought 5 acres at Black Point, down the coast from Waikiki, and began to build and furnish the first home that would be all her own. She called it Shangri La. For more than 50 years, the home was a work in progress as Duke traveled the world, buying art and furnishings, picking up ideas for her Mughal Garden, for the Playhouse in the style of a 17th-century Irani pavilion, and for the water terraces and tropical gardens. When she died in 1993, Duke left instructions that her home was to become a public center for the study of Islamic art.

Outside of minor conservation-oriented changes and more extensive 2017 renovations to the courtyard and pool, the house and gardens have remained much as Duke left them. To walk through them is to experience the personal style of someone who saw everything as raw material for her art. With her trusted houseman, Jin de Silva, she helped build the elaborate Turkish Room, trimming tiles and painting panels to retrofit the existing space (including raising the ceiling and lowering the floor) and building a fountain of her own design.

Among many aspects of the home inspired by the Muslim tradition is the entry: an anonymous gate, a blank white wall, and a wooden door that bids you, "Enter herein in peace and security" in Arabic script. Inside, tiles glow, fountains tinkle, and shafts of light illuminate artwork through arches and high windows. In 2014, after years of renovation, Duke's bedroom (the Mughal Suite) opened to the public. This was her private world, entered only by trusted friends.

When Doris Duke died in 1993, her estate, Shangri La, became a museum of Islamic culture and art. Tours leave from the Honolulu Museum of Art in downtown Honolulu.

■ TIP→ **The house is open only via the guided tours that depart from downtown's Honolulu Museum of Art, take about 2½ hours including transit time, and require reservations.** Book your spot as early as possible, and note that children under eight are not permitted. ⊠ *Hawaii Kai* ☎ *808/532–3853 for Honolulu Museum of Art* ✆ *tickets@honolulumuseum. org* ⊕ *www.shangrilahawaii.org* ⊠ *$25* ⊘ *Closed Sun.–Tues.* ⊑ *$5 parking at Honolulu Museum of Art.*

Beaches

Much of Southeast Oahu is surrounded by reef, making most of the coast uninviting to swimmers, but the spots where the reef opens up are true gems. The drive along this side of the island is amazing, with its sheer lava-rock walls on one side and deep-blue ocean on the other. There are plenty of restaurants in the suburbs of Hawaii Kai and Kahala, so you can make a day of it, knowing that sustenance isn't far away.

Halona Beach Cove

BEACH | Also known as *From Here to Eternity* Beach and "Pounders," this little beauty is never crowded due to the short, treacherous climb down to the sand. But what a treat it is for the intrepid—perfect for packing a lunch and holing up for the day. It's in a break in the ocean cliffs, with the surrounding crags providing protection from the wind. Open-ocean waves roll up onto the sand (thus the second nickname), but a gently sloping sand bottom takes much of the punch out of them before they hit the shore. Turtles frequent the small cove, seeking respite from the otherwise blustery coast. ⚠ **The current is mellow inside the cove but dangerous once you get outside it. Amenities:** parking (no fee). **Best for:** sunrise. ⊠ *8699 Kalanianaole Hwy., Hawaii Kai* ⊹ *Below Halona Blow Hole Lookout parking lot.*

★ Hanauma Bay Nature Preserve

BEACH | FAMILY | Picture this as the world's biggest open-air aquarium. You come to see fish, and fish you'll see. Due

If you're a snorkeler, head straight for Hanauma Bay, the best and most popular place to snorkel on Oahu.

to their exposure to thousands of visitors every week, these fish are more like family pets than the skittish marine life you might expect. An old volcanic crater has created a haven from the waves where the coral has thrived. Note that there's a fee for nonresidents to enter the preserve; make reservations and prepay online ahead of time. You must also watch a nine-minute video about the nature preserve in its educational center before being allowed down to the bay. Snorkel equipment and lockers are available for rent, and you can walk the short distance from the parking lot or take a tram. ■TIP➜ It's best to visit early in the morning (around 7), as it's difficult to park later in the day. Need transportation? Take TheBus each way from anywhere on the island. **Amenities:** food and drink; lifeguards; parking (fee); showers; toilets. **Best for:** snorkeling; swimming. ✉ 7455 Kalanianaole Hwy., Hawaii Kai ☎ 808/768–6861 ⊕ hanaumabaystatepark.com ✉ Nonresidents $25 (excluding tram from parking lot); parking $3 (cash only); snorkel rental $20

⊘ Closed Mon. and Tues. ⊰ Reservations must be made in advance.

★ Sandy Beach Park
BEACH | Very popular with locals, this broad, sloping beach is covered with sunbathers who come to soak up the rays and watch "The Show"—a shore break that's like no other in the Islands. Monster ocean swells rolling into the beach combined with the sudden rise in the ocean floor causes waves to jack up and crash magnificently. Expert surfers and bodyboarders young and old brave the dangers to enjoy some of the biggest barrels around. ⚠ **Use extreme caution when swimming here. The stretch is nicknamed Break-Neck Beach for a reason: many neck and back injuries are sustained here each year. Amenities:** lifeguards; parking (no fee); showers; toilets. **Best for:** walking. ✉ 7850 Kalanianaole Hwy., Hawaii Kai ⊹ Makai (toward ocean) of Kalanianaole Hwy., 2 miles east of Hanauma Bay.

🍴 Restaurants

Liko's Tap & Table

$$ | AMERICAN | This open-air, upscale taproom puts a local spin on classic American dishes and has an excellent waterfront view from its otherwise nondescript strip-mall location. A long beer, wine, and cocktail menu includes locally sourced drinks. **Known for:** great views in a surprising location; generous servings; local favorite. $ *Average main: $25 ⊠ 377 Keahole St., Suite C2, Hawaii Kai ☎ 808/394–5456 ⊕ www.likoshawaii. com.*

Roy's Hawaii Kai

$$$ | MODERN HAWAIIAN | Roy Yamaguchi is one of the 12 founding chefs of Hawaiian regional cuisine, a culinary movement that put the state on the food map back in 1991. Opened in 1988, his flagship restaurant across the highway from Maunalua Bay is still packed every night with food-savvy visitors and well-heeled residents, all of whom come for classics like smoked Szechuan baby back ribs or blackened ahi with soy mustard butter sauce. **Known for:** signature menu items like blackened ahi with a cultlike following; spectacular sunset views and a tiki torch–lit lanai and bar area; small and large portions available for many dishes. $ *Average main: $34 ⊠ Hawaii Kai Corporate Plaza, 6600 Kalanianaole Hwy., Hawaii Kai ☎ 808/396–7697 ⊕ www. royyamaguchi.com/roys-hawaiikai ⊗ No lunch.*

☕ Coffee and Quick Bites

Kokonuts Shave Ice & Snacks

$ | ICE CREAM | FAMILY | Why not stop for shave ice like President Barack Obama did while visiting the island after the 2008 election? This spot in Koko Marina Center serves fluffy shave ice, açai bowls, bubble drinks, ice cream, and more. **Known for:** acai bowls; shave ice with syrup flavors such as strawberry, coconut, and lilikoi (passionfruit); bubble

drinks. $ *Average main: $5 ⊠ Koko Marina Center, 7192 Kalanianaole Hwy., Unit E121, Hawaii Kai ☎ 808/396–8809 ▭ No credit cards.*

Uncle Clay's House of Pure Aloha

$ | HAWAIIAN | FAMILY | Located in a strip mall in the residential neighborhood of Aina Haina, Uncle Clay's is a happy place. This shave-ice stand specializes in home-made all-natural syrups made from cane sugar and locally sourced fruits, including "kalespin"—a combination of kale and spinach. **Known for:** Uncle Clay's big personality; shave ice that's gone trendy; fun, and kids love it. $ *Average main: $5 ⊠ Aina Haina Shopping Center, 820 W. Hind Dr., Unit 116, Hawaii Kai ✛ Right off Kalanianaole Hwy. ☎ 808/373–5111 ⊕ houseofpurealoha.com.*

Nightlife

BARS

Kona Brewing Pub

BREWPUBS | This massive Kona Brewing Co. restaurant and bar on the docks of Koko Marina has long been a hot spot. In addition to serving the company's signature brews, this authentic pub offers live music Thursday to Sunday nights. It's a lively spot, especially on the weekends when it's standing-room-only at the bar. ⊠ *Koko Marina Center, 7192 Kalanianaole Hwy., Honolulu ☎ 808/396–5662 ⊕ www. konabrewinghawaii.com.*

Waimanalo

11 miles north of Hawaii Kai.

This modest little seaside town flanked by chiseled cliffs is worth a visit. Home to more Native Hawaiian families than Kailua to the north or Hawaii Kai to the south, Waimanalo's biggest draws are its beautiful beaches, offering glorious views to the windward side. Bellows Field Beach Park is great for swimming, bodysurfing, and camping, and

East (Windward) Oahu

KEY

1 *Exploring Sights*

1 *Restaurants*

1 *Quick Bites*

1 *Hotels*

PACIFIC

OCEAN

Lanikai Beach

Bellows Field
Beach Park

Waimanalo Beach Park

72

Kalanianaole Hwy.

MANANA ISLAND
(RABBIT ISLAND)

Makapuu Beach Park

12 8

Koko
Crater 5

Sandy Beach Park

9 Hawaii 3
Kai

11 4 7

Halona Beach Cove

Hanauma Bay
Nature Preserve

Hanauma Bay

KOKO
HEAD

G   H   I

Waimanalo Bay Beach Park is also safe for swimming.

Down the side roads, as you head *mauka* (toward the mountains), are little farms that grow a variety of fruits and flowers. Toward the back of the valley are small ranches with grazing horses. ■**TIP**➜ **If you see any trucks selling corn, and you're staying at a place where you can cook it, be sure to get some. It may be the sweetest you'll ever eat, and prices are the lowest on Oahu.**

GETTING HERE AND AROUND

The drive from Waikiki in Honolulu takes approximately 30 minutes.

Sights

★ Makapuu Point

VIEWPOINT | This spot has breathtaking views of the ocean, mountains, and the windward Islands. The point of land jutting out in the distance is Mokapu Peninsula, site of a U.S. Marine base. The spired mountain peak is Mt. Olomana. On the long pier is part of the Makai Undersea Test Range, a research facility that's closed to the public. Offshore is Manana Island (Rabbit Island), a picturesque cay said to resemble a swimming bunny with its ears pulled back. Ironically enough, Manana Island was once overrun with rabbits, thanks to a rancher who let a few hares run wild on the land. They were eradicated in 1994 by biologists who grew concerned that the rabbits were destroying the island's native plants.

Nestled in the cliff face is the Makapuu Lighthouse, which became operational in 1909 and has the largest lighthouse lens in America. The lighthouse is closed to the public, but near the Makapuu Point turnout you can find the start of a paved mile-long road (it's closed to vehicular traffic). Hike up to the top of the 647-foot bluff for a closer view of the lighthouse and, in winter, to do some whale-watching. ⊠ *Ka Iwi State*

Scenic Shoreline, Kalanianaole Hwy., Waimanalo ✢ *At Makapuu Beach* ⊕ *dlnr.hawaii.gov/dsp/hiking/oahu/ makapuu-point-lighthouse-trail.*

Sea Life Park

AQUARIUM | **FAMILY** | Dolphins leap and spin, and penguins frolic at this marine-life attraction 15 miles from Waikiki at scenic Makapuu Point. The park has a 300,000-gallon Hawaiian reef aquarium, a breeding sanctuary for Hawaii's endangered *honu* sea turtles, penguin and Hawaiian monk seal habitats, an aviary, a seabird sanctuary, and many more marine attractions. Sign up for a dolphin, sea lion, or shark encounter to get up close and personal in the water with these sea creatures. ⊠ *41-202 Kalanianaole Hwy., Waimanalo* ☎ *808/259–2500* ⊕ *sealifeparkhawaii.com* ⊠ *$45; parking $10.*

Beaches

★ Bellows Field Beach Park

BEACH | Bellows is the same beach as Waimanalo, but it's under the auspices of the military, making it more friendly for visitors—though that also limits public access on weekends. The park area is excellent for camping, and ironwood trees provide plenty of shade. There are no food concessions, but McDonald's and other takeout options are right outside the entrance gate; there's also a weekend farmers' market. ■**TIP**➜ **The beach is best before 2 pm. After 2, trade winds bring clouds that get hung up on steep mountains nearby, causing overcast skies.** **Amenities:** lifeguards; parking (no fee); showers; toilets. **Best for:** solitude; swimming; walking. ⊠ *520 Tinker Rd., Waimanalo* ✢ *Enter on Kalanianaole Hwy. near Waimanalo town center.*

Makapuu Beach Park

BEACH | A magnificent beach protected by Makapuu Point welcomes you to the windward side. Hang gliders circle above, and the water is filled with bodyboarders.

Just off the coast you can see Bird Island, a sanctuary for aquatic fowl, jutting out of the blue. The currents can be heavy, so check with a lifeguard if you're unsure of safety. Before you leave, take the prettiest (and coldest) outdoor shower available on the island. Being surrounded by tropical flowers and foliage while you rinse off that sand will be a memory you will cherish from this side of the rock. **Amenities:** lifeguards; parking (no fee); showers; toilets. **Best for:** sunrise; walking. ⊠ *41-095 Kalanianaole Hwy., Waimanalo* ✛ *Across from Sea Life Park, 2 miles south of Waimanalo.*

Waimanalo Bay Beach Park

BEACH | FAMILY | One of the most beautiful beaches on Oahu, Waimanalo is a local pick, busy with picnicking families and active sports fields. Expect a wide stretch of sand; turquoise, emerald, and deep-blue water; and gentle shore-breaking waves that are fun for all ages. Theft is an occasional problem, so lock your car. **Amenities:** lifeguards; parking (no fee); showers; toilets. **Best for:** sunrise; swimming; walking. ⊠ *41-849 Kalanianaole Hwy., Waimanalo* ✛ *South of Waimanalo town center.*

Kailua

6 miles north of Waimanalo.

Upscale Kailua is the most easily accessed town on the windward side. It has two of Oahu's best beaches as well as great shopping and dining opportunities in its central core. You could easily spend a day visiting the stunning beaches, kayaking, exploring a hidden *heiau* (shrine), picnicking, or dining out with locals.

GETTING HERE AND AROUND

The easiest way to reach Kailua from Waikiki, roughly 15 miles to the southwest, is to take the H1 interstate to Highway 61 (best known as the Pali Highway). On your way, stop for a breathtaking view

at the Pali Lookout. Emerging from the tunnels, you'll immediately see what all the fuss is about—a turquoise bay lies to your left while you hug the emerald-green serrated mountains of the Koolau Range.

 ## Sights

Ulupo Heiau State Historic Site

RUINS | Find this spot—where signs near a *heiau* (shrine) also explain Kailua's early history—tucked next to the Windward YMCA. Although they may look like piles of rocks to the uninitiated, heiau are sacred stone platforms for the worship of the gods and date from ancient times. *Ulupo* means "night inspiration," referring to the legendary Menehune, a mythical race of diminutive people who are said to have built the heiau under the cloak of darkness. ⊠ *Kalanianaole Hwy. and Kailua Rd., Kailua* ✛ *Behind Windward YMCA* ⊕ *dlnr.hawaii.gov/dsp/parks/oahu/ulupo-heiau-state-historic-site.*

 ## Beaches

★ Kailua Beach Park

BEACH | FAMILY | A cobalt-blue sea and a wide continuous arc of powdery sand make this one of the island's best beaches, as illustrated by the crowds of local families who spend their weekend days here. The water is calm, a line of palms and ironwoods provides shade on the sand, and a huge park has picnic pavilions where you can escape the heat. This is also the "it" spot for windsurfing or kiteboarding, and you can rent kayaks nearby at Kailua Beach Adventures (⊠ *130 Kailua Rd.*) for day trips to the Mokulua Islands. **Amenities:** lifeguards; parking (no fee); showers; toilets; water sports. **Best for:** swimming; walking; windsurfing. ⊠ *437 Kawailoa Rd., Kailua* ✛ *Near Kailua town, turn right on Kailua Rd. After Kalapawai Market, cross bridge, then turn left into beach parking lot.*

Windward Oahu Villages

Tiny villages—generally consisting of a sign, a store, a beach park, possibly a post office, and not much more—are strung along Kamehameha Highway on the windward side. Each has something to offer. In **Waiahole**, look for fruit stands and the Waiahole Poi Factory, which is worth a stop for Hawaiian food and their famous poi. In **Kaaawa**, there's a convenience store/gas station. In **Punaluu**, get a plate lunch at Keneke's, or visit the venerable Chings' General Store. **Hauula** has the gallery of fanciful landscape artist Lance Fairly; the Shrimp Shack; Hauula Gift Shop, a clothing shop where sarongs wave like banners; and, at Hauula Kai Shopping Center, Penny's Malasadas and Tamura's Market, with excellent seafood and the last liquor before Mormon-dominated Laie.

★ Lanikai Beach

BEACH | Think of the beaches you see in commercials: peaceful jade-green waters, powder-soft white sand, families and dogs frolicking, and offshore islands in the distance. It's an ideal spot for camping out with a book. Though the beach hides behind multimillion-dollar houses, by state law there is public access every 400 yards. Street parking is available but very difficult to find (and prohibited on holiday weekends). Consider parking at Kailua Beach Park and walking along the paved pathway into Lanikai. Just don't block the boat ramp stalls. There are no shower or bathroom facilities here—but you'll find both at Kailua Beach Park. ■TIP➔ **Look for walled or fenced pathways every 400 yards, leading to the beach. Be sure not to park in the marked bike/jogging lane. Amenities:** none. **Best for:** sunrise; swimming; walking. ⊠ *974 Mokulua Dr., Kailua* ✛ *Past Kailua Beach Park.*

🍴 Restaurants

Baci Bistro

$$ | **ITALIAN** | A long-time local favorite, elegant, inviting Baci Bistro is a classic Italian restaurant offering an extensive range of pastas, antipasti, mains, and really excellent desserts. Consider the ravioli *del giorno* followed by *vitello* (veal) cooked with a variety of sauces. **Known for:** cozy, romantic setting; a wide variety of antipasti; homemade pasta. ⑤ *Average main: $23* ⊠ *30 Aulike St., Kailua* ☎ *808/262–7555* ⊕ *www.bacibistro.com.*

Big City Diner

$ | **AMERICAN** | **FAMILY** | This outlet of the popular retro diner chain—with four locations, including one at Windward Mall in neighboring Kaneohe—is across the street from a small bird sanctuary and has outdoor lanai seating and a bar. It's a hot spot for breakfast and Sunday football; popular dinner items include grilled steak with onions and mushrooms, baby back ribs, meatloaf, and salads. **Known for:** nice indoor and outdoor bar; big portions; happy families returning again and again. ⑤ *Average main: $16* ⊠ *108 Hekili St., Kailua* ☎ *808/263–8880* ⊕ *bigcitydinerhawaii.com.*

Buzz's Original Steak House

$$$ | **STEAKHOUSE** | Virtually unchanged since opening in 1967, this neighborhood institution opposite Kailua Beach Park is filled with the aroma of grilling steaks and plumeria blooms. It doesn't matter if you're a bit sandy and beach bedraggled (though bare feet are a no-no, as are tank tops after 4:30 pm)—just find a spot in the cozy maze of rooms; stop

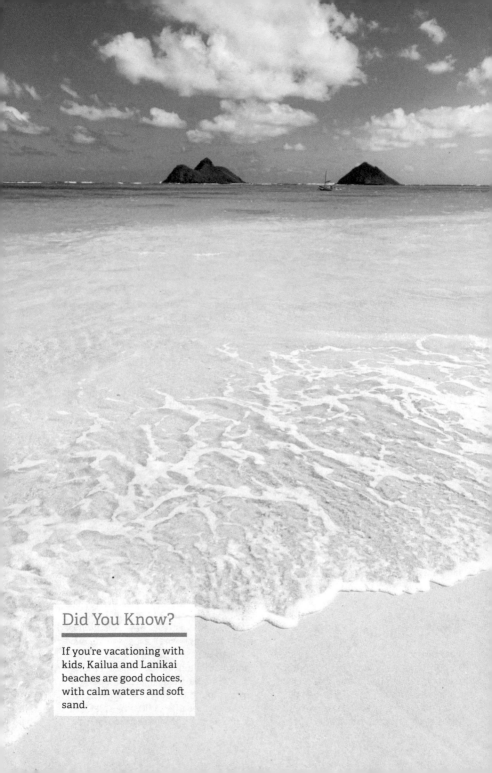

Did You Know?

If you're vacationing with kids, Kailua and Lanikai beaches are good choices, with calm waters and soft sand.

at the salad bar; and order a steak, a burger, teriyaki chicken, or the fresh fish special. **Known for:** excellent fruity beach cocktails, including very strong mai tais; local institution; the views from the lanai at lunch. ⑤ *Average main: $35 ⊠ 413 Kawailoa Rd., Kailua* ☎ *808/261–4661* ⊕ *buzzsoriginalsteakhouse.com.*

Cinnamon's Restaurant

$ | **AMERICAN** | **FAMILY** | Known for uncommon variations on common breakfast themes, this neighborhood favorite is tucked into a hard-to-find Kailua office park (call for directions). Local-style lunch plates are good, but the main attraction is breakfast, when you don't want to miss the guava chiffon and red velvet pancakes or the signature cinnamon macadamia-nut rolls. Be prepared to wait. **Known for:** long waits; endless variations on pancakes, eggs Benedict, and waffles; cinnamon rolls (of course). ⑤ *Average main: $16 ⊠ 315 Uluniu St., Kailua* ☎ *808/261–8724* ⊕ *cinnamons808. com* ⊗ *No lunch on Sun. and holidays. Takeout only on Wed. and Thurs.*

GOEN Dining + Bar

$$ | **ASIAN FUSION** | This chef Roy Yamaguchi spinoff serves elevated Hawaii regional cuisine and cocktails in the Lau Hala Shops complex, right where the old Macy's used to be. The kids' menu goes above and beyond the typical fare. **Known for:** yummy cocktails; open-air and patio seating; friendly, attentive service. ⑤ *Average main: $25 ⊠ 1175 Lunahaneli Pl, 573 Kailua Road, Kailua* ☎ *808/263–4636* ⊕ *royyamaguchi.com/goen-kailua* ⊗ *No lunch Mon.–Thurs.*

Kailua Town Pub & Grill

$ | **AMERICAN** | Looking for pub grub? This is the spot in Kailua for enormous gourmet hamburgers, fish-and-chips, and, of course, an ever-changing selection of craft beers on tap. **Known for:** friendly atmosphere; happy hour; craft beer. ⑤ *Average main: $14 ⊠ 26 Hoolai St., Suite 1100, Kailua* ☎ *808/230–8444* ⊕ *www.kailuatownpub.com.*

Kalapawai Cafe & Deli

$$ | **ECLECTIC** | **FAMILY** | This one-stop, green-and-white, Mediterranean-leaning café, wine bar, bakery, and gourmet deli is the creation of the Dymond family, two generations of restaurateurs who have shaken up the windward food scene. Come in on your way to the beach for a cup of coffee and bagel, and stop back for a gourmet pizza or bruschetta for lunch or a candlelight dinner at night. **Known for:** impressive wine list for such a small spot; signature dishes by night; good coffee and sandwiches by day. ⑤ *Average main: $20 ⊠ 750 Kailua Rd., Kailua* ☎ *808/262–3354* ⊕ *kalapawaimarket.com.*

☕ Coffee and Quick Bites

★ Agnes' Portuguese Bake Shop

$ | **BAKERY** | This food truck in the Manuhealii parking lot serves delicious, made-to-order *malasadas* (Portuguese donuts) that are crispy and dark brown on the outside and soft, chewy, and sweet on the inside. They're also denser than those found at some other bakeries on the island. **Known for:** convenient location; authentic malasadas; no-fuss takeout. ⑤ *Average main: $15 ⊠ 5 Ho'ola'i St., Kailua* ⊹ *In the parking lot of Manuhealii across from Kalapawai Cafe* ⊗ *Closed Sun.* ☞ *Just over $1 a malasada.*

Island Snow

$ | **ICE CREAM** | **FAMILY** | This hole-in-the-wall has been creating shave ice perfection in its tiny original spot since 1979, but when two young girls named Obama discovered the luscious flavors in 2008, it was really put on the map. A favorite spot for both locals and storied visitors (and these days lots of regular tourists), it makes a mean shave ice, whether you stick with standard flavors like cherry or go for lilikoi guava with a snowcap on top. **Known for:** long lines of locals and tourists; the best shave ice on the windward side; the Obama girls, who grew up on this stuff (look for their photos on the wall).

$ *Average main: $6* ✉ *130 Kailua Rd., Kailua* ☎ *808/263–6339* ⊕ *islandsnow. com.*

Kalapawai Market

$ | SANDWICHES | FAMILY | Generations of children have purchased their beach snacks and sodas at Kalapawai Market near Kailua Beach. A Windward Oahu landmark since 1932, the green-and-white market has distinctive charm. **Known for:** a great selection of wine; takeout deli sandwiches; good coffee. $ *Average main: $7* ✉ *306 S. Kalaheo Ave., Kailua* ☎ *808/262–4359* ⊕ *www. kalapawaimarket.com.*

Hotels

Sheffield House Bed & Breakfast

$$ | B&B/INN | Close to Kailua Beach, this cozy bed-and-breakfast has been around since the 1990s and has two suites that are attached to the main house but have their own private entrances. **Pros:** boutiques and dining abound in Kailua; one of the few legal B&Bs in Kailua; best beaches on the island. **Cons:** rental car a must; don't expect luxury; B&Bs aren't for everybody. $ *Rooms from: $180* ✉ *131 Kuulei Rd., Kailua* ☎ *808/262–0721* ⊕ *www.hawaiisheffieldhouse.com* ⇆ *2 rooms* ⦿ *Free Breakfast* ☞ *Breakfast included on the first morning only.*

Nightlife

BARS

Tap & Barrel

BREWPUBS | Lanikai Brewing Company's taproom features its island-centric beer, including seasonal varieties that incorporate unusual ingredients like surname cherry, mushrooms, and white tea. It also serves Valentina's wood-fired pizza and sometimes has a food truck out front. In addition to beer, there are spirits from the brewery's new distillery line, homemade sangria, Paradise Ciders, and other sips from which to choose. Kids are welcome, and there are board games

available to play. ✉ *167 Hamakua Dr., Kailua* ⊕ *www.lanikaibrewing.com.*

Shopping

Shopping on the windward side is one of Oahu's best-kept secrets. The trip here takes a half hour by car or about an hour on TheBus. The real treats lie in the small boutiques and galleries in the heart of Kailua—the perfect place to find unique gifts. ■**TIP→ Stop by Kalapawai Market, at Kailua Beach near the entrance to Lani-kai, for sandwiches and cold drinks, as well as souvenirs, and finish the day relaxing on a less bustling white-sand beach.**

BOOKS

★ Bookends

BOOKS | FAMILY | Shop for gifts or yourself at this cozy, independent bookstore, which feels more like a small-town library, welcoming browsers to linger. It sells new and secondhand books, and its children's section is filled with both books and toys. ✉ *600 Kailua Rd., Unit 126, Kailua* ☎ *808/261–1996* ⊕ *instagram. com/bookendskailua.*

CLOTHING

Manuhealii

MIXED CLOTHING | For modern and authentic aloha attire made in Hawaii, Manu-healii is your place. The Kailua storefront is one of two physical locations (the other is in Honolulu). The clothes aren't inexpensive, but their quality is superb. ✉ *5 Ho'ola'i St., Kailua* ☎ *808/261–9865* ⊕ *manuhealii.com.*

HEALTH AND BEAUTY PRODUCTS

Lanikai Bath and Body

OTHER HEALTH & BEAUTY | Take home the fragrances of the Islands with this shop's organic body lotions, hand creams, soaps, sprays, bath salts, and scrubs. Botanical extracts, such as papaya, mango, sea kelp, and calendula, are combined with essential oils, including from macadamia and kukui nuts, to produce the shop's refined line of products. ✉ *Kailua Shopping Center, 600 Kailua*

Rd., Suite 119, Kailua ☏ 808/262–3260
⊕ lanikaibathandbody.com.

HOME DECOR
★ Under a Hula Moon
HOUSEWARES | Exclusive tabletop items
and Pacific home decor, such as shell
wreaths, shell night-lights, Hawaiian
beach sheets, frames, and unique one-
of-a-kind gifts with an Islands influence,
define this eclectic shop. ⊠ Kailua
Shopping Center, 600 Kailua Rd., Kailua
☏ 808/261–2200 ⊕ underahulamoonkai-
lua.com.

Kaneohe

6 miles west of Kailua.

The largest community on Oahu's windward side, Kaneohe (meaning "bamboo
man" in Hawaiian) is a sprawling community with malls, car dealerships, and a
few worthwhile restaurants. At the base
of the Koolau Range, Kaneohe sees a lot
more rain than neighboring Kailua and is
the greener for it. Two noteworthy sights
take advantage of their proximity to the
mountains: the Byodo-In Temple and
Hoomaluhia Botanical Garden.

GETTING HERE AND AROUND
Kaneohe is a 30-minute drive or one-hour
bus ride from Waikiki. If driving, you can
take any of the three highways across
the Koolau Mountains: the H3, the Pali,
or the Likelike.

Sights

★ Byodo-In Temple
TEMPLE | Tucked away in the back of the
Valley of the Temples Memorial Park
is a replica of the 11th-century temple
at Uji in Japan. A 2-ton, carved-wood
statue of the Buddha presides inside the
main building. Next to the temple are a
meditation pavilion and gardens set dra-
matically against the sheer, green cliffs
of the Koolau Mountains. You can ring
the 5-foot, 3-ton brass bell for good luck;

feed some of the hundreds of koi, ducks,
and swans that inhabit the garden's
2-acre pond (buy fish food at the gift
shop); and relax and enjoy the peaceful
surroundings. Call ahead to schedule
a guided tour. ⊠ 47-200 Kahekili Hwy.,
Kaneohe ☏ 808/239–9844 ⊕ byodo-in.
com ☒ $5.

★ Hoomaluhia Botanical Garden
GARDEN | FAMILY | The name, which
means "a peaceful refuge," describes
the serenity and feeling of endless space
you find in this verdant garden framed
by the stunning Koolau Range. Its 400
acres contain specimens from such
tropical areas as the Americas, Africa,
Melanesia, the Philippines, and Hawaii.
Not just for the botanist, Hoomaluhia
also has a 32-acre lake, easy walking
trails, and open lawns ideal for picnicking
and camping by permit. Families can
also take advantage of the park's catch-
and-release tilapia fishing program; free
bamboo fishing poles are sometimes
available for borrowing at the visitor
center. If you see unusually dressed-up
visitors, they are likely selfie seekers
doing it for the 'gram. Hoomaluhia is very
photogenic; just make sure you're not
blocking the roadways in search of the
perfect shot. ⊠ 45-680 Luluku Rd., Kaneohe ☏ 808/233–7323 ⊕ www.honolulu.
gov/parks/hbg.html ☒ Free.

★ Nuuanu Pali State Wayside
VIEWPOINT | This panoramic perch looks
out to expansive views of Windward
Oahu—from Kaneohe Bay to a small
island off the coast called Mokolii ("little
lizard," also known as Chinaman's Hat). It
was in this region that King Kamehameha I drove defending forces over the
edges of the 1,200-foot-high cliffs, thus
winning the decisive battle for control of
the island.

Temperatures at the summit are several
degrees cooler than in warm Waikiki, so
bring a jacket along. Hang on tight to any
loose possessions, and consider wearing
pants; it gets extremely windy at the

lookout, which is part of the fun. After arriving in the pay-to-park lot, remove valuables from your car and lock it; break-ins have occurred here (this wayside is in the most trafficked state park in Hawaii). ✉ *Pali Hwy., Kaneohe ✛ at very top of Pali Hwy.* ⊕ *dlnr.hawaii.gov/dsp/parks/ oahu/nuuanu-pali-state-wayside* ▣ *Parking $7 per car.*

Restaurants

Haleiwa Joe's Haiku Gardens

$$$ | AMERICAN | The Haleiwa location may be the namesake and claim the surf, but this windward-side branch offers knock-'em-dead views and a tiki torch–lit atmosphere after dark along with the friendly vibe and grilled seafood. In addition to surf-and-turf favorites, look for special preparations of each day's catch, which is delivered straight from the Honolulu Fish Auction. **Known for:** excellent daily specials; stunning views of Haiku Gardens; reliable for both seafood and meat. ⑤ *Average main: $28* ✉ *44-336 Haiku Rd., Kaneohe* ☏ *808/274–6671* ⊕ *www. haleiwajoes.com/kaneohe-menu.*

Pah Ke's Chinese Restaurant

$ | CHINESE | FAMILY | If you happen to be on the windward side at dinner time, this out-of-the-ordinary Chinese restaurant—named for the local pidgin term for "Chinese" (literally translated, this is "Chinese's Chinese Restaurant")—is a good option. Ebullient owner and chef Raymond Siu, a former hotel pastry chef, focuses on healthier cooking techniques and local ingredients. **Known for:** a big dining room with bright lights and not much atmosphere; dependable spot for the family; house specials that are usually better than standard menu fare. ⑤ *Average main: $15* ✉ *46-018 Kamehameha Hwy., Kaneohe* ☏ *808/235–4505* ⊕ *pahke.com* ☞ *BYOB.*

Hotels

Paradise Bay Resort

$$ | RESORT | Right on picturesque Kaneohe Bay amid the junglelike fauna of the windward side, this resort offers apartment-style units ranging from cozy studios to spacious two-bedroom suites with breathtaking views of the majestic Koolau Mountains; there's also one stand-alone cottage in a remote area not generally frequented by tourists. **Pros:** en suite kitchens or kitchenettes; local, authentic experience; beautiful views over the bay. **Cons:** rental car a necessity (but parking included in $35 nightly resort fee); neighborhood is a bit run-down; remote location not near most other attractions. ⑤ *Rooms from: $200* ✉ *47-039 Lihikai Dr., Kaneohe* ☏ *808/239–5711* ⊕ *www.paradisebayresort.com* ⇆ *46 rooms.*

🛍 Shopping

HOME DECOR

Jeff Chang Pottery & Fine Crafts

ART GALLERIES | This family-owned and -operated gallery offers the artist's functional and decorative pottery as well as the works of approximately 200 other American artisans. Jeff has worked with clay for more than 40 years and his wife, Karon, operates the gallery and selects other works, including jewelry, glass pieces, metal sculpture, wall art, wooden items, musical instruments, chimes, suncatchers, sand globes and pictures, holiday decor, and ornaments. ✉ *Windward Mall, 46-056 Kamehameha Hwy., 2nd fl., Theatre Wing, Kaneohe* ☏ *808/235–5150* ⊕ *www.windwardmall. com/stores/jeff-chang-pottery.*

Kualoa Point is in Kualoa Regional Park in Kaaawa, a beautiful but windy area overlooking Kaneohe Bay and the towering Koolau Mountains.

Kaaawa

14 miles north of Kaneohe.

Less a village than a collection of homes, Kaaawa consists of little more than a post office, bus stop, and gas station—bookended by an elementary school and a fire station. Of course, there's a beach park, too.

GETTING HERE AND AROUND

With its location on Kamehameha Highway, you'll pass through Kaaawa immediately before or after you pass Kualoa Ranch.

Sights

Ahupuaa O Kahana State Park

NATURE PRESERVE | FAMILY | This park offers the true Hawaiian experience: a beautiful windward bay sits a short walk away from the Huilua Fishpond, a National Historic Landmark (note that it's undergoing restoration to reinforce the rock walls). There are rain-forest hikes through lots of local fruit trees, a hunting area for pigs, and a coconut grove for picnicking. The water is suitable for swimming and bodysurfing, though it's a little cloudy for snorkeling. ✉ *52-222 Kamehameha Hwy., near Kahana Bay, Kaaawa* ⊕ *dlnr.hawaii.gov/dsp/parks/oahu/ahupuaa-o-kahana-state-park.*

★ Kualoa Ranch

FARM/RANCH | FAMILY | Encompassing 4,000 acres, about 45 minutes by car from Waikiki, this working ranch offers a wide range of activities—from ATV and horseback tours to ziplining or expeditions into the valley on an electric bike. The mountains that serve as the backdrop here may seem familiar: the ranch has served as the set for movies such as *Jurassic Park* and *Windtalkers,* as well as TV shows like *Magnum P.I.* and *Lost* (and you can take a film sites tour). From the grounds, you'll have a wonderful view of the ocean and Mokolii (Chinaman's

The 4,000-acre Kualoa Ranch may look familiar to you: it's been featured in several movies and TV shows. You can even take a film sites tour of the ranch.

Hat). You can drop by the visitor center anytime, but it's best to book activities and tours two or three days in advance. ✉ 49-560 Kamehameha Hwy., Kaaawa ☎ 808/237–7321 ⊕ www.kualoa.com ⊠ From $48.

Mokolii

NATURE SIGHT | As you drive the windward and northern shores along Kamehameha Highway, you'll note a number of interesting geological features. At Kualoa, look to the ocean at the uniquely shaped little island of Mokolii ("little lizard"), a 206-foot-high sea stack also known as Chinaman's Hat (for its hat-like shape). According to Hawaiian legend, the goddess Hiiaka, sister of Pele, slew the dragon Mokolii and flung its tail into the sea, forming the distinct islet. Other dragon body parts—in the form of rocks, of course—were scattered along the base of nearby Kualoa Ridge. ✉ 49-479 Kamehameha Hwy., Kaaawa.

Beaches

Kahana Bay Beach Park

BEACH | FAMILY | Local parents often bring their children here to wade in safety in the very shallow, protected waters. This pretty beach cove, surrounded by mountains, has a long arc of sand that is great for walking and a cool, shady grove of tall ironwood and pandanus trees that is ideal for a picnic. An ancient Hawaiian fishpond, which was in use until the 1920s, is visible nearby. Note, though, that the water here is not generally a clear blue due to the runoff from heavy rains in the valley. **Amenities:** parking (no fee); showers; toilets. **Best for:** swimming; walking. ✉ 52-201 Kamehameha Hwy., Kaaawa ⊹ North of Kualoa Park.

★ Kualoa Regional Park

BEACH | Grassy expanses border a long, narrow stretch of sand with spectacular views of Kaneohe Bay and the Koolau Mountains, making Kualoa one of the island's most beautiful picnic, camping, and beach areas. Dominating the view is an islet called Mokolii, better known as Chinaman's Hat, which rises 206 feet above the water. You can swim in the shallow areas of this rarely crowded beach year-round. The one drawback is that it's usually windy here, but the wide-open spaces are ideal for kite flying. **Amenities:** lifeguards; showers; toilets. **Best for:** solitude; swimming. ⊠ *49-479 Kamehameha Hwy., Kaaawa ✛ North of Waiahole.*

Punaluu Beach Park

BEACH | If you're making a circle of the island, this is a great place to stop, stretch your legs, and get your toes wet. It's nice (there is a sandy bottom and mostly calm conditions) and easy (the sand literally comes up to your parked car). Plus there are full facilities, shops for picnic supplies, and lots of shade trees. Often overlooked, and often overcast, Punaluu can afford you a moment of fresh air before you get back to your sightseeing. **Amenities:** food and drink; parking (no fee); showers; toilets. **Best for:** solitude; swimming. ⊠ *53-400 Kamehameha Hwy., Hauula.*

Laie

10 miles north of Kaaawa, 33 miles north of Honolulu.

Visiting Laie—over an hour by car and a world away from bustling Waikiki and Honolulu—is like taking a trip to another island. Home to a Mormon temple and the Mormon-founded Polynesian Cultural Center, Laie is a "dry town."

GETTING HERE AND AROUND

From Waikiki, getting here will take a little more than an hour by car or up to two hours by bus. By car you can take the H2 past Haleiwa, until it joins Kamehameha Highway. Along the route, you'll pass Haleiwa town and world-famous North Shore surf spots. Alternatively, take any of the highways going over the Koolau Range (Likelike, Pali, or H3) to Kaneohe and follow Highway 83 north. This road will then meet up with the two-lane Kamehameha Highway, which leads you to all points north.

Sights

Polynesian Cultural Center

MUSEUM VILLAGE | FAMILY | Re-created individual villages showcase the lifestyles and traditions of Hawaii, Tahiti, Samoa, Fiji, the Marquesas Islands, New Zealand, and Tonga. In addition, the 42-acre center, which is 35 miles from Waikiki and which was founded in 1963 by the Church of Jesus Christ of Latter-day Saints, has restaurants, hoots luau, and demonstrates cultural traditions, such as hula, fire dancing, and ancient ceremonies. The Hukilau Marketplace carries Polynesian handicrafts.

There are multiple packages available, from basic admission to an all-inclusive deal. Every May, the Center hosts the World Fireknife Championships, an event that draws the top fireknife dance performers from around the world. Get tickets for that event in advance. ■TIP→ If you're staying in Honolulu, see the Center as part of a van tour so you won't have to drive home late at night after the two-hour evening show. ⊠ *55-370 Kamehameha Hwy., Laie* ☎ *800/367–7060* ⊕ *www. polynesia.com* ⊠ *From $70* ⊗ *Closed Sun. and Wed.*

Beaches

Malaekahana State Recreation Area

BEACH | FAMILY | The big attraction here is tiny Goat Island, a bird sanctuary just offshore. At low tide the water is shallow enough—never more than waist-high—for you to wade out to it. Wear sneakers or aqua socks so you don't cut yourself on the coral. The beach itself is fairly narrow but long enough for a 20-minute stroll, one-way. The waves are never too big, and sometimes they're just right for novice bodysurfers. The entrance gates, which close at 7:45 pm in summer and 6:45 pm the rest of the year, are easy to miss, and you can't see the beach from the road. It's a great rural getaway: families love to camp in the groves of ironwood trees at Malaekahana State Park, and there are also cabins here. **Amenities:** parking (no fee); showers; toilets. **Best for:** swimming; walking. ⊠ *56-207 Kamehameha Hwy., Laie* ✛ *Enter at gates ½ mile north of Laie on Kamehameha Hwy.* ⊕ *dlnr.hawaii.gov/dsp/parks/oahu/malaekahana-state-recreation-area.*

 # Hotels

Courtyard Oahu North Shore

$$$ | HOTEL | FAMILY | This property offers reliable and affordable accommodations close to the Polynesian Cultural Center and a short drive to some of the North Shore's most iconic beaches and surfing spots. **Pros:** near the beach; best bet for North Shore exploring; reliable, modern, and clean. **Cons:** a car is needed, and parking is not free; no alcohol served in the hotel or nearby establishments; a long drive to the rest of Oahu's attractions. ⑤ *Rooms from: $270* ⊠ *55-400 Kamehameha Hwy., Laie* ☎ *808/293-4900* ⊕ *marriott.com* ⤢ *144 rooms* ¶⊙¶ *No Meals.*

Chapter 7

ACTIVITIES AND TOURS

Updated by
Powell Berger

Although much is written about the water surrounding this little rock known as Oahu, there is as much to be said for the rock itself. It's a wonder of nature, thrust from the ocean floor thousands of millennia ago by a volcanic hot spot that is still spitting out islands today.

Hawaii is the most remote island chain on Earth, with creatures and plants that can be seen here and nowhere else. And there are dozens of ways for you to check them all out.

From the air, you can peer down into nooks and crannies in the mountains—where cars cannot reach and hikers don't dare. Whether flitting here and there amid a helicopter's rush and roar or sailing by in the silence of a glider's reverie, you glimpse sights that few have experienced. Or, if you would rather, take a step back in time and take off from the waters of Keehi Lagoon in a World War II–era seaplane. Follow the flight path flown by the Japanese Zeros as they attempted to destroy Pearl Harbor and the American spirit.

If you prefer to stay grounded, Oahu is covered in hiking trails that traverse everything from tropical rain forest to arid desert. Even when in the bustling city of Honolulu, you are but minutes from hidden waterfalls and bamboo forests. Out west, you can wander a dusty path that has long since given up its ability to accommodate cars but is perfect for hikers. You can admire sea arches and gape at caves opened by the rock slides that closed the road. You can also camp out on many of these treks and beaches.

If somewhat less rugged and less vigorous exploration is more your style, how about letting horses do your dirty work? You can ride them on the beaches and in the valleys, checking out ancient holy sites, movie sets, and brilliant vistas.

Finally, there is the ancient sport of Scotland. Why merely hike into the rain forest when you can slice a 280-yard drive through it and then hunt for your Titleist in the bushy leaves instead? Almost 40 courses cover this tiny expanse, ranging from the target jungle golf of the Royal Hawaiian Golf Club to the pro-style links of Turtle Bay. There is no off-season in the tropics, and no one here knows your real handicap.

Aerial Tours

Taking an aerial tour of the Islands opens up a world of perspective. Look down from the sky at the outline of the USS *Arizona,* where it lies in its final resting place below the waters of Pearl Harbor, or get a glimpse of the vast carved expanse of a volcanic crater—here are views only seen by an "eye in the sky." Don't forget your camera.

⚠ **All helicopter tour companies in Hawaii are under increasing legislative and regulatory scrutiny due to multiple fatal accidents**

Take a helicopter tour for a unique perspective of the island.

since 2018, so it's possible that they will undergo further regulations and limitations in the near future.

HONOLULU

Blue Hawaiian Helicopters

AIR EXCURSIONS | This company stakes its claim as Hawaii's largest helicopter operation, with tours on all the major Islands and more than two-dozen choppers in its fleet. The 45-minute Oahu tour seats up to six passengers and includes narration from your friendly pilot along with sweeping views of Waikiki, the beautiful windward coast, and the North Shore. If you like to see the world from above or are just pinched for time and want to get a quick overview of the whole island without renting a car, this is the way to go. Discounts are available if you book online in advance. ⊠ *99 Kaulele Pl., Airport Area* ☎ *808/831–8800, 800/745–2583* ⊕ *www. bluehawaiian.com* ⌕ *From $129.*

Magnum Helicopters

AIR EXCURSIONS | For the adventurous, this *Magnum P.I.*, doors-off helicopter tour offers sweeping views of Keehi Lagoon through urban Honolulu and the harbor, including the Aloha Tower and Waikiki Beach. Soar past and over Diamond Head Crater and up the scenic coast by Makapuu Lighthouse and Sandy Beach and over Windward Oahu's iconic Lanikai and Kailua Beaches. The breathtaking finale takes you inland to Sacred Falls, known for its stunning, 1,000-foot drop and its starring role in *Jurassic Park*, before returning to the airport via North Shore surf spots and a bird's-eye view of Pearl Harbor and the USS *Arizona* Memorial. If you're looking for more thrill (or a cool proposal site), opt for the exclusive mountain-top landing. And if water is your thing, your Navy SEAL guide will join you in plunging into the ocean for some scuba diving. ⊠ *130 Iolana Pl., Airport Area* ☎ *808/833–4354* ⊕ *www.magnum-helicopters.com* ⌕ *From $295.*

NORTH SHORE

Most aerial tour and skydiving operators on the North Shore work out of Kawaihapai Airfield (formerly known as Dillingham Airfield). Controversially, the airfield may be closed to most of these operators. Though the activity and tour outfitters object, the issue continues to be considered. If you book a glider or skydiving adventure, definitely reconfirm with your outfitter closer to the time of any reservation to ensure that it is operational.

Honolulu Soaring — The Original Glider Rides

AIR EXCURSIONS | "Mr. Bill" has been offering piloted glider (sailplane) rides over the northwest end of Oahu's North Shore since 1970. Scenic rides for one or two passengers are in sleek, bubble-top, motorless aircraft with aerial views of mountains, shoreline, coral pools, windsurfing sails, and, in winter, humpback whales. Seeking more thrills? You can also take a more acrobatic ride or take control yourself in a mini-lesson. Flights run 15–60 minutes long. The company operates two days a week, and reservations are requested. ✉ Dillingham Airfield, 69-132 Farrington Hwy., Waialua ☎ 808/637–0207 ⊕ www.honolulusoaring.com 🖃 From $85.

Paradise Helicopters

AIR EXCURSIONS | Paradise offers tours on several islands, with Oahu tours departing from two helipads: Kalaeloa (near the Ko Olina resorts on the west side) and Turtle Bay Resort on the North Shore. Kalaeloa options range from a one-hour trip over Diamond Head to a two-hour island circle (daytime and sunset) to specialized trips that focus on World War II history. Turtle Bay choices include several 1½-hour North Shore adventures, with vistas of beaches as well as inland waterfalls. ✉ Honolulu ☎ 866/300–2294 ⊕ paradisecopters.com 🖃 From $295.

Animal Encounters

Pods of dolphins surround the Islands and spotting them can be as easy as just getting yourself out in—or on—the ocean. They are wild animals, of course, and do not follow a schedule, but a catamaran sail off Waikiki will usually net you a sighting. Dolphins also generally make appearances shortly after sunrise on the west shore and can be clearly observed from beaches like Makua and Makaha. And while they won't have the peppy music of Sea World in the background, their jumping and spinning is even more awe-inspiring when you realize they are just doing it as a natural part of their lives rather than for a reward.

Some tour operators offer opportunities to swim with dolphins, but keep in mind that these are federally protected marine mammals, so you should always follow the instructions given by the tour operator if you take one of these trips. The National Oceanographic and Atmospheric Administration (NOAA) provides specific guidelines for tour operators encountering dolphins through their Dolphin Safe program.

The cost for dolphin encounters ranges from $130 for a chance to swim with wild dolphins on a snorkel cruise to $700 for getting in the pool with them as trainer-for-a-day. Both Dolphin Quest at The Kahala Hotel in Honolulu and Sea Life Park in Waimanalo offer opportunities to view and interact with captive dolphins. See Chapter 3, Honolulu, and Chapter 4, Windward Oahu, for more information.

Similarly, you can also swim with sharks, though you do so in a protective cage.

LEEWARD (WEST) OAHU

Dolphin Excursions

WILDLIFE-WATCHING | FAMILY | Oahu's leeward coast offers an abundance of spinner dolphins, as well as whales (in the winter months) and other marine wildlife. This company's three-hour Dolphin

Adventure departs from Waianae Boat Harbor and includes round-trip transportation from Waikiki and Ko Olina. Early morning tours are suggested for better dolphin sightings, and whale-watching tours in the winter, leading into sunset, are sure to take your breath away. Snorkeling adventures are also available. ✉ *Waianae Boat Harbor, 85-491 Farrington Hwy., Waianae* ✛ *Check in at Spinners Café* ☎ *808/239-5579* ⊕ *dolphinexcursions.com* 🎫 *From $140.*

NORTH SHORE
North Shore Shark Adventures
WILDLIFE-WATCHING | "You go in the cage, cage goes in the water, you go in the water. Shark's in the water." You remember these lines from *Jaws,* and now you get to play the role of Richard Dreyfuss, as North Shore Shark Adventures provides you with an interactive experience out of your worst nightmare. The tour allows you to swim and snorkel in a cage as dozens of sharks lurk just feet below and around you in the open ocean off the North Shore. No swimming is required.

The company provides transportation from Waikiki for an additional charge, and discounts are available if you book online. ■TIP➜ **If you go, go early: the sea is calmer and clearer in the morning, and the sitings are more plentiful.** ✉ *Haleiwa Small Boat Harbor, 66-105 Haleiwa Rd., Haleiwa* ✛ *Check in at Shark Shack in harbor* ☎ *808/228-5900* ⊕ *sharktourshawaii.com* 🎫 *From $96.*

Biking

Oahu's coastal roads are flat, well-paved, and, unfortunately, awash in vehicular traffic. Frankly, biking is no fun in either Waikiki or Honolulu, but things are a bit better outside the city. Your best bet is to cycle early in the morning, or get off the road to check out the island's bike trails.

Honolulu City and County Bike Coordinator
BIKING | This office can answer many of your biking questions concerning trails, permits, and state laws. ✉ *Honolulu* ☎ *808/768-8335* ⊕ *www.honolulu.gov/bicycle.html.*

BEST SPOTS
HONOLULU
Maunawili Demonstration Trail
BIKING | Locals favor biking this 10-mile trail that has breathtaking views as you descend into Waimanalo. There are many flat portions, but the trail does have some uneven ground to negotiate unless you're willing to carry your bike for small stretches. The main trailhead is at the Pali Lookout on the blacktop of Old Pali Road. Be aware that the trail is also popular with hikers and dog walkers. Note, too, that there have been closures, so check ahead on the trail's status before heading out. ✉ *Nuuanu Pali Dr., at Pali Lookout, Honolulu.*

NORTH SHORE
Kaena Point Trail
BIKING | If simply pedaling up a mountain road is not your idea of mountain biking, then perhaps Kaena Point Trail is better suited to your needs. This 10-mile trail takes you oceanside around the westernmost point on the island. You pass sea arches and a mini-blowhole, then finish up with some motocross jumps right before you turn around. There's no drinking water available on this ride, so remember to bring your own, and then cool off at the Yokohama Beach showers. ✉ *69-385 Farrington Hwy., Waialua* ⊕ *dlnr.hawaii.gov/dsp/hiking/oahu/kaena-point-trail.*

Kaunala Trail
BIKING | Biking the North Shore may sound like a great idea, but the two-lane road is narrow and traffic-heavy. Consider trying the West Kaunala Trail. It's a little tricky at times, but with the rain-forest surroundings and beautiful ocean vistas, you'll hardly notice your legs burning on

the steep ascent at the end. It's about 5½ miles round-trip. Bring water because there's none on the trail unless it comes from the sky. (Also remember it gets really muddy and slippery after heavy rains.) ⊠ *59-777 Pupukea Rd., at the end of Pupukea Rd., Haleiwa* ⊹ *Pupukea Rd. is next to Foodland, the only grocery store on North Shore* ⊕ *hawaiitrails. hawaii.gov/trails/#/trail/kaunala-trail/171.*

North Shore Bike Park

BIKING | Wind around 12 miles of trails plus seven professionally designed, single-track loops at the North Shore's Turtle Bay Resort. Trails lead to protected wildlife areas and ancient Hawaiian sites, a World War II pillbox, a giant banyan tree, and secluded beaches and bays. Purchase day passes at the Hele Huli Adventure Center, and rent bikes right on site. ⊠ *57-091 Kuilima Dr., Kahuku* ☎ *808/293–6024* ⊕ *www.turtlebayresort. com* ✉ *Rates vary depending on season, trails, and bikes rented.*

EQUIPMENT AND TOURS
HONOLULU
Bike Hawaii

BIKING | Whether you want to tackle road tours of the North Shore or muddy off-road adventures in the Koolau Range, this company can help, and it offers combination packages that pair cycling with snorkeling, sailing, or hiking, too. Its Rainforest to Reef Tour (half- or full-day options) is often cited as one of the island's best outings, taking you 2,000 feet up into the Koolau Mountains so you can coast downhill through tropical woodlands before getting on a catamaran to swim and snorkel with turtles. Other options include a three-hour road excursion and a six-hour mountain-biking foray. Tours include equipment, transportation, and water; some also include lunch. The company will pick you up at central locations in Waikiki. ⊠ *Honolulu* ☎ *808/734–4214* ⊕ *bikehawaii.com* ✉ *From $62.*

Biki

BIKING | In late 2017, nonprofit Bikeshare Hawaii launched a Honolulu bikesharing system equipped with 1,300 bikes docked at solar-powered kiosks throughout urban Honolulu. The comfortable, easy-to-maneuver bikes accommodate riders of all sizes and include a basket to carry your farmers' market goodies. The procedure is easy: pay at a kiosk, hop on a bike, and dock it at the kiosk closest to your destination. You can do a one-time rental for 30 or 60 minutes or prepurchase a pool of minutes to use during the course of your trip. Helmets are not required by law, but you can purchase or rent one. ⊠ *Honolulu* ☎ *888/340–2454* ⊕ *gobiki.org* ✉ *From $4.*

Hawaii Bicycling League

BIKING | Don't want to go cycling by yourself? Visit this shop online, and you can get connected with rides and competitions, including the annual circle island ride. ⊠ *3442 Waialae Ave., Ste. 1, Honolulu* ☎ *808/735–5756* ⊕ *hbl.org.*

NORTH SHORE
North Shore Explorers

BIKING | Rent cruisers, fat-tire bikes, mountain bikes, or mopeds at this outfitter's Hele Huli Adventure Center at Turtle Bay Resort. The company also runs an array of guided adventure tours, plus disc and foot golf, tennis, and mountain bike lessons. If you want to do it, they probably offer it. ⊠ *Kahuku* ☎ *808/293–6024* ⊕ *northshoreexplorers.com* ✉ *Bike rentals from $50.*

Birding

Victor Emanuel Nature Tours, the largest company in the world specializing in birding tours, has two 10-day Fall Hawaii and Spring Hawaii trips to Oahu, Kauai, and the Big Island that cost $6,195, including double-occupancy accommodations, meals, inter-island air, ground transportation, and guided excursions.

Camping in Oahu

If you are looking for a more rugged escape from the resorts of Waikiki, consider pitching a tent on the beach or in the mountains, where you have easy access to hiking trails and the island's natural features.

■ TIP→ Camping here is not as highly organized as it is on the Mainland: expect few marked sites, scarce electrical outlets, and nary a ranger station.

What you find instead are unblemished spots in the woods and on the sand. Both the Division of Forestry and Wildlife and the Division of State Parks offer recreation areas at which you can camp. All such campsites can now be reserved up to 90 days in advance online (⊕ *www.hawaiistateparks.org*). The fee is $18 per night per campsite for up to six people.

As for the county spots, there are 17 campgrounds currently available, and all require a permit. The good news is that the permits are only $32 for three days and $52 for five days, always beginning on a Friday, with no camping allowed on Wednesday or Thursday. They are also easy to obtain, as long as you're not trying to go on a holiday weekend. Visit ⊕ *camping.honolulu.gov* for more information.

Victor Emanuel Nature Tours
SPECIAL-INTEREST TOURS | This Mainland-based tour company offers periodic Hawaii bird-watching tours that often sell out, so book quickly! ☎ *800/328–8368* ⊕ *www.ventbird.com.*

Boat Tours and Charters

Being on the water can be the best way to enjoy the Islands. Whether you want to see the fish in action or experience how they taste, there is a tour for you.

For a sailing experience, you need go no farther than the beach in front of your Waikiki hotel. Strung along the sand are several catamarans that offer one-hour rides during the day (about $35) and 90-minute sunset sails ($49–$120).
■ TIP→ Feel free to haggle, especially with the smaller boats.

Some operators provide drinks for free, some charge for them, and some let you pack your own, so keep that in mind when pricing the ride. Or choose to go the ultraluxe route and charter a boat for a day or week. These run from less than $100 per person per day to more than $1,000 *(see also, Deep-Sea Fishing)*.

HONOLULU
Hawaii Duck Tours
BOATING | FAMILY | These unique tours in amphibious vehicles take advantage of the ducks' dual means of travel by navigating the streets of Waikiki and then gliding into the surrounding waters. The tour starts in Waikiki and travels on land to Kapiolani Park, Diamond Head, and the Ala Wai Canal. Then it's out to sea for views of the district's famous beaches and landmarks from the water. Tours last approximately 75 minutes and run throughout the day and at sunset. ⊠ *Ala Wai Yacht Harbor, 1651 Ala Moana Blvd., Waikiki* ☎ *808/988–3825* ⊕ *hawaiiducktours.com* ☑ *From $35.*

Hawaii Nautical
BOATING | With two locations—one in Waikiki and one on the Waianae coast—this outfitter offers a wide variety of cruise options, including guaranteed-sighting dolphin and whale-watching (in season), gourmet dinners, lunches, snorkeling,

scuba diving, and sunset viewing. Three-hour cruises, including lunch and two drinks, depart from the Kewalo Basin Harbor just outside Waikiki. (The company's Port Waikiki Cruises sail from the Hilton Pier off the Hilton Hawaiian Village in Waikiki.) For those interested in leaving from the Waianae coast, snorkel tours are available from the Waianae Boat Harbor on Farrington Highway (⊠ *85-471 Farrington Hwy.*). Prices include all gear, food, and two alcoholic beverages. The dock in the Waianae Boat Harbor is a little more out of the way, but this is a much more luxurious option than what is offered in Waikiki. Both morning and afternoon snorkel tours include stops for observing dolphins from the boat and a visit to a snorkel spot well populated with fish. All gear, snacks, sandwiches, and two alcoholic beverages make for a more complete experience. Pickup in Ko Olina is free. ⊠ *Kewalo Basin Harbor, 1125 Ala Moana Blvd., Waikiki* ☎ *808/234-7245* ⊕ *www.hawaiinautical.com* ✉ *From $59.*

Honolulu Sailing Company

BOATING | With a small fleet of mono- and multihull sail and power boats, the Honolulu Sailing Company offers both boat charters and sailing instruction opportunities. Itineraries include private chartered day or sunset sails, snorkeling adventures, powerboating around Oahu, offshore fishing adventures, and special events like weddings. Remember that these are all private, full-ship charters, so you'll want at least a small group to make it affordable. ⊠ *Kewalo Basin Yacht Harbor, 1025 Ala Moana Blvd., Honolulu* ☎ *808/239-3900* ⊕ *honsail.com* ✉ *From $585.*

Maitai Catamaran

BOATING | Taking off from the stretch of sand between the Sheraton Waikiki and The Halekulani, this 44-foot cat is the fastest and sleekest on the beach. There are a variety of tours to choose from, including a sunset sail and a snorkel excursion. If you have a need for speed and want a more upscale experience, this is the boat for you. ⊠ *Sheraton Waikiki, 2255 Kalakaua Ave., Waikiki* ✛ *On beach behind hotel* ☎ *808/922-5665, 800/462-7975* ⊕ *www.maitaicatamaran.net* ✉ *From $49.*

Makani Catamaran

BOATING | The 65-foot *Makani* is the top catamaran in Hawaii for luxury, from its Bose stereo system to its LCD TVs to its freshwater bathrooms. It sails out of Kewalo Basin four times daily, offering snorkel cruises that include lunch, afternoon "fun" sails, "Honolulu City Lights/Sunset" dinner cruises, and more. ⊠ *Kewalo Basin Harbor, 1009 Ala Moana Blvd., Slip F31, Ala Moana* ☎ *808/591-9000* ⊕ *sailmakani.com* ✉ *From $92.*

Star of Honolulu Cruises

BOATING | **FAMILY** | Founded in 1957, this company anchors Oahu's dinner-cruise market with its 232-foot *Star of Honolulu,* featuring four floors of walk-around decks and a 60-foot-high observation deck. Enjoy views, live entertainment, cocktails, and dinner. The company also offers several cruise experiences—from casual to luxury—to fit your needs and whims. On some cruises you can even learn how to string lei, play ukulele, or dance hula. Transportation from all hotels on the island can be arranged. ⊠ *Honolulu* ☎ *808/983-7827, 800/334-6191* ⊕ *starofhonolulu.com* ✉ *From $69*Italicize.

Tradewind Charters

BOATING | This company's half-day private excursions can include sailing, snorkeling, reef fishing, sunset dinner cruises, whale-watching, and even spa treatments, all on luxury yachts that can accommodate from 2 to 49 people. Traveling on these vessels not only gets you away from the crowds, but also gives you the opportunity to take the helm if you wish. The cruises may include snorkeling at an exclusive anchorage, as well as hands-on snorkeling and sailing instruction. All charters are for the full ship. ⊠ *Kewalo Basin Harbor, 1125 Ala Moana*

Blvd., Ala Moana ☎ *808/227–4956, 800/829–4899* ⊕ *www.tradewindcharters.com* ✉ *From $495.*

Bodyboarding and Bodysurfing

Bodyboarding (or sponging) has long been a popular alternative to surfing for a couple of reasons. First, the start-up cost is much less—a usable board can be purchased for $30–$40 or rented on the beach for $5 an hour. Second, it's a whole lot easier to ride a bodyboard than a surfboard. All you have to do is paddle out to the waves, then turn toward the beach as the wave approaches and kick like crazy.

Most grocery and convenience stores sell bodyboards. Though these boards don't compare to what the pros use, beginners won't notice a difference in how they handle on smaller waves.

Though they are not absolutely necessary for bodyboarding, fins do give you a tremendous advantage when you're paddling. If you plan to go out into bigger surf, get a leash, which reduces the chance you'll lose your board. The smaller, sturdier versions of dive fins used for bodyboarding sell for $25–$60 at surf and sporting-goods stores. Most beach stands don't rent fins with the boards, so if you want them, you'll probably need to buy them.

Bodysurfing requires far less equipment—just a pair of swim fins with heel straps—but it can be a lot more challenging to master. Typically, surf breaks that are good for bodyboarding are good for bodysurfing.

If the direction of the current or dangers of the break are not readily apparent to you, don't hesitate to ask a lifeguard for advice.

BEST SPOTS

Bodyboarding and bodysurfing can be done anywhere there are waves, but due to the paddling advantage surfers have over spongers, it's usually more fun to go to surf breaks exclusively for bodyboarding. For more information on Oahu beaches, see the individual regional chapters.

Bellows Beach. On Oahu's windward side, Bellows Field Beach Park has shallow waters and a consistent break that makes it an ideal spot for bodyboarders and bodysurfers. (Surfing isn't allowed between the two lifeguard towers.) But take note: the Portuguese man-of-war, a blue jellyfishlike invertebrate that delivers painful and powerful stings, is often seen here. ✉ *41-043 Kalanianaole Hwy., Waimanalo.*

Kuhio Beach. This beach park offers an easy spot for first-timers to check out the action. A break near the large pedestrian walkway that's called Kapahulu Groin is the quintessential bodyboarding spot. The soft, rolling waves make it perfect for beginners. Even during summer's south swells, it's relatively tame because of the outer reefs. ✉ *Waikiki Beach, between Sheraton Moana Surfrider Hotel and Kapahulu Groin, Honolulu.*

Makapuu Beach. With its extended waves, this beach park is a sponger's dream. If you're a little more timid, go to the far end of the beach to Keiki's, where the waves are mellowed by Makapuu Point. Although the main break at Makapuu is much less dangerous than that at Sandy's, mind the ocean floor—the sands are always shifting, sometimes exposing coral heads and rocks. Always check (or ask lifeguards about) the currents, which can be strong. ✉ *41-095 Kalanianaole Hwy., across from Sea Life Park.*

Sandy Beach. The best spot for advanced bodyboarding is Sandy Beach on Oahu's eastern shore. That said, even when the shore break here is small, it can be

The windward side has many good spots for bodyboarding.

extremely dangerous. As lifeguards will attest, there are more neck injuries suffered here than at any other surf break in the United States. It's awesome for the advanced, but know its danger before paddling out. ⊠ *8800 Kalanianaole Hwy., 2 miles east of Hanauma Bay, Honolulu.*

Waimanalo Beach. With the longest sand beach on Oahu's windward side, Waimanalo Bay Beach Park has a shallow sandbar at the water's edge that provides good waves for bodyboarding and bodysurfing. It's an ideal break for novices because of its soft waves. Like Walls in Waikiki, this area is protected by an outer reef. And like Bellows, it's favored by the dangerous Portuguese man-of-war. ⊠ *Aloiloi St., Waimanalo.*

EQUIPMENT

The more than 30 rental spots along Waikiki Beach all offer basically the same prices. But if you plan to bodyboard for more than just an hour, consider buying an inexpensive board for $20–$40 at an ABC Store—there are almost 40 in the Waikiki area—and giving it to a kid at the end of your vacation. It will be more cost-effective for you, and you'll be passing along some aloha spirit in the process.

Deep-Sea Fishing

Fishing isn't just a sport in Hawaii, it's a way of life. A number of charter boats with experienced crews can take you on a sportfishing adventure throughout the year. Sure, the bigger yellowfin tuna (ahi) are generally caught in summer, and the coveted spearfish are more frequent in winter, but you can still hook them any day of the year. Plus, the dolphinfish (mahimahi), wahoo (ono), and skipjacks, not to mention the king—Pacific blue marlin—are ripe for the picking on any given day. The largest Pacific blue marlin ever caught, weighing in at 1,805 pounds, was reeled in along Oahu's coast.

When choosing a fishing boat in the Islands, look for veteran captains with decades of experience. Better yet, find those who care about Hawaii's fragile marine environment. Many captains now tag and release their catches to preserve the state's fishing grounds.

The general rule for the catch is an even split with the crew. Unfortunately, there are no "freeze-and-ship" providers in the state, so unless you plan to eat the fish while you're here, you'll probably want to leave it with the boat. Most boats do offer mounting services for trophy fish; ask your captain.

Prices vary greatly, but expect to pay from around $65 per person for a spot on a boat with more than 20 people to $2,000 for an overnight trip for up to 6 people. Besides the gift of fish, a gratuity of 10%–20% is standard, but use your own discretion based on the overall experience.

BOATS AND CHARTERS
HONOLULU
Maggie Joe Sport Fishing

FISHING | The oldest sportfishing company on Oahu boasts landing one of the largest marlins ever caught out of Kewalo Basin. It offers a variety of offshore fishing packages, including exclusive or shared charters, and has a fleet of three boats. Half-day exclusives on the 41-foot *Sea Hawk* or the 38-foot *Ruckus* can accommodate up to six people and are the cheapest options for daytime fishing. The 53-foot *Maggie Joe* embarks on three-quarter- or full-day sails; can accommodate up to 15 anglers; and is equipped with air-conditioned cabins, hot showers, and cutting-edge gear. A marine taxidermist can mount the monster you reel in. ⊠ *Kewalo Basin, 1025 Ala Moana Blvd., Ala Moana* ☎ *808/591–8888, 877/806–3474* ⊕ *www.maggiejoe.com* 🖃 *From $200.*

Magic Sport Fishing

FISHING | This 50-foot Pacifica fishing yacht, aptly named *Magic,* boasts a slew of sportfishing records, including some of the largest marlins caught in local tournaments and the most mahimahi hooked during a one-day charter. The yacht, which can accommodate up to six passengers for both shared or full charters, is very comfortable, with air-conditioning, a cozy seating area, and a smooth ride thanks to twin diesel engines. ⊠ *Kewalo Basin Harbor, 1125 Ala Moana Blvd., Slip G, Ala Moana* ☎ *808/596–2998* ⊕ *www. magicsportfishing.com* 🖃 *From $220 per person for a shared charter; from $1,190 for a private charter.*

Golf

Unlike elsewhere in Hawaii, most of Oahu's golf courses aren't associated with hotels and resorts. In fact, of the island's more than three dozen courses, only five are tied to lodging, and none is in the tourist hub of Waikiki.

Although municipal courses are a good choice for budget-conscious golfers, they're more crowded than (and not always as well maintained as) private courses. Your best bet is to call the day you want to play and inquire about walk-on availability. Greens fees are standard at city courses: walking rate $66 for visitors, riding carts $20 for 18 holes, pull carts $4.

Greens fees listed here are the highest course rates per round on weekdays and weekends for U.S. residents. (Some courses charge non–U.S. residents higher prices.) Discounts are often available for resort guests and for those who book tee times online. Twilight fees are usually offered.

HONOLULU

There is only one spot to golf near Waikiki, and it is the busiest course in America. Although not a very imaginative layout, the price is right, and the advantage of walking from your hotel to the course is not to be overlooked. If you don't make a reservation, bring

Tips for the Green

Before you head out to the first tee, there are a few things you should know about golf in Hawaii:

■ All resort courses and many daily-fee courses provide rental clubs. In many cases, they're the latest lines from Titleist, PING, Callaway, and the like. This is true for both men and women, as well as for left-handers, which means you don't have to schlep clubs across the Pacific.

■ Most courses offer deals varying from twilight deep-discount rates to frequent-visitor discounts, even for tourists. Ask questions when calling pro shops, and don't just accept the first quote—deals abound if you persist.

■ Pro shops at most courses are well stocked with balls, tees, and other accoutrements, so even if you bring your own bag, it needn't weigh a ton.

■ Come spikeless—very few Hawaii courses still permit metal spikes.

■ Sunscreen. Buy it, and apply it (minimum 30 SPF). The subtropical rays are intense, even in December.

■ Resort courses, in particular, offer more than the usual three sets of tees, sometimes four or five. So bite off as much or little challenge as you can chew. Tee it up from the tips, and you'll end up playing a few 600-yard par 5s and see a few 250-yard forced carries.

■ In theory, you can play golf in Hawaii 365 days a year. But there's a reason the Hawaiian Islands are so green. Better to bring an umbrella and light jacket and not use them than not to bring them and get soaked.

■ Unless you play a muni or certain daily-fee courses, plan on taking a cart. Riding carts are mandatory at most courses and are included in greens fees.

something to read because it will be a little while before you tee off.

Ala Wai Golf Course

GOLF | Just across the Ala Wai Canal from Waikiki, this municipal golf course is said to host more rounds than any other U.S. course—up to 500 per day. Not that it's a great course, just really convenient. The best bet for a visitor is to show up and expect to wait at least an hour or call up to three days in advance for a tee time. (The jury is out on whether online reservations have made securing a time any easier.) The course itself is flat, though Robin Nelson did some redesign work in the 1990s, adding mounding, trees, and a lake. The Ala Wai Canal comes into play on several holes on the back nine, including the treacherous 18th. There's

also an on-site restaurant and bar. ⊠ 404 Kapahulu Ave., Waikiki ☎ 808/207– 6856 for reservations ⊕ www.honolulu.gov/des/golf/alawai.html ☞ $66 ⚐ 18 holes, 5861 yards, par 70.

Moanalua Golf Club

GOLF | Said to be (not without dispute) the oldest golf club west of the Rockies, this 9-holer is semiprivate, allowing public play except on weekend and holiday mornings. Near Pearl Harbor and nestled in the hardwoods, this course will remind you more of golf in Pennsylvania than in the tropics, but it offers the lowest greens fees in the area, and by the time you get here, you'll probably be over the whole palm-tree theme anyway. The course is a bit quirky, but the final two holes, a par 3 off a cliff to a smallish

The North Shore's Turtle Bay Resort attracts golfers who come for the prized Palmer Course.

tree-rimmed green and a par 4 with an approach to a green set snugly between stream and jungle, are classic. Although carts are not required, they are recommended, as this course is a bit steep in places. ⊠ *1250 Ala Aolani St., Salt Lake* ☎ *808/839–2411 for starter's office, 808/839–2311 for pro shop and clubhouse* ⊕ *moanaluagolfclub.com* ⊠ *$41* ⌢ *9 holes, 2972 yards, par 36.*

WEST (LEEWARD) OAHU

On the leeward side of the mountains, shielded from the rains that drench the Kaneohe side, West Oahu is arid and sunny and has a unique kind of beauty. Indeed, golfers generally choose courses in Ewa and Kapolei because they provide a totally different landscape from that found in Waikiki or the North Shore. Although west side resort courses are a long drive from town, the beaches are magnificent, and you can find deals if you're combining a room with a round or two on the greens.

Coral Creek Golf Course

GOLF | On the Ewa Plain, 4 miles inland, this course is cut from ancient coral left from when this area was still underwater. Robin Nelson (1999) did some of his best work in making use of the coral—and of some dynamite—blasting out portions to create dramatic lakes and tee and green sites. They could just as easily call it Coral Cliffs because of the 30- to 40-foot cliffs Nelson created. They include the par-3 10th green's grotto and waterfall and the vertical drop-off on the right side of the par-4 18th green. An ancient creek meanders across the course, but there's not much water, just enough to be a babbling nuisance. Carts are required and are included in the greens fee. ⊠ *91-1111 Geiger Rd., Ewa Beach* ☎ *808/441–4653* ⊕ *www.coralcreekgolfhawaii.com* ⊠ *$80 for 9 holes, $155 for 18 holes* ⌢ *18 holes, 6347 yards, par 72.*

Ewa Beach Golf Club

GOLF | A private course open to the public, Ewa is one of the delightful products of the too-brief collaboration of Robin

Nelson and Rodney Wright (1992). Trees are very much part of the character here, but there are also elements of links golf, such as a double green shared by the 2nd and 16th holes. Carts are required and are included in the greens fee. ✉ *91-050 Fort Weaver Rd., Ewa Beach* ☎ *808/689–6565* ⊕ *ewabeachgc.com* ✉ *From $167* ⚐ *18 holes, 5861 yards, par 72.*

Hawaii Prince Golf Club

GOLF | Affiliated with the Prince Waikiki hotel, the Hawaii Prince Golf Club (not to be confused with the Prince Course at Princeville, Kauai) has a links feel to it, and it is popular with local-charity fundraiser golf tournaments. Arnold Palmer and Ed Seay (1991) took what had been flat, featureless sugarcane fields and sculpted 27 challenging, varied holes. Mounding breaks up the landscape, as do 10 lakes. Water comes into play on six holes of the A course, three of B, and seven of C. The most difficult combination is A and C (A and B from the forward tees). Carts are required and are included in the greens fee. ✉ *91-1200 Fort Weaver Rd., Ewa Beach* ☎ *808/944– 4567* ⊕ *www.hawaiiprincegolf.com* ✉ *From $149 for 18 holes; $175 for 18 holes including rental clubs* ⚐ *A Course: 9 holes, 3138 yards, par 36. B Course: 9 holes, 3099 yards, par 36. C Course: 9 holes, 3076 yards, par 36.*

Kapolei Golf Club

GOLF | This is a Ted Robinson aquatic wonderland with waterfalls and four lakes—three so big they have names— coming into play on 10 holes. Set on rolling terrain, Kapolei is a serious golf course, especially when the wind blows. Carts are required and are included in the greens fee. ✉ *91-701 Farrington Hwy., Kapolei* ☎ *808/674–2227* ⊕ *www.kapoleigolf.com* ✉ *$185* ⚐ *18 holes, 6586 yards, par 72.*

Ko Olina Golf Club

GOLF | Hawaii's golden age of golf-course architecture came to Oahu when Ko Olina Golf Club opened in 1989. Ted Robinson, king of the water features, went splash-happy here, creating nine lakes that come into play on eight holes, including the par-3 12th, where you reach the tee by driving behind a Disney-like waterfall. Tactically, though, the most dramatic is the par-4 18th, where the approach is a minimum 120 yards across a lake to a two-tiered green guarded on the left by a cascading waterfall. Today Ko Olina has matured into one of Hawaii's top courses. You can niggle about routing issues—the first three holes play into the trade winds (and the morning sun), as do two consecutive par 5s on the back nine play—but Robinson does enough solid design to make those of passing concern. ■TIP→ **The course provides free transportation from Waikiki hotels.** ✉ *92-1220 Aliinui Dr., Ko Olina* ☎ *808/676– 5300* ⊕ *koolinagolf.com* ✉ *$115 for 9 holes, $225 for 18 holes* ⚐ *18 holes, 6432 yards, par 72.*

Makaha Valley Country Club

GOLF | This course (William F. Bell, 1968), known locally as Makaha East, is indeed a valley course, taking great advantage of the steep valley walls and natural terrain. The double-dogleg, downhill-up-hill, par-5 18th is a doozy of a closer. Carts are required and are included in the greens fee. ✉ *84-627 Makaha Valley Rd., Waianae* ☎ *808/695–7111* ⊕ *www. makahavalleycc.com* ✉ *$37 for 9 holes, $89 for 18 holes* ⚐ *18 holes, 6260 yards, par 71.*

★ West Loch Golf Course

GOLF | The best of Honolulu's municipal courses, this Robin Nelson (1991) design plays along Pearl Harbor's West Loch. In the process of building the course, wetlands were actually expanded, increasing bird habitat. ✉ *91-1126 Okupe St., Ewa Beach* ☎ *808/675–6076* ⊕ *www.honolulu. gov/des/golf/westloch.html* ✉ *$66* ⚐ *18 holes, 6335 yards, par 72.*

CENTRAL OAHU

In Central Oahu, plantations morphed into tract housing, and golf courses were added to anchor communities. The vegetation is much sparser, but some of the best greens around can be found here. Play early to avoid the hot afternoons. If, however, you can handle the heat, note that most courses offer substantial discounts for twilight hours.

Hawaii Country Club

GOLF | Also known as Kunia—but not to be confused with Royal Kunia a few miles away—this course is in the middle of former sugarcane fields and dates from plantation times. Several par 4s are drivable, including the 9th and 18th holes. This is a fun course, but it's a bit rough around the edges. You can walk it on weekdays only. Reservations can be made online two weeks in advance. ⊠ *94-1211 Kunia Rd., Wahiawa* ☎ *808/621–5654* ⊕ *www.hawaiicc.com* ⌨ *$45* ⅈ *18 holes, 5910 yards, par 71.*

Mililani Golf Club

GOLF | Located on Oahu's central plain, Mililani is usually a few degrees cooler than downtown, 25 minutes away. The eucalyptus trees through which the course plays add to the cool factor, and stands of Norfolk pines give Mililani a "mainland course" feel. Bob and Robert L. Baldock (1966) make good use of an old irrigation ditch reminiscent of a Scottish burn. Carts are required and are included in the greens fee. ⊠ *95-176 Kuahelani Ave., Mililani* ☎ *808/623–2222* ⊕ *mililanigolf.com* ⌨ *$160* ⅈ *18 holes, 6274 yards, par 72.*

Pearl Country Club

GOLF | Carved in the hillside high above Pearl Harbor, the 18 holes here are really two courses. The front nine rambles out along gently sloping terrain, while the back nine zigzags up and down a steeper portion of the slope as it rises into the Koolau Mountains. The views of Pearl Harbor are breathtaking. Hawaii residents consistently rank it their #1 choice in the *Honolulu Star-Advertiser* annual rankings of state courses. Carts are required and are included in the greens fee. ⊠ *98-535 Kaonohi St., Aiea* ☎ *808/487–3802* ⊕ *www.pearlcc.com* ⌨ *$120* ⅈ *18 holes, 6232 yards, par 72.*

Royal Kunia Country Club

GOLF | At one time, the PGA Tour considered buying the Royal Kunia Country Club and hosting the Sony Open here. It's that good. Robin Nelson's eye for natural sight lines and his dexterity with water features add to the visual pleasure. ■ TIP→ **Every hole offers fabulous views from Diamond Head to Pearl Harbor to the nearby Waianae Mountains.** Carts are required and are included in the greens fee. ⊠ *94-1509 Anonui St., Waipahu* ☎ *808/688–9222* ⊕ *www.royalkuniacc. com* ⌨ *From $85* ⅈ *18 holes, 6507 yards, par 72.*

Ted Makalena Golf Course

GOLF | The flat layout of this bare-bones municipal course with Bermuda grass fairways appeals to all levels of players, but especially those just starting to learn the sport. ⊠ *93-059 Waipio Point Access Rd., Waipahu* ☎ *808/675–6052, 808/207–6735 for reservations* ⊕ *www.honolulu. gov/des/golf/makalena.html* ⌨ *$66* ⅈ *18 holes, 5976 yards, par 71.*

Waikele Country Club

GOLF | Outlet stores are not the only bargain in Waikele. The adjacent, daily-fee golf course offers a private club–like atmosphere and a terrific Ted Robinson (1992) layout. Robinson's water features are less distinctive here but define the short par-4 4th hole—with a lake running down the left side of the fairway and guarding the green—and the par-3 17th, which plays across a lake. The par-4 18th is a terrific closing hole, with a lake lurking on the right side of the green. Carts are required and are included in the greens fee. ⊠ *94-200 Paioa Pl., Waipahu* ☎ *808/676–9000* ⊕ *www.golfwaikele. com* ⌨ *$170* ⅈ *18 holes, 6261 yards, par 72.*

NORTH SHORE

The North Shore has both the cheapest and the most expensive courses on the island. You can play nine holes in your bare feet, and you can chunk up the course played by both the LPGA and Champions Tour here, too. Don't try to go the barefoot route on the LPGA course, or the only course in the Islands you may be allowed on will be the Kahuku muni.

Kahuku Golf Course

GOLF | The only true links course in Hawaii, this 9-hole municipal course is not for everyone. Maintenance is an ongoing issue, and, in summer, it can look a bit like the Serengeti. It's walking-only (a few pull carts are available for rent); there's no pro shop, just a starter who sells lost-and-found balls; and the 19th hole is a soda machine and a covered picnic bench. And yet the course stretches out along the blue Pacific where surf crashes on the shore, the turf underfoot is spongy, sea mist drifts across the links, and wildflowers bloom in the rough. ⊠ *56-501 Kamehameha Hwy., Kahuku* ☎ *808/293–5842* ⊕ *www.honolulu.gov/des/golf/kahuku.html* ✉ *$22* ✶ *9 holes, 2699 yards, par 35.*

Turtle Bay Resort

GOLF | When the Lazarus of golf courses, the Fazio Course (George Fazio, 1971), rose from the dead in 2002, Turtle Bay on Oahu's rugged North Shore became a premier golf destination. Two holes had been plowed under when the Palmer Course (Arnold Palmer and Ed Seay, 1992) was built, while the other seven lay fallow, and the front nine remained open. Then new owners came along and re-created holes 13 and 14 using Fazio's original plans, and the Fazio became whole again.

Check on the status of the temporarily closed Fazio Course. The gem at Turtle Bay, though, is the Palmer. The front nine is mostly open as it skirts Punahoolapa Marsh, a nature sanctuary, while the back nine plunges into the wetlands and winds along the coast. The short par-4 17th runs along the rocky shore, with a diabolical string of bunkers cutting diagonally across the fairway from tee to green. Carts are required and are included in the greens fee. ⊠ *57-091 Kamehameha Hwy., Kahuku* ☎ *808/293–8574* ⊕ *www.turtlebaygolf.com* ✉ *$209 ($139 twilight, staring at 1PM)* ✶ *Palmer Course: 18 holes, 7200 yards, par 72.*

HAWAII KAI

Prepare to keep your ball down on this windy corner of Oahu. You'll get beautiful ocean vistas, but you may need them to soothe you once your perfect drive gets blown 40 yards off course by a gusting trade wind.

Hawaii Kai Golf Course

GOLF | The Championship Golf Course (William F. Bell, 1973) winds through a Honolulu suburb at the foot of Koko Crater. Homes (and the liability of a broken window) come into play on many holes, but they are offset by views of the Pacific and a crafty routing of holes. With several lakes, lots of trees, and bunkers in all the wrong places, Hawaii Kai really is a "championship" golf course, especially when the trade winds howl. Greens fees for this course include a mandatory cart. The Executive Course (1962), a par-54 track, is the first of only three courses in Hawaii built by Robert Trent Jones Sr. Although a few changes have been made to his original design, you can find the usual Jones attributes, including raised greens and lots of risk-reward options. You may walk or use a cart on this course for an additional fee. ⊠ *8902 Kalanianaole Hwy., Hawaii Kai* ☎ *808/395–2358* ⊕ *hawaiikaigolf.com* ✉ *Championship Course: $150. Executive Course: $50* ✶ *Championship Course: 18 holes, 6207 yards, par 72. Executive Course: 18 holes, 2196 yards, par 54.*

EAST (WINDWARD) OAHU

Windward Oahu is what you expect when you think of golfing in the Islands. Lush, tropical foliage will surround you, with towering mountains framing one shot and the crystal-blue Pacific framing the next. Although it's a bit more expensive, and a good deal wetter, on this side, the memories and pictures you take on these courses will last a lifetime.

Olomana Golf Links

GOLF | Bob and Robert L. Baldock are the architects of record for this layout, but so much has changed since it opened in 1969 that they would recognize little of it. A turf specialist was brought in to improve fairways and greens, tees were rebuilt, new bunkers were added, and mangroves were cut back to make better use of natural wetlands. But what really puts Olomana on the map is that this is where wunderkind Michelle Wie learned the game. A cart is required at this course and is included in the greens fee. ⊠ *41-1801 Kalanianaole Hwy., Waimanalo* ☎ *808/259–7926* ⊕ *www.olomanalinks. com* ⊠ *$75 from 2 pm to close, $105 for 18 holes* ⚑ *18 holes, 6306 yards, par 72.*

Pali Golf Course

GOLF | Panoramic views of the Koolau Mountains and Kaneohe Bay enhance the many challenges at this popular municipal course between Kaneohe and Kailua. ⊠ *45-050 Kamehameha Hwy., Kaneohe* ☎ *808/207–7099 reservations, 808/262–2911 pro shop* ⊕ *www.honolulu. gov/des/golf/pali.html* ⊠ *$66* ⚑ *18 holes, 6524 yards, par 72.*

★ Royal Hawaiian Golf Club

GOLF | In the cool, lush Maunawili Valley, Pete and Perry Dye created what can only be called target jungle golf. In other words, the rough is usually dense jungle, and you may not hit a driver on three of the four par 5s, or several par 4s, including the perilous 18th that plays off a cliff to a narrow green protected by a creek. Mt. Olomana's twin peaks tower over the course. ■TIP→ **The back nine wanders deep into the valley and includes an island green (par-3 11th) and perhaps the loveliest inland hole in Hawaii (par-4 12th).** ⊠ *770 Auloa Rd., at Luana Hills Rd., Kailua*

☎ *808/262–2139* ⊕ *royalhawaiiangc.com* ⊠ *$160* ⚑ *18 holes, 5541 yards, par 72.*

Hiking

The trails of Oahu cover a full spectrum of environments: desert walks through cactus, slippery paths through bamboo-filled rain forest, and scrambling rock climbs up ancient volcanic calderas. The only thing you won't find is an overnighter, as even the longest of hikes won't take you more than half a day. In addition to being short in length, many of the prime hikes are within 10 minutes of downtown Waikiki, meaning that you won't have to spend your whole day getting back to nature.

Hawaii Department of Land and Natural Resources

HIKING & WALKING | Go to the website for information on all major hiking trails on Oahu. You can also obtain camping permits for state parks here. ■TIP→ **Make sure to follow DLNR recommendations regarding personal safety and environmental impact in these fragile areas.** ⊠ *1151 Punchbowl St., Room 310, Downtown* ☎ *808/587–0300* ⊕ *dlnr.hawaii.gov/dsp/ hiking/oahu.*

Na Ala Hele Trail & Access Program

HIKING & WALKING | Contact the Na Ala Hele (Trails to Go On) folks for a free hiking-safety guide and trail information. The interactive website has maps and information about the current status of trails on all the Islands. You can also stop in at their office for free printed maps and information. ⊠ *1151 Punchbowl St., Room 325, Downtown* ☎ *808/587–0166* ⊕ *hawaiitrails.hawaii.gov.*

BEST SPOTS
HONOLULU
Aiea Loop Trail

HIKING & WALKING | This 4.8-mile loop begins and ends in the Keaiwa Heiau State Recreation Area, running along the ridge on the west side of Halawa

Valley. It's a fairly easy hike that lasts about 2½ to 3 hours and brings many rewards, including views of the southern coastline of Oahu from Pearl Harbor and the Waianae Range to Honolulu and Diamond Head. Foresters replanted this area with various trees in the 1920s, so scents of lemon eucalyptus, pine, koa, and other trees enhance the trek. There's ample parking near the trailhead, close to restrooms and a picnic pavilion. ✉ *Aiea District Park, 99-350 Aiea Heights Dr., Aiea* ✛ *At upper east corner of park, at top of Aiea Heights Rd.* ☎ *808/587–0300* ⊕ *dlnr.hawaii.gov/dsp/hiking/oahu/ aiea-loop-trail.*

Diamond Head State Monument

HIKING & WALKING | Every vacation has requirements that must be fulfilled, so that when your neighbors ask, you can say, "Yeah, did it." Climbing Diamond Head is high on that list of things to do on Oahu. It's a moderately easy hike if you're in good physical condition, but be prepared to climb many stairs along the way. Also be sure to bring a water bottle, because it's hot and dry. Only a mile up, a clearly marked trail with handrails scales the inside of this extinct volcano. At the top, the fabled final 99 steps take you up to the pillbox overlooking the Pacific Ocean and Honolulu. It's a breathtaking view and a lot cheaper than taking a helicopter ride for the same photo op. Last entry for hikers is 4:30 pm. ✉ *Diamond Head Rd. at 18th Ave., Diamond Head* ✛ *Enter on east side of crater; there's limited parking inside, so most park on street and walk in* ☎ *808/587– 0300* ⊕ *dlnr.hawaii.gov/dsp/parks/oahu/ diamond-head-state-monument* ✑ *$5 per person, $10 to park.*

★ Manoa Falls Trail

HIKING & WALKING | Travel up into the valley beyond Honolulu to make the Manoa Falls hike. Though only a mile long, this well-trafficked path, with an estimated 100,000 visitors a year, passes through so many different ecosystems that you feel as if you're in an arboretum—and you're not far off. The beautiful Lyon Arboretum is right near the trailhead, if you want to make another stop. Walk among the elephant ear (ape) plants, ruddy fir trees, and a bamboo forest straight out of China. At the top is a 150-foot waterfall, which can be an impressive cascade or, if rains have been light, little more than a trickle, but this hike is more about the journey than the destination. Make sure you bring mosquito repellent because they grow 'em big up here. ✉ *3998 Manoa Rd., Manoa* ✛ *West Manoa Rd. is behind Manoa Valley in Paradise Park. Take West Manoa Rd. to end, park on side of road or in parking lot for a small fee, follow trail signs* ⊕ *hawaiitrails. hawaii.gov/trails/#/.*

LEEWARD (WEST) OAHU

★ Kaena Point Trail

HIKING & WALKING | Kaena Point is one of the island's last easily accessible pockets of nature left largely untouched. For more than a quarter century, the state has protected nearly 60 acres of land at the point, first as a nature preserve and then, more recently, as an ecosystem restoration project for endangered and protected coastal plants and seabirds. The uneven 5-mile trail around the point can be accessed from two locations— Keawaula Beach (aka Yokohama Bay) at the end of Farrington Highway on Oahu's western coastline, or Mokuleia at the same highway's northern coast endpoint. It's a rugged coastline hike without much shade, so bring lots of water and sunscreen. (Or, better yet, start early!) ■**TIP**➔ **Keep a lookout for the Laysan albatrosses, and don't be surprised if these enormous birds come in for a closer look at you, too.** ✉ *81-780 Farrington Hwy., Waianae* ✛ *Take Farrington Hwy. to its end at Yokohama. Hike in on old 4x4 trail* ⊕ *dlnr.hawaii.gov/dsp/hiking/oahu/ kaena-point-trail.*

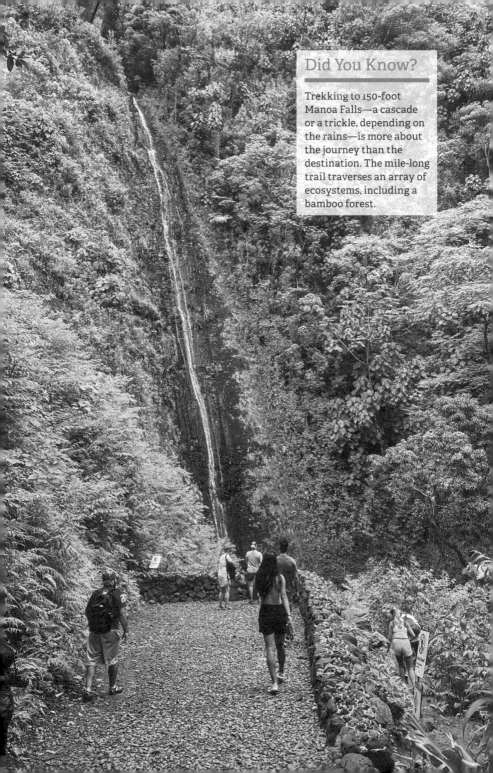

Did You Know?

Trekking to 150-foot Manoa Falls—a cascade or a trickle, depending on the rains—is more about the journey than the destination. The mile-long trail traverses an array of ecosystems, including a bamboo forest.

NORTH SHORE
Maunawili Falls

HIKING & WALKING | Want to find a waterfall that you can actually swim in? Then Maunawili Falls is your trip. In fact, plan on getting wet even if that's not your goal: you have to cross Maunawili Stream several times to get to the falls, and the route is pretty muddy. Along the 1½-mile trek enjoy the ginger, vines, and heliconia before greeting fern-shrouded falls that are made for swimming. The water is not the clearest, but it's cool and refreshing after battling the bugs to get here. Bring mosquito repellant. Walking sticks are helpful, too; if you don't have one, use the loaner sticks often left by hikers at the trailhead. ■TIP→ On weekends, the trail can be very crowded. Prepare to park far from the trailhead as regulations are strictly enforced. ⊠ 1221 Kelewina St., Kailua ✛ Take Pali Hwy. (Rte. 61) from Honolulu through tunnels, then take 3rd right onto Auloa Rd., then take left fork immediately. At dead end, climb over vehicle gate to find trailhead.

Trails at Turtle Bay Resort

HIKING & WALKING | When on the North Shore, check out Turtle Bay Resort, which has more than 12 miles of trails and oceanside pathways. Maps of the property are available. ⊠ 57-091 Kamehameha Hwy., Kahuku ☎ 808/293–8811 ⊕ www. turtlebayresort.com.

HAWAII KAI
Makapuu Lighthouse Trail

HIKING & WALKING | For the less adventurous hiker and anyone looking for a great view, this paved trail that runs up the side of Makapuu Point in Southeast Oahu fits the bill. Early on, the trail is surrounded by lava rock, but as you ascend, foliage—the tiny white koa haole flower, the cream-tinged spikes of the kiawe , and, if you go early enough—the stunning night-blooming cereus—begins taking over the barren rock. At the easternmost tip of Oahu, where the island divides the sea, this trail gives you a spectacular view of the cobalt ocean meeting the land in a cacophony of white caps.

To the south is the lighthouse; to the east are the Manana (Rabbit) and Kaohikaipu islets, two bird sanctuaries just off the coast. The 2-mile round-trip hike is a great break on a circle-island trip. From late December to early May, this is a marvelous perch to see migrating humpback whales. Note that you can no longer access the tidal pools here. The trail to them is closed as the descent was treacherous (steep, rocky, and very slippery), and there were incidences of rogue waves sweeping people out to sea. ■TIP→ Heed trail closure signs. Also, don't leave valuables in your car; break-ins, even in the parking lot, are common. ⊠ Makapuu Lighthouse Rd., Hawaii Kai ✛ Take Kalanianaole Hwy. to base of Makapuu Point, then look for parking lot ⊕ dlnr.hawaii.gov/dsp/hiking/oahu/makapuu-point-lighthouse-trail.

GOING WITH A GUIDE
HONOLULU
Hawaii Nature Center

HIKING & WALKING | FAMILY | This center in the upper Makiki Valley conducts a number of programs for both adults and children, including guided hikes into tropical settings that reveal hidden waterfalls and protected forest reserves. Activities aren't offered every day, so it's a good idea to check ahead and make reservations. ⊠ 2131 Makiki Heights Dr., Makiki Heights ☎ 808/955–0100 ⊕ hawaiinature-center.org.

Oahu Nature Tours

HIKING & WALKING | Guides explain the native flora and fauna and history that are your companions on the various walking and hiking tours of the North Shore, Diamond Head, and Windward Oahu. The company also offers much more expensive private birding tours, perfect for those interested in spotting one of Hawaii's native honeycreepers. Tours include pickup at centralized Waikiki

Tips for the Trail

- When hiking the waterfall and rain-forest trails, use insect repellent. The dampness draws huge swarms of bloodsuckers that can ruin a walk in the woods.

- Volcanic rock is very porous and therefore likely to be loose. Rock climbing is strongly discouraged, as you never know which little ledge is going to go.

- Avoid hiking after heavy rains and check for flash-flood warnings. Keep in mind that those large boulders in the idyllic pools beneath the waterfalls were carried by torrential flows high up in the mountains.

- Always let someone know where you're going, and never hike alone. The foliage gets very dense, and, small as the island is, hikers have been known to get lost for a week or longer.

locations and are discounted if booked online in advance. ☎ *808/924–2473* ⊕ *www.oahunaturetours.com* ✉ *From $125.*

NORTH SHORE
North Shore Eco Tours
HIKING & WALKING | Native Hawaiians own and operate this business, the only one allowed to lead guided small-group adventures in private conservation lands. Options range from 2- and 3½-mile round-trip hikes to pools and waterfalls (lunch included) to an off-road expedition in all-terrain vehicles. Excursions, which are described in detail on the company's website, have minimum age requirements for children. The pickup point for hikes is the North Shore Marketplace in Haleiwa town; off-road tours begin in Waimea Valley. ✉ *North Shore Marketplace, 56-250 Kamehameha Hwy., Haleiwa* ☎ *877/521–4453* ⊕ *www.northshoreecotours.com* ✉ *From $95.*

Horseback Riding

A great way to see the island is atop a horse, leaving the direction to the pack while you drink in the views of mountains or the ocean. It may seem like a cliché, but there really is nothing like riding a

horse with spectacular ocean views to put you in a romantic state of mind.

WEST (LEEWARD) OAHU
Happy Trails Hawaii
HORSEBACK RIDING | FAMILY | Take a guided horseback ride above the North Shore's Waimea Bay along trails that offer panoramic views from Kaena Point to the famous surfing spots. Groups are no larger than 10, and instruction is provided. The rides are particularly family-friendly, and children six and older are welcome. You can take either a 1½- or a 2-hour ride, which includes a 15-minute mini-lesson. Local fruits grown on the property are offered for tasting when available. Reservations are required. ✉ *59-231 Pupukea Rd., Pupukea* ✛ *Go 1 mile mauka (toward mountain) up Pupukea Rd.; the office is on right* ☎ *808/638–7433* ⊕ *happytrailshawaii.com* ✉ *From $109.*

NORTH SHORE
Turtle Bay Stables
HORSEBACK RIDING | FAMILY | Trail rides follow the 12-mile-long coastline and even step out onto sandy beaches fronting this luxe resort on Oahu's fabled North Shore. The stables here are part of the resort but can be utilized by nonguests. The sunset ride is a must. Private rides, group rides, and educational (horsemanship) classes are among the many options.

A basic trail ride lasts 45 minutes and visits filming sites for ABC's *Lost* and the film *Pirates of the Caribbean.* ✉ *Turtle Bay Resort, 57-091 Kamehameha Hwy., Kahuku* ☎ *808/293–6024* ⊕ *turtlebaystables.com* ⬛ *From $85.*

EAST (WINDWARD) OAHU
Gunstock Ranch
HORSEBACK RIDING | FAMILY | This working cattle ranch encompasses nearly 800 acres on the northeastern shore, in the foothills of the Koolau Mountains. Choose among 5 to 10 small-group guided trail rides a day (1–2½ hours, or longer) for riders of all skill levels. Rides are designed to replicate the experience of the *paniolo,* or Hawaiian cowboy. Some climb high enough to view (on clear days) 30 miles of coastline—sometimes as far as Maui and Molokai. The ranch also offers private 30-minute horse experiences for ages two to seven, private and group advanced trail rides, and private romantic couples tours with picnics. Reservations are required. ✉ *56-250 Kamehameha Hwy., Laie ✛ 2 miles North of the Polynesian Cultural Center, between Laie and Kahuku.* ☎ *808/341–3995* ⊕ *gunstockranch.com* ⬛ *Trail rides from $87.*

Kualoa Ranch
HORSEBACK RIDING | FAMILY | This 4,000-acre working ranch across from Kualoa Beach Park offers two-hour trail rides in the breathtaking Kaaawa Valley, which was the site of such movie back lots as *Jurassic Park, Godzilla,* and *50 First Dates,* as well as numerous television shows, including *Lost.* Kualoa has other activities—bus, boat, and Jeep tours; electric mountain bike tours; kayak adventure tours; ATV trail rides; canopy zipline tours; and children's activities—that may be combined for full-day package rates. The minimum age for horseback rides is 10. ✉ *49-479 Kamehameha Hwy., Kaneohe* ☎ *800/231–7321, 808/237–7321* ⊕ *www.kualoa.com* ⬛ *From $144.*

Jet Skiing and Waterskiing

HONOLULU
Aloha Jet Skis
JET SKIING | Skip across the surface of the immense Keehi Lagoon as planes from Honolulu International Airport soar above you. After an instructional safety session, you can try your hand at navigating the buoyed course. The Yamaha deluxe wave runners can be operated either tandem or solo. Reservations are required. ✉ *Keehi Lagoon, 1640 Sand Island Access Rd., Honolulu* ☎ *808/721–1754* ⊕ *www.alohajetski.com* ⬛ *From $115.*

Hawaii Water Sports Center
JET SKIING | FAMILY | This company transforms Maunalua Bay into a water park with activities for all ages. You can bounce around in a bumper tube, zoom around on Jet Skis, wakeboard, waterski, scuba dive, or ride the six-person banana boats. ✉ *Koko Marina Center, 7192 Kalanianaole Hwy., Honolulu* ☎ *808/395–3773* ⊕ *hawaiiwatersportscenter.com* ⬛ *From $69.*

HAWAII KAI
H2O Sports Hawaii
WATER SPORTS | FAMILY | Parasailing, Jet Skiing, snorkeling, and scuba diving, plus banana boats, bumper boats, and packages: this company offers a wide variety of activities on the water. All of them launch in Maunalua Bay near Hawaii Kai. ■**TIP→ Make your reservations early.** ✉ *Hawaii Kai Shopping Center, 377 Keahole St., near Longs Drugs, Hawaii Kai* ☎ *808/396–0100* ⊕ *www.h2osportshawaii.com* ⬛ *From $60.*

Kayaking

Kayaking is an easy way, even for novices, to explore the ocean—and Oahu's natural beauty—without much effort or skill. It offers a vantage point not afforded by swimming or surfing and a workout you won't get lounging on a catamaran.

The ability to travel long distances can also get you into trouble. ■ TIP→ **Experts agree that rookies should stay on the windward side.** Their reasoning is simple: if you get tired, break or lose an oar, or just plain pass out, the onshore winds will eventually blow you back to the beach. The same cannot be said for breezes off the North Shore and West Oahu.

Kayaks are specialized: some are better suited for riding waves while others are designed for traveling long distances. Your outfitter can address your needs depending on your skill level. Sharing your plans with your outfitter can lead to a more enjoyable—and safer—experience. Expect to pay from $35 for a half-day single rental to $139 for a guided kayak tour with lunch. Some kayaking outfitters also rent stand-up paddleboards *(see also Stand-Up Paddleboarding)*.

BEST SPOTS
Bellows Field Beach Park, near Waimanalo Town Center on the windward side, and **Mokuleia Beach Park,** across from Kawai-hapai Airfield (formerly Dillingham Airfield) on the North Shore, are two great spots to try surf kayaking. Hard-to-reach breaks, the ones that surfers exhaust themselves trying to reach, are easily accessed by kayak. The buoyancy of the kayak also lets you catch the wave earlier and get out in front of the white wash. If you're green, stick to Bellows with those onshore winds. Also, you don't want to be catching waves where the surfers are (in Waikiki, however, pretty much anything goes).

Because of its calm waters and onshore winds, **Lanikai Beach,** tucked away in a windward side residential area, is popular with amateur kayakers. More adventurous paddlers can head to the Mokulua Islands, two islets less than a mile from

Kayaking to The Mokes

The Mokulua Islands (aka The Mokes) are two islets off Lanikai Beach. The larger Moku Nui is a perfect kayaking destination and a popular place for picnics. The islands are state-protected bird sanctuaries, and sometimes you can glimpse one of the 11 different kinds of seabirds that nest there. Some outfitters offer guided tours. But as it would be impossible to miss the islets and the water between them is typically calm, spend your money on sunscreen and snacks instead, and enjoy the paddle.

the beach. You can land on Moku Nui, which has surf breaks and small beaches great for picnicking. Take a dip in Queen's Bath, a small saltwater swimming hole.

For something a little different, try Windward Oahu's Kahana Stream, which empties into the ocean at **Kahana Bay Beach Park.** The riverlike stream may not have the blue water of the ocean, but the majestic Koolau Mountains, with waterfalls during rainy months, make for a picturesque backdrop. It's a short jaunt, about 2 miles round-trip from the beach, but it's tranquil and packed with rain-forest foliage. Bring mosquito repellent.

EQUIPMENT, LESSONS, AND TOURS
HONOLULU
Go Bananas Kayaks
KAYAKING | Staffers make sure that you rent the appropriate kayak for your abilities and can also outfit your rental car with soft racks (included in the rental fee) to transport your boat to the beach. You can rent either a single or a double kayak. The store also carries clothing and

kayaking accessories and rents stand-up paddleboards. A second location in Aiea is closer to the North Shore. ⊠ *799 Kapahulu Ave., Kapahulu* ☎ *808/737–9514* ⊕ *gobananaskayaks.com* ⊠ *From $35.*

NORTH SHORE
Surf N Sea

KAYAKING | This outfitter is located in a rustic wooden building on the beach, so in minutes you can start paddling on a single or double kayak. ■TIP➔ **Keep in mind that these plastic boats are great from spring to fall, but winter weather can be hazardous for even veteran kayakers. This outfitter's proximity to a protected stream makes kayaking in any sea conditions possible.** In addition to kayaking, this company also offers just about any surf-related activity you can imagine on the North Shore. ⊠ *62-595 Kamehameha Hwy., Haleiwa* ☎ *808/637–9897* ⊕ *www.surfnsea.com* ⊠ *From $60 for a half-day rental.*

EAST (WINDWARD) OAHU
Hawaiian Watersports

KAYAKING | FAMILY | This multifaceted outfitter emphasizes ocean safety with fully guided 90-minute tours to either the Mokes or Flat Island that include both instruction and equipment rental. Experienced paddlers can also rent a single or double kayak and venture out on their own. In addition, the company rents windsurfing equipment, surfboards and bodyboards, snorkel equipment, and stand-up paddleboards. Discounts are available if you reserve online. ⊠ *171 Hamakua Dr., Kailua* ☎ *808/262–5483* ⊕ *hawaiianwatersports.com* ⊠ *Rentals from $29, tours from $74.*

Kailua Beach Adventures

KAYAKING | One of the best places for beginners to kayak is Kailua Beach, and this outfitter has an ideal location just across the street from it. The company offers two- and five-hour guided kayak tours (the longer tour includes lunch, time for kayaking, and time for the beach). More adventurous visitors can rent a kayak (double or single for a half or full day) and venture to the Mokulua Islands off Lanikai. Other rental options include snorkeling equipment, stand-up paddleboards, and bikes. Discounts are given if booked online. ⊠ *Kailua Beach Shopping Center, 130 Kailua Rd., Kailua* ☎ *808/262–2555* ⊕ *www.kailuasailboards.com* ⊠ *From $69 for rental, $179 for tours.*

Sun & Salt Adventures Hawaii

KAYAKING | The outfitter offers kayak rentals (single or double), lessons, and guided tours. Guides are trained in the history, geology, and birds of the area. Fully guided kayak excursions are either 2½ or 5 hours and include lunch, snorkeling gear, and transportation to and from Waikiki. ⊠ *134B Hamakua Dr., Kailua* ☎ *808/262–5656* ⊕ *www.twogoodkayaks.com* ⊠ *Rentals from $49, tours from $147.*

Running

In Honolulu, the most popular places to jog are the two parks, Kapiolani and Ala Moana, at either end of Waikiki. In both cases, the loop around the park is just less than 2 miles. You can also run a 4-mile ring around Diamond Head Crater, past scenic views, luxurious homes, and herds of other joggers.

BEST SPOTS
HONOLULU
Healthy Hawaii Initiative

RUNNING | FAMILY | This statewide initiative by the Hawaii Department of Health provides a free downloadable Fitness Fun Map, which lists a dozen walking and jogging routes and suggested itineraries. ⊠ *1250 Punchbowl St., Room 422, Downtown* ☎ *808/586–4488* ⊕ *www.healthyhawaii.com/wp-content/uploads/2015/05/fun_map.pdf.*

Honolulu Marathon

RUNNING | The Honolulu Marathon is a thrilling event to watch as well as to participate in. Join the throngs who cheer at the finish line at Kapiolani Park as internationally famous and local runners tackle the 26.2-mile challenge. It's held on the second Sunday in December and is sponsored by the Honolulu Marathon Association. ✉ *Honolulu* ☎ *808/734–7200* ⊕ *www.honolulumarathon.org.*

Running Room

RUNNING | Once you leave Honolulu, it gets trickier to find places to jog that are both scenic and safe. It's best to stick to the well-traveled routes, or ask the experienced folks at this outpost of the international chain for advice. ✉ *819 Kapahulu Ave., Kapahulu* ☎ *808/737–2422* ⊕ *www. runningroomhawaii.com.*

Scuba Diving

Not all of Hawaii's beauty is above water. What lurks below can be just as magnificent. Although snorkeling provides adequate access to this underwater world, nothing gives you the freedom—or depth, quite literally—as scuba.

The diving on Oahu is comparable with any you might do in the tropics, but its uniqueness comes from the isolated environment of the Islands. There are literally hundreds of species of fish and other marine life that you can find only in this chain. In fact, about 25% of Hawaii's marine life can be seen here only—nowhere else in the world. Adding to the singularity of diving off Oahu is the human history of the region. Military activities and tragedies of the 20th century filled the waters surrounding Oahu with wreckage that the ocean creatures have since turned into their homes.

Although instructors certified to license you in scuba are plentiful in the Islands, it's best to get your PADI certification

before coming, as a week of classes may be a bit of a commitment on a short vacation. Expect to pay around $150 for a two-tank boat dive (provided that you are certified). ■ **TIP→ You can go on short, shallow introductory dives without the certification, but the best dives require it and cost a bit more.**

BEST SPOTS

Hanauma Bay Nature Preserve. On Oahu's southeast shore, about a 30-minute drive east of Waikiki, this preserve is home to more than 250 different species of fish, a quarter of which can be found nowhere else in the world. This has made this volcanic crater bay one of the state's most popular dive sites. It's a long walk from the parking lot to the beach—even longer lugging equipment—so consider hooking up with a licensed operator. Preservation efforts have aided the bay's delicate ecosystem, so expect to see various butterfly fish, surgeonfish, tangs, parrot fish, and endangered Hawaiian sea turtles. ✉ *7455 Kalanianaole Hwy., Hawaii Kai, 808/396–4229, $7.50 per person and $1 parking.*

***Mahi* Wreck.** Hawaii's waters are littered with shipwrecks, but one of the most intact and accessible is this 165-foot minesweeper that was sunk in 1982 off the leeward coast. It lies upright in about 90 feet of calm, clear water, encrusted in coral and patrolled by white spotted eagle rays and millet seed butterfly fish. The wreck also serves as an artificial reef for such Hawaii aquatic residents as blue-striped snappers, puffer fish, lionfish, moray eels, and octopuses. Visibility averages about 100 feet, making this one of the most popular dives on the island. ✉ *Waianae.*

Maunalua Bay. Stretching about 7 miles, from Portlock Point to Black Point, and teeming with marine life, this bay has several accessible dive sites of varying difficulty. The shallow-water Turtle Canyon is home to endangered Hawaiian green sea turtles. Fantasy Reef is another shallow dive, with three plateaus of volcanic rock lined with coral that is home to fish, eels, and sea turtles. In about 85 feet of water, *Baby Barge* is an easy-to-penetrate sunken vessel encrusted in coral. An advanced dive, the wreck of a Vought F4U Corsair attracts garden eels and stingrays. ⊠ *Southeast Oahu.*

100 Foot Hole. Once an ancient Hawaiian fishing ground reserved for royalty, this cluster of volcanic boulders, which is accessible from shore, features ledges, caves, and a large open-ended cavern perfect for diving. The spot attracts octopuses, manta rays, and the occasional white-tip shark. ⊠ *Off Diamond Head, Honolulu.*

Shark's Cove. Oahu's best shore dive is accessible only during the summer months. Shark's Cove, on the North Shore, churns with monster surf during the winter, making this popular snorkeling and diving spot extremely dangerous. In summer, the cavernous lava tubes and tunnels are great for both novices and experienced divers. Some dive-tour companies offer round-trip transportation from Waikiki. ⊠ *Haleiwa.*

Three Tables. A short walk from Shark's Cove is Three Tables, named for a trio of flat rocks running perpendicular to shore. There are lava tubes to the right of these rocks that break the surface and extend out about 50 feet. Although this area isn't as active as Shark's Cove, you can still spot octopuses, moray eels, parrot fish, green sea turtles, and the occasional shark. ⊠ *Haleiwa.*

EQUIPMENT, LESSONS, AND TOURS
WEST (LEEWARD) OAHU
Hawaii Nautical
SCUBA DIVING | With operations throughout the Islands, this eco-focused operator follows strict guidelines to protect marine mammals and wildlife. Its full-service offerings include refresher, introductory, and more advanced dives, with all trips departing from the Waianae Boat Harbor. Transportation from the Ko Olina hotels is free; transit to/from Waikiki is offered at an additional charge. All equipment is included. This outfitter also offers other water adventures; check out its website for details. ⊠ *Waianae Boat Harbor, 85-491 Farrington Hwy., Waianae* ☎ *808/234–7245* ⊕ *www.hawaiinautical. com* ⊠ *From $159 for 2-tank dives.*

NORTH SHORE
Surf N Sea
SCUBA DIVING | This is the North Shore headquarters for all things water-related, including diving. One interesting perk: upon request, the dive guides can shoot a video of your adventure. It's hard to see facial expressions under the water, but it still might be fun for those who want to prove that they took the plunge. Two-tank shore dives are the most economical choice (prices for noncertified divers are higher), but the company also offers boat dives, and in the summer, night dives are available for only slightly more. ⊠ *62-595 Kamehameha Hwy., Haleiwa* ☎ *808/637–3483* ⊕ *www.surfnsea.com* ⊠ *From $120 (2-tank shore dives).*

EAST (WINDWARD) OAHU
Aaron's Dive Shop
SCUBA DIVING | This friendly and well-equipped dive shop caters to everyone. Take an "introductory" dive if you're not certified, get certified, or sign up for an offshore day or night dive excursion if you're experienced. In addition to organized group dives, the company's "dive concierge" can arrange private charters for those who want a completely customized experience. Snorkelers can go along on many dives as well. ⊠ *307 Hahani St., Kailua* ☎ *808/262–2333* ⊕ *www.aaronsdiveshop.com* ⊠ *From $140 for 2-tank dive.*

Hanauma Bay in Southeast Oahu has more than 250 different species of marine life; you'd be hard pressed to find a better place to snorkel.

Snorkeling

If you can swim, you can snorkel. You don't need any formal training, and you can do it anywhere there's enough water to stick your face in. A mask, snorkel, and fins will run you about $35 at any corner ABC Store. At the other end of the price spectrum, luxurious snorkel cruises cost up to $175, including lunch and drinks.

Conditions at each snorkeling spot vary, depending on the weather and time of year, so consult with the purveyor of your gear for tips on where the best viewing is that day. Keep in mind that the North Shore should be attempted only when the waves are calm, namely in the summertime. Also, be sure to put plenty of sunscreen on your back (or better yet, wear a T-shirt): once you start gazing below, your head may not come back up for hours.

BEST SPOTS

Electric Beach. This haven for tropical fish is on the island's western side, directly across from an electricity plant—hence the name (aka Kahe Beach Park). The expulsion of hot water from the plant raises the temperature of the ocean, attracting Hawaiian green sea turtles, spotted moray eels, and spinner dolphins. Although visibility is not always the best, the crowds are small, and the fish are guaranteed. ⊠ *Farrington Hwy., 1 mile west of Ko Olina Resort, Kapolei.*

Hanauma Bay Nature Preserve. What Waimea Bay is to surfing, Hanauma Bay in Southeast Oahu is to snorkeling. It's home to more than 250 different species of marine life. Due to the protection of the narrow mouth of the cove and the prodigious reef, you would be hard-pressed to find a place you would feel safer while snorkeling. ⊠ *7455 Kalanianaole Hwy., Honolulu, 808/396–4229, $7.50 per person and $1 parking.*

Did You Know?

Shark's Cove is a wonderful place for young snorkelers to spend time exploring the ocean's bottom in shallow waters, as the area is protected by a huge reef just offshore.

Queen's Surf Beach. On the edge of Waikiki, between the Kapahulu Groin and the Waikiki Aquarium, this marine reserve isn't as chock-full of fish as Hanauma Bay, but it has its share of colorful reef fish and the occasional Hawaiian green sea turtle. Just yards from shore, it's a great spot for an escape if you're stuck in Waikiki and have grown weary of watching the surfers. ⊠ *Kalakaua Ave., Honolulu.*

Shark's Cove. Great shallows protected by a huge reef make Shark's Cove on the North Shore a prime spot for snorkelers, even young ones, in the summer. You'll find a plethora of critters, from crabs to octopuses, in water that's no more than waist deep. When the winter swells come, this area can turn treacherous. ⊠ *Kamehameha Hwy., across from Foodland, Haleiwa.*

EQUIPMENT AND TOURS
HONOLULU
Snorkel Bob's
SNORKELING | FAMILY | This place has all the stuff you'll need—and more—to make your water adventures more enjoyable. Bob makes his own gear and is active in protecting reef fish species. Feel free to ask the staff about good snorkeling spots, as the best ones can vary with weather and the seasons. You can either rent or buy gear (and reserve it in advance online). ⊠ *700 Kapahulu Ave., Kapahulu* ☎ *808/735–7944* ⊕ *snorkelbob. com* ⊠ *Rentals from $42 per wk.*

HAWAII KAI
★ **Hanauma Bay Rental Stand**
SNORKELING | FAMILY | You can rent masks, fins, and snorkels here. The stand also has lockers that are just large enough to stash your valuables. Bring ID or car keys as a deposit for rental. ⊠ *Hanauma Bay Nature Preserve, 7455 Kalanianaole Hwy., Hawaii Kai* ☎ *808/396–3483* ⊕ *hanaumabaystatepark.com* ⊠ *Rentals from $20, lockers from $10* ☉ *Closed Mon. and Tues.*

Stand-Up Paddleboarding

From the lakes of Wisconsin to the coast of Lima, Peru, stand-up paddleboarding (or SUP, for short) is taking the sport of surfing to the most unexpected places. Still, the sport remains firmly rooted in the Hawaiian Islands.

Back in the 1960s, Waikiki beachboys would paddle out on their longboards using a modified canoe paddle. It was longer than a traditional paddle, enabling them to stand up and stroke. It was easier this way to survey the ocean and snap photos of tourists learning how to surf. Eventually it became a sport unto itself, with professional contests at world-class surf breaks and long-distance races across treacherous waters.

Stand-up paddleboarding is easy to learn—though riding waves takes some practice—and most outfitters on Oahu offer lessons for all skill levels starting at about $55. It's also a great workout; you can burn off yesterday's dinner buffet, strengthen your core, and experience the natural beauty of the island's coastlines all at once. Once you're ready to head out on your own, half-day rentals start at $50.

If you're looking to learn, go where there's already a SUP presence. Avoid popular surf breaks, unless you're experienced, and be wary of ocean and wind conditions. You'll want to find a spot with calm waters, easy access in and out of the ocean, and a friendly crowd that doesn't mind the occasional stand-up paddleboarder.

BEST SPOTS
Ala Moana Beach Park. About a mile west of Waikiki, Ala Moana is the most SUP-friendly spot on the island. In fact, the state installed a series of buoys in the flat-water lagoon to separate stand-up paddlers and swimmers. There are no waves here, making it a great spot to

learn, but beware of strong trade winds, which can push you into the reef.

Anahulu Stream. Outfitters on the North Shore like to take SUP beginners to Anahulu Stream, which empties into Waialua Bay near the Haleiwa Boat Harbor. This area is calm and protected from winds, plus there's parking at the harbor, and surf shops nearby rent boards.

Waikiki. Several south shore outfitters take beginners into the waters off Waikiki. Canoes, the surf break fronting the Duke Kahanamoku statue, and the channels between breaks are often suitable for people learning how to maneuver their boards in not-so-flat conditions. But south swells here can be menacing, and ocean conditions can change quickly. Check with lifeguards before paddling out, and be mindful of surfers in the water.

White Plains Beach. If you've got a car with racks, you might want to venture to White Plains, a fairly uncrowded beach about 27 miles west of Waikiki. It's a long, sandy beach with lots of breaks and plenty of room for everyone. There are lifeguards, restrooms, and lots of parking, making this a great spot for beginners and those just getting comfortable in small waves.

EQUIPMENT AND LESSONS
HONOLULU
Hans Hedemann Surf School
STAND UP PADDLEBOARDING | FAMILY | Get professional instruction in stand-up paddleboarding right in Waikiki, where the sport originated. This school offers group lessons, semiprivate lessons, and private training. Instruction is also offered at Turtle Bay Resort in Kahuku. ⊠ *Queen Kapiolani Hotel, 150 Kapahulu Ave., Honolulu* ☎ *808/924–7778* ⊕ *www.hhsurf.com* ⊠ *From $90.*

NORTH SHORE
Rainbow Watersports Adventures
STAND UP PADDLEBOARDING | FAMILY | When you spot this company's colorful van at the bay near Haleiwa Beach Park, you'll know you're in the right place. You can get a two-hour private or group lesson on Oahu's North Shore. All lessons are held in a spot popular with the resident green sea turtles. The company also offers a 3½-hour coastal eco-adventure trip, including snorkeling and lunch. Its Twilight Glow Paddle lets you glide through calm waters illuminated by lights mounted to your board. ⊠ *Haleiwa Beach Park, Kamehameha Hwy., Haleiwa* ☎ *800/470–4964, 808/470-4332* ⊕ *rainbowwatersports.com* ⊠ *Group lessons from $99; private lessons from $119.*

Surf N Sea
STAND UP PADDLEBOARDING | FAMILY | With stand-up paddleboarding lessons for every skill level, Surf N Sea is a great place to start. Beginners can take the introductory lesson to learn proper paddling technique. A one-hour session focuses on honing your skills. More advanced paddlers can book surf trips out to several North Shore breaks. ⊠ *62-595 Kamehameha Hwy., Haleiwa* ☎ *808/637–3008, 800/899–7873* ⊕ *www.surfnsea.com* ⊠ *Rentals from $60 (includes paddle).*

EAST (WINDWARD) OAHU
Hawaiian Watersports
STAND UP PADDLEBOARDING | FAMILY | Paddle off the shore of picturesque Kailua Beach. This safety-conscious outfitter offers both equipment rentals and 90-minute and 3-hour group or individual lessons. The one-stop shop for water sports also offers kiteboarding, surfing, and windsurfing lessons as well as kayak tours and equipment rentals. Discounts are available online if you book ahead. ⊠ *171 Hamakua Dr., Kailua* ☎ *808/262–5483* ⊕ *hawaiianwatersports.com* ⊠ *Rentals from $59.*

Submarine Tours

HONOLULU

Atlantis Submarines

BOATING | FAMILY | This is the underwater adventure for the unadventurous. Not fond of swimming, but want to see what you've been missing? Board this high-tech 64-passenger vessel for a ride past shipwrecks, turtle breeding grounds, and coral reefs. Little kids really seem to love it, though there's a 36-inch height minimum. The tours, which depart from the pier at the Hilton Hawaiian Village, are available in several languages, and discounts are available if booked online. ⊠ *Hilton Hawaiian Village Beach Resort & Spa, 2005 Kalia Rd., Honolulu* ☎ *808/973–9800, 800/381–0237 for reservations* ⊕ *atlantisadventures.com* 🖅 *From $143.*

Surfing

Perhaps no word is more associated with Hawaii than surfing. Every year, the best of the best gather on Oahu's North Shore to compete in their version of the Super Bowl: the prestigious Vans Triple Crown of Surfing. The pros dominate the waves for a month, but the rest of the year belongs to folks just trying to have fun.

Oahu is unique because it has so many famous spots: Banzai Pipeline, Waimea Bay, Kaiser Bowls, and Sunset Beach. These spots, however, require experience. Waikiki is a great place for beginners to learn or for novice surfers to catch predictable waves. Group lessons on Waikiki Beach start at $50, but if you really want to fine-tune your skills, you can pay up to $500 for a daylong private outing with a former pro.

The island also has miles of coastline with surf spots that are perfect for everyday surfers. But remember this surfer's credo: when in doubt, don't go out. If you're unsure about conditions,

stay on the beach, and talk to locals to get more info about surf breaks before trying yourself.

⚠ **To avoid a confrontation with local surfers, who can be very territorial about their favorite breaks, try some of the alternate spots listed below. They may not have the name recognition, but their waves can be just as great.**

BEST SPOTS

Makaha Beach Park. If you like to ride waves, try this west side beach. It has legendary, interminable rights that allow riders to perform all manner of stunts: from six-man canoes with everyone doing headstands to Bullyboards (oversize bodyboards) with whole families along for the ride. Mainly known as a longboarding spot, it's predominantly local but respectful to outsiders. Use caution in winter, as the surf can get huge. It's not called Makaha—which means "fierce"—for nothing. ⊠ *84-369 Farrington Hwy., Waianae.*

Sunset Beach Park. Impress your surfing buddies back home by catching a wave at the famous Sunset Beach on Oahu's North Shore. Two of the more manageable breaks are Kammie Land (or Kammie's) and Sunset Point. For the daring, Sunset is part of the Vans Triple Crown of Surfing for a reason. Thick waves and long rides await, but you'll need a thick board and a thicker skull. Surf etiquette here is a must, as it's mostly local. ⊠ *59-104 Kamehameha Hwy., 1 mile north of Ehukai Beach Park, Haleiwa.*

Ulukou Beach. In Waikiki you can paddle out to Populars—or Pops—a break at Ulukou Beach. Nice and easy, it never breaks too hard and is friendly to both newbies and veterans. It's one of the best places to surf during pumping south swells, as this thick wave breaks in open ocean, making it more rideable. The only downside is the long paddle out from Kuhio Beach, but that keeps the crowds

This surfer is doing a stellar job of riding the world-famous Banzai Pipeline on Oahu's North Shore.

manageable. ✉ *Waikiki Beach, in front of Sheraton Waikiki hotel, Honolulu.*

White Plains Beach. Known among locals as "mini Waikiki," the surf at White Plains breaks in numerous spots, preventing the logjams that are inevitable at many of Oahu's more popular spots. It's a great break for novice to intermediate surfers, though you do have to watch for wayward boards. ✉ *From the H1, take the Makakilo exit. Off H1, Kapolei.*

EQUIPMENT AND LESSONS
HONOLULU
Aloha Beach Services
SURFING | FAMILY | It may sound like a cliché, but there's no better way to learn to surf than from the iconic beachboys in Waikiki, a Waikiki fixture since 1959. In fact, it's often where locals take their visitors who want to surf because it's really got it all. There's no one better than Harry "Didi" Robello, a second-generation beachboy and owner of Aloha Beach Services. Learn to surf in an hour-long group or semiprivate lesson or with just you and an instructor. You can also rent a board here. ✉ *2365 Kalakaua Ave., on beach near Moana Surfrider, Waikiki* ☎ *808/922–3111 (ask for Aloha Beach Services)* ⊕ *www.alohabeachservices. com* ✉ *Lessons from $100, board rentals from $20.*

Faith Surf School
SURFING | FAMILY | Professional surfer Tony Moniz started his own surf school in 2000, and since then, he and his wife, Tammy, have helped thousands of people catch their first waves in Waikiki. The Moniz family is iconic in Hawaii's surf culture, and their stories are as good as their lessons. The 90-minute group lessons include all equipment and are the cheapest option. You can pay more (sometimes a lot more) for semiprivate lessons with up to three people or for private lessons. You can also book an all-day surf tour with Moniz, riding waves with him at his favorite breaks. ✉ *Outrigger Waikiki Beach Resort, 2335 Kalakaua Ave., Waikiki* ☎ *808/931–6262* ⊕ *faithsurf-school.com* ✉ *Lessons from $95, board rental from $20.*

NORTH SHORE

Hans Hedemann Surf School

SURFING | FAMILY | Hans Hedemann spent 17 years on the professional surfing circuit. He and his staff offer surfing, bodysurfing, and stand-up paddleboarding instruction; multiday intensive surf camps; and fine-tuning courses with Hedemann himself. Two-hour group lessons are the cheapest option, but private lessons are also available. There are also locations on the North Shore. ✉ *Queen Kapiolani Hotel, 150 Kapahulu Ave., Waikiki* ☎ *808/924–7778* ⊕ *hhsurf. com* 🖼 *From $78.*

Surf N Sea

SURFING | This is a one-stop shop for surfers (and other water-sports enthusiasts) on the North Shore. Rent a short or long board by the hour or for a full day. Two-hour group lessons are offered, as are four- to five-hour surf safaris for experienced surfers. ✉ *62-595 Kamehameha Hwy., Haleiwa* ☎ *800/899–7873* ⊕ *www. surfnsea.com* 🖼 *Lessons from $85, rentals from $35 per day.*

Tennis

Although tennis has given way to golf as the biggest resort attraction, and many of the hotel courts have closed, there are still locations in Waikiki to get your tennis match on. Both sides of Waikiki are framed by tennis complexes, with 10 courts at Ala Moana Beach Park and four at Kapiolani Regional Park. Play is free at public courts, which are readily available during the day—but they tend to fill up after the sun goes down and the asphalt cools off.

HONOLULU

Ala Moana Beach Park Tennis Courts

TENNIS | The 10 public courts in Ala Moana Beach Park are the closest to the *ewa* (west) end of Waikiki. ✉ *Ala Moana Park, 1201 Ala Moana Blvd., Ala Moana* ☎ *808/768–3029.*

Diamond Head Tennis Center

TENNIS | Across the street from Kapiolani Park, this center has 10 courts open to the public. ✉ *3908 Paki Ave., Waikiki* ☎ *808/971–2525.*

Kapiolani Tennis Courts

TENNIS | There are four lighted courts for play here, just beyond Waikiki Beach. ✉ *2740 Kalakaua Ave., Waikiki* ☎ *808/765–4626.*

Volleyball

With no shortage of sand, beach volleyball is an extremely popular sport on the Islands.

BEST SPOTS

There are sand-volleyball courts in Waikiki near **Fort DeRussy.** These are open to the public, so talent levels vary; however, the winner-plays-on policy here guarantees a higher level of play as the day progresses. For more advanced play, go to **Queen's Beach,** where you must bring your own net (which can lead to court possessiveness). This is the area where college kids and pros come when they're in town.

Whale-Watching

December is marked by the arrival of snow in much of North America, but in Hawaii it marks the return of the humpback whale. These migrating behemoths move south during the winter months for courtship and calving, and they put on quite a show. Watching males and females alike throwing themselves out of the ocean and into the sunset awes even the saltiest of sailors. Newborn calves riding gently next to their 2-ton mothers will stir you to your core. These gentle giants can be seen from the shore as they make a splash, but there's nothing like having a boat rock beneath you in the wake of a whale's breach.

HONOLULU

Atlantis *Majestic* Cruises

WILDLIFE-WATCHING | FAMILY | The 150-foot cruise vessel *Majestic* bills itself as the smoothest whale-watching tour on Oahu and guarantees a whale sighting. The boat has three decks, and you can choose from indoor or outdoor viewing while listening to Hawaiian music and an onboard naturalist who provides information as you search for the leviathans. Included among the offerings are 2½-hour lunch cruises. Departures are from the historic Aloha Tower Marketplace at Pier 6. Transportation from Waikiki can be arranged. ■TIP→ **Check-in begins 30 minutes before departure. Arrive early to get a table near a window for the best views while you dine.** ⊠ *Aloha Tower Marketplace, 1 Aloha Tower Dr., Pier 6, Downtown* ☎ *800/381–0237* ⊕ *www. atlantisadventures.com* ⛴ *From $65.*

WEST (LEEWARD) OAHU

Wild Side Specialty Tours

WILDLIFE-WATCHING | FAMILY | Boasting a marine-biologist/naturalist crew, this company takes you to undisturbed snorkeling areas. Along the way you may see dolphins and turtles. The company promises a sighting of migrating whales year-round on some itineraries. Tours may depart as early as 8 am from Waianae, so it's important to plan ahead. The three-hour deluxe wildlife tour is the most popular option. ⊠ *Waianae Boat Harbor, 85-471 Farrington Hwy., Waianae* ☎ *808/306–7273* ⊕ *sailhawaii.com* ⛴ *From $205.*

Windsurfing and Kiteboarding

Those who call windsurfing and kiteboarding cheating because they require no paddling have never tried hanging on to a sail or kite. It will turn your arms to spaghetti quicker than paddling ever could, and the speeds you generate earn these sports the label of "extreme."

Windsurfing was born here in the Islands. For amateurs, the windward side is best because the onshore breezes will bring you back to land even if you're not a pro. The newer sport of kiteboarding is tougher but more exhilarating, as the kite will sometimes take you in the air for hundreds of feet.

■TIP→ **Changes to local laws restrict lessons on the beach, so outfitters offering lessons are few and far between.**

EAST (WINDWARD) OAHU

Hawaiian Water Sports

WINDSURFING | Learn to kiteboard, windsurf, kayak, surf, or ride a stand-up paddleboard with this multifaceted outfitter. This is the only shop to offer kiteboarding and windsurfing lessons on Oahu, and the location of your lessons—off Kailua Beach—is one of the best and most beautiful on the island. For experienced kitesurfers, rentals are available, and the company offers equipment rentals for other water sports as well. You'll get a discount by booking your lessons or rentals online in advance. ⊠ *171 Hamakua Dr., Kailua* ☎ *808/262–5483* ⊕ *hawaiianwatersports.com* ⛴ *Group lessons from $120, equipment rental from $100.*

Index

Photo Credits

Notes

Notes

Notes

Notes

Notes

Fodor's OAHU

Publisher: Stephen Horowitz, *General Manager*

Editorial: Douglas Stallings, *Editorial Director*; Jill Fergus, Amanda Sadlowski, Caroline Trefler, *Senior Editors*; Kayla Becker, Alexis Kelly, *Editors*; Angelique Kennedy-Chavannes, *Assistant Editor*

Design: Tina Malaney, *Director of Design and Production;* Jessica Gonzalez, *Graphic Designer;* Erin Caceres, *Graphic Design Associate*

Production: Jennifer DePrima, *Editorial Production Manager*; Elyse Rozelle, *Senior Production Editor;* Monica White, *Production Editor*

Maps: Rebecca Baer, *Senior Map Editor*; David Lindroth, Mark Stroud (Moon Street Cartography), *Cartographers*

Photography: Viviane Teles, *Senior Photo Editor;* Namrata Aggarwal, Payal Gupta, Ashok Kumar, *Photo Editors;* Eddie Aldrete, *Photo Production Intern*

Business and Operations: Chuck Hoover, *Chief Marketing Officer*; Robert Ames, *Group General Manager;* Devin Duckworth, *Director of Print Publishing*

Public Relations and Marketing: Joe Ewaskiw, *Senior Director of Communications and Public Relations*

Fodors.com: Jeremy Tarr, *Editorial Director;* Rachael Levitt, *Managing Editor*

Technology: Jon Atkinson, *Director of Technology;* Rudresh Teotia, *Lead Developer*; Jacob Ashpis, *Content Operations Manager*

Writers: Powell Berger, Marla Cimini, Cheryl Crabtree, Tiffany Hill, Anna Weaver

Editor: Laura M. Kidder

Production Editor: Elyse Rozelle

9th Edition

ISBN 978-1-64097-521-7

ISSN 1559-0771

All details in this book are based on information supplied to us at press time. Always confirm information when it matters, especially if you're making a detour to visit a specific place. Fodor's expressly disclaims any liability, loss, or risk, personal or otherwise, that is incurred as a consequence of the use of any of the contents of this book.

SPECIAL SALES
This book is available at special discounts for bulk purchases for sales promotions or premiums. For more information, e-mail SpecialMarkets@fodors.com.

PRINTED IN CANADA

10 9 8 7 6 5 4 3 2 1

MIX
Paper from responsible sources
FSC® C016245

About Our Writers

Powell Berger lives in the heart of Honolulu's Kakaako neighborhood, where she's ever in search of the best poke bowl. Her wanderlust has taken her to more than 50 countries around the world, and her writing appears in numerous state and regional publications, AAA magazines, *The Atlantic,* and various websites, in addition to Fodor's. Powell updated the Activities and Tours chapter for this edition.

Marla Cimini (⊕ *www. marlacimini.com*) is an award-winning writer with a passion for travel, beaches, music, and culinary adventures. As an avid globetrotter and frequent Oahu visitor, she has covered topics such as Hawaii's luxury hotels, fascinating and fun surf culture, and the innovative restaurant scene on the islands. She appreciates Oahu's unique dichotomy, and enjoys the bustling Waikiki neighborhood as much as exploring the island's quieter beaches. And she's always up for surfing or an outrigger canoe ride in Waikiki! Marla's articles have appeared in numerous publications worldwide, including *USA Today* and many others. Marla updated the Experience chapter and the Waikiki portion of the Honolulu and Pearl Harbor chapter.

Cheryl Crabtree first visited Hawaii as a kindergartner, a trip that sparked a life-long passion for the islands and led to frequent visits. She spends months at a time in residence on the North Shore and updated The North Shore and the West (Leeward) and Central Oahu chapters for this edition. Cheryl has also contributed to *Fodor's*

California for nearly two decades and is a regular updater for *Fodor's National Parks of the West* and *Complete National Parks.* She also contributes to numerous regional and national publications.

Tiffany Hill, who updated Travel Smart, grew up on Oahu and has lived on both the Leeward and Windward sides, but today she calls Portland, Oregon, home. She specializes in travel, culture, and business. Her work is regularly published in regional and national publications, as well as online. When she's not on assignment, you can find her playing roller derby.

Writer and multimedia journalist **Anna Weaver** is a sixth-generation *kamaaina*, born and raised in Kailua, Oahu. She can never get enough of Spam *musubi, malassadas,* or the gorgeous Koolau mountains in her home state. Anna has written for *Slate, Simplemost,* and such Hawaii publications as the *Honolulu Advertiser* (now *Star-Advertiser*), *Honolulu Magazine,* and *Pacific Business News.* In this guide, she updated all but Waikiki in the Honolulu and Pearl Harbor chapter, the East (Leeward) Oahu chapter, and the feature on Hawaiian cultural traditions.